BARRON'S

Pass Key to the ACT®

SECOND EDITION

Brian W. Stewart, M.Ed.
Founder, BWS Education Consulting

D1502739

Dedication
Dedicated to my wife Caitlin, my son Andrew, and my daughter Eloise—without your love and support, this book would not have been possible. I would like to especially thank my mom, my dad, Andy, Mitchell, Alaina, Andrew, and Mercedez for their help with this undertaking. I am grateful to everyone at Barron's, especially my editor Kristen Girardi.

Thanks so much to all of my students over the years—I have learned far more from you than you have learned from me.

About the Author
Brian W. Stewart is the founder and President of BWS Education Consulting, Inc., a boutique tutoring and test preparation company based in Columbus, Ohio. He has worked with thousands of students to help them improve their test scores and earn admission to selective schools. Brian is a graduate of Princeton University (A.B.) and The Ohio State University (M.Ed.). You can connect with Brian at www.bwseducationconsulting.com.

© Copyright 2016, 2014 by Barron's Educational Series, Inc.

All rights reserved.
No part of this publication may be reproduced or distributed
in any form or by any means without the written
permission of the copyright owner.

All inquiries should be addressed to:
Barron's Educational Series, Inc.
250 Wireless Boulevard
Hauppauge, New York 11788
www.barronseduc.com

ISBN: 978-1-4380-0800-4

Library of Congress Control Number: 2016931076

Printed in Canada
9 8 7 6 5 4 3 2 1

10%
POST-CONSUMER
WASTE
Paper contains a minimum
of 10% post-consumer
waste (PCW). Paper used
in this book was derived
from certified, sustainable
forestlands.

Contents

Introduction

FREQUENTLY ASKED QUESTIONS ABOUT THE ACT

What is the ACT?

The ACT is a test accepted by all colleges and universities in the United States for consideration in the admissions process. It is a test of the general skills you have developed over your academic career. It is approximately 4 hours long and is offered on six Saturdays throughout the year. For a list of upcoming dates and registration deadlines, go to:

www.actstudent.org/regist/dates.html

The ACT is made up of the following sections:

- English, 45 minutes, 75 questions—test of grammar, usage, and rhetorical skills
- Math, 60 minutes, 60 questions—test of problem-solving skills in algebra, geometry, and trigonometry
- Reading, 35 minutes, 40 questions—test of reading comprehension skills
- Science, 35 minutes, 40 questions—test of scientific analytical and reasoning skills
- Writing, 40 minutes, 1 essay question (This section is optional.)

There is a 10-minute break between the Math and Reading sections, and a 5-minute break between the Science and Writing sections.

How do I sign up?

It is easiest to sign up online, although there are a variety of options given on the ACT website:

QUICK LINK TO THE ACT

www.actstudent.org/regist/

If you receive extended time or other special accommodations on school tests, be sure to look into extended time and/or accommodations on the ACT.

The ACT has a process to ensure that those who deserve extended time receive it. Find the latest details on what services may apply to your situation here:

http://www.actstudent.org/regist/disab/

The ACT also allows students whose families are experiencing economic hardship to take the test twice at no cost. You will need to ask your guidance counselor for a Fee Waiver Form. The most updated information on ACT Fees can be found here:

http://www.actstudent.org/regist/actfees.html

When should I take it?

Most students take the test in their Junior year of high school since they will have completed most of the math they will need, but you can certainly take it earlier if you are interested in seeing where you stand. Unless a college specifically requires that you submit all of your test scores from the ACT (which is quite rare), you will only send in the results from the test date(s) you choose. Check out the ACT test dates to see what works well with your schedule, and take the ACT when you will have adequate time to be well-rested and well-prepared.

WHEN'S THE NEXT TEST?

Where should I take it?

The ACT is offered at a wide variety of schools and universities throughout the United States and around the world. They make it relatively easy for you to take the test at a location not too far away. In fact, even if you are in prison, the ACT allows for special accommodations for you to be tested. There are four things most students should consider when picking a location:

1. Register early to ensure you don't get closed out of a location that appeals to you.
2. High schools often have larger desks than colleges, which makes it easier to fully open your test booklet instead of only being able to have a single page open at a time.
3. If you are someone who likes to take the test in familiar surroundings, see if the test is offered at your high school. If it is not, you may want to

check out your test location before the actual ACT so you can be calmer on test day.

4. If you find that being around people you know makes you feel more competitive stress during the ACT, take the test at a location where you won't know many people.

How is it scored?

There is <u>NO GUESSING PENALTY</u> on the ACT, so be certain that you do not leave any answer blank!

The ACT is scored on a curved scale from 1–36, with 1 being terrible and 36 perfect. The average test taker scores around 21–22. Each of the four required sections—English, Math, Reading, and Science—is scored from 1–36. The ACT adjusts the curve with each test to ensure that the results from one test indicate the same level of ability as the results from another. The overall composite score is found by taking a simple average of the four section scores and is rounded up if applicable. The ACT Writing section is reported separately on the score report, but it does not affect the overall composite score.

WHAT COLLEGES REQUIRE A WRITING TEST?

Should I take the Writing Test?

If you don't know where you are planning to apply to school, go ahead and take the Writing Test so you can keep your options open. If you know where you will be applying to school, take a look at the ACT website for the latest information on how particular colleges use the ACT Writing results:

https://actapps.act.org/writPrefRM/

How do I receive my scores?

If you register online, you will typically be able to access your score report approximately 3 weeks after your test date. If you choose, you can also have your scores mailed to you.

An incredibly helpful tool is the ACT Test Information Release. For a fee, cur-

I'D LIKE A COPY OF MY TEST, PLEASE.

rently $20, the ACT will send you a copy of your answers and the test booklet for the test you took. They offer this service for three of the test dates in a given year. When you receive this booklet, it will be a highly valuable resource in seeing where you need further focus in your preparation. You can sign up for this service when you register, or you can do it after testing by using this form:

www.actstudent.org/scores/release.html

Don't some colleges prefer the ACT to the SAT and vice versa?

All U.S. colleges will now accept either the ACT or SAT. You can look at your results from ASPIRE to see how you might perform on the ACT and your results from the PSAT to see how you might perform on the SAT. If you have similar percentiles on each test, you may want to try both the SAT and ACT at least once to see which is a better fit. If one test has significantly better results than the other, you may want to focus only on that test. If you have any doubt about what to do, you may want to give both the SAT and ACT a try since either test will be accepted by colleges. If you have test anxiety, knowing that you have two tests to show what you are capable of can help you relax and perform better since you won't have all of your eggs in one basket.

How do I send my scores to colleges?

Up to four colleges can receive your test scores free of charge—just select the colleges you want to receive your scores when you register. You can send the scores to more colleges if you pay an extra fee. They will only receive the scores from the particular test date you choose. You can also send scores after you have taken the test—go into your online account to pick the test date and the colleges, and pay any associated fees.

What are the differences between the ACT and SAT?

With the major recent overhaul of the SAT, the two tests are more similar than they were in the past. There is no guessing penalty on either test, and both have an optional analytical essay. The general differences between the tests are

Material Covered: Both tests evaluate Reading, Math, and Grammar. The SAT evaluates more vocabulary in context than the ACT. The ACT has a stand-alone Science section, while the SAT has graph analysis questions distributed throughout the test. The ACT will have more geometry and trigonometry than the SAT, and the SAT provides a math formula sheet, whereas the ACT does not.

Speed: The SAT is generally easier to finish than the ACT, as there are fewer questions per minute of provided test time.

Critical Thinking: The ACT is a bit more straightforward than the SAT, but both evaluate critical thinking skills.

What kind of calculator can I use?

IS MY CALCULATOR PERMITTED?

You can use most any scientific or graphing calculator on the Math section, with the most prominent exception being the TI-89 graphing calculator. Be sure you check if your calculator is permitted by looking at this updated list:

www.actstudent.org/faq/calculator.html

Do they give me any information sheets or math formulas?

There are no reference sheets on the ACT for any of the sections. (The SAT does give you a few math formulas.) Be sure you know your math formulas and grammar concepts going into the test. If there is an unusual math concept, such as the Law of Sines, they will typically give you the information you need. The Math chapter has extensive information on what concepts you will need to know.

How has the ACT changed from years past?

The ACT continuously makes changes to the test based on the results of its National Curriculum Survey to ensure that the ACT tests what students should know for college. In 2015, there were many major changes from the tests in years past. Even though this book is completely updated to reflect what the ACT is currently like, be very careful if you practice with materials from other sources, as they may not be updated to reflect these important changes.

1. **The Essay Is Completely Different.** You will have 40 minutes to do the new ACT Writing. It will be an "issue analysis" instead of a mere opinion essay. You will need to consider three different points of view on a topic of general interest and then develop and defend your own view on the topic. This book is completely updated for the new ACT Writing section.
2. **The Reading Section Will Almost Certainly Have a Comparative Passage.** One of the four reading passages will have two smaller passages, labeled

Passage A and Passage B. The questions for Passage A will come first, the questions for Passage B second, and the questions about both passages last. *You may find it helpful to read Passage A first and do its questions, then read Passage B and do its questions, and finally do the questions regarding both passages.* This way, you could focus on just one passage at a time. This book has been completely updated to include a comparative passage in every practice test.

3. **The Science Section Could Have 6 or 7 Passages.** There will still be 40 questions and 35 minutes total, but given this change, you should change your timing strategy. *Time yourself by taking about **9 minutes for every 10 questions on the Science**.* Alternatively, you could spend about 6 minutes per passage if there are 6 passages, and 5 minutes per passage if there are 7 passages—you will just need to check at the end of the science test to see how many passages there are before starting. This book will give you practice with both the 6-passage format and 7-passage format.

4. **The Allocations of Questions on the English and Math Sections Could Vary.** In the past, there have been firm percentages of question topics; now, the question topics could vary. Here are the possible ranges of topics on the new ACT English and ACT Math:

ACT English	ACT Math
Punctuation: 10–15%	Pre-Algebra: 20–25%
Grammar and Usage: 15–20%	Elementary Algebra: 15–20%
Sentence Structure: 20–25%	Intermediate Algebra: 15–20%
Strategy: 15–20%	Coordinate Geometry: 15–20%
Organization: 10–15%	Plane Geometry: 20–25%
Style: 15–20%	Trigonometry: 5–10%

5. **There Will Be More Statistics and Probability Questions in the Math.** Make sure you are familiar with concepts like probability calculations, mean, median, and mode. The tests in this edition of the book are completely updated to reflect the current proportion of these types of questions.

6. **The Act Now Allows Many Schools the Option of Administering the Test in a Computer-Based Format.** The core part of the test will remain the same as the paper-based test, but the computer-based test will have some optional free-response questions. Many schools may offer these free-response questions as a way of meeting Common Core Curriculum

requirements. These optional questions will not impact the overall 1–36 score. Don't worry if you don't want to take the test on a computer—the ACT will continue to offer the paper-based test for the foreseeable future.

7. **There Will Be Additional Feedback on Your Score Report.** ACT will add the following four reporting categories to score reports:

- **STEM Score:** This will compile the performance from the math and science parts of the ACT, helping students to determine their readiness for STEM (Science, Technology, Engineering, Mathematics) professions. It is an average of the math and science sections scores.
- **English Language Arts Score:** This will compile the performance from the English, Reading, and Writing sections of the test to help students assess their college readiness. It is an average of the English, Reading, and Writing section scores.
- **Understanding Complex Texts Indicator:** This will help students determine their level of proficiency in understanding the main ideas and purposes in a range of increasingly difficult texts.
- **Progress Toward Career Readiness Indicator:** This will help students assess their readiness for different career possibilities.

It is a good idea to check out *actstudent.org* to see if there are any additional changes to the test that have occurred after this book's printing.

What should I take with me to the test?

Your ACT Registration ticket has a printout of what you are permitted to have. Some things to be sure you don't forget follow:

- Your photo identification (The ACT has much more rigorous security procedures than in years past.)
- Your registration ticket
- Plenty of number 2 pencils (they are not allowed to be mechanical)
- A permitted calculator that has fresh batteries
- A snack to have during the break
- A watch that doesn't make any noise
- Do NOT bring your cell phone or any other wireless device. If it rings during the test or if you are caught using it at any point, even during breaks, you may be disqualified from testing.

What else can I do besides test prep to prepare for the ACT?

Since the ACT is a test of your overall academic skill development, most everything you are doing in your coursework in school will directly or indirectly help improve your ACT performance capacity over the long term. Here are some specific things beyond using this book that you can use to improve the skills on which you will be evaluated:

- **Read, read, read!** The ACT is very much a literacy test. Students who read frequently find it much easier to read at the speed and with the comprehension necessary to do well on the Reading section, as well as the other test sections.
- **Take rigorous courses.** Even though taking the easy course where you will get the easy "A" is very appealing, you will ultimately be grateful that you pushed yourself with more challenging classes when it comes time to take the ACT.
- **Have fun while building your writing skills.** Start your own blog, leave comments on websites, e-mail your friends. The more comfortable you are with expressing yourself, the better you will be at the ACT Writing and the ACT English.

OVERCOMING MISTAKEN THOUGHTS ABOUT THE ACT: FOUR BIG IDEAS

Have you ever had any of these thoughts when you think about the dreaded ACT?

- "I just don't know all the tricks to the test."
- "I wish I knew which choice they like the best."
- "I haven't learned everything I need to do well on this."
- "I know how to do well in school, but I am a bad test taker."
- "These questions don't make any sense—I have to read them over and over to understand."
- "I hate it when I get it down to two answers and they both look right."
- "I can't do the test quickly enough to finish everything in time."
- "I feel like this is all or nothing—either I'll do well enough to accomplish my goals, or I'm going to do terribly."

If you have, you are not alone, and you've come to the right place. In order to have a test-taking strategy that works, you must first eliminate any misconceptions you have about the ACT. Then, with a clear mind, you can learn strategies that are *helpful, doable, and personalized*. So, let's begin!

> ### WORRY #1
> I don't know all the tricks to the test, and I wish I knew what choice they like the best.

Imagine that your very best friend has had absolutely terrible experiences in dating. Everyone that he or she has dated in the past has been deceptive, treating your friend with great disrespect. Now, let's say that your friend has met someone who is actually nice and trustworthy. What will your friend be thinking about this new person? "He is going to trick me and hurt me just like everyone else in the past." But is this concern warranted with this new person? The worry is *understandable* because of past heartaches, but it is not *applicable* because this is a very different person.

What was the point of that example? The past bad experiences are like the poorly written tests you have taken in the past. You have learned that sometimes there can be several correct answers, and that there are lots of tricks you can play (using the test to solve itself, seeing what choices the teacher has liked in the past). The ACT, however, represents the new person—there simply are no games or tricks to be found on the ACT. It is understandable that you would think that the same mindset would apply to the ACT as it would to school tests. After all, they are both administered in schools, and they both test academic accomplishment. But as we will see, what works in school won't work so well on the ACT.

Let's start by learning some facts about the ACT:

Fact #1: It is taken by approximately 1.9 million students each year.

Fact #2: It is accepted by all U.S. colleges and universities for admissions consideration.

Fact #3: The ACT is used by colleges to help them predict how students will perform once they enroll.

Do you *really* think that a test that is given to so many people, accepted by all colleges, and used by colleges to predict freshman success will have a bunch of games and tricks that you can play? No. Believe it or not, the ACT is a really well-written test. In fact, as a general rule, when in doubt about what strategy would be helpful on the ACT, *think about what thought process would actually be useful in college* and that is likely what will work the best!

In the world in which we live, information is readily available thanks to technology. What is lacking, however, is the capacity to critically analyze all of this information. Compare this to a test you take in school—it's given to just a few students, one teacher creates it, and if there is a bad question, the teacher will just toss it out, or give everyone a free point. Let's consider some of the games that school tests often have that you WON'T have on the ACT:

School	ACT
If a choice hasn't been used in a while, it's going to be used very soon.	Take each question on its own—don't look for any patterns. It is completely random.
The longest answer is often right.	They mix it up so that you can't make a prediction based on the length of an answer.
Forget about "no change" or "none of the above." Teachers typically hate these answers.	Consider "no change" and other unusual answers just as likely as any other answer.
Several answers can sometimes work, and it can sometimes be a matter of opinion.	You'll find a couple of answers that SEEM correct, but, in fact, only one of them is definitively correct.

So when you are taking the ACT, remember big idea #1:

> **BIG IDEA #1**
>
> There are no games on the ACT, and there is always one definitive answer to each question.

If you remember this, your mind can focus on what matters instead of what doesn't matter: clearing your mind and using your critical thinking ability to solve the problems, instead of looking for tricks.

> **WORRY #2**
>
> I haven't learned everything I need to do well on this. I know what I have to do to do well in school, but I am a bad test taker.

Virtually every test you've taken in school tests your ability to remember information. Even in math, if you can't remember several formulas, you are totally out of luck. It might seem to make sense that the ACT would operate the same way, but it is very, very different. If you look at the test summaries that ACT puts together, you'll find an emphasis on one key word: "skills." Colleges will care more about your problem-solving skills than what you have memorized because they want students with great *academic potential* to come to their schools. What if someone is really intelligent but has not had the opportunity to attend a high school that has dynamic teachers and top-notch resources? Colleges want to find students like this and give them the opportunity to realize their potential. In the right academic environment, students with excellent critical thinking skills will flourish because they have the ability to take full advantage of all the resources available—to learn new things and think in new ways. If you don't believe this, believe Harvard University: "We regard test results as helpful indicators of academic ability and achievement when considered thoughtfully among many other factors."

Don't be intimidated by the notion of critical thinking skills. If you have a cell phone, laptop, or tablet computer, did you spend hours and hours reading through manuals before you started using it? No! You simply jumped in and *figured things out*. The mindset of jumping in and fearlessly figuring things out is much more constructive on the ACT—the mindset of memorizing facts for a recall test is *not* what is called for here.

A good ACT question that tests critical thinking skills is really difficult to write. Why? Because it must be simultaneously challenging yet provide the test taker with almost all that he or she needs to figure it out. Now don't misunderstand—you need to know some English grammar, some math formulas, and even a few science concepts. However, if you are able to completely understand what is being asked and you are able to think through it correctly, you'll be in good shape.

Let's break this down by examining a tough school-style question. If someone is teaching history and wants to make his students miserable, all he has to do is pick a fact that is really obscure and test his students on it. How about this question?

What is the first name of the 19th U.S. President's spouse?

A. Mary
B. Lucy
C. Agnes
D. Elizabeth

If you know this off the top of your head, you have just earned an imaginary gold star.

The correct answer is B.

The ACT, on the other hand, does not expect this type of knowledge from students. Why? Because the point of the ACT is to test academic potential for college. Demonstrating knowledge of trivial facts would give colleges a poor idea of your academic potential. Demonstrating an ability to critically think through problems, on the other hand, would most certainly do it. Check out an ACT-style question.

In the following equation, the profit per unit (**P**) is expressed in terms of the total cost of all units (**C**), where (**R**) represents the total revenue and (**N**) represents the number of units sold.

$$P = \frac{R-C}{N}$$

What is the total cost of all units in terms of the other variables?

F. $C = R + P + N$
G. $C = R - PN$
H. $C = RP + N$
J. $C = P - \frac{R}{N}$
K. $C = R + PN$

In case you were wondering, the answer is G. We will discuss how to break down a question like this when we reach the Math chapter. Right now, let's focus on this key idea:

> **BIG IDEA #2**
> The test is more about thinking than knowledge.

On the above math question, do you need to know difficult math formulas? Absolutely not. Do you need to approach the question extremely carefully and think through it well? Absolutely yes. The worst thing you can tell yourself on an ACT question is *"I don't know how to do it."* While this will be true in some rare cases (e.g., you've forgotten a grammar rule or a math formula), in the vast majority of cases this attitude will make you shut down your thought process and totally give up. A much more empowering attitude is to think *"I can't quite figure it out right now."* This attitude places the emphasis on what you *can* control during the test—your thought process.

But how are you supposed to better think through the questions? Let's find out as we address this next piece of baggage from above:

> **WORRY #3**
>
> These questions don't make any sense—I have to read them over and over to understand. I hate it when I get it down to two answers and they both look right.

In the school question we checked out previously, we could read it fairly quickly and understand it without any issue. With the ACT-style question, we probably needed to read it two or three times before fully grasping what is going on. That brings us to:

> **BIG IDEA #3**
>
> Give more focus to the questions than the answers.

The conventional test-taking wisdom in school tests tells you to "go with your first gut instinct." You look at the choices, doing process of elimination based on whether the fact mentioned was something you (A) read in the book or (B) heard the teacher mention in class. Yet on the ACT, we need to shift our energy toward what is being asked. This key difference is summed up in this visual:

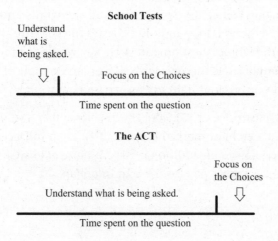

If you read the question too quickly, you will develop a defeatist attitude where you assume the question is harder than it actually is, which in turn makes it harder to see what's going on, which in turn makes you think the question is harder than it actually is, and so on. It is critical that you are PATIENT in breaking down what is being asked.

To illustrate this idea, check out this picture:

If you are like most people, you missed the second "THE" in the drawing. It is important to realize that we humans are not equipped to read everything super-carefully, and we must recognize this weakness and come up with a way of coping with it while taking the ACT. How can we do this?

- Read the question ONE TIME WELL, instead of three or four times poorly. It's strange but true—the slower you go the faster you will go!
- Keep your eyes and your brain in sync with each other. Don't let your eyes go any faster than your mind can fully keep up with what is being asked.
- Use your pencil to keep you focused on key words by "coasting the question," so named since if you underline all the words and loop the key words, it resembles a looping roller coaster track. Many students like to underline the whole question and circle key words as they go, but most prefer to simply circle the key words. Here is an example of the key words you would want to highlight as you "coast a question":

A coat has a list price of $325.00. During November, it did not sell and the merchant marked it down 20%. Then in December, she marked it down an additional 10%. What would a Christmas shopper in December pay for the coat in dollars?

- A. $6.50
- B. $227.50
- C. $230.00
- D. $234.00
- E. $286.00

Some people find that underlining all of the question and circling every key word is too "busy," and find that they would simply like to underline key words. Other students find that they naturally read slowly enough that doing coasting or underlining is not necessary. Whatever you do, you must fully understand what is being asked or you will be eaten alive on the questions. A theme of this text will be *how to use writing* on the test to achieve this understanding. It is a carryover from school that we want to avoid writing on the test so that it can be saved for the next class, but you can write ALL OVER the ACT with no penalty whatsoever. Take advantage of this!

So we know that we shouldn't play games on the test, we need to think well to do well, and we need to understand what is being asked. This would be great if we had plenty of time to do all the questions, but how on earth are we supposed to finish? This brings us to:

WORRY #4

I can't do the test quickly enough to finish everything in time. I feel like this is all or nothing—either I'll do well enough to accomplish my goals, or I'm going to do terribly.

We will discuss many ways to pick up speed, but the best general advice is:

BIG IDEA #4

Do what you can, do it well, and don't do too much.

It would be great if there were a magical strategy to rapidly increase your reading and thinking speed. Unfortunately, that is not possible. What works the best is to manage your time by going into the test already having decided that you will not attempt to do every question or even every passage. Even if your goal is to score a 36, you can still miss questions and achieve your goal.

Let's think about what a good goal for you would be. DO NOT say to yourself, "I want to earn a perfect score on the ACT so I have all my options open!" This is a recipe for disaster because you will spread yourself WAY too thin on the questions and make lots of careless errors. DO ask yourself, "What score do I need to have a solid chance for admissions to a school I would enjoy attending?" This is a far better thing to ask yourself because it will focus your energies on where you have the biggest bang for your buck on the test, instead of squandering it on questions you will likely miss.

We will break this down section by section, but here is a summary of how well you need to do to accomplish your goals, keeping in mind that your ACT score is only one component of the overall college admissions process:

1. If you are thinking about an Ivy League or similar school where scores are around a 33, you should shoot for an "A" on the ACT—answer about 95% of the questions correctly.

2. If you are thinking about a school at the level of an elite state school, like University of Texas or Ohio State, where scores are around a 29, you should aim for a "B" on the ACT—answer about 85% of the questions right.

3. If you would be happy at an average state school where the scores are around a 24, go for around a "C" or "D"—answer around 65–75% of the questions correctly.

4. If you want to go to college in general, safely shoot for a 20, which a solid "F" will make possible—you only need about 50% of the questions right to accomplish your goal.

Be aware of how many you can miss, and develop a personalized plan for how many questions and passages you will attempt when you do the ACT. If you don't go in with the mindset that you will do what you can and do it well, here is what will happen:

- You will read questions way too quickly and make many careless mistakes.
- You will waste time on super-hard questions that you will still miss.
- Your test anxiety will go through the roof because you know, deep down, that you are biting off more than you can chew.

What we have just covered is likely different from advice you have heard on other tests you have taken. Don't be alarmed by this. Take a look at some common test-taking suggestions you have likely heard from friends and teachers, understand where they do work, and understand how you should be careful using them on the ACT:

Common Testing Advice	Where does it work?	How should you adjust it for the ACT?
Go with your first instinct!	On memorization-based fact recall tests. You either know it or you don't, so don't overthink it.	Go with your first instinct after *really understanding the question* and setting things up well. Don't jump to conclusions without thinking through the problem.
Use process of elimination!	On tests where the questions are straight-forward, and where you can easily plug in answers (like on many Math tests).	Be careful to keep an open mind. Don't eliminate choices too quickly, and don't go to the choices without fully understanding what you are being asked to do.
Double-check your answers!	When you have *plenty* of time to take the test (like many tests you take in school).	Since time is of the essence on the ACT, spending time double-checking is time that could have been spent much more effectively getting the question right *the first time*. Try to finish the test *right when time is called* rather than having several minutes to go back and look over things.

This book is packed with practice questions, strategies, and in-depth explanations. But if you learn nothing else from this text, please remember these four key ideas:

1. There are no games on the ACT, and there is always one definitive answer to each question.
2. The test is more about thinking than knowledge.
3. Give more focus to the questions than the answers.
4. Do what you can, do it well, and don't do too much.

ATTAINING AN OPTIMAL, BALANCED MINDSET FOR THE ACT

In any performance situation, feeling a bit of stress is both understandable and helpful—it gives you the edge you need to perform your best. If you are too relaxed, you won't try hard enough to give it your all. If you are too stressed, you focus too much on the results instead of on the task at hand. The key is to avoid being too relaxed or too stressed—like Goldilocks in the fairy tale about the Three Bears, we can't be too cold or too hot. We need to get it *just right*. Let's explore several issues that often cause ACT test takers to feel either too relaxed or too stressed, and how to instead have a more *balanced mindset*.

What's the point of the ACT?

Too Relaxed: "The ACT is stupid. Who cares?"

Too Stressed: "The ACT assesses everything about my academic abilities. How I do on this is a measure of how I measure up as a person."

Just Right: "The ACT gives a fair assessment of my general academic abilities but says nothing about me as a person."

Virtually no other test you will take will have the amount of time, money, and resources invested in its development to ensure its fairness and usefulness to colleges. The ACT carefully aligns its content by doing extensive surveys of educators. This ensures that the types of questions on the ACT measure skills and knowledge that will be critical to success in college. If you check out the ACT's job postings, they have positions for "Fairness Consultants"—people who evaluate the test to make sure it doesn't discriminate against any group who will take it. Also, if any test takers have a documented disability—from ADHD to traumatic brain injury—the ACT will allow them to have accommodations to give them a fair shot. It is impossible to create a perfect measure of student academic ability, but the resources and care that go into the ACT's development can assure you that this test will fairly assess your general academic skill level.

Your general academic skill level, however, is not a full measure of your academic abilities and your character. The ACT only measures general ability to edit papers, solve math problems, understand what you read, and analyze scientific information. If your academic abilities are outside of these areas, demonstrate your abilities to colleges in different ways. In your application, send in a recording of your music or dance if you are a performer. Send a link to an online portfolio if you are an artist or blogger. If you have a strong work ethic and outstanding character, show how you have started a business or worked with the less fortunate. The ACT measures abilities that are much easier to measure. If your abilities are less easy to measure—how on earth could you do a standardized test on painting?—it does not mean that they are unimportant abilities. You just need to make a bit more effort in your application to help the admissions officers see that you do indeed have these abilities. The measure of your abilities and character will be up to what you do and how you respond in the years to come.

How does the ACT affect your chances of getting into school?

Too Relaxed: "The ACT doesn't matter."

Too Stressed: "If I don't do well on the ACT, I'm not getting into college and I will be a complete failure."

Just Right: "The ACT is about one fourth to one third of what admissions officers consider. It is the easiest admission measure to quantify, but it is only a component of what is considered."

In many countries, a single standardized test determines one's collegiate future. Such a test does not exist in the United States—the ACT is just one of many components that colleges take into account. The ACT can be an incredible opportunity for students who may not be considered by admissions officers; otherwise:

- Students who had an extensive illness or family tragedy that caused their grades to plummet for an extended time. The ACT can show that they do possess significant skills despite abnormalities in their grades.
- Students who might never even think about applying to a top college because no one in their circle of friends/family has done so. After a great performance on the ACT, colleges might send them mail that could encourage them to broaden their horizons and apply.
- Students who have had a bad experience in a particular high school class. Since the ACT assesses more general abilities instead of specific knowledge, you can show that you have the *potential* to do well in science or English even though you didn't have the best instruction in that subject.

Even though colleges find the ACT to be a useful tool, know that you have many options in case you're not the world's greatest test taker:

- Several hundred colleges do not require ACT or SAT test results. You can find an updated list at *www.fairtest.org*.

- If you do have a learning disability or physical disability that prevents you from completing the ACT under typical conditions, be sure you look into accommodations. Colleges will have no record that you took the test with extended time or under special conditions, so if you are legitimately entitled to special testing, be sure to use it. Go to *www.actstudent.org* for extensive details on the latest requirements.
- Make personal contacts with the college. Try to schedule an interview with an admissions staff member to give an in-person explanation of issues you may face when testing, as well as to highlight the strong aspects of your background.
- All colleges accept the ACT and SAT. If you have significant issues finishing the ACT, the SAT might be a better fit as it is quite a bit easier to finish than the ACT.
- Be sure you apply to a wide range of colleges—don't put all your eggs in one basket by only applying to highly selective schools.

In the whole college admissions process, control what you can control. Put plenty of energy into your coursework, extracurricular activities, college essays, and the ACT. A good score on the ACT is not make or break for college admissions, just as graduating from a particular college is not make or break for success in life. Keep things in perspective.

How often should I take the ACT?

Too Relaxed: "Take the test once and be done with it."

Too Stressed: "Take it *six or seven* times."

Just Right: "Two to four times is probably good."

Most students do improve after taking the ACT at least once, but the gains tend to level off on the third attempt. As much as you can prepare for the ACT, there is nothing like actually taking it in order to see what issues with test anxiety you may encounter. Plan on taking it at least a couple of times, but if you start taking it five, six, or seven times, you might want to find a better way to spend your Saturdays. As a general rule, most colleges do not take the best score from each section of the test, also known as "super-scoring." If the college to which you are applying *does* take the best score from each section, it can make sense to retake the test until you achieve the section scores you want. A final consideration: some students find it helpful in managing their test anxiety to (1) not have their scores automatically sent to colleges and (2) go ahead and register for the next ACT. Doing these two things often helps students avoid having annoying thoughts while taking the ACT about what colleges are going to think of their test performance.

How are my parents/guardians affecting my performance?

Too Relaxed: "I don't care what my parents think."

Too Stressed: "I feel like if I don't do well, I will be a disappointment to my parents."

Just Right: "My parents had a very different system when they applied—easier to get in, less expensive. If they can understand how things have changed and how much pressure there is, it will help me out."

Just a generation ago, getting into a good state college was almost as easy as filling out the application. You could pay your way through school with part-time jobs and graduate debt-free. College is more competitive and more expensive than ever before—no wonder so many students find the ACT and college admissions so stressful. Talk to your parents about what you are going through and help them understand how things have changed. If your parents went to college in a different country, know that they may put *too* much importance on the ACT, since they may not fully understand that U.S. college admissions have a more holistic process than the admissions systems elsewhere. U.S. college admissions are fairly unique worldwide in that *many* factors are considered—not just test results.

How much should I practice?

Too Relaxed: "I won't do anything to prepare."

Too Stressed: "I can only get better by doing dozens and dozens of tests."

Just Right: Rigorous academic coursework, review of key content, learning optimal strategies, and realistic practice will make a big difference in the end."

As with most endeavors, it's not just putting in the time that makes a difference. Rather than practice making perfect, *it's perfect practice that makes perfect*. This book is designed to give you the tools to continually evaluate your thought process so that you don't repeat the same mistakes over and over again. It is also designed to replicate the same thought processes you will need when you take the actual ACT. Beyond this book, know that the more problem solving and critical thinking you do in your coursework and beyond will ultimately help you do better on the ACT.

What should I do leading up to the test?

Too Relaxed: "Who cares how much sleep I get or what I eat?"

Too Stressed: "I need to prep up to the last second."

Just Right: "I will do long-term preparation focused on improving my critical thinking."

If the ACT were a memorization-based test, studying up to the last minute could be quite helpful. Since it is a critical thinking and skill test, it is essential that you put yourself in the best position you can to think well when you take the test. Gradually prepare over a longer time period, and as the test approaches, scale things back. The night before the test is the last time you want to do a bunch of practice. Would you go run a marathon the night before an actual marathon? Of course not—you would be exhausted! Perfectionists can get into trouble by over-preparing leading up to the test so that they have very little energy left for the real thing. Those who do not care about the test may be guilty of "self-sabotage"—rather than admitting that they can't score highly on the ACT, they subconsciously take actions that result in poor performance so that they have an excuse if anyone asks how they did. Don't be overly worried about prepping constantly, and don't be so relaxed that you end up hurting your potential to perform well.

What should I do about guessing?

Too Relaxed: "I'll just randomly guess."

Too Stressed: "I have to get it right."

Just Right: "I will do what I can do and do it well—I will guess on everything else."

There is no guessing penalty on the ACT, so be certain that you put down an answer for every question. As you will see in the coming chapters, there are clear patterns as far as where the more difficult questions of a section will be—take advantage of this by guessing on questions that will be too time-consuming. Since the ACT questions are more critical thinking puzzles than factual recall questions, it is critical that you give questions a good try. On the one hand, don't immediately give up on it if you don't see what you are supposed to do right away. On the other hand, don't obsess over a question so that you leave several easier questions unanswered. Use this book to help you develop a personalized, balanced guessing strategy.

How should I think while taking the test?

Too Relaxed: "I'm thinking about my friends or the weekend ahead. I'm figuring out my strategies as I go."

Too Stressed: "I can't stop thinking about how I'm doing and comparing myself to others, trying to remember what to do. My mind is cluttered."

Just Right: "My strategies and timing are internalized. I'm able to focus on the task at hand with a clear and clean mind."

Mental clutter is the enemy on a thinking test like the ACT. If you are too relaxed, you will have to waste time during the test reviewing the directions and basic facts and experimenting with which strategies work and which ones don't work. For example, you might go into the Reading section and try one passage where you read the passage before going to the questions, and another passage where you just go right to the questions. Given the predictability of the test, you don't want to waste any time making basic strategic decisions about your test-taking approach during the ACT itself—you want to figure this out ahead of time so you can use your mental energy to solve the problems.

If you are too stressed, you will fill your mind with worries about your test-taking performance and comparisons to other test takers. You'll also feel that you need to remember a ton of strategies and facts in order to do well. What should you do instead? Use the practice tests in this book to determine a *reasonable* goal for your performance and to focus on getting the best score for *your situation.* Avoid the dangerous mindset of "I want to keep all my options open, so I need to get a nearly perfect score." Instead, ask yourself, "Based on where I would actually be happy attending college, what score do I need?" Go online and find out what its average ACT score is and go with that. Most students find that the first time they take the test they go "all-out" and sometimes try to do more questions than they should. This is completely understandable—why wouldn't you want to do the best you can? After the first test-taking experience, most students then formulate more reasonable goals. You will ultimately have the highest score possible if you aim for the best score based on your abilities and where you would be happy attending college. In order to do your best, your strategies need to be internalized, automatic, and straightforward. Experiment with different strategies and practice in a reflective way so that you know exactly what is going to work for you when taking the test. Get to the point where you are able to stay in the moment as you solve the problems without thinking too far ahead or letting past questions nag at you. Mentally rehearse "worst-case scenarios" with respect to timing and problem solving so nothing surprises you (for example: What will you do if you encounter a really tough passage or get stuck on a question? Figure this out *ahead* of time—not during the test.).

Your thought process should ultimately be like that of an athlete in a big game. Know your plays and practice your fundamentals ahead of time. Avoid looking at the scoreboard and beating yourself up for small mistakes. Focus on one play at a time and do the best that you can.

How will where I've gone to high school impact how I will do?

Too Relaxed: "My school and teachers weren't good, I have no reason to succeed. I might as well not even try."

Too Stressed: "My school and teachers have been excellent. I should know how to do every single problem that comes my way, and if I don't, there's something wrong with me."

Just Right: "The ACT is more about figuring things out than having been taught specific information. I'm going to think my way through things instead of assuming that I should have been taught exactly how to do a specific problem."

Don't let your high school background make you give up too easily on a problem or stay stuck on a problem way too long. Students who are not confident in their academic backgrounds often do not give themselves enough credit for their natural problem-solving abilities. The ACT is designed to help colleges find students who do have strong academic potential, even though they haven't gone to world-class schools. Students who have gone to really great schools often become easily frustrated if they can't figure out a question, resenting their teachers for not having taught them how to do a specific problem. Understand that school will prepare you by helping your overall skill development, not as much by filling your head with endless facts. This book is carefully designed to review the content you need to know while focusing primarily on your critical thinking skill development.

Does the test change much?

Too Relaxed: "It's always the same. No big deal."

Too Stressed: "They are going to trick me, I need to take it on a certain date."

Just Right: "The ACT is generally predictable, but since it is assessing my critical thinking ability, I will need to have flexibility and creativity in my thought process. The test is curved, so a score from one test means the same as a score from another."

The ACT would be of little use to colleges if scores from one test date represented a different level of skills than scores from another date. It's impossible to make every single ACT test exactly the same level of difficulty. That's why they curve the ACT in order to account for minor differences among tests. They make this curve based on how students actually perform on the assessment. If the ACT seems easier a particular day, many students end up becoming overly excited and end up making lots of careless errors. If the ACT seems more challenging on a particular day, students often get depressed and anxious about their performance and cannot think clearly. If the test seems easier or more difficult when you take it, don't let it bug you—know that the test will be curved, and it will all work out in the end.

Should I get advice from other people?

Too Relaxed: "I don't need to think about stress or talk to anyone else."

Too Stressed: "I talk to people about the ACT all the time. I'm so confused with what strategies I should use. Everyone else seems to have it together."

Just Right: "I should think about what has worked for me elsewhere (sports, music, life), and also ask for tips from parents and good friends. What works for one person may not work for me. An experienced tutor can sometimes be good at helping me figure out what will work."

Just a few years ago, students could take the ACT and scores would only be sent in the mail to their homes. Now, so many people have smartphones so that students are able to compare ACT scores anywhere, anytime. It is very difficult to not let what other people are saying about their test results bug you. Do your best to stay focused on your personal situation and not to worry about comparing yourself to everyone else. Talk to parents and good friends about how they have managed test and performance anxiety—they know you well and might be able to help you see your tendencies clearly. A good tutor or teacher can also help you determine what personalized strategies would work the best. The strategies that work for one student can be quite different from those that work for another. Be careful with trying to replicate what some of your high-scoring friends have done because it may not be what will help you do your best. This book will help you determine the strategies that work best *for you*.

SELF-REFLECTION

Perhaps the most important thing you will learn from preparing for the ACT will be how to manage your emotions in a high pressure performance situation. With almost anything you study in college and with virtually any career you choose, you will need to know how to think clearly and process information under time constraints. Take a few moments and reflect on any test anxiety or testing mindset issues you might face, and think about how you will deal with them in the best way possible:

Problems I Encounter with Test Anxiety or My Testing Mindset When I Take the ACT	Ways I Will Approach Things Differently to Overcome These Issues

English

1

WHAT ARE THE BASIC FACTS ABOUT THE ACT ENGLISH SECTION?

→ 45 minutes
→ 75 questions total
→ 5 passages, typically 15 questions each, with a typical question breakdown as follows:
   • 10 Punctuation questions
   • 12 Grammar and Usage questions
   • 18 Sentence Structure questions
   • 12 Writing Strategy questions
   • 11 Writing Organization questions
   • 12 Writing Style questions
→ Questions are in a random order of difficulty

ACT ENGLISH STRATEGIES

To do our best on the English, we must remember the fundamental skill that is being assessed:

How well can we edit a paper?

An editor would certainly be able to pick up on grammar errors, but he or she can also determine the intent of the author, make sure a paper has a nice flow, and check that things make sense. An editor has an eye on both the nit-picky details as well as the big picture of an essay. Here are 10 key strategies that will help you think like a great editor as you go through the ACT English section:

1. Hear It in Your Head.

It is important to remember one of the big strategy ideas: *The ACT is more about Thinking than Knowledge*. Although there are certainly quite a few rules of grammatical usage and mechanics that we must know, the most important thing we can do is to tap into the familiarity we have with the English language from our speaking, reading, and writing. The best way to do this is to **mouth things out in your head**. (Do it in your head or at least mouth it silently so that you aren't asked to leave by the proctor!) Students who do well on the English section are not taking the time to say to themselves, "this particular question reminds me of grammar rule #47"—instead, like anyone else who knows a topic well, they trust their instincts first. If something *sounds bad, that is often enough to know* that it is incorrect. The grammar rules we have reviewed will give you the knowledge and confidence to know what to do in situations where you are feeling indecisive. Fundamentally, however, nothing can help us more in our editing than hearing what sounds good or bad.

Why is this point so important? Because when we read in other areas of the ACT—the science, math, and reading—we can read things much more *visually*. There is not a need to sound things out because taking time to do this will often slow us down. When editing papers, it is *imperative* that we take the time to mouth things out because quick scans of things will enable us to pick up on the general meaning of things but will prevent us from really understanding if something has careless errors.

Take this paragraph and read it quickly and visually—without mouthing things out and hearing them—and see how many spelling and grammar errors you can find.

> I went to a concert this weekend with my friends Jeanie Beth and Sam. It was amazing we saw our favorite preformer do his most popluar song. I am so excited to go on tuor with my friends this summer to follow him throughout the country. My parents are worried that we wont be responsable but I wouldn't want to do anything stupid that wood prevent us for following him all the way to August.

How many errors did you find? Now, read it again, ***hearing all the words*** as **you read, really taking your time to look for errors:**

> I went to a concert this weekend with my friends Jeanie Beth and Sam. It was amazing we saw our favorite preformer do his most popluar song. I am so excited to go on tuor with my friends this summer to follow him throughout the country. My parents are worried that we wont be responsable but I wouldn't want to do anything stupid that wood prevent us for following him all the way to August.

Here is the corrected Paragraph with 11 total errors, all of which are underlined:

> I went to a concert this weekend with my friends Jeanie, Beth, and Sam. It was amazing—we saw our favorite performer do his most popular song. I am so excited to go on tour with my friends this summer to follow him throughout the country. My parents are worried that we won't be responsible, but I wouldn't want to do anything stupid that would prevent us from following him all the way to August.

Most people find that they locate many more errors when they take their time. Just because speedy visual reading works well elsewhere on the ACT, know that when it comes to the English section, hearing things will make all the difference in the world.

For those who would argue that the ACT is not connected to actual academic skills, understand that in order to be successful on the ACT English, we must not take shortcuts that procrastinating students often do—namely, simply doing the spell check or grammar check on the word processer and expecting this to pick up on all potential errors. Most all of us have been guilty of this at some point when we haven't had the time to thoroughly edit a paper. The ACT will have many errors that a grammar check would *not* pick up on, and mouthing things out is the easiest way to ensure that mistakes don't slip through the cracks. Take this lesson and apply it to your school paper editing—instead of simply giving the paper a quick grammar check and skim before turning it in, take the time to read the paper *out loud* before turning it in. You will be amazed at how much the quality of your writing improves.

2. Trust Your Instincts

The English section tests your ability to edit things written in a fundamentally typical style of prose writing. You are not editing poetry or narrative fiction. So, don't waste your time thinking that answers might be strangely written, outside-of-the-box styles. Spend your time trying to make things sound like they would need to sound in a well-written high school or college paper assignment.

More important with this is to let go of the need that so many of us have to try to *explain why* we pick each and every answer. Consider this analogy... If you are in a restaurant and the cook gives you something that tastes terrible, all you need to do is send it back and ask for something new. Although it would be helpful for the cook if you could explain why you didn't like it, the fact that you didn't like it is more than a sufficient reason to reject it. Have that same standard here with the ACT English. For many of us—particularly math/science people who love being able to give extensive explanations to justify their answers—it is difficult to pick an answer simply on the basis that it sounds good. Even though there is indeed an explanation for every answer, on the ACT there is no need to be able to explain everything thoroughly in order to feel comfortable picking something.

Consider these examples:

The married couple is excited to get hitched.
When the teacher is talking, please try to keep a straight face.
I had a brush with death this morning—a car nearly ran over me!

TIP

Wouldn't it be nice if English made sense all the time? Unfortunately, English has more random exceptions to rules than we can begin to cover here. Use your experience in speaking the language as your guide to what sounds correct.

Imagine trying to explain why these phrasings work to someone who is not familiar with the English language. The person to whom you are explaining these things might ask the following: "Why would a couple of people want to join together like a trailer joins a car?" "Aren't faces round?" and "How can death brush up against you?" The explanation is that the English language, like other languages, has many exceptions to its general rules. We have reviewed the general rules in the grammar sections above, but it would be impossible to review every possible idiom and exception to the general rules without making this book thousands of pages in length. So, even though you should use the grammar rules we have discussed for general help, use your overall feel for the sound and flow of the English language as your ultimate guide.

Another reason that trusting our instincts is so important is the fact that in many high schools today, grammar is not emphasized in English classes. What grammar we cover is done in foreign language classes or at the elementary and middle school level. What we do cover in high school English classes is typically a mixture of reading literature and writing papers. (If you have been fortunate enough to have an English teacher who has emphasized quite a bit of grammar, consider yourself an exception!) These assignments will definitely help your capacity to perform well on the ACT English by (1) helping you become more familiar with what good writing looks like by reading the works of excellent authors and (2) making you apply good writing habits by writing journals, papers, research assignments, etc. What most of us will lack is an ability to *explain why* certain things sound good and sound bad. So, use what you have as a strength: *a thorough familiarity with the way that good writing should look, sound, and feel*. The modern high school English student is much like a jazz musician who can certainly determine the quality of a musical piece but would not be as comfortable giving a music theory explanation as to why it worked. Fortunately on the ACT, the questions are multiple choice and no explanation is needed.

A final note on this… If you are not a native English speaker or you simply have not had much exposure to quality English writing, know that in order to maximize your potential on the ACT English, you should make reading some good books a long-term priority. There is not a shortcut to learning all the nuances and complexities of the English language. Read high-quality books and magazines in addition to doing focused test preparation.

3. Think About the Meaning

There is a temptation to want to have a "small-picture" focus when editing papers and also on the ACT English section (i.e., a focus only on minor punctuation issues, spelling issues, apostrophes, etc., without thinking about the big picture). The ACT English will test our ability to determine whether things *make sense* on a bigger scale. It is great that the ACT assesses this because it is a vital skill to have in college and in the workforce. If you had a paper with no small spelling and grammar issues, yet it was not cohesive, having illogical structure, your paper would be superficially good but fundamentally poor.

Big-picture thinking questions throw us off because for question after question, we are focused on small-picture grammar issues. Be ready at any point, but particularly at the end of passages and paragraphs, to *think* in addition to listening to the flow and sound of things.

Our capacity to edit on a bigger level can be tested in a variety of ways—let's look at a couple of situations that come up frequently.

First, we need to be able to put sentences and phrases in a logical order. Consider this paragraph, and think about the arrangement of sentences we would need in order to have the paragraph be as logical as possible.

(1) When she left home for college, she resolved to make her future better than her past. (2) Sarah had a challenging childhood, in which regular meals were an irregularity and poverty was the norm. (3) Graduating from college in only 3 years, she was able to land a great job with a start-up firm. (4) Sarah is well on her way to ensuring that the childhoods of her future kids will be more comfortable and prosperous than what she experienced. (5) Even though many of her classmates saw Thursday, Friday, and Saturday nights as times to party, Sarah saw them as times when the library would be less busy.

What order is most logical for these sentences?
(Try not to look ahead!)

_____

Here is the corrected order of the sentences:

(2) Sarah had a challenging childhood, in which regular meals were an irregularity and poverty was the norm. (1) When she left home for college, she resolved to make her future better than her past. (5) Even though many of her classmates saw Thursday,

Friday, and Saturday nights as times to party, Sarah saw them as times when the library would be less busy. (3) Graduating from college in only 3 years, she was able to land a great job with a start-up firm. (4) Sarah is well on her way to ensuring that the childhoods of her future kids will be more comfortable and prosperous than what she experienced.

The ACT English will also test our ability to think about the meaning of things with questions that ask us to determine whether a sentence or paragraph has accomplished a given task. See if you can figure out the correct answer to the following big-picture thinking questions.

EXAMPLE

Given that all of the choices are true, which of the following would provide the most specific detail in expressing how the cake should be baked?
A. The oven should be set at a very high temperature, hot enough to bake the cake thoroughly.
B. Set the oven to 350 degrees Fahrenheit, place the cake on the center rack, and cook it for 45 minutes.
C. Put the cake in the middle of the oven and bake it until it feels and smells like it is completely cooked.
D. Set the oven to a moderate heat, put the cake in the middle of the oven, and bake it for about 45 minutes until it is finished.

Answer: **B** provides the most *specific detail*, as the question requires. The other options are grammatically fine—as will be the case on such questions on the ACT English—but B does exactly what is asked.

Let's take a look at a question that involves even greater big-picture thinking. Consider the following paragraph and answer the question that follows.

EXAMPLE

When choosing the best college for you, be sure you are doing it for the right reasons. (1) College is a four-year educational program that prepares people for a variety of careers. (2) Many students choose a college simply based on its reputation and ranking. (3) Some choose a college based on where their high school friends are going. (4) You should pick a college based on what is the best fit for your academic and professional goals, not just on the opinions of other people.

Which of the following sentences in the paragraph above should be removed due to irrelevance to the narrative?
A. 1
B. 2
C. 3
D. 4

> Answer: **Sentence 1.** It interrupts the flow of the paragraph by inserting information that is widely known. Specialized terminology would be fine to clarify, but "college" is hardly a specialized term.

The small-picture grammar was fine on these examples, but only one answer correctly addressed the big-picture question that was asked. On both the ACT English and in your editing in general, be sure that you have an eye on both how things sound and if they make sense.

4. Consider Covering the Answers

This is not a strategy for everybody, but it can be a great thing for people who find themselves doing any of the following:

- Rushing through the English section and having several minutes left at the end of the test.
- Frequently getting it down to two choices and can't make a solid decision.
- Making careless mistakes by misreading questions and not considering enough context.

If the ACT English were a memorization-based recall test, it would make sense to look at the choices and immediately go with your first instinct. Since it is a skill-based test, you need to do whatever you can to be certain you fully understand what you are being asked. Consider covering up the answers as a way to make yourself slow down to give the questions the focus they require.

Covering answers can be particularly helpful on big-picture questions that ask you to determine whether a passage has addressed a given prompt. An example:

> Suppose the writer's goal had been to write an essay focusing on the various ways in which animals demonstrate human characteristics. Would this essay fulfill that goal?

Rather than jumping into the choices that would follow such a question, take time to really think about how *you* would respond to that question if asked. Create a *general, flexible* idea of what might work, and then evaluate which of the choices addresses the prompt in the best way.

One more thing to consider with covering answers . . . Although we can practice and practice for the ACT, nothing can fully simulate the pressure we will feel when we are in the middle of the actual test setting. Although you may not feel a need to cover up answers while practicing, during the morning of the ACT, you will likely feel much more pressure to move things along. You will worry about finishing, you will see people around you going more quickly, and you will revert to the "pick the first answer" mindset that works on school-based tests. So, you may find it helpful to plan on covering up the answers on the ACT English so that you can keep yourself under control and do your very best.

5. Pace Yourself to Finish Right on Time

A big danger we face on the ACT English is that of the "unknown unknown"— missing questions where we are not even aware that we misread things. When we do the ACT Math, we can often predict which questions we have missed since they seem much more challenging. On the ACT English, on the other hand, we can feel great about our performance but then get our scores back and realize that we must have made a ton of careless mistakes. It is much like when we receive our graded papers and realize, when it's too late, that we have quite a few grammatical errors.

The best way to prevent careless mistakes from happening is to *use all the time that you are given and pace yourself.* Few students have trouble finishing the ACT English, unlike the other sections of the test, so they unintentionally rush through this section. Having time at the end of the test to go back and recheck answers does not make much sense because of the following:

- We are typically not aware of the questions we have missed on the English, and so we spend time inefficiently.
- We spend time *convincing* ourselves that we have answered questions correctly just to feel better.
- We often change answers we have correctly answered due to second-guessing.
- It is highly unlikely that we made a gridding error on the answer document because of the ACT helping us by alternating the "ABCD" and "FGHJ" responses.

What are our options for pacing? There are 75 questions, 45 minutes, and 5 passages on the ACT English, so here are two suggestions:

Option #1

15 minutes for 25 questions
This divides the English test into thirds. If you have a bit more trouble doing mental math, this could be a simple way of pacing yourself correctly since you have nice, clean numbers to remember.

Option #2

9 minutes per passage

Each passage usually has 15 questions, with some having 14 or 16 on occasion. Since they are of relatively uniform length, taking 9 minutes a passage divides the test into fifths. This could be a better option if you are better at mental math and wouldn't have trouble quickly and accurately calculating that if you start at an odd time, like 8:17, that you should be done with the first passage at 8:26. Having a timer on your watch might make this easier.

With either option that you choose, something that can help you *keep your mind clear and avoid multitasking* would be to **start the English section by writing the times down for where you need to be.** If, for example, you were doing Option #1, you could start the test by writing "15" next to question 25, "30" next to question 50, and "45" next to question 75. Doing this would take a few seconds at the beginning of the test, but if you are (A) someone who goes way too quickly or way too slowly or (B) someone who is *constantly worried about the time*, this can be worth the relatively small investment.

If you are someone worried about finishing the ACT English, the easiest way to handle things is to guess on the *longer problems with a written question typically at the ends of passages*. These questions will take you the most time because you have to determine what they are asking and look at quite a bit of context to determine an answer. Since all of the questions are worth the same number of points, you will improve your performance by *skipping and guessing on* the questions that would take you the most time. If you spread yourself too thin and try to answer every question quickly, you will end up performing worse because you will make too many careless mistakes. Remember the big idea: *do what you can and do it well!*

If you are someone who is able to finish the ACT English with plenty of time to spare—10 minutes or more—you may want to *read each passage from beginning to end before doing the questions*. This will help you get the big-picture context that can help with questions about transitions, strategy, and style. Rather than going back and double-checking your work, getting the questions right the first time through will be more likely to lead to a higher score.

6. Consider Enough Context

Grammar is a lot like food or fashion—in isolation, most anything is fine, but in *context,* things may not work. Eating sushi can be delicious. Wearing a clown costume in and of itself is not a problem. But if you went to a Mexican restaurant and they were serving sushi, or if you went to a wedding dressed in a clown costume, these options would *not* fit the context of the situations. Similarly, the word "him" is perfectly fine by itself, but if we said "Him is my friend," that would clearly be wrong. We need to look around the phrase we are considering correcting to determine what will work.

If we were pressed for time, like we are on the ACT Science section, we would not have the opportunity to consider context. For most students, however, the ACT English is relatively easy to finish in the given time so *please* take the time to look at enough of the wording around the phrase under consideration. Here are some general tips about how much context to consider:

- **At a minimum, we will need to take into account at least the full sentence.** Many times, we will be tempted to jump to an answer without considering an entire sentence. Be certain that you hold off on committing to an answer until you have looked at the flow of the sentence as a whole.

  For example, consider a correction to the underlined portion below:

  On one's vacation, be certain that you bring an extra copy of your passport.

  If we were in a hurry, we might think, "Looks good how it is, since *one's* is a more formal and proper way of writing." When we look at the context that follows in the sentence, we realize that in order to be consistent, we would need to change the underlined phrase to "On your." Be sure that you are keeping an open mind and at least taking the full sentence into account. If you find that you are jumping to answers too quickly, consider covering up the answers as discussed previously.

- **Look at more context with the beginnings of sentences and paragraphs.** It is easy to get a bit lazy when examining the beginnings of sentences and paragraphs. After all, many questions can be answered without having to check out greater context so it is easy to let our guard down. When dealing with the beginnings of sentences and paragraphs, be sure to look at *the sentence before* and possibly the sentence after to be sure you are making a good *transition*.

  For example, this sentence sounds fine in isolation:

  On the other hand, the beautiful sunrise portended a great start to the morning.

  Now look how this would *not* work if we consider a sentence that comes before it:

  The birds are chirping away, showing their excitement at a new day. On the other hand, the beautiful sunrise portended a great start to the morning.

We can only know that the "*On the other hand*" phrase is incorrect by looking at the sentence that comes before. Our best option would be to simply omit this phrase, since the sentences are similar in what they express.

TIP

You can even use context that is not in the passage at all! When trying to determine what wording is appropriate, use the words in sentences of your own to test out what sounds good. Don't limit yourself to what is right in front of you on the page.

- **Topic Sentences (i.e., the first sentences of each paragraph) are almost always adequate when you need to answer questions about the entire English passage.** Remember that this is a test of editing skills, not of reading comprehension. *It is not necessary to read the entire passage before you start doing the questions.* Just look at context for particular questions as you go. Consider a question like this that could come at the end of an English passage:

  If the author had been assigned to write an essay that discusses the contributions of an artist to the Italian Renaissance, would this essay fulfill the assignment?

  Two things will be sufficient to enabling you to answer such a question. (1) *You can go back and read over the topic sentences of the essay to understand the general meaning of the essay.* If you don't do this, you will often be trapped by only taking into account the information in the very last paragraph of the passage. You can be assured that the ACT English will have an answer that will trap you on a question like this that you would pick if you only considered the paragraph that comes right before the question. (2) *Keep the general meaning of the passage in the back of your mind as you work through the early questions.* Know that you will often have a big-picture question at the end of English passages, so as you do the questions leading up to the last one, try to gather a sense of the passage as a whole. This does not require a concerted effort, since so many of the questions you will answer involve looking at greater context as you go along. Just be prepared to answer a big-picture question by being mindful of the general structure and topic of the passage.

To summarize, **when in doubt, check it out**. Look at enough context until you feel satisfied that you understand what is needed to answer the question. It would be nice if we could know ahead of time *exactly* how much of the passage we will need to consider to answer a given question, but the ACT does a great job of testing your editing skills. To be a good editor, you will need to think on your feet and determine how much context is needed on a case-by-case basis. Since most students find it easy to finish the English, as a general rule you should err on the side of reading a bit too much context than not reading enough. You may not finish as quickly as other test takers, but you will have more correct answers, which is obviously the ultimate goal.

7. Roller Coast Long Questions

Even though most of the questions on the ACT English simply involve picking the best grammatical option and don't specifically ask you a question, there are quite a few questions that ask us to consider what would best accomplish particular tasks, given the intent of the author. For example,

> Given that all of the choices are true, which answer would most specifically convey the rapid pace with which the author is completing her task?

If we read this quickly, we might miss the word "specifically," causing us to pick the incorrect answer. If we Coast the question, we are far less likely to miss important parts of the question:

> Given that all of the choices are true, which answer would most specifically convey the rapid pace with which the author is completing her task?

Some of the key words that we frequently miss if we read questions too quickly include words like "not," "except," "detailed," and so forth. We need to be certain that we are answering the question that is asked, since a careless mistake in reading the question will still be a mistake when it comes to your score. In almost every case, the grammar and usage in the answers are perfectly fine—simply examining the choices would not be sufficient for picking an answer. While the more frequent error correction questions would be equivalent to an English teacher correcting grammar mistakes in your essay, these bigger-picture questions are equivalent to an English teacher writing a comment or question on your essay about the extent to which you properly communicated your intention. As a result, we must remember the big idea: *Give more focus to the questions than to the answers.*

8. Write Down Potential Placements and Underline Potential Deletions

To put it simply, *write* = **right**. Unlike school tests, where we must do our work in our head or on scratch paper, on the ACT, there is no reason to not write all over the test if it helps you keep organized. Multitasking may work in theory, but in practice, we tend to lose focus and make careless mistakes. Having to simultaneously think about both *where* something should be placed and *whether* it sounds good can cause confusion. Instead, you may find it helpful to physically write down where the choices would go in the passage on questions like these:

> Where should sentence 5 be placed in the paragraph in order to improve the logic and cohesion of the essay?
> A. Before sentence 1
> B. Before sentence 2
> C. After sentence 3
> D. After sentence 6

Before answering a question like this, write an (A) at the beginning of sentence 1, a (B) before sentence 2, a (C) after sentence 3, and a (D) after sentence 6. Having done this, you can try plugging sentence 5 into the different spots to see where it makes the most sense without having to simultaneously think about where you are placing the option.

Additionally, if a question asks you to determine whether deleting something from the passage would make sense, <u>underline</u> the phrase or sentence in question so that you can devote your full attention to determining whether it contributes to the essay or detracts from it.

EXAMPLE

> Many aspiring novelists enjoy doing their work at coffee shops so that they can both feel isolated in their own creative world and feel connected to others, more so than they would if they worked at a library. [1]

1. The author is considering deleting the phrase "at coffee shops" from the preceding sentence. Should the author make this deletion?
   A. Yes, because it distracts from the primary topic of the sentence.
   B. Yes, because it introduces irrelevant information to the novel-writing process.
   C. No, because it provides clarifying details about the place of work.
   D. No, because the information is provided elsewhere in the sentence.

This question is FAR easier to answer by underlining the phrase in question:

EXAMPLE

Many aspiring novelists enjoy doing their work at coffee shops so that they can both feel isolated in their own creative world and feel connected to others, more so than they would if they worked at a library. [1]

1. The author is considering deleting the phrase "at coffee shops" from the preceding sentence. Should the author make this deletion?
   A. Yes, because it distracts from the primary topic of the sentence.
   B. Yes, because it introduces irrelevant information to the novel-writing process.
   C. No, because it provides clarifying details about the place of work.
   D. No, because the information is provided elsewhere in the sentence.

The answer, by the way, is (C). Writing down placements and underlining potential deletions are very simple techniques, but they can really pay off on the ACT English. Many students who are very bright often believe that writing down is a waste of their time because they don't customarily have to write things down on high school tests. Don't look at writing things down as a sign of weakness or low intelligence. Know that it can help you avoid careless errors, and if you have ambitious goals for your ACT performance, each careless mistake you make can have a sizable impact on your score. Do *all that you can* to ensure that no careless mistakes occur.

9. Synonymous Answers Will Not Be Correct

A great way to break ties on tough ACT questions is to see if there are any answers that mean essentially the same thing. If 2 or 3 of the answers are similar in what they mean, they *cannot* be correct. Here are some examples of questions on which you can use this strategy:

WORDINESS EXAMPLE

The delicious pizza, which tasted great, was an excellent thing to have at the party.

   A. No change
   B. , which was absolutely yummy,
   C. , which was enjoyable to eat,
   D. OMIT the underlined portion

The correct answer is (D) because all of the other answers are repetitive, telling us again that the pizza is delicious. The similarities among (A), (B), and (C) can really help us determine that *none* of them would work.

TRANSITION EXAMPLE

My sister was extremely disappointed <u>because</u> the amusement park closed early that day.

    A. No change
    B. however
    C. in contrast
    D. on the other hand

The correct answer is (A) since it is the only one that provides a cause and effect relationship between the two parts of the sentence. The other words are all synonymous in that they show a contrast between the two parts of the sentence, which would not be warranted here. When dealing with transition questions, consider if the choices are synonymous with one another—some frequent possibilities are when multiple answers are synonymous with one of the big three transitional words: "but," "also," or "because."

PUNCTUATION EXAMPLE

We are thrilled to go to the store <u>opening</u>—we've been waiting for that store to come to our town for years.

    Which of the following would NOT work as an alternative to the underlined portion?
    A. opening, since we've
    B. opening; we've
    C. opening. We've
    D. opening, we've

The answer is (D) because the other answers all are similar in providing a clean break between two independent clauses (i.e., complete sentences). (D) is a comma splice, which is why it does NOT work. Use the similarities among what options (A), (B), and (C) accomplish to help you answer correctly.

You can also use differences among the answers to help you determine the concept that is being tested. If all of the answers are long and have the same information, it might be a question about word order. If all of the questions have the same wording but different punctuation, surely punctuation is being tested. So you can use answer similarities *and* answer differences to look for patterns that might help you solve the problem.

10. Don't Play Any Games

We can free up a great deal of mental energy and time by not looking for games or tricks to work through these questions. Here are some games we can avoid playing on the ACT English:

- *Don't they usually dislike commas and like it when things are shorter?* The ACT will mix things up enough so that we cannot plan on there being a particular pattern to the answer choices the ACT English will favor. Don't waste your time looking for a gimmick—instead, make sure you actually understand the grammar concepts being tested. Many other test prep books will recommend that you do simple tricks like avoiding commas or picking short answers, but the ACT is not so easily dissected. If it were, why would virtually all colleges bother looking at it for admissions and scholarships? The pattern of the types of answers the test will favor will vary from test to test, making you think on your feet and actually know what you are doing.

- *Don't worry about "pet peeves."* Many teachers have particular ways of writing and expression that they favor. If what they favor is merely a preference, don't worry about it. If what they favor is a true grammatical rule, please do worry about it. The ACT English will only test well-recognized grammatical rules, not subjective preferences. Here are some of the most common pet peeves that should not worry you:

  - *Starting a sentence with "because."* Many people find this annoying, but it is grammatically fine, and the ACT will often have sentences that do this.
  - *Worrying about the "Oxford comma."* This is an optional comma that comes between the second and third items in a list. For example:

    I love to have chocolate, whipped cream, and a cherry on my sundae.

    Although English teachers will fight over this, the ACT does not care one way or another about having a comma between the second and third items.

– *Avoiding the more informal "you" as opposed to "one."* The ACT English will sometimes have essays that use a more relaxed, personal tone. Look at the context to determine if "one" or "you" would be more appropriate. If "one" is being used, *keep using it.* If "you" is being used, *keep using it.* Don't make a determination based on the general advice that using "you" is a poor choice in essay writing.

- **Everything will be true.** There is absolutely, positively no need to think about whether an answer is factually true on the ACT English. Every question is only about the grammar, usage, and rhetorical skills. Never avoid picking an answer because you are not sure whether it is true or false. The ACT English is a skill test, not a factual knowledge test, so approach it accordingly.
- **"No error" has just as much of a chance as anything else.** A game that students often play on the ACT English is to convince themselves that it will *never be "no error."* The faulty logic goes like this: *It's probably not "no error," since it only has a 25 percent chance. So, I should never pick "no error."* This is like saying that on any given day, there is a 25 percent chance it will rain—so, it will *never rain.* Don't let yourself go down this mistaken path. Treat "no error" just like you would any of the other choices.

There is more than enough on the ACT English to keep your mind busy without wasting time on dead ends and pet peeves. See the ACT English for what it is: a well-written test that will assess valuable English editing skills. By seeing it for what it is, you will avoid overthinking and will improve your performance.

SAMPLE ENGLISH PASSAGE

Let's put together all of our strategies by breaking down a sample English passage one question at a time. Remember that you *don't* need to read the whole passage before you begin—this is not a reading comprehension test. Also, you want to take things *very patiently* so that you don't miss any potential errors. Let's begin!

The Development of Modern

Gourmet Cuisine

If we go back a <u>century</u> to one
1
hundred years ago, the philosophy of the

1. **A.** NO CHANGE
   B. in time
   C. to the grand time of French Prominence
   D. OMIT the underlined portion

Look at the context of what comes immediately after this—it says "one hundred years." What is a century? It's a time period of one hundred years! So, (A) and (B) would be repetitive. If we sneak a peek at what follows in the sentence by looking at question 2 below, we can see that (C) would also be repetitive. So, **(D)** is the correct answer because removing this phrase would make the sentence the most concise. The ACT will *not* always favor the shortest answer, so make sure you actually think about the meaning of the sentence to determine whether extra details are needed.

great French <u>Chefs, like Carême and</u>
2
<u>Escoffier, was</u> prominent throughout the
2
culinary world. Complex

2. **F.** NO CHANGE
   G. Chefs like Carême and Escoffier
   H. Chefs, like Carême, and Escoffier
   J. Chefs like Carême and Escoffier,

If we mouth this out, we can hear that pauses to set "like Carême and Escoffier" out of the way would be appropriate, making **(F)** the correct answer. If your mouthing of things out loud isn't sufficient, understand that the phrase "like Carême and Escoffier" provides a clarification of who a couple of the great French Chefs were. It is not essential to making this a complete, understandable sentence, but it certainly adds helpful details. (G) and (J) would not provide needed pauses, and (H) is way too choppy. Punctuation questions like this can be broken down by both *hearing* it and *thinking* about the structure of it.

sauces, elaborate presentations, and lots

of calories <u>was</u> the norm for gourmet

       3

cuisine. Into the twentieth

3. **A.** NO CHANGE
    B. is
    C. are
    D. were

We need to determine the correct tense by looking at other verbs close by. The previous sentence uses "was," so it is logical to conclude that this would be in the past tense as well. Both (A) and (D) are in the past tense, but the subject of the sentence is the multipart "Complex sauces, elaborate presentations, and lots of calories," so we need to have a *plural* verb. The only answer that uses a plural, past tense verb is **(D)**. (B) and (C) are both in the present tense. Context is *everything* when it comes to English grammar.

century, cooks moved more toward cuisine

that was clean, diverse, and experimental

<u>in response to cultural processes.</u>

       4

4. **F.** NO CHANGE
    G. as a result of changes throughout world cultures.
    H. due to the fact that culture has developed significantly over the years.
    J. OMIT the underlined portion.

Good writing is neither too wordy nor too vague—it is *descriptive*. This question demands that we think about what would give us the best description. (G) and (H) have the same information expressed in (F), but they are way too wordy. If we removed the phrase, as in (J), we would not understand *why* the chefs made these changes to their cooking. We never have to worry about whether the answers are true or false, so just pick what works based on what is grammatically correct and what would add helpful information to the passage. **(F)** is the correct answer because it gives us helpful information without being too wordy.

As the last century unfolded, people

became more and more concerned about

the dangers of heart disease, diabetes, and

high blood pressure. <u>These diseases were</u>
                                        5
<u>related to obesity.</u> As a result, customers
        5

5. Which of the following alternatives to
   the underlined portion would NOT be
   acceptable?
   A. pressure, which were diseases
      related to obesity.
   B. pressure; these diseases were
      related to obesity.
   C. pressure, however these diseases
      were related to obesity.
   D. pressure—these diseases were
      related to obesity.

It is extremely helpful to coast on questions like this—underline and circle key words so that you don't miss anything. If you don't do this, it is possible that you can miss the NOT in the question. To paraphrase what is being asked, we want to see which of these, if substituted for the underlined part, would NOT work. Think about what the underlined portion has—it has a clean break between the sentence that comes before and the sentence that comes later by putting a period between "pressure" and "These." (B) and (D) have punctuation that also can be used to separate two complete sentences. (A) changes what comes after the comma to make it work, since the phrase "which were diseases related to obesity" would no longer be a complete sentence. A comma *can* be used to separate an independent clause (which comes before the comma in this case) from the dependent clause (which comes after the comma in this case). A comma can NOT be used by itself to separate two complete sentences because it would be a comma splice. (C) is the correct answer because we would need a semicolon or period before the "however," and a comma after the "however" to make this work.

<u>demand</u> food that had quite a bit of flavor,
   6
while not having all of the calories. We see

this trend reflected in

6. F. NO CHANGE
   G. demanded
   H. demands
   J. had demanded

We need to look around to determine what tense is appropriate here. Based on this sentence and the previous sentences, we see that this needs to be in the *past* tense. (F) and (H) are both in the present tense, so they are both incorrect. (J) is in the past perfect tense, which would indicate that this occurred prior to something else in a series of past events. This is not what we need to express since it is simply stating something that happened in the past. So, the simple past tense of **(G)** would be correct.

the widespread incorporation of Asian

cooking styles, like sushi and spices.

Not from fat and salt but from unique
                          7
flavorings comes flavor.
          7

7. **A.** NO CHANGE
   B. From unique flavorings, but not fat and salt, comes flavor.
   C. Flavor comes not from fat and salt, but from unique flavorings.
   D. Flavor comes from fat and salt, but not from unique flavorings.

Let's be careful that we don't sound like the *Star Wars* character Yoda! Although these sentences all have the same information, we need to put them in a logical sequence so that the reader can easily understand what is meant. If you mouth this out and also think about the logical flow of the sequence, (C) is the only option that makes sense. It puts the subject of "flavor" right at the beginning of the sentence. (A) and (B) put "flavor" at the end. Even though (D) also has "flavor" at the beginning, it changes the meaning of the original sentence to mean the *opposite* of what it currently does.

Consumers have also become far more

open to the cuisine of other cultures. As
                        8
people have traveled the world through

tourism and military service, they have been

exposed to the culinary delights that

other countries

8. **F.** NO CHANGE
   G. of various peoples and nationalities
   H. and food of the world
   J. OMIT the underlined portion.

Wouldn't it be nice if we could simply measure the length of the answers to determine whether something is too wordy? The ACT doesn't make it that easy—you actually need to think about what level of detail is needed. Getting rid of a phrase here would cause the sentence to lose clarity as to what kind of cuisine consumers are willing to try, so (J) would not work. A culture involves people and nationalities, so (G) is too wordy, since the same information is expressed in (F). (H) mentions "food," but this has already been stated by the word "cuisine." So, **(F)** would provide the needed information without being unnecessarily wordy.

can offer. <u>Because</u> French cuisine was

      9

once considered the only true gourmet

possibility, diners now enjoy the flavors of

Vietnam, Thailand, Ethiopia, and Mexico.

9. **A.** NO CHANGE
   B. Since
   C. On the other hand,
   D. While

What kind of transitional word is most appropriate to have here? We need to think about what the sentence is expressing—it is pointing out that even though French food was once the only food considered "gourmet," now diners also consider foods from other cultures to be excellent. So, we have a contrast in the sentence. (A) and (B) would demonstrate cause and effect, so they are not right. (C) would work in a contrast, but it would not make sense as an introduction to the sentence—"on the other hand" would only work if we clearly stated the first item in the contrast beforehand. So, **(D)** gives a contrast in a way that works as an introduction to the sentence.

Many top chefs, like John-Georges

Vongerichten, don't limit <u>themselves, to</u>

                  10

<u>one country, they do "fusion" cuisine,</u>

           10

which combines flavors from all over the

world to create surprisingly wonderful

dishes.

10. **F.** NO CHANGE
    G. themselves to one country, they do "fusion" cuisine
    H. themselves to one country they do "fusion" cuisine
    J. themselves to one country; they do "fusion" cuisine

By mouthing this out loud and thinking about the meaning, you can tell that unless we break this sentence up somehow, it is going to be a massive run-on. (F) uses commas to break it up, but it ends up being way too choppy—we certainly wouldn't want to break "themselves to one country" into different parts. (G) would be a comma splice, since what comes before the comma and what comes after the comma are *both* complete sentences. A comma by itself is not enough to join two complete sentences together. (H) provides no breaks or pauses whatsoever. (J) places a semicolon between the two independent clauses in the sentence and would be the correct option.

<u>As well</u>, science has taken cooking
   11

to a new level. "Molecular gastronomy"

is a recent innovation in cooking, in

which chefs use advanced knowledge of

chemistry to create such wonders as

floating foods.

11. Which of the following is the best placement for the underlined phrase in this sentence?
A. NO CHANGE
B. After the word "has"
C. After the word "cooking"
D. After the word "level"

A helpful approach on the above question would be to *write the possible placements down* in the sentence. Write an "A" where (A) would be, a "B" where (B) would be, etc. Take advantage of being able to write all over the ACT. When we do this, we can then plug in the potential placement for the phrase "as well." Leaving it where it is would make for an awkward introduction to the sentence and would prevent us from clearly understanding the subject right from the start. So, (A) would not work. (B) and (C) would put this phrase in a spot that would interrupt phrases that need to be continuous: "has taken" and "taken cooking to a new level." **(D)** is the only option that puts the phrase in a logical place relative to the sentence and the essay as a whole.

The restaurant, El Bulli, with its chef,
12

Ferran Adrià, is world-renowned for this
12

type of food, amazing dinners with

35-course tasting menus.

12. **F.** NO CHANGE
G. The restaurant El Bulli, with its chef Ferran Adrià,
H. The restaurant El Bulli with its chef Ferran Adrià,
J. The restaurant El Bulli with its chef Ferran Adrià

This is clearly a comma placement question. How do we sort this out? The phrase "restaurant" is too vague by itself, making (F) incorrect. The phrase "The restaurant El Bulli" is sufficiently clear on its own, and the phrase about the chef Ferran Adrià provides a helpful detail about the restaurant. So, we can separate the phrase "with its chef Ferran Adrià" by surrounding it with commas. (G) does this, making it correct, and (H) and (J) do not.

Diners find that the ultra-modern cuisine

of El Bulli stimulates their senses of
13

taste, smell, and of touch.
13

13. **A.** NO CHANGE
B. stimulate their senses of taste, smell, and touch.
C. stimulates their senses of taste, smell, and touch.
D. stimulates their senses of taste, of smell, and touch.

All of these choices have the same information, but it is *how they express* the information that is up for debate. It is essential that we write these listed items in a *parallel* way. (A) and (D) are not parallel in the way they list the items. (A) has an "of" with the first and third items, but not with the second one. (D) has an "of" with the first and second items, but not with the last one. (B) would work if the subject were plural, but the subject is the singular "cuisine." (C) is correct because it is parallel through putting the "of" in front of only the first listed item, making the "of" apply to all the items in the list. (C) also works because it uses "stimulates," which matches with the singular subject of "cuisine."

With all that has changed in this past
<u>14</u>
century in the world of food, one can only
<u>14</u>
hope to live another hundred years to see
<u>14</u>
what unfolds in the twenty-first century.
<u>14</u>

14. If the author were to delete the underlined sentence, the essay would primarily lose:

F. a concluding sentence that ties the essay together while looking toward the future.

G. a conclusion that gives the reader a concrete prediction for where culinary development will go in the future.

H. a sentence that analyzes the causes of culinary changes in the past century and into the next.

J. a sentence that summarizes each of the main body paragraphs by helping the reader consider the future.

On questions like these, don't jump into the choices until you have thought about an answer in your own words. Otherwise, it is very easy to become swept up in the wrong options because they are written in such a convincing way. We can start by *paraphrasing* what this sentence says. For example, we could say "Food has changed a lot in the past century—I can't wait to see what will come next." What does this sentence serve to do? (1) It wraps up the essay with a conclusion. (2) It looks forward to what the future might hold for the world of food. So, **(F)** would be the most logical choice. It is not (G) because it does not provide a "concrete prediction" of what will happen in the future, instead giving a vague sense of hope. (H) is wrong because it provides no analysis (i.e., an exploration of the reasons why something might happen). (J) is incorrect because it provides a conclusion to the essay as a whole—it does not provide a summary of each of the body paragraphs. Be sure you are looking for a *flawless* answer rather than just the "best" answer. Find contamination in the wrong choices and you'll be in great shape!

15. Suppose the author had been assigned to write an essay answering the question, "How did a great chef change modern cooking?" Would this essay fulfill the prompt?

   A. Yes, because the essay discusses Ferran Adrià, a great chef who created huge tasting menus.

   B. Yes, because the essay talks about the role that several chefs have had on the development of modern cuisine.

   C. No, because the essay primarily discusses chemistry, such as when it mentions molecular gastronomy.

   D. No, because the essay briefly mentions several chefs, rather than doing an in-depth study of one.

A question like this makes you think that you may need to go back and reread the entire passage. There is no need for this. Why? First, you have already become quite familiar with the passage based on having done the previous questions! Second, if need be, you can go back and skim over the passage to get a general feel for what the passage is like as a whole. If you go back and skim through the passage, you will realize that the author is not focusing on the chef throughout. Instead, the essay briefly discusses the contributions of *several* different chefs throughout history. Because of this, it would NOT fulfill the prompt in the question, making (A) and (B) incorrect. (C) is wrong because the essay only briefly discusses chemistry—it is certainly not a primary focus of the essay. **(D)** is correct because it gives the correct reason *why* this would not fulfill the given prompt, namely, that it does in fact mention several chefs instead of focusing on just one.

ENGLISH GRAMMAR SUMMARY

Sentence Basics
A complete sentence has a subject and a verb.

Subject-Verb Agreement
Be sure that nouns and verbs are consistent in being singular or plural depending on context.

Punctuation
- Use commas where a breath is needed. If it's a long item, no commas are needed. If it's extra information, separate it with commas.
- Use semicolons to separate two related, complete sentences.
- A colon comes after a complete sentence, and before a list or clarification.
- A dash provides an interruption.

Possession
- 1 dog's toys (to show singular possession, put the apostrophe before the "s")
- 2 dogs' toys (to show plural possession, put the apostrophe after the "s")
- "Their," "Whose," and "Its" all show possession. "They're" = *They are.* "Who's" = *Who is.* "It's" = *It is.*

Tense
Look at other verbs close by to see if it makes sense to put it in the past, present, or future tense.

Parallelism
Example: "I love reading, learning, and studying." NOT: "I love reading, learning, and the process of going to study."

Transitions
Look at what comes before *AND* after the underlined portion to see what type of transition is needed (e.g., "also," "but," or "because").

Wordiness
Find a balance between repetition/irrelevance and effective description.

Illogical Comparisons
Be sure that what you mean to compare is what you actually compare (e.g., "The paintings by Da Vinci are better than those by John Smith." NOT "The paintings by Da Vinci are better than John Smith.").

Proper Wording
Since there are so many exceptions in the English language, *mouth things out and trust your instincts* when trying to decide the correct wording.

🗝 ENGLISH STRATEGY SUMMARY

- It is typically easy to finish the English section—don't rush!
- Pace yourself in one of two ways:

  - 9 minutes a passage
  - 15 minutes for every 25 questions

- By taking your time, you can

  - Mouth things out
  - Think about the meaning
  - Consider enough context

- On problems where there are written questions, *really focus on what they ask you to do*.
- Even if you don't know the exact grammar rule, knowing that something seems odd is often enough to figure it out.

Mathematics

2

⊙━ WHAT ARE THE BASIC FACTS ABOUT THE ACT MATH SECTION?

→ 60 minutes
→ 60 questions
→ Pre-Algebra: 20–25%; Elementary Algebra: 15–20%; Intermediate Algebra: 15–20%; Coordinate Geometry: 15–20%; Plane Geometry: 20–25%; Trigonometry: 5–10%
→ Questions generally increase in difficulty from the beginning to the end.
→ No formulas provided
→ No calculator provided, so you should bring your own.
→ Most scientific and graphing calculators permitted, except for ones like the TI-89. (Check on *www.actstudent.org* for a fully updated list of calculators you cannot use.)

⊙━ MATH STRATEGIES

Although the ACT Math requires a good bit of math knowledge, the quality of your *thinking* is what will enable you to earn the best possible score. The three biggest hurdles to high-quality thinking on the ACT Math are:

• Time management problems
• Overthinking the questions
• Careless mistakes

We will examine each of these issues and discuss a variety of tools that you can use to optimize your thought process. Choose from the suggestions below based on what will best help your personal situation.

Time Management Ideas

The ACT Math is a tough test to finish for the vast majority of students. It is vitally important that you do no more than the number of questions you can *do well*. To determine a realistic number of questions you would like to complete, think about a realistic *goal score* for the Math section. Are you trying for a 20? A 25? Maybe something in the 30s? Sure, we'd all like to score a 36 on the Math. If you want to do your best, however, don't be an optimist—be a realist. If a student who is best capable of scoring a 25 tries to go for a 35, he will often end up scoring an 18 because of so many careless mistakes on easy questions. Take a look at this table to determine how many questions you would like to aim to do well on the ACT Math:

ACT Math Score, 1–36	Number of Correct Answers on a Typical Test	ACT Math Score, 1–36	Number of Correct Answers on a Typical Test
36	60	18	24–26
35	58–59	17	22–23
34	57	16	19–21
33	55–56	15	16–18
32	54	14	13–15
31	52–53	13	9–12
30	50–51	12	7–8
29	49	11	6
28	47–48	10	5
27	45–46	9	4
26	43–44	8	3
25	40–42	7	–
24	37–39	6	2
23	35–36	5	–
22	34	4	1
21	32–33	3	–
20	30–31	2	–
19	27–29	1	0

If your goal is to score a 30, you can miss 10 questions; if you would like to score a 25, you can miss 20; if a 20 will be fine for your goals, you only need to answer half of the questions correctly. When we are used to school tests in which missing a few questions can have a tremendous negative impact on our grade, it can be very difficult to adjust to the ACT Math, where missing a few questions still results in a top score.

Now that we have a goal score in mind and know about how many questions we can afford to miss, let's understand three important things.

1. **The ACT Math Questions generally become harder further in the test.** There will be exceptions to this general rule—it is possible that question 18 could be quite a bit more difficult than question 55. But if we look at questions 1–10 and compare them to questions 51–60, questions 51–60 will be *much more challenging* as a group. (The ACT Math is the only test where this pattern of difficulty is found for the test as a whole.)

2. **Doing questions "half-way" is a bad idea.** When students rush through the last few questions on the test, they typically do much worse than if they would have just guessed on some of the tougher questions and given a good try to the easier ones. Sure, they wouldn't get all of the questions right. But, they would almost certainly end up with a better result than they would if they spread themselves too thin. If you are going to try a question, give it a solid try by reading the question thoroughly and writing out your work. If you are not going to give a question a solid try, *don't even read the question—just pick a letter and move on.* Don't try to have it both ways.

3. **Use all your time to do the questions ONE TIME WELL instead of double-checking.** Rushing through the questions so that you have quite a bit of time at the end to double-check your answers is not a sensible approach. If the ACT consisted of questions that consistently enabled you to plug in your answers to equations to check your calculations, then it would make sense to allow plenty of checking time. As we will discuss in a bit, the difficulty in the ACT Math questions comes in *properly setting them up and figuring out what they want you to do.* Because of this, you will be much better off *finishing the test questions right when time is called* instead of having several minutes at the end to go back and check your work.

Now, let's discuss a variety of ways you can approach the ACT Math timing. See which of these approaches feels like the right fit for you.

Option 1

If your goal is *to complete every question*, spend 25 minutes on the first 30 questions and 35 minutes on the last 30 questions.

This makes sense if you are trying to score in the 30s, since you will need to attempt most every question. If you can allot your time in this way, you will not dwell on easier questions at the beginning, and you will likely have sufficient time to solve the more challenging questions toward the end.

Option 2

If you are not going to do every question and you tend to RUSH, start by guessing on some of the last questions.

Since every question is worth the same amount, it makes sense to pick your battles wisely. Why waste time on tougher questions when just a bit more time on easier questions will allow you to fully understand them and avoid careless errors? If this approach makes sense to you, think of the number of questions you want to guess on, and *start* the math test by bubbling in the same letter for every single one of these ending questions. Many students find that guessing on the last column on the answer sheet, questions 51–60, is a great approach. You will find that taking these tough questions off of the table will help you relax and focus on the questions you are choosing to do.

Option 3

If you are not going to do every question and you tend to GET STUCK ON QUESTIONS, plan on having some THROWAWAYS.

Maybe it's five questions, maybe it's ten—if you tend to get stuck on tougher questions, plan ahead to guess on them, and you will avoid becoming stuck. Even though the Math test gets harder as you go, since there are some tough questions that will appear every so often earlier in the test, planning to guess on a few questions can help you do your best. Getting stuck is really tough for perfectionists, because they are used to typically having the luxury of taking as much time as they need for homework assignments and in-school tests. Don't let the perfect stand in the way of the good—as we saw above, you can usually score a 30 and still miss 10 questions.

Option 4

If you are just not a math person and can be easily overwhelmed by the ACT Math, DO ALL THE EASY QUESTIONS FIRST, THEN COME BACK FOR THE LEFTOVERS.

If you tend to give up easily when it comes to math, building positive momentum is absolutely key. This approach can make a lot of sense if you know there will be at least 15–20 questions on which you will likely guess. It can also be a good approach if you tend to have quite a bit of difficulty with *word problems*. Word problems are scattered throughout the test, and if these slow you down, save them for the end or go ahead and guess on them the first time through.

Option 5

If you are a top math student who can finish the math with several minutes to spare but find the problems at the end tough to solve, consider *doing the test backwards.*

This is a risky approach, because there is a danger that you will have trouble finishing since you may end up having to rush the beginning questions if you get stuck on the tough questions with which you start. If you are going to do this option, *be sure you practice it a couple of times before trying it on the actual test.* By starting with the later questions, you will give your subconscious mind the opportunity to solve the problem if you are unable to solve it the first time through. It is very rare that this will be a strategy that will be effective, but every so often it can work for somebody, so it deserves mention.

No matter what timing strategy you decide to use, keep in mind a couple of key ideas:

1. **Don't look at coming back to questions as a sign of weakness.** If you stay on a tougher question for more than a couple of minutes, you are taking time away from doing questions you might be able to solve more easily. When you decide to come back to a question, it does not mean it is a lost cause. In fact, you are allowing your *subconscious mind* the chance to more fully digest what was asked and to come up with a solution.

2. **Plan your strategy AHEAD of time and stick to it.** If you don't plan ahead on your timing approach, you will almost certainly *do more questions than you have business doing.* It is only natural to try to do as many questions as you possibly can. It takes a conscientious effort to realize that to do your best, you may need to pick your battles and do what will result *in your personal best.* When students take the ACT for the first time, they often set unrealistic goals and attempt more questions than they should. Use the practice tests in this book to determine the number of questions that it makes sense for you to try in order to maximize your performance.

Overcoming Overthinking

Overthinking a question can be one of the most frustrating things about taking the ACT Math. It is very common for us to get in a cycle like this:

We don't see how to do the problem right away → We assume the problem must be hard → Since we assume it's hard, we can't see how to do it → Since we can't see how to do it, we assume it's hard → Cycle goes on and on...

When this happens to us, we will spend forever on a tough problem and get nowhere, only to find that when we see the solution, it was *far, far* easier than we initially thought. What are some bad beliefs that lead to consistently over-thinking questions and some good beliefs that can help us avoid this

Bad Belief #1	**Good Belief #1**
There are REALLY TOUGH MATH CONCEPTS on the ACT that I've never learned.	I have the tools—I just need to put the right ones to use.

Why? The ACT is designed fundamentally as a critical thinking test first, a knowledge test second. This allows the ACT to show colleges that someone who may not have had the best opportunities to learn math but who has quite a bit of math talent and ability would be worth admitting so that she can realize her full potential. Because of this, the math content goes no further than Algebra II, Geometry, and Trigonometry. If you review the concepts earlier in the chapter, you can be assured that you will have the tools to figure out any problem that comes your way.

On the ACT Math, think of yourself as a carpenter who will need to make a unique item using simple tools like a hammer and screwdriver. You will need to solve challenging problems, but you will only need to use relatively easy math concepts to do so. The difficulty is not with the material but in figuring out what is being asked and how to set up your problem-solving approach.

Once in a while, the ACT Math will give you a problem with concepts like imaginary numbers, the law of cosines, the law of sines, or some formula from physics. If you are too easily intimidated, you will give up before you will realize that *they will give you the information you need to solve problems with more advanced concepts like these*. If it wasn't covered earlier in the chapter and you find it on the ACT Math, know that they will almost certainly give you the information you need to figure it out.

Bad Belief #2	**Good Belief #2**
I don't KNOW how to do it.	Let me FIGURE IT OUT.

On many math tests in school, you can tell right away whether you will be able to solve a given problem. If you (1) know the formula the problem uses and (2) can solve it without making a careless error, you are virtually guaranteed a correct answer. When we bring this mindset to the ACT Math, it can cause problems, since we will *give up way too quickly if we think we don't KNOW how to do it.*

A much more helpful approach is to think of the ACT Math problems less like the problems we face in school and more like problems that demand more patience and creativity:

Treat a problem like a puzzle or maze. The idea that you would "know" how to solve a maze prior to playing around with it is nonsense. On many of the ACT Math problems, you will only see how to figure them out after you have taken a step that seems like a natural step to take. For example:

If $5x - 4y = y$, what is $x - y$?

It would be very easy to simply give up on a problem like this, since we have two variables and only one equation. Instead, treat it like a *maze* and take a first step without complete knowledge of where it will take you. Start by doing whatever you can to simplify it. How about we subtract y from both sides so that we can group like terms together?

$$5x - 5y = 0$$

Now, since we want to end up with $x - y$, all we need to do is divide both sides by 5.

$$\frac{5x - 5y}{5} = \frac{0}{5}$$

This means that $x - y = 0$. You will only see the way to get through a problem like this by taking the first step.

In solving the ACT Math problems, break out of the mindset of a cook who can only cook with a recipe. Instead, be a cook who can go into a kitchen, see what looks good, and make something work based on what is available. Even if you do every single practice question in this book and in all the other ACT test preparation books available, you will *still* see problems on the actual ACT that will differ from what you have previously seen, since the ACT is more of a thinking than a knowledge test. While you need to know quite a bit, your *mathematical skill* is what will ultimately enable you to think on your feet and improvise, no matter what concepts or wording are thrown your way.

Bad Belief #3	**Good Belief #3**
I should save time by DOING THINGS IN MY HEAD.	I should WRITE IT ALL OUT SO I CAN MAKE CONNECTIONS.

Why do we often do too much in our head on math problems? Frankly, we do it because we have gotten away with it in the past.

Even though our teachers preach it, we can often get away with not writing out all of our work. This is particularly true for students who are bright and have solid "working memory," meaning they can keep quite a bit straight in their head at once. Some smart students take pride in the fact that they can do quite a bit in their head, and perhaps subconsciously like to have the excuse in advance that if their score isn't as high as they would like, they can blame it not on their ability but on "stupid mistakes." Stupid mistakes are still mistakes—do whatever you have to do to have the best performance possible. Be confident, not arrogant, and put everything in front of you.

We often don't write much on school tests so we can save the test for the next class. This saves schools money and is great for the environment, but on the ACT, your test booklet will not be reused by another student. They even provide half a page of blank space on which to do your figuring. Use it or lose it!

Why is writing out your work so important to setting up ACT math problems?

You won't fully understand what is being asked. As you read the question, write as you go so that you can *paraphrase* the question. If you misread or misinterpret even one word in the problem, you will probably miss the question.

If you do misunderstand the question, the ACT will likely have what you come up with as a wrong answer. The ACT Math questions will have wrong answers that students who go down an incorrect path are likely to choose. The ACT takes it a step beyond just coming up with numbers close to the right answer. If they only did this, as long as you came up with an answer that was there, you could feel comfortable that you were correct. You have to really put your energy and emphasis on *carefully reading and carefully setting up the problem*. You don't want to just feel good about your answer while taking the test only to receive your scores and realize how many careless mistakes you must have made.

Instead of thinking about writing out your work as a pointless, time-wasting chore, look at writing out your work as being like a *crime detective who puts all the evidence on a big table so that he can see how to solve a mystery*. Detectives don't just stare off into space hoping to have a miraculous insight pop into their heads—they put all the crime photographs and information in front of them to put their minds in a position to make connections. On the ACT Math, if you put down what is being asked, write out relevant formulas, and don't skip problem-solving steps, you will put your mind in a position to make connections too.

Let's do an example problem that shows how important it is to write out your work:

An elevator capacity cannot equal or exceed 1,800 pounds in order to function properly. The elevator is currently 300 pounds overweight. There are 7 people on board of identical weight. What is the least number of people needed to get off the elevator for it to function properly?

A. 0
B. 1
C. 2
D. 3
E. 4

Paraphrase the problem: The elevator has a capacity of 1,800 pounds, and is 300 pounds OVER capacity.

So, the elevator has 1,800 + 300 = 2,100 pounds currently.

If there are 7 people on the elevator, each person would weigh

$$\frac{2,100}{7} = 300 \text{ pounds}$$

The question says that the elevator cannot EQUAL OR EXCEED 1,800 pounds. So, if we take just one person out of the elevator, the elevator would *still* be at 1,800 pounds, which is not permitted. So, we have to take a TOTAL OF 2 people out of the elevator, making the correct answer (C). If we had rushed through the question and done too much in our head, here are some of the things we might have misread:

• That the elevator is 300 pounds OVER capacity, not UNDER capacity.
• That the elevator cannot EQUAL OR EXCEED 1,800 pounds, not that it only must not exceed 1,800 pounds.
• That the people are all of the same weight, and that to figure out their individual weights, we need to divide 2,100 by 7.

You don't have to go overboard in writing out every single solitary step. Most students find that they write way too little, so it is important to get more in balance by being certain to write out enough.

Bad Belief #4
I need to JUMP ON MY CALCULATOR right away to save time.

Good Belief #4
Problems involve MORE THINKING THAN COMPUTATION—I will use my calculator when needed.

Computation and memorization are skills that are becoming relatively less important as technology advances and can do the work for us. The ACT and colleges know this and want to test your ability to problem solve rather than your ability to remember a simple formula and plug in a bunch of numbers into your calculator to solve it.

Here is an example of a problem you would **NOT** find on the ACT:

$$\text{Solve for } x: 5x^4 + 3x^3 - 14x^2 + 17x - 1 = 15$$

This would involve a very long and tedious calculation, or the use of an equation-solving program on your calculator. The answers end up being −2.485 *and* 1.207, which are weird, not "clean" numbers. You will never have a problem like this on the ACT.

Here is an example of a problem you *WOULD* find on the ACT:

$$\text{Solve for } x: x^2 - 6x + 9 = 0$$

To solve this problem, you can look for patterns and can avoid tedious calculations. First, factor the equation:

$$(x - 3)(x - 3) = 0$$

The answer is simply **3** since if we plug 3 in for x, the entire expression would equal 0.

If you find yourself going down a path where you are doing a really in-depth multistep computation, know that you are doing something wrong. Retrace your steps, or even start over to see what you misread.

Bad Belief #5	Good Belief #5
IF I DON'T SEE IT RIGHT AWAY, THERE IS NO HOPE.	I WILL GIVE MYSELF PERMISSION TO NOT SEE IT RIGHT AWAY.

Solving ACT Math problems is an ***intuitive, creative*** process. While you don't want to dwell on a tough problem too long, if you find that you throw in the towel too easily, here are five things to consider:

1. **If you are doing too many questions, you will set yourself up for failure.** You need to give yourself enough time based on *your* personal abilities and situation to solve the problems you can. Revisit the timing guidelines earlier in the chapter if you need some guidance.
2. **Mistakes can lead to success.** If the ACT had problems that required 10 or more steps to solve, a small mistake would end up wasting quite a bit of

time. Since the problems typically involve 1–3 steps to solve, realize that *the first step forward can be a step backward*. If you make a small mistake in your initial setup, don't get down on yourself—recover from it and move forward.

3. **You only need to get it right—not to explain it to someone.** If you tend to overanalyze problems, set a different standard for yourself. Instead of feeling that you can only pick an answer if you give a detailed justification as to why you picked it, know that students who do extremely well on the Math often *solve the problems more intuitively*. They can get the correct answer but would have difficulty showing someone else how to do it. Embrace this mindset for yourself.

4. **There are multiple ways to solve problems.** There are usually several ways that you *can* approach solving ACT Math problems. From plugging numbers in to drawing pictures, be open-minded to all of the possible ways you might solve the problem.

5. **Give your subconscious mind a chance.** Perhaps more than any other section, coming back to questions on the ACT Math will give your mind the opportunity to think through the problems more thoroughly. Trust your feelings and instincts—if you don't feel comfortable with your answer but are holding your nose while you pick the answer, something is wrong. Go ahead and bubble in an answer so that if you run out of time, you will at least have it answered, but be open to coming back to it after your subconscious mind has given the problem more consideration.

Avoiding Careless Mistakes

The bottom line with avoiding careless mistakes is:

WRITE = RIGHT!

The more you put in front of you, the better you will do on the questions. You need to read the questions slowly, visualizing every step of the way in order to do your best. Watch the danger of the "unknown unknowns," much like we must do throughout the test. There will probably be some questions on the Math that most students know they cannot figure out; however, students can really improve their performance on those questions with *just a little more care*. They will be able to get them right because they are very doable. Here are five techniques that will enable you to avoid careless errors on the ACT Math.

1. Roller Coaster the Questions

It is essential that you read the questions *only as quickly as you fully understand what is being asked.* "Coasting" the question can force you into reading the question one time well instead of reading it over and over again, only to waste time and end up misreading the question. All you need to do is, as you read the question, underline everything and circle the key words. The ACT Math questions incorporate a great deal of wording that is not essential to solving the problems, but is inserted so that there can be no doubt as to what is being asked. Coasting the question will enable you to focus on what is really important while being certain that you don't miss anything. Here is an example of what a coasted math question looks like:

> The previews for the film take 20 minutes. The actual film is 110 minutes long. If Bill watches all of the previews and all of the film and spends no other time at the theater, what percent of his time in the theater is spent watching previews?

2. Draw Pictures

Many of the problems that incorporate geometry in particular can be solved by drawing pictures—don't just do them in your head. For example:

> What fraction of the area of a circle is covered by a square that is inscribed in the circle (i.e., all four of the square's vertices intersect the circle)?
>
> A. $\dfrac{2}{\pi}$
>
> B. $\dfrac{1}{2}$
>
> C. $\dfrac{4}{\pi}$
>
> D. $\dfrac{\pi}{4}$
>
> E. $\dfrac{2\pi}{3}$

Drawing a picture is extremely helpful to solving this problem:

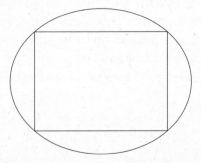

This is the square inscribed in the circle. To solve it, one of the easiest things to do is to come up with some concrete numbers you can use as values for the radius of the circle and the side of the square:

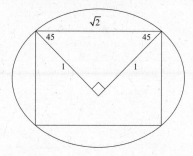

Then, solve for the fraction by calculating the area of the square and dividing it by the area of the circle:

$$\frac{\text{Area of Square}}{\text{Area of Circle}} = \frac{\sqrt{2} \times \sqrt{2}}{\pi 1^2} = \frac{2}{\pi}\text{ , making (A) the correct answer.}$$

3. Label Drawings

Other than when having the drawing drawn to scale would make solving the problem a complete joke, such as if they are asking you about what side lengths are congruent in a geometry problem, you can almost certainly count on the drawings on the ACT being to scale. As a result, labeling the drawings can be a huge help in solving the problems. For example:

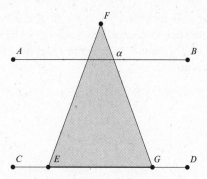

In the above figure, lines AB and CD are parallel, and the triangle, EFG, is isosceles, with sides EF and FG congruent. How many angles in the figure are congruent to angle α?

A. 4
B. 5
C. 6
D. 7
E. 8

Since the answers are all so close to one another, if we miscount by even one angle, we will likely miss the question. Instead, take the time to label every equivalent angle by hand:

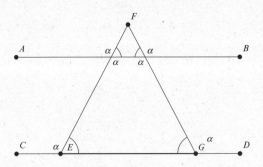

Careless mistakes are still mistakes, so if you label things as above, you will find that you have 5 angles equivalent to α, making the correct answer **(B)**.

4. Turn Words into Algebra

Students are often much more accustomed to problems where they can go on "autopilot" and simply solve for a variable, since that is what they typically have for in-school homework and test assignments. In-depth word problems are usually less frequent. On the ACT, word problems are *everywhere*. Don't rush through them and expect to solve them quickly without writing anything down. Instead, take the time to turn words into equations. For example:

A red balloon starts at a height of 150 feet in the air, and is losing height at a rate of 5 feet per minute. A blue hot-air balloon starts at a height of 60 feet and gains height at a rate of 4 feet per minute. At how many feet will the heights of the red and the blue balloon be equal?

A. 50
B. 100
C. 150
D. 200
E. 250

The equation for the height of the red balloon is height = 150 – 5 × minutes. The equation for the height of the blue balloon is height = 60 + 4 × minutes.

Then, we can solve for the number of minutes by setting these two expressions equal to one another:

$$150 - 5 \times \text{minutes} = 60 + 4 \times \text{minutes}$$

Simplify by grouping like terms together, subtracting 60 from both sides, and adding 5 to both sides:

$$90 = 9 \times \text{minutes}$$

We can then divide both sides by 9, giving us 10 minutes for the amount of time that will go by for these to equal one another. Then, to figure out the height, plug 10 minutes back into one of the equations. Let's do it for the red balloon:

$$\text{height} = 150 - 5 \times \text{minutes}$$
$$\text{height} = 150 - 5 \times 10 \text{ minutes}$$
$$\text{height} = 100 \text{ feet}$$

So, the correct answer is **B**. Had we done this in our head, we might have made a careless mistake along the way.

5. Plug in Numbers

Teachers are smart to give you the general advice to make sure you actually know how to solve problems, rather than plugging in choices and plugging in sample numbers. On the ACT, however, shortcuts like these can be quite effective. There are a couple of situations where plugging in numbers will be a good idea:

- **When you can easily work backwards from the answers rather than going forward by setting up an equation.** *Start with the MIDDLE ANSWER (C or H) since the answers are almost always in order from least to greatest.* That way you can see if you need an answer that is smaller or larger than what you have chosen, making you have to test a maximum of *three* answers instead of all five.

Here is an example problem where plugging in your choices may make things much easier, helping you to avoid the careless mistakes that may come from elaborate calculations.

What values of x are solutions for $x^2 - 21 = 4x$?

A. −8, −3
B. −5, −1
C. −3, 7
D. 7, 8
E. 8, 14

Even though we could solve this using the quadratic formula or factoring, if we plug in the numbers for x, we will be able to figure it out without difficulty. When we start with (C) in this case, we luck out, because both 7 and – 3 work, making (C) the correct answer.

- **Plug in numbers for variables to see how an expression will behave.** This is particularly helpful when you can't see an easy way to approach the problem algebraically. Make up some sample values that you can test in the expression. Here is an example problem where this technique would work:

If m has a value between 2,000 and 3,000 in the function $f(m) = \dfrac{1}{m^3}$, the value of $f(m)$ will be closest to which of the following?

A. –200
B. –150
C. –10
D. 0
E. 100

To figure this out, pick a number that we can plug in for m that falls in the range between 2,000 and 3,000. How about 2,500? When we put 2,500 in for m, let's see what we get:

$$\frac{1}{2500^3} = 0.000000000064$$

This is closest to 0, giving us **(D)** for the correct answer.

> **TIP**
>
> Putting in a certain amount of time to solve a problem is no guarantee you will figure it out. Mathematical problem solving demands creativity and flexibility, not just hard work.

Putting It All Together: Simplicity Underneath the Complexity

Throughout the ACT Math, you will find that you will often be initially intimidated, but if you can see that the difficulty is in **setting up the problem and not in the calculations or concepts**, you will be in great shape. Let's look at a few problems to illustrate how you should always be on the lookout for the simplicity underneath the complexity. There are lots of ways to solve problems, but *much of the time* (not always! Just much of the time!), there is a puzzle-like efficient approach you can take instead of a long, involved inefficient approach.

1. **The midpoint of line xy is given by (3, 2) and point y is (–2, –1). What are the coordinates of point x?**

Inefficient approaches: Either create a careful graph and sketch out where the different points would be, or plug all of these points into the midpoint formula to eventually solve.

Efficient approach: Realize that the differences between the x/y coordinates of the midpoint and point y will be the same as they are between the midpoint and point x. If you see this, you can get it done more quickly. Check out the table below for a detailed description:

	Point y Coordinates	Midpoint	How Far Are They Apart?	Now, Add the Differences to the Midpoint to Get Point x	Point x Coordinates
x coordinate	–2	3	+5	3 + 5	8
y coordinate	–1	2	+3	2 + 3	5

Obviously, you wouldn't need a table like this to solve it as long as you can quickly see the connection in your mind. The final answer would be (8, 5).

2. **What is the value of $16a^2$ if $(4a + 5)(4a – 5)= 7$?**

Inefficient approach: FOILing this all the way through, and then solving by using the quadratic formula or factoring.

Efficient approach: Go ahead and FOIL this and see what you have:

$$(4a + 5)(4a - 5) = 7$$
$$16a^2 - 25 = 7$$
$$16a^2 = 32$$

The question doesn't ask for the value of a, but simply wants the value of $16a^2$. So, as long as you can get that expression equal to a number, you are all done! When we look at this expression, we can see that the outer and inner terms from FOILing it will cancel. The final answer is 32.

3. **How many points will satisfy the equation $(x - 3)^2 + (y - 4)^2 = 212$?**

Inefficient Approach: Try different combinations of numbers until you eventually get a firm answer.

Efficient Approach: Realize that since there are two variables and one equation, there are infinitely many solutions! We need to have the same number of variables as equations in order to solve something like this. So, the final answer is "infinitely many."

4. **The Ideal Gas Law states that $PV = nRT$, where P stands for the absolute pressure of the gas, V is the volume of the gas, n is the number of moles of gas, T is the absolute temperature of the gas, and R is the universal gas constant. What is the value of the universal gas constant R in terms of the other values?**

Inefficient Approach: Assume that you need to have a background in chemistry to answer this question, and find yourself overwhelmed by all the wording and variables.

Efficient Approach: Get R by itself by dividing both sides by nT and you're done!

$$PV = nRT$$

Divide both sides by nT

$$\frac{PV}{nT} = R$$

And that is your final answer. Don't let the ACT Math intimidate you by making you think you need to know more equations than necessary, and don't let yourself get bogged down in elaborate wording.

5. **A set of unique integers, sorted from least to greatest, consists of A, B, C, D, E, and F. If G and H are added to this set, and they are greater than E, and X and Y are added, and they are less than B, what is the median of the new set of integers?**

Inefficient Approach: Plug in concrete values for every single variable and compute the median of the set before the changes and after the changes.

Efficient Approach: Realize that with an even number of unique integers, we need to find the median (the middle value) by taking the average of the values in the middle. The median of the original set will therefore be $\frac{C+D}{2}$. Because we are adding two values *greater* than E and two values *less* than B, the median of the new set *will not change at all!* So, the final answer is simply $\frac{C+D}{2}$.

So please be on the lookout for the simplicity underneath the complexity. The ACT is interested in your ability to *think*, not so much your ability to *remember* or *calculate*. Although there will be some problems in which doing a brute force calculation or remembering a tough formula will be essential, they are not nearly as frequent as those problems where you can think your way through them just as you would a puzzle.

MATH FORMULAS SUMMARY

Rectangle Area

$$Length \times Width = Area$$

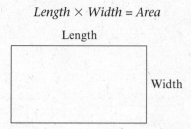

Triangle Area

$$Area = \frac{1}{2}\ Base \times Height$$

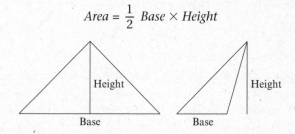

Parallelogram Area

$$Base \times Height = Area$$

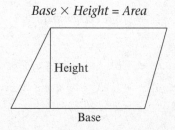

Trapezoid Area

$$\frac{(B1 + B2)}{2} \, Height = Area$$

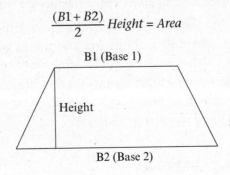

Triangle Types

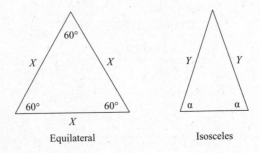

Degrees in a Polygon

(Number of Sides – 2) × 180 = Number of Degrees

Angle Rules

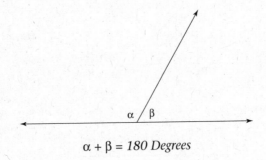

$\alpha + \beta = 180 \, Degrees$

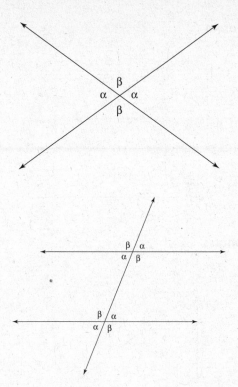

Circle Rules

$\pi r^2 = Area$

$2\pi r = Circumference$

$(x - h)^2 + (y - k)^2 = r^2$

$h = X\ center$

$k = Y\ center$

$r = radius$

$(x - 3)^2 + (y - 2)^2 = 9$ would be

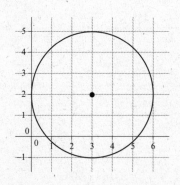

Pythagorean Theorem

$A^2 + B^2 = C^2$

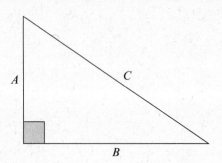

Special Right Triangles

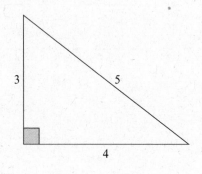

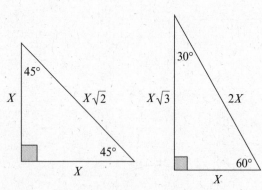

Cylinder Volume

$\pi r^2 h$ = Volume

Box Volume

$l \times w \times d$ = Volume

$$\text{DISTANCE} = \text{RATE} \times \text{TIME}$$

$$\frac{\text{PART}}{\text{WHOLE}} \times 100 = \text{PERCENTAGE}$$

$$y = mx + b \qquad\qquad (x_1, y_1), (x_2, y_2)$$

m = Slope

$b = y$ intercept $\qquad$ Slope $= \dfrac{(y_2 - y_1)}{(x_2 - x_1)} = \dfrac{\text{Rise}}{\text{Run}}$

Parallel lines = same slope

Perpendicular lines = negative reciprocal

POINTS: $(x_1, y_1), (x_2, y_2)$

$$\text{DISTANCE} = \sqrt{\left(x_2 - x_1\right)^2 + \left(y_2 - y_1\right)^2}$$

$$\text{MIDPOINT} = \left(\frac{x_1 + x_2}{2}, \frac{y_1 + y_2}{2}\right)$$

$$x^2 x^3 = x^{(2+3)} = x^5 \qquad (x^2)^3 = x^{(2 \cdot 3)} = x^6$$

$$x^{-3} = \frac{1}{x^3} \qquad\qquad x^{\frac{2}{3}} = \sqrt[3]{x^2}$$

$$\frac{\text{Radians}}{\pi} = \frac{\text{Degrees}}{180°}$$

$$\log_a x = b \text{ is the same as } a^b = x$$

$$\log_a xy = \log_a x + \log_a y$$

$$\log_a \frac{x}{y} = \log_a x - \log_a y$$

$$\log_a x^y = y \cdot \log_a x$$

$$\text{Mean} = \frac{\text{Sum of parts}}{\text{Number of parts}}$$

Median = Middle

Mode = Most frequent

$$\cos^2 x + \sin^2 x = 1 \quad \text{and} \quad \tan\theta = \frac{\sin\theta}{\cos\theta}$$

S-O-H	C-A-H	T-O-A
$\sin\theta = \dfrac{\text{Opposite}}{\text{Hypotenuse}}$	$\cos\theta = \dfrac{\text{Adjacent}}{\text{Hypotenuse}}$	$\tan\theta = \dfrac{\text{Opposite}}{\text{Adjacent}}$
Their respective reciprocals are . . .		
$\csc\theta = \dfrac{1}{\sin\theta}$	$\sec\theta = \dfrac{1}{\cos\theta}$	$\cot\theta = \dfrac{1}{\tan\theta}$

MATH STRATEGY SUMMARY

- Be sure you memorize all the formulas for the test since they are not provided.
- ACT Math problems are difficult in terms of figuring out what they are asking and setting them up. They are typically not difficult in terms of what you need to know or in the calculations.
- The more you write as you think through the problems, the fewer careless errors you will make, and the more likely you will recognize patterns.
- Don't overthink the questions—there is always a relatively straightforward method to solving them, although it typically won't be obvious.
- The questions generally become more difficult later in the test.
- Determine your timing strategy ahead of time. Some options:

  - Do all 60 questions, spending 25 minutes on the first 30 questions and 35 minutes on the second 30 questions.
  - If you tend to rush, guess on some of the last questions so you avoid careless errors.
  - If you tend to get stuck on problems, plan on having some "throw-away" questions as you go.

Reading

3

🔑 WHAT ARE THE BASIC FACTS ABOUT THE ACT READING SECTION?

→ 35 minutes, 40 questions
→ 4 passages—one each from Prose Fiction, Social Science, Humanities, and Natural Science
→ One passage will likely have two smaller passages you will compare
→ 10 questions follow each passage
→ Questions are in a random order of difficulty

If you are like most students, you have concerns about the following when you approach the reading section:

• Time constraints
• Being able to stay focused on the passage
• Second-guessing on the questions

The source of most of these issues is that students assume that they should use the *same approach to the reading test as they do when they read for school.* Let's explore the way that you read things for school so that you can see the differences. . . .

In school, you find that the following strategies work well to help you prepare for tests and quizzes:

• Take your time to read—you have plenty of it!
• Memorize key details, since your teachers will ask you *lots* of highly specific questions to make sure that you haven't simply looked at Cliffsnotes©, Sparknotes©, or Wikipedia©.
• When you are answering test questions about what you have read, you simply think "Did I hear this in lecture?" or "Did I see this in the book?" The name of the game is to *match* information in the choices with information you have studied. You answer the questions quickly, trusting your gut instincts.

All of the above assumptions will result in *serious* trouble on the ACT Reading test. If you have made these assumptions previously and the results weren't what you would have liked, realize that the mistakes say nothing about **you**—they only reflect **your method**. You need to completely change your assumptions:

- Time is critical—you can't do ACT Reading as you would do textbook reading.
- Don't sweat the small stuff—focus on the big picture.
- Be very methodical and patient on the questions.

Let's first examine how we need to read, and then how to answer the questions.

METHODOLOGY FOR READING THE PASSAGES

How do you change how you read so that you can move through the reading more quickly? Understand that the way you normally read *works in school* but *does NOT work on the ACT!* Instead of trying to memorize every little detail of the passage, focus *on the areas that give you the biggest return for your efforts!*

The easiest way to think about this is to pretend you are studying for an open book test. This is hard to do because you are so used to studying for closed book tests for school! For closed book tests, you have to memorize all the little details because your teacher will want to make sure you have actually read the material and haven't used an online resource to prepare. With a different test, you need a different approach. Here are the three things to focus on while you read the ACT reading passages, keeping in mind that it is open book:

1. **What is the gist of the passage?** When you read it, don't worry about all the small stuff. Read it so that at the end of the passage, if someone asked you "What was the story about?" you would be able to give a couple of sentences to summarize it. *See the forest, not just the trees!*
2. **Do you have a mental map of the passage?** You should expect to go back and look at context to answer about 75% of the questions. Although some of the questions will give you particular lines and paragraphs, several will refer to a specific item without telling you where it is. If you are going to answer *specific* questions well, you have to know where to go without having to reread the whole passage. So, when you read, focus on **organization** instead of **memorization**.
3. **Know how to alternate between reading carefully and quickly.** If you can read at a pace of 200–250 words a minute, you will have no trouble

finishing the ACT Reading. So, there is not a need to "skim" the passages. However, there will be a need to read some parts of the passages more carefully and other parts more quickly so that you can focus your time and energy most effectively. Here are some of the major differences between careful and quick reading:

Careful Reading	Quick Reading
Your eyes move *side to side* like a typewriter as you read. You are processing one word at a time.	Your eyes widen and flow *like a waterfall* over the words. You are processing several words at a time.
You *hear* all the words, one by one. It is like listening to the radio.	You *see* the words. In your mind, it transforms into watching a movie!
What you do when you read a textbook!	What you do when you read social media!

The ability to alternate between careful and quick reading will serve you well not only on the ACT but in college. In college, you will have some classes where you could have 300 pages *a week* for ONE CLASS! Perhaps this is why the ACT wants to make sure you can read efficiently so that colleges can see if you are truly ready for a college curriculum. Be mindful of the careful/quick reading distinctions as we explore the different passage types on the ACT and break down what needs to be read carefully and what can be read more quickly.

HOW TO READ DIFFERENT TYPES OF PASSAGES

The immediately following strategies are recommended for the *average* test taker—after the strategies are broken down, a thorough explanation of how you can change your approach *based on your personal situation* will follow. There is definitely not a one-size-fits-all approach to the reading section!

TIP

You might be a faster reader or a slower reader than you think. Practice the ACT Reading with time to find out where you stand and adjust your strategy as needed.

You may be wondering, "Do I have to read everything BEFORE I do the questions, or should I just go to the questions first?" The short answer is "**read the passages first in an 'open-book' way, unless you face significant read-**

ing comprehension challenges, or are in a huge time crunch." Why do this? If you were taking a test that you had never seen before, then, yes, it would make sense to read the questions first since you would have NO IDEA what the questions were like!

On the ACT, however, we know what the questions are going to be like: *a mixture of general, specific, and line questions that test your ability to comprehend the meaning of what you read, and to make inferences based on context clues.* Since the questions rely so heavily on your ability to see the big picture, if you only see the "trees" instead of the "forest," you will be in a lot of trouble on the questions. In school, you often encounter many poorly written multiple-choice questions where you can easily go back and *match* information to what your teacher said in lecture, or a word you heard in a book. Here, you need to really lock into the big picture, or you will become lost.

The ACT Reading always has **four** types of passages in the following order:

- **Prose Fiction**—A fiction piece you would read in English class—a short story or excerpt from a novel.
- **Social Science**—Something you would read in your social studies classes.
- **Humanities**—A mixture of artistic, social, and biographical texts. It is tough to predict what exactly this will be.
- **Natural Science**—A nontextbook-style selection from any of the sciences: astronomy, biology, geology, etc.

Note that any one of these types of passages could be the one with a comparative Passage A and Passage B format. For whichever one it is, be sure you focus on the relationship between the passages as you read because there will likely be three questions about the relationship. You may want to do Passage A and its questions first, Passage B and its questions second, and the comparative questions last. They always go in this order, making this an easy strategy to implement.

Due to its predictable structure, you can have a solid plan of attack going into the test. It would be delightful if you could read each passage the exact same way, but you need to change your approach depending on what you are reading. Here's what to do for each passage type.

Prose Fiction

Focus heavily on the beginning paragraph; then read the rest of the passage at a normal pace. With any story, if you do not understand the beginning, the rest of it will be complete nonsense to you. To illustrate this, consider this situation:

You go to the movies, and you have a desperate craving for popcorn. So, instead of going right into the theater, you wait in the enormous line for your snack. Then, you finally make it into the theater 20 minutes into the film. At this point, you are totally lost. The only thing entertaining you is the consumption of your buttery popcorn because the story doesn't make any sense.

The prose fiction passage is like this, only without the popcorn! You will be tempted to move too quickly in the beginning of the fiction—i.e., the *first paragraph or two* (if the first couple of paragraphs are short), but if you do, you will miss out on:

- The setting of the story
- The characters that will be acting and speaking later on
- The beginning of the plot

Take your time at the beginning, locking into the start of the story, and you will be in great shape going forward. It takes more time to do this up front, but it will definitely save you time in the long run.

When you read the body paragraphs, quick reading is not a good idea. Important plot points and character development are embedded within the text. So, in the body paragraphs, *read them at a normal pace.*

Social Science and Natural Science

Focus heavily on the first paragraph, topic sentences, and last paragraph. Nonfiction reading is structured differently from the fiction passages. When you encounter a nonfiction experience in your daily life, you can see this clearly:

- If you come late to a class, like history or science, in which the teacher is giving a lecture on a nonfiction topic, it is not difficult at all to pick up on what is going on. "Oh yeah! They're talking about cell reproduction!" or "Oh yeah! They're talking about World War II!" Compare this situation to trying to piece together a story when someone has already been telling it for a few minutes. You will be hopelessly lost!
- It is FAR easier to outline nonfiction reading than fiction. That's why your English teachers will usually have you do annotations, and your history/science teachers will usually have you do chapter outlines! The two types of reading demand different strategies.

In order to understand the most from nonfiction, take the following steps:

STEP 1 *Focus heavily on the first paragraph.* This is where you will find the thesis and general overview of the passage.

STEP 2 Then, *read the body paragraphs by reading the topic sentences super-carefully, and the other sentences of the body paragraph by reading quickly.* The topic sentences give you the main idea of each paragraph and the other sentences provide supporting details. As long as you know *where* the information can be found, there is no need to remember exactly *what* the information was.

STEP 3 Finally, be sure to *read the concluding paragraph carefully.* This is where the big picture of the passage will be tied together.

Now, there are a couple of situations where you would want to change your approach. . . .

First, if the body paragraphs are longer, read two or three sentences of the beginning of each paragraph more carefully. Then, read the remaining part of the body paragraph more quickly. Some ACT nonfiction passages have as few as three or four paragraphs (although this is fairly rare), so be prepared to improvise!

Second, if you are a strong reader, don't worry about having to read through the body paragraphs quickly. "If it ain't broke, don't fix it!" If you can read with solid comprehension in a timely fashion, stick to what you are doing. You may still want to *be absolutely certain* you have fully comprehended the key parts of the passage (i.e., the first paragraph), the topic sentences, and the last paragraph.

Humanities

Read it like the fiction if it is a first-person story, and read it like the nonfiction if it is a third-person passage.

Humanities requires that you change it up, depending on what you see in front of you on a particular test that morning. It could go either way between being a story-telling passage or a nonfiction passage. You will be able to tell which way it is going within the first paragraph. The key word to look for is "**I**"! If you see several "I"s, then you know that it is written in *first-person*. So, it is likely to be some sort of autobiographical piece that you will want to read like the prose fiction. If there are no "I"s, read it like the social science and natural science.

To sum all of this up, take a look at this table:

Prose Fiction	Humanities	Social/Natural Science
Focus on the *beginning* of the passage, then read the rest at a normal pace.	Do it like the fiction if you see that it is in *first-person* (I), and like the social/natural science if you don't.	Carefully read the *first paragraph*, *topic sentences*, and *last paragraph*. Read the rest at a quicker pace.
Passage A and Passage B: Focus on the relationship between the passages— consider doing Passage A and its questions first, Passage B and its questions second, and the comparative questions last.		

An enormous problem that people face when reading is *staying focused* on what is in front of them instead of daydreaming. You will find that by reading the passages in the ways described above, you will be able to *read more quickly* and *with greater comprehension* than how you normally read. You can do this because you are being reasonable about what your capabilities are. Unless you have a photographic memory, which *very, very* few people have, then you will find it much more helpful to focus on the *big picture and mental map* while you read, rather than trying to memorize a lot of little details. Reading with a focus on tiny details is a recipe for trouble because it is extraordinarily boring and will easily lead to daydreaming and losing focus.

> **TIP**
>
> In today's society, with information at our fingertips thanks to technology, remembering lots of facts is not as important as it once was. Being able to quickly comprehend the general idea of a text and use information within it is. These are exactly what the ACT Reading evaluates.

Another mindset that may help you stay focused while you read is to apply *an attitude of impatience* to what you are reading. If you were reading a letter from a long-lost friend and wanted to savor every detail, then you would definitely take your time. If, however, you were reading something that was boring, you could respond in one of two ways:

- Distraction—you think of *anything but* the passage in front of you as a way of coping with having to do something you don't want to do.
- Impatience—you want to *hurry up and get to the point* so that you can move onto other things.

Impatience is clearly a better attitude. It's strange, but when you read in a slow, distracted way, you end up spending *very little time actually reading!* Allow yourself to focus on the most important parts of the passage, move quickly through the rest, and you will be more successful.

METHODOLOGY FOR ANSWERING QUESTIONS

All of the Big Ideas about the ACT apply to how you do the questions on the reading section, so let's review.

1. **There are no games on the ACT, and there is always one definitive answer to each question.**
   The reading questions will strike you as having multiple correct answers, but liberate yourself by knowing that although something may FEEL 99 percent correct, it will still be 100 percent wrong.
2. **Give more focus to the questions than the answers.**
   If you misread a question and fail to focus on the key things that it is asking you to do, you will think you got it right when it was actually incorrect.
3. **The test is about thinking rather than knowledge.**
   The test does not have a bunch of "recall" questions that have you match up with the words in the text—you need to think very carefully about what it might be before you jump in and pick an answer.
4. **Do what you can, do it well, and don't do too much.**
   It is very tough to finish the reading section, so go into the test knowing how much of it you can reasonably attempt.

Let's go in-depth by examining how most people without any preparation approach ACT Reading questions. First, they read the question quickly, and then they immediately look at the choices and try to eliminate the choices one by one. This approach works well if you were doing a *rapid recall test* in one of your classes in high school—having to remember facts, dates, formulas, etc. It works in school because the questions are usually *short*, and they are based *purely on your memory* from lectures or the reading. *You cannot approach the ACT Reading questions this way because they are totally different!*

The ACT Reading questions are far more complex than the reading comprehension questions you have on tests for school. They are longer, ask you to make more inferences, and have some *very* persuasive wrong answers. As such, you need to *slow the process down* so that you can be successful.

"But wait!" you may ask, "How on earth can I slow the process down on the reading questions and finish the test in time?!" Great point, and here's the answer:

> **It is far better to do the question *one time through perfectly* than it is to have to reread it several times and *still* miss the point of the question!**

You want to control the test rather than let the test control you. You do this by focusing on the questions, breaking them down piece by piece, and creating your own answer. This approach is fleshed-out in the **4-C Method**. Follow these steps to succeed on the reading questions.

> **Cover** your choices with your nondominant hand (i.e., if you are right-handed, cover the choices with your left hand). This will ensure that you do not look too hastily at the answer choices, which would allow the wrong answers to distract you.

Have you ever been grocery shopping when you (a) had no list and (b) were extremely hungry? You inevitably end up buying far more than you need, and you come home and ask yourself, "why did I get this giant box of cookies?" Contrast this with when you go to the grocery and you *have a list*! It takes more time up front to write the list, but it saves you time in the long run because you don't waste time agonizing over what to buy—you simply go in to the store, find what you need, and go home.

Your approach to ACT Reading questions should be similar. If you don't know what you want before you look, you will become trapped by what they put in front of you. Just like a sneaky advertiser, they know what sort of incorrect answers will tempt you. You will avoid problems if you "know before you go"!

> **Coast the question**—read the questions carefully to pick up exactly what is being asked.

To do this, underline the entire question, and highlight key words as you read it. Here is an example of what this could look like:

> We can infer from the passage as a whole, that the term "incense," as it is used in line 45, most nearly means which of the following?

Here are some things to keep in mind as you roller coaster the reading questions:

- Be sure you pick up on key words that ask you to do something *differently from just figuring out what something means*. Some examples of these words are: **not, except, infer, suggests, function of, serves to, theme, tone,** etc. If you are going too quickly, you will definitely skip over these, and there will be a distractor (wrong answer) ready to trap you.

- Use the coasting to ensure you read the question *one time well* rather than several times poorly. Be sure that your brain and your eyes are in sync with one another—don't allow your eyes to race ahead of where your brain is.

- Don't worry too much about which words to circle and which to just underline. If you understand what you are reading, you are doing it the right way.

- If you don't like underlining and circling because you find it to be *too busy on the page*, you can modify it by merely underlining the key words and leaving everything else blank.

TIP

The thought process to succeed on the ACT Reading is much like that of the Scientific Method: you make observations and a hypothesis before concluding what theory applies.

When you do this, you will avoid *second-guessing*, having to *reread the question*, and making *careless mistakes*. The key is to read each question only one time and to do it **perfectly**! Do not read past a phrase of a question *unless you fully comprehend what you have just read*!

- **CREATE a GENERAL answer using CONTEXT.** This is the *most important step*. It is by far the easiest step to skip if you are in a hurry, but it will be the most vital thing you can possibly do to be successful on the questions.

  - *Create* an answer in your own words. If you are more of a visual thinker, a picture in your mind will suffice. Make sure you at least have *something* that you can use.

- **Keep it *General***: There are literally thousands of answers that the test makers could create that would be correct. Keep what you create in your head very general and flexible so that no matter what the right answer is, you are prepared to recognize it.
- ***Context.*** With context, follow one of the following two paths:

  1. If it is a *general* question about the passage as a whole, it will be sufficient to simply stop and think of an answer in your own words. After having read the passage, you should have a good sense of the meaning of the passage as a whole so that you can do these types of questions without having to go back.
  2. If it is a question that refers to *specific lines* or to a *specific thing mentioned in the passage*, be sure to go back and look at the *context*! (Unlike the SAT, the line questions do not necessarily go in order.) The specific item questions will refer to a person, idea, or event that you may recall from the passage, but don't rely on your memory. Go back and check it out for yourself! With both of these situations, at a minimum, look at *the sentences that are before and after the excerpt.* You will find over and over again that if you rely on your memory, you will be steered the wrong way by the ever-so-persuasive wrong answers.

People who are zooming along feel the pressure of the time and go too quickly on this particular step. Paradoxically, they find that the faster they jump to look at the choices, the longer it takes them to answer the question. Don't let this happen to you.

TIP

If you get it down to two answers, look for the flaws in one of the choices. There will always be something in the wrong answer that keeps it from being perfect.

Critically look at the choices. At this point, you finally look at the choices. You must allow yourself to *gradually* come to an answer—do not "leap" to an answer too rapidly. There are a few things to consider:

1. **If it is partially right, it is 100 percent wrong.** Allow the fact that there is one *perfect* answer to liberate you from latching onto anything too quickly. Fight the tendency that comes from your high school tests to immediately go with your gut instinct. Be on the lookout for parts of an answer that *contaminate* the rest of the choice. The ACT Reading questions will sometimes be 95 percent correct, with only *one word* that ruins the meaning of the whole thing. A test that is given to well over 1,900,000 test takers a year will simply *not have questions* that have more than one answer that is correct! (If they do, it will be a major news story!) This is not like what you often have in high school, where sometimes questions will actually have two viable answers, and the teacher will simply give everyone a freebie or throw out the question to make up for it. *There is only one perfect answer, and if you are not finding it, there is a problem with your strategy and not with the test!*

2. You will be more attracted to answers that are more *specific* and *long*. In the same way that you would assume that someone who used large words and spoke for a greater length of time was more intelligent, you will be more inclined to think longer and more specific answers are correct. There is nothing wrong in and of itself with a long answer, but do not pick a long and specific answer for that reason alone. Be certain that the content of what is needed is there, not just the superficial form of it.

3. Most importantly, focus on *meaning, not matching*. Don't pick an answer *simply because it has words that match up with words in the passage*. If the sole reason you are choosing an answer is that the answers match up with some random words in the passage, then you are going down the wrong path. Think about the *big picture* and *general meaning* of what you want. As an analogy, let's think once again about shopping. If you are going to buy a *Wizard of Oz* DVD as a present for a friend and the store doesn't have it, you will panic because you can't find a perfect match for what your friend wants. Instead, you will be better off going to the store with the mindset that you want "a classic movie." This more *general* mindset will give you the flexibility you need to find something that really works as an answer to the question. Often if you are not flexible, you will panic because the exact match is not there.

Like learning any new skill, executing a step-by-step method may seem overwhelming. Allow yourself to *take it slowly* the first few times. These steps will not come to you at full speed right away, but, with enough practice, you will find that your accuracy and speed will increase dramatically.

OPTIONS FOR YOUR PERSONAL SITUATION

The Reading section, more than any other, demands that students adjust their technique depending on their strengths and weaknesses. Here are some ways that you can adjust your approach depending on the problems you are running into. . . .

If you are a GREAT, FAST READER, congratulations! You will be able to finish the reading test without too many problems.

- Be sure that you spend about *NINE minutes per passage* (including reading the passage and answering the questions).
- Don't be overconfident and skip the steps on the questions.

If you are close to being able to read everything and answer the questions in time, then BOUNCE the questions from easy to hard! Instead of doing the questions in numerical order, fight for every point you can and save the tough ones for later. Do the questions in **this** order:

- *Short Questions and/or Line Reference Questions **First***. These questions are almost certainly easier than other ones because you don't have to spend much time reading them, and/or you don't have to spend much time looking for the context that you will need to put an answer in your own words. Since every question is worth the same amount, do these right away.
- *Long Questions and/or General Interpretation Questions **Later***. This is essentially the opposite of the above questions. They will take longer to read and understand, and it will be more difficult to find where the information is in the passage. If you are having trouble finishing up the reading section, perhaps you can even *skip* a few of these more challenging questions! Whatever you do, *do not get bogged down on anything!* You can do extraordinarily well even if you miss a few questions, so *let the tough ones go!* Once again, this is hard to do based on your high school class testing experience—teachers typically will let you stay after class for a few minutes to finish if need be, and more often than not, the tests are not that long.

Don't overanalyze the bouncing. Make sure you are **decisive**—quickly pick the first question that you are going to do, and immediately look for the next one that seems easy. That is why we call it "bouncing," since you will bounce from one question to the next! Whatever you do, don't spend a bunch of time reading a question and then deciding, "Oh, this question looks too tricky for me!" You will have already wasted much of your time. (If you have gone through the question-answering process as described through the 4-C approach, and you STILL are stuck on a question, then let it go after you have given it a good try.) Your pace doing it this way should still be *nine minutes per passage*, including the questions and the reading.

If you are a GOOD but SLOW reader, then pick THREE of the passages to do instead of doing all four. It is very easy to earn a score in the mid 20s on the ACT Reading by only doing three of the passages and simply guessing on the questions on the fourth one. Will you be able to score a 36 doing it this way? No. But, if that is not your goal, it is far better to aim for a 25 and actually score it than it is to aim for a 36, spread yourself too thin, and score an 18. *Be realistic about your situation!*

When picking three, there are three ways that you can choose which passages to do. Think about which of the following would work the best for you:

1. **Consider what subject in school you dislike the most.** Think about *English*, *History*, and *Science*. If you find the reading from one of these subjects *really boring*, then you should be able to go into the test knowing which passage to skip all together. If you don't like English, skip the Prose Fiction. If you don't like History, skip the Social Science. And if you dislike Science, then skip the Natural Science. Since the Humanities passage is pretty variable, you should probably go ahead and do this one. Also, if the comparative passage format gives you quite a bit of difficulty, you may want to skip that passage, wherever it falls.

2. **Read some sample passages.** In the practice test samples, take a look at some passages for yourself and determine which type gives you the most difficulty. If there is a clear one that you have trouble with, then skip that one. For most people, it is either the Prose Fiction or the Natural Science. The Prose Fiction is tough if you have difficulty "reading between the lines" (i.e., picking up on inferences when you read). The Natural Science is usually the least "story-like" of the passages and often has the material that you would be least likely to read on your own. See for yourself and determine which one will make the most sense to skip.

3. Take a few seconds at the beginning of the test to determine your order. If there is not a passage that consistently gives you the most difficulty, then this might be what you should do. Take no more than 20–30 seconds at the beginning of the ACT Reading to skim the topics of each of the passages. Determine which three passages look the most interesting to you. Do them in order from "most interesting" to "least interesting." If you are someone who is easily bored and loves to have control over what you are doing, this may be the best approach for you.

If you do the "Pick Three" method, then you will have approximately *11–12 minutes per passage*, including the reading and the questions. This extra bit of time will allow you to read the passages at a more comfortable pace and to answer the questions in a careful manner. If you happen to finish the three passages with a few minutes to spare, then go to the last passage and *go directly to the questions*, answering them in the order described below. You can expect to score a maximum of a 25–29 approaching the test by doing 3–3.5 passages.

TIP

Most students overestimate their abilities to read quickly and comprehend well. Be realistic about what you can do and adjust your strategy accordingly.

If you are an extremely slow reader with poor comprehension, then go DIRECTLY to the questions. You can likely score around a 20 or so doing it this way. Spend a little under a minute per question.

If you have no idea which way will work best for you, not to worry. Start by doing the diagnostic test in this book and then examine what makes the most sense for you based on the results.

It is so important to be realistic about what you are capable of doing. People inevitably struggle on the test when they try to do too much. If you know that when you read (even if you do the approaches outlined above) the words go "in one ear and out the other," then it *does not make sense to waste time reading the passage*! Trying to read the passage will compound your trouble, since you will have little time left to answer the questions in a careful way. Here is how you should attack the passages/questions doing it this way:

First, determine which order makes the most sense for you. In all likelihood, you will want to do the passages in this order:

1. Natural Science
2. Social Science
3. Humanities
4. Prose Fiction

This will be the fourth, the second, the third, and then the first passage. Why? It is *far* easier to answer the questions without having read the passage with *nonfiction* reading than it is with *fiction* reading. Without having a sense of the big picture on the fiction, you will often be completely lost on many of the questions. With the nonfiction, you have a good chance on several of the questions because nonfiction does not rely so much on inferences. This order is recommended for most people doing the "straight-to-the-questions" method, but you will need to decide for yourself what works best for you. Allow yourself flexibility in coming up with the optimal order.

Now, let's talk about the questions. You will want to do them in this order:

1. **Line Questions.** Do any questions that refer to specific lines or paragraphs in the passage, since you will not have to have read any of the passage to know exactly where to go. When you do this, it is vital that you *read around the line reference* in order to have adequate context to answer the question.
2. **Specific Questions.** Do questions that refer to specific items in the passage. This can include virtually anything—characters, ideas, events—that is mentioned in the reading. You will be tempted to do these without looking back at the reading, but that will cause you to have no idea what they are talking about.
3. **General Questions.** These questions ask you about the passage as a whole. Even though you are answering the first two types of questions, in the back of your mind, you should be thinking about how the specific items you are reading fit together in a big picture. It is like watching a movie a bit here and a bit there—pretty soon you have an idea of the whole plot of the film!

What to do if time is running out, and things are falling apart. . .

When you are doing the Reading section, have a *mental game plan of flexibility*. You want to plan for best case and worse case scenarios. If things do not go to your liking, allow yourself to modify your approach accordingly.

The **line**, **specific**, **general** approach (outlined above) will work in ANY situation in which you are running out of time and cannot read the passage. In particular, if you have five minutes remaining and you have just begun the very last passage, you can skip reading the passage, and do the questions in the **line**, **specific**, **general** order. Be sure that you DO NOT SPREAD YOURSELF TOO THIN—don't do a question unless you take the time to do it right. You may only finish 5–6 out of all 10 in a passage, but it is much more likely they will be correct. Here are a couple of other ways you may need to change based on the circumstances:

- If you are getting stuck on questions, "bounce" on them instead of doing them in order.
- If a particular passage seems extremely boring right from the start, be decisive and move on to another passage. Build positive momentum by doing passages that are easier and more interesting.
- If you know that you won't finish all the questions, DO NOT try to read all the questions really quickly and do them all. Instead, allocate your time so that you can do a few questions well while completely guessing on the other questions. Remember—there is no guessing penalty on the ACT. The ACT is too well written for you to be able to quickly guess on several questions and get them right. The easiest thing to do is to pick a letter and stay with it—that way you won't be indecisive on test day.

The bottom line is that you should know going into the test that things may not go as well as you imagine, and be prepared to change!

TIP

Have a backup plan in case you are not able to read as quickly as you would hope. Practice what you will do before you take the test so you do not panic.

If you are still feeling indecisive about how you should approach the Reading, try thinking about what score you would like to aim for and see about how many questions you need to answer correctly to earn the score:

Number of Questions Correct	Approximate ACT Reading Score
38–40	36
37	35
36	34
35	33
34	32
—	31
33	30
32	29
30–31	28
29	27
28	26
27	25
26	24
25	23
24	22
23	21
22	20
21	19
20	18

Number of Questions Correct	Approximate ACT Reading Score
19	17
17–18	16
16	15
14–15	14
12–13	13
10–11	12
08–09	11
07	10
06	9
05	8
—	7
04	6
03	5
02	4
—	3
01	2
00	1

It is pretty surprising to most students just how many questions they can miss in order to earn the score they want!

PRACTICE READING PASSAGES

Don't forget the different ways to read the passages:

Prose Fiction	Humanities	Social/Natural Science
Focus on the *beginning* of the passage, then read the rest at a normal pace.	Do it like the fiction if you see that it is in *first-person* (I), and like the social/natural science if you don't.	Focus on the *first paragraph*, *topic sentences*, and *last paragraph*.
Passage A and Passage B: Focus on the relationship between the passages—consider doing Passage A and its questions first, Passage B and its questions second, and the comparative questions last.		

Don't forget the steps in answering the questions:

(STEP 1) Cover your answers.

(STEP 2) "Coast" the question.

(STEP 3) Create a General answer using Context.

(STEP 4) Critically look at your choices.

PUTTING IT ALL TOGETHER

Here is a Social Science passage you can do to put all the strategies and techniques together. If you are going to read the passage first because you are shooting for a Reading score in the 20s or higher, remember to *read everything*, but to *slow down* on the *first paragraph, topic sentences,* and *last paragraph.* Why? Because this is a nonfiction passage that is easier to *outline* in your mind. In reading it, don't get bogged down in the details but focus on getting the overall *gist* of the passage. If you plan on attempting every question on the ACT Reading, take about 3–3.5 minutes to read this. If you plan on not reading one of the passages, you can allow 4–5 minutes to read this. Let's begin!

SOCIAL SCIENCE

Technological Eurocentrism in the Cult of Ancient Astronauts

In assembling a chronology for the development of the world's ancient cultures, there are, invariably, anomalies to the artifact record—unusual, misfit pieces that refuse to conform within the emergent puzzle that is
Line a culture's accepted historical profile. Predictably, such artifacts tend to
(5) attract unprecedented public attention, along with the profusion of theories—from the evidentiary to the ludicrous—that so often accompany history's famed enigmas. Very few of these so-called "out-of-place-artifacts" carry much academic weight within the archeological community; many are the result of hoaxes, of mistakes in archeological dating, or are
(10) discovered under circumstances too obscure for authentication; and the notorious "science-fiction" status attached to many of these artifacts by a startlingly large coterie of imaginative laymen compels most historical anthropologists to dismiss the pieces—and their potential historical consequences—altogether.
(15) Easily the most ubiquitous and outrageous popular culture response to curiosities such as ancient Egyptian orthopedic surgery, Han dynasty

seismology, and the Mesopotamian galvanic cell is the claim of extraterrestrial origin. It should be mentioned that our purpose here is not to
prove nor disprove the legitimacy of these artifacts; nor to debate the
(20) possibility of intelligent life existing on extrasolar planets. The vulgar
popularity of the idea that "ancient astronauts" produced these technologies is outrageous not because it is absurd to think that extraterrestrial
beings may exist, but because of what it implies about Western civilization's sociopsychological attitude toward the sophistication of preexist-
(25) ing and independent world cultures. And the engineering capabilities of
ancient, non-Western civilizations are perhaps nowhere more freely and
consistently dismissed than in those indigenous to the Americas.

It is, to a shockingly large sector of society, more ridiculous to suggest that the Nazca lines—the remarkably intricate and expansive
(30) 2,000-year-old geoglyphs in southern Peru—indicate a need to reform
our understanding of the technological, mathematical, and—dare we
say—*scientific* sophistication of ancient American civilizations than it is
to suggest that, because the pre-Columbian cultures were so primitive,
another—*any other*—explanation for their construction must be sought.
(35) This egregiously irrational pattern of thought is likely rooted in the social
narrative of Western progress. It would perhaps not be too bold to say
that there is a penetrating, subconscious attitude in the Euro-American
world that understands technological innovation and science as solely
Western novelties at best, and evidence of extraterrestrial encounters at
(40) worst.

In 2006 Dr. Joe Nickell—an English professor at the University of Ken-
tucky known for debunking paranormal theories—managed to recreate
large portions of the Nazca lines with a precision exceeding that of the
originals using only simple, wooden tools, some basic surveying equip-
(45) ment, and rudimental calculations—all of which, there is ample reason
to believe, were available to the ancient Nazca. The obdurate notion
that American cultures could not have developed even the most basic of
applications for arithmetic prior to the arrival of the Europeans demonstrates a sordid and persisting tradition of cultural arrogance.

(50) As a control in our little social investigation, let us consider another,
slightly less-known "out-of-place-place-artifact" dating from nearly the
same period as the Nazca lines of Peru. The Antikyethera Mechanism—
discovered in an ancient shipwreck off the Greek Isles—is an astonish-
ingly sophisticated scientific calculator and astronomical clock, the likes
(55) of which did not reappear in Europe until the 14th century. Its mechani-

cal complexity and accuracy is remarkable to the extent that it has often been referred to as the first known analog computer. What's more, it is the only one of its kind; the artifact record contains no other fragments or references to such technologies in the Hellenistic period.

(60)   The Mechanism, one might venture, should be an ideal target for the proponents of "ancient astronaut" technology—it is unique, sophisticated, concerns the celestial bodies, and incongruous with our concept of the limits to ancient Greek engineering. And yet, no such "cult of the extraterrestrial" surrounds the Mechanism. The public response—quite

(65) simply and quite rationally—has been instead to expand its opinion of Hellenistic technology. It should not, in some sense, be surprising—the narrative of Western technological exceptionalism derives from the Greek and Roman tradition, and even today Western science proudly traces its lineage to the rationalism of ancient Greece.

There are five general types of questions you will encounter on the ACT Reading, ranging from *small picture* to *big picture*.

1. Meanings of words
2. Supporting details
3. Sequential, comparative, and cause-effect relationships
4. Generalizations and conclusions
5. Main ideas and author's approach

Now, let's do a couple of questions of each type. If you are planning on doing the ACT Reading questions *out of order* on a passage (**Lines**, **Specific**, **General**), the order that we are doing these will mimic the way you will want to attack the actual test. If you are doing the questions *in order*, know that on the actual test, the questions will be in a random order of difficulty. You may want to consider skipping a question that looks like it is going to take you a good bit of time.

Don't forget to cover your answers up, comprehend the question, create your own answer, and critically examine the choices. Let's begin!

Meanings of Words

1. As it is used in line 26, "freely" most nearly means:
   A. easily.
   B. generously.
   C. spontaneously.
   D. inexpensively.

On a question like this, be sure to look back not just at line 26, but at the lines that are around it. The context leading into this line points out that Western civilization has often dismissed the incredible architectural creations of Native Americans as having an extraterrestrial origin. In doing so, Western civilization is dismissing the capabilities of Native Americans. Based on this understanding, the only answer that makes sense is (A), because it would be easy for Western civilization to dismiss the contributions of Native Americans. If we can find flaws in any of the other answers, they are 100 percent wrong, even if they seem partially correct. It is not (B) because Western civilization is being the opposite of "generous" in its assessment of Native American capabilities. It is not (C) because based on the context, this is an attitude that Western civilization consistently has. It is not (D) because although "free" is often associated with having no cost, there is nothing related to economics in this context.

2. The word "complexity" in line 56 could be successfully replaced with all of the following terms EXCEPT:
   F. intricacy.
   G. sophistication.
   H. difficulty.
   J. cleverness.

Be sure that you read the question carefully so that you do not miss the EXCEPT. We are looking for a word that could NOT work as a replacement for "complexity." Let's use the context around line 56 to clearly determine what "complexity" is supposed to mean. It is referring to the way that the Antikythera Mechanism is designed. It would be accurate to call a clock/calculator design "intricate," "sophisticated," or "clever." It would NOT make sense to call it a "difficult" design. Perhaps it was difficult to build, but it would be very odd to describe the design as being difficult. So, (H) is the correct answer.

SUPPORTING DETAILS

3. To what country or region does the author suggest that most anthropologists will look as the source of Western Scientific thought?
   A. China
   B. Greece
   C. Peru
   D. Egypt

On supporting details questions, it is very tempting to try to *remember* the answer. If you do this, you will likely make a bad decision because the level of specificity that they want is at a very high level. Instead, go back and *scan the passage* to find where this information is discussed, and read the context around it. Although we generally want to wait on looking at our answers until we have formulated our own idea, on a question like this, we will need to check out the answers. Don't let yourself *jump* to any conclusions prematurely, however. If we scan around for mentions of these countries, we find that Greece is mentioned with the most frequency. In the last sentence of the passage, it states that "Western science proudly traces its lineage to the rationalism of ancient Greece." So, based on this, we can safely state that **(B)** is the only logical choice. The second and third passages discuss China, Peru, and Egypt as cultures with creations that many people in Western civilization have dismissed as being of extraterrestrial origin.

4. All of the following are cited by the author as culturally flawed intellectual assumptions on the part of researchers EXCEPT:
   F. Pre-Columbian cultures must have been primitive.
   G. Human technological and scientific sophistication are solely of European origin.
   H. Many ancient Greek and Roman innovations had extraterrestrial sources.
   J. American cultures could not have developed arithmetic without European support.

This is another question where we should notice the EXCEPT, and check out the answers without allowing ourselves to jump to a conclusion prematurely. Paraphrasing the question, we need to determine which of these is NOT discussed by the researchers as a faulty assumption. The correct answer is **(H)** because the passage spends a good bit of time discussing how Greek creations are analyzed far differently from the way non-European creations are. The discussion of the Antikyethera Mechanism in lines 50–59 particularly does this. So, it is not the case that researchers made the assumption that Greek and Roman creations had an extraterrestrial origin. (F) is discussed in line 33, (G) in lines 36–40, and (J) in lines 46–48.

SEQUENTIAL, COMPARATIVE, AND CAUSE-EFFECT RELATIONSHIPS

5. The main purpose of the phrase "the remarkably intricate . . . in southern Peru" in lines 29–30 is to:
   A. counter an objection.
   B. define a term.
   C. provide anthropological analysis.
   D. provide a transition.

On questions like this, be sure you are focusing on the key words that clarify what the question is asking. Many times we will read a question like this and think that it is simply asking us to give the "meaning," when in fact it is asking us to give the "main purpose." To determine the purpose, look at the context surrounding the phrase. Immediately before this, the author mentions "Nazca lines." This is not an ancient creation that is generally known (like the Pyramids in Egypt or the Great Wall of China), so it is very helpful to clear up what this is so the reader can understand the passage. Thus, **(B)** is correct because this phrase defines what the Nazca lines are. There is no objection in the surrounding context, so (A) is incorrect. It does not provide any anthropological analysis (anthropology is the general study of humankind), so (C) is incorrect. It is not (D) because what comes before and after this phrase are on the same topic, so no transition would be needed.

6. The author suggests that the underlying cultural biases of North American and European people would most likely lead them to rank the following peoples in what order, in increasing order of intellectual sophistication?
   A. Ancient Mesopotamians, Ancient Greeks, Ancient Americans
   B. Ancient Greeks, Ancient Mesopotamians, Ancient Americans
   C. Ancient Americans, Ancient Greeks, Ancient Mesopotamians
   D. Ancient Americans, Ancient Mesopotamians, Ancient Greeks

Read the question very, very carefully so you are certain to not get this backwards. We want to list how biased Europeans and North Americans would rank these cultures from *least to most* sophisticated according to the passage. You may recall from the passage that Greeks are considered the most sophisticated by the biased researchers, so they would have to come last. At this point you could go with **(D)** because it is the only option that has Greeks listed last. Just so you know, lines 23–25 point out that the biased researchers would put Ancient Americans at the bottom of their list. On a question like this, you may feel you answered it correctly, but because of going too quickly or getting things mixed around, you made a mistake. Careless mistakes are still mistakes, so don't try to save time by taking shortcuts in reading the questions.

GENERALIZATIONS AND CONCLUSIONS

7. What would the author most likely assert would be the reaction by a typical person to the discovery of a unique cultural artifact that conflicts with the historical record of a given society?
    A. Interest in the artifact coupled with hypothesizing about an unusual origin
    B. A patient reluctance to jump to unwarranted conclusions
    C. Desire to ignore an object that would conflict with previously held beliefs
    D. Deference to the opinions of historical and scientific experts in the field

Before answering this question, we should carefully think about what the general characteristics of a person's reaction would be. We find information about this in the first paragraph of the essay, where the author discusses how "misfit pieces" in the archaeological record tend to "attract unprecedented public attention, along with the profusion of theories" that people create to explain how these objects originated. So, we can infer that the author would think that a typical person would have *interest in the artifact* along with *hypothesizing about* its unusual origin, making **(A)** correct. Based on the first paragraph, a typical person would not likely have much patience in coming to conclusions, making **(B)** incorrect. It is not **(C)** because people seem to have curiosity about these objects. It is not **(D)** because people tend to have a wide variety of theories, some of which are "ludicrous," in order to explain an object's origin.

8. Which of the following, if true, would most significantly undermine the primary argument of the author?
    F. The Nazca lines are actually approximately 500 years older than the author asserts, putting them at about 2,500 years of age.
    G. Europeans and North Americans, when surveyed, felt that the ancient Stonehenge in Europe was just as likely to be of extraterrestrial origin as the Nazca lines.
    H. Some of the leading scientific and historical minds at the best universities in the United States and Europe dispute the notion that the Nazca lines were crafted by aliens.
    J. A newly discovered "out-of-place" artifact is found in a European city, and journalists believe it to demonstrate the technological sophistication of the ancient Europeans.

We need to carefully think about what the primary argument of the author is before we go to the choices. From a more general reading of the passage, we can conclude that the argument is that Western civilization tends to dismiss the scientific know-how of non-Western civilizations. We can pick this up from the way researchers have contemplated the possible extraterrestrial origins of non-Western creations while believing the Western creations to be almost certainly of human origin. The question asks us what would *undermine,* or harm, the argument of the author. **(G)** is the correct answer because if Europeans and North Americans thought that *both* a European and a Native American artifact had just as much likelihood of being extraterrestrial in origin, it would be incorrect to state that there would be a cultural bias in favor of the European creations. (F) would be irrelevant to proving or disproving the author's thesis. (H) and (J) would both *support* the author's primary argument.

MAIN IDEAS AND AUTHOR'S APPROACH

9. What is the overall structure of the essay?
    A. Analysis of historical facts followed by the presentation of an expert opinion
    B. An in-depth argument coupled with an equally in-depth counterargument
    C. Presentation of an unsettling trend further developed through a comparative case study
    D. Sociological condemnation of cultural beliefs justified by a scientific experiment

On this question, you may be tempted to jump into the answers prematurely, but be certain to have *some* general idea before doing so or you are likely to get trapped. The essay starts by introducing the idea of how many people tend to dismiss the creations of non-European societies by supposing that any of their technologically magnificent artifacts may have had extraterrestrial origins. The essay then goes on to discuss the different treatments of the Nazca lines and the Antikyethera Mechanism to illustrate his point. This general structure is best described by **(C)**, since the unsettling trend is the tendency to dismiss non-European creations, and the comparative case study is that of the Nazca and Greek artifacts. It is not (A) because an expert opinion is not presented. It is not (B) because there is not an argument and a counterargument, since the author is consistent in his viewpoint throughout. It is not (D) because no scientific experiment is conducted later in the passage.

10. The tone of the author throughout the essay as a whole can best be described as:

    F. impassioned and rational.

    G. serious and subjective.

    H. reserved and impartial.

    J. critical and grave.

When it comes to tone questions, be sure you do not confuse the subject matter of the essay and the author's tone. For example, if the author is talking about a tragic event, her tone could be very calm and rational while the *topic* is very disturbing. Also, be sure that you pick the most *precise* description of tone—there are lots of words that can generally mean "good" or "bad," but you want to be sure to pick the word that most clearly describes how the author is communicating. In this question, the author passionately advocates for the idea that non-Western artifacts are unfairly dismissed by researchers. The author does so in a calm, rational way, carefully demonstrating his view by presenting in-depth examples. So, the tone can best be described as "impassioned and rational," making (F) correct. It is not (G) because although the author has a clear viewpoint, he presents his argument in a more objective than subjective way. It is not (H) because the author is not "reserved" or "impartial," since he has a strong viewpoint on the issue. It is not (J) because even though the author is a bit critical, he is far from being "grave," which would imply a dreary seriousness.

> **TIP**
>
> Students who are strong in math and science often find "tone" questions difficult because they would prefer more black and white answers than the more nuanced descriptions that tone will typically require.

Now, let's do a Prose Fiction passage. Be sure to read the *beginning* of it more in-depth so you don't miss the introduction of the characters and setting, and read the rest of it at a normal pace so that you don't miss important plot points.

PROSE FICTION

Fiat Lux

For seven summers Angela and I preferred stargazing to all other evening pastimes. In the soft hills above Bryson City, we'd trudge out at
night between the heavy spruces and the shaggy, redolent firs until we
Line came to some clear summit—overgrown in clover, ivy, wild violets, or
(5) any other tender vegetation whereupon we could lay ourselves supine
and look skyward.

The sun, I sometimes thought along those treks, was greedy—or perhaps instead, a prima donna. All day it outshines the other celestial
bodies, but by night the stars reveal the worth of harmony. Twinkling
(10) together subtly, symphonically; their dim light is more spectacular in its
multiplicity than daylight, for all its caprice, could ever be. I suppose that
in the sun there is great volume, but in the stars there is depth.

The way up was not especially difficult. Even at night, the hillsides
were alive with light—the flashbulb abdomens of a thousand fireflies,
(15) and the unworldly glow of foxfire guided our footsteps. Moonlight, too,
would abet one's way through the woods, though an overzealous moon
could also ruin even the clearest summer sky. The majesty of manifold
starlight is in its gracefulness and delicacy, and invariably the finest
stargazing was always sealed between our darkest and most treacherous
(20) journeys.

Sometimes as we walked, Angela spoke of the Rockies, of the valley town in Utah where she spent the other nine months of the year.
She spoke of their fearsome, infinite ranges and their towering, alpine
heights—almost baroque in scale and intricacy. Having naught but the
(25) Great Smoky Mountains to compare, I imagined the Rockies as a colossal
beast: all gnashing fangs, metallic scales, and long, ice-coated talons. The
Smokies meanwhile are warm, ancient and gentle—like a wise, Creta-
ceous tortoise. Once, I attempted to articulate this sentiment to Angela,
whispering, "The grass is like a turtle's shell."

(30) Immediately, I felt the warm dilations of embarrassment invade my
cheeks.

But Angela didn't scoff. She remained transfixed on the sky, and
answered, "And that star is like a sad, stray dog."

Venus in retrograde was emerging as the dominant evening star in
(35) the west, climbing her azimuth circle toward the Pleiades cluster—but
it didn't much matter: we knew none of this. To the two of us the stars
were not a specimen to be studied, but a canvas: a damp, plaster ceiling

from which new frescoes were endlessly and magically emerging. Each night we re-constellated the sky from scratch. We erected floating cit-
(40) ies, filling them with the tragedies and romances of exiled kings, ship-wrecked explorers and lonely, forgotten enchantresses.

Near the end of our last summer together, I was gesturing to indicate a formation which, with a generous imagination, resembled a windmill, when I became aware that Angela was crying. I turned my head. My
(45) eyes, which so recently had been peering into the impossible distances of space, gradually adjusted to see the weeping girl beside me. Her cheeks, glazed in steady, silent tears, glimmered silver in the starlight. I watched her, quietly, and it was a long while before she spoke.

"I can't come back next summer."
(50) I didn't respond, but continued watching—it was difficult, almost, to tell whether she spoke to me, or to the stars. Before we left that night, we made a pact, as any stargazing children might, that we would reunite, wherever and however old we were, when the fans of the windmill had made one full revolution. It was ridiculous, of course; I've long forgot-
(55) ten which stars we swore upon, and the crude machinations of a child's astronomy are hardly to be trusted. There are just too many stars, and when I see them now I no longer perceive the orchestrated, celestial waltz we once envisioned, but broad confusion—huge, empty and desolate.

Tonight there are no stars, and in a way I'm glad. A low cloud cover
(60) veils the sky; the only light visible spills from the red windows of a blast furnace across the ridge. But even now, as winter yields and the leaves across the Smokies begin to bud, I wonder about Angela, and whether she ever managed to find our windmill atop some awful precipice in Utah. I wonder what we expected to happen when, at long last, our stars
(65) aligned—an eruption of silver light, perhaps; a metamorphosis and a blossoming of primordial darkness into a larger and more vacuous darkness: a new beginning, another *fiat lux*.

On the actual test, the questions won't be in the following order—they are in a random order of type of question and difficulty. If you find doing the questions in this order helpful, you should consider doing the questions in order from *small picture* to *big picture*, doing the line questions first, then specific ones, and finally the general ones. If you have trouble picking up on the big picture of the storyline in fiction, going out of order on the questions could be a big help.

MEANINGS OF WORDS

1. As it is used in line 19, "sealed" most nearly means:
   A. fastened.
   B. bounded.
   C. conserved.
   D. finalized.

Take a look at the sentence where "sealed" is found, and create your own general idea for what kind of word would work in the context. The sentence in lines 17–20 discusses how the best stargazing is found when they go on the darkest and most treacherous journeys because they don't have any light interference from the moon. (B) makes the most sense here because the best stargazing is found within the boundaries of dark and treacherous journeys. (A), (C), and (D) all give valid dictionary definitions of "sealed," but they do not fit the context of its use in this sentence.

2. It can reasonably be inferred that the windmill mentioned in line 43 is a:
   F. star.
   G. nearby building.
   H. constellation.
   J. childhood drawing.

Look at the context surrounding line 43 to establish what is happening. If we look at the previous paragraph, we see that they are discussing visualizing constellations in the night sky. So, it makes sense that the windmill formation they are observing would also be a constellation, making (H) the correct choice. It is not (F) because one star alone would not make a windmill formation. It is not (G) because they are looking at formations in the sky at night. It is not (J) because they are visualizing nature, not looking at artistic creations on paper.

SUPPORTING DETAILS

3. The narrator and Angela created imaginary star formations of all of the following items EXCEPT:
   A. floating cities.
   B. exiled kings.
   C. shipwrecked explorers.
   D. a stray dog.

It is very easy to miss the EXCEPT on a question like this, so be sure to read the question carefully. Frequently on EXCEPT and NOT questions, you will find the potential answers clustered relatively close together in the passage. Knowing this can put your mind at ease, since it is very unlikely that you will have to go back and reread the whole passage. If these types of questions give you difficulty, you may find it helpful to read them over and put them in the back of your mind as you do other questions. That way you can be on the look-out for relevant information to answer this question while you are answering other questions. We see evidence of (A), (B), and (C) in lines 39–41, so these would not work as the answer. Angela refers to a *single star*, not a formation of stars, as resembling a "stray dog" in line 33, so **(D)** is the correct answer.

4. According to the passage, the Rockies and the Smokies can best be described in which of the following respective ways?
   F. formidable, tranquil.
   G. terrifying, sincere.
   H. majestic, kindly.
   J. groaning, passive.

Paraphrasing the question, the first adjective should describe the Rockies and the second adjective should describe the Smokies. Don't base this on mem-ory—go back and check out the discussion of the Rockies and Smokies by scanning for where these two words are mentioned and reading the surround-ing context. Lines 21–29 discuss the differences between these two mountain ranges, with the Rockies having "fearsome, infinite ranges and . . . towering, alpine heights." These could be described as "formidable," "majestic," with "terrifying" being a stretch. The Smokies are described as "warm, ancient and gentle." Since they are mountains, not people, "tranquil" would be the only logical adjective. So, **(F)** is the correct answer.

SEQUENTIAL, COMPARATIVE, AND CAUSE-EFFECT RELATIONSHIPS

5. When it was not the season during her childhood that Angela spent with the Narrator, she primarily spent her time:
   A. in Bryson City.
   B. in the Great Smokey Mountains.
   C. in a valley town in Utah.
   D. atop a mountain in the Rockies.

The question essentially asks, when Angela was not with the Narrator, where did she live? You can scan back through the passage to find any information about where Angela may have lived. If you find it difficult to scan for information, put this question in the back of your mind and be on the lookout for information related to it as you do other questions. Lines 21–22 explicitly speak of "the valley town in Utah where she (Angela) spent the other nine months of the year." So, (C) is the correct answer. (A), (B), and (D) are tempting because they involve words mentioned elsewhere in the passage, but they do not express where Angela lived when she was not in the same town as the Narrator.

6. The passage suggests that the Narrator and Angela differ from one another with respect to their understanding of:
   F. the emotional significance of their interpersonal relationship.
   G. whether stargazing can be an enjoyable activity.
   H. astronomical terminology.
   J. whether metaphorical references are fitting in conversation.

This is a tough question on which to create your own answer before looking at the choices, but don't let yourself jump to or eliminate any answer prematurely. Some process of elimination may be in order here. It is not (G) because the first sentence of the passage expresses that they "preferred stargazing to all other evening pastimes." It is not (H) because as lines 34–41 state, they do not have specialized understanding of astronomical terminology, but do share a love for imagining astronomical formations. It is not (J) because in lines 21–33, they both exhibit a comfort with describing mountain ranges and stars in metaphorical ways. The correct answer is (F) because the Narrator is far more stoic in his reaction to the news of Angela's plans to not come back than Angela is, as demonstrated by Angela's crying and the Narrator's lack of emotion in lines 42–48. Also, later in the passage the Narrator speaks of how little he remembers some of the specifics of their time spent together. So, it can reasonably be inferred that the Narrator places *less* value on their relationship than Angela does.

GENERALIZATIONS AND CONCLUSIONS

7. The narrator initially reacts to his comment in lines 28–29 with a feeling that it was:
   A. appropriate.
   B. scholarly.
   C. offensive.
   D. awkward.

This is an excellent example of how the ACT Reading will assess your ability to paraphrase. Be sure to look at the context surrounding these lines. Immediately after these, the Narrator finds that he is blushing, given the "warm dilations of embarrassment" invading his cheeks. So, it would be most accurate to call his initial reaction "awkward," making **(D)** the correct choice. He would not feel this embarrassment if his reaction were "appropriate," making (A) incorrect. Their entire interaction has nothing to do with scholarship, so (B) is incorrect. And his comments do not reach the extreme of being "offensive," so (C) is incorrect.

8. As discussed in the second paragraph (lines 7–12), the sun's relationship relative to the stars most resembles which of the following situations?
   F. An opera singer who sings harmoniously with the other performers
   G. A stereo that drowns out all the delicate sounds of nature when it is turned on
   H. A large ocean of water and a small river of water that flow into one another
   J. A business owner and bitter employees perpetually in conflict with one another

This question involves a good bit of critical thinking—we need to capture the essence of the relationship between the sun and the stars as portrayed in these lines. Paraphrasing these lines, we gather that the sun tends to drown out the beautiful starlight behind it. **(G)** is the only option that expresses a similar relationship, with the stereo acting like the sun, and the sounds of nature acting like the subtle light of stars. (F) involves a balance between two things. (H) does not involve one thing drowning out another, but one item contributing to the other. (J) expresses a constant conflict, which the sun and stars would not have between one another.

Main Ideas and Author's Approach

9. What is the primary purpose of the first paragraph of the essay?
   A. To establish the setting for most of the essay's events
   B. To analyze the vegetation of a particular place
   C. To explain the appeal of stargazing to young lovers
   D. To discuss the geographical features of Bryson City

Be sure you focus on the *primary* purpose of the first paragraph, not a minor purpose of it or something that is simply mentioned in it. We need to avoid just *summarizing* the paragraph and instead think about the paragraph's function in the essay as a whole. The first paragraph introduces the setting of the wooded hills above Bryson City as a place where Angela and the Narrator would spend time looking at the sky. The purpose is best described as **(A)** because it establishes the setting for most of the essay's events. (B) and (D) are too narrowly focused. (C) is not explicitly discussed and does not represent a primary focus of the first paragraph.

10. The point of view of the Narrator is that of:
    F. a child discussing the intricacies of astronomical observation.
    G. a young adult recalling what led to an ongoing relationship.
    H. an adult contemplating what might have come of an earlier friendship.
    J. an adult analyzing his intellectual progression in understanding astronomy.

This is a good type of question to save to the end because it involves understanding virtually all the passage as a cohesive whole. The Narrator spends most of the essay recalling his interactions with his childhood friend Angela, and the last paragraph contemplates what may have become of her. So, **(H)** best expresses the Narrator's point of view—he is looking back on his childhood from a more mature perspective, and he muses on what Angela could be up to in the present day. It is not (F) because the narrator is clearly not a child. While the narrator could possibly be a "young" adult, the narrator is not focusing on what led to an *ongoing* relationship because Angela and the Narrator have ceased to be in contact with one another. The word "ongoing" serves as contamination in this answer choice. It is not (J) because this choice ignores the interactions between Angela and the Narrator, focusing on the superficial discussion of astronomy in the passage.

Comparative Passages

The comparative passage could be any one of the four passages—it will be at most one of them. The same reading and question strategies apply on this type of passage, with two important additions:

- Be sure you focus on *summarizing the similarities and differences* between the passages since there will definitely be questions that ask you to compare the texts.

- The format will consistently have the Passage A questions first, the Passage B questions second, and the comparative passages last. Because of this, you may want to read Passage A and do its questions first, then do Passage B and its questions, and end with the comparative passages. This is a great strategy to use if you need more time to process what you have read.

Here is a sample passage followed by 3 sample comparative questions:

NATURAL SCIENCE—Passage A is about child safety in motor vehicles. Passage B is about child safety in aircraft.

PASSAGE A

Much progress has been made in the field of car seat safety in recent decades. People who are becoming parents today may not have even used a car seat as an infant. Their children, however, have the benefit of
Line the best technology and understanding of skeletal development to date.
(5) Motor vehicle accidents are the leading cause of death for children under 18 years old and kill more children than all other accidental causes of death combined. For young children, however, rear-facing in a properly installed car seat is especially crucial to the prevention of injury or death. This is because young children have proportionally larger heads
(10) compared to their bodies than adults and because the bones in their spine are not hardened, or ossified, like that of an adult. Ossification of the spine is complete between three and six years old. The American Academy of Pediatrics recommends children remain in a rear-facing infant or convertible car seat until a minimum of two years old or until the height
(15) or weight limits of the car seat are exceeded. The National Highway Safety and Transportation Administration goes further and recommends children remain in a rear-facing car seat until four years old or the height or weight limits of their car seat are exceeded. In Sweden, widely considered the world leader in car seat safety, children typically ride in rear-facing car seats
(20) until six years old. Between 1992 and 1997, only nine properly restrained rear-facing Swedish children died in motor vehicle accidents.
The next step after a rear-facing car seat is a forward-facing car seat. Children should remain in a forward-facing five-point harnessed car seat until a minimum of five years old. If the car seat is outgrown by weight
(25) or height before five, a new car seat that will accommodate the height and weight of the child must be purchased. After five years old, there is

inconclusive evidence about the difference in safety among a forward-facing harnessed car seat, a high back belt positioning booster, and a low back belt positioning booster, provided all are used correctly. When using (30) either type of booster, children must sit correctly and not lean or slouch as it affects the seat belt fit. A high back booster is necessary in vehicles that do not have an appropriate headrest as it prevents whiplash.

Children may transition to the seatbelt alone when they are a minimum of 10 years old provided the vehicle seat has an appropriate head-(35) rest. To be safe, the seat belt must fit low across the hips and comfortably across the torso. The child must sit all the way back in the vehicle seat with feet flat on the floor and must be able to maintain this position for the entire vehicle ride.

PASSAGE B

Children under two are permitted to ride on aircraft in their parent's (40) lap. This practice is commonly referred to as "lap babies," and it is dangerous for the child and everyone else on board the aircraft.

Runway emergencies and turbulence during the flight are much more common than a catastrophic crash. Runway emergencies are simply car crashes at a much greater speed. During these emergencies, parents will (45) not be able to securely hold their lap baby, and the child could become a projectile. For example, a 15 pound infant in a 150 mph runway emergency would become a projectile with 2,250 pounds of force.

Aircraft seatbelts are designed to fit appropriately at a body weight of approximately 40 pounds. Before 40 pounds, the AAP, FAA, and NTSB (50) agree the only safe way for children to fly is in a properly installed car seat. Children should face the direction they do in the car. FAA policy gives children and their parents protections to use car seats on domestic carriers provided the car seats are FAA approved. For example, if the car seat does not fit in a certain seat, the airline should provide a different (55) aircraft seat within the same class of service to accommodate the car seat. Additionally, within the limits of the car seat, parents may choose to rear- or forward-face their child.

In addition to the clear safety benefits of using a car seat on an aircraft, in many situations children will need a car seat at their destination. (60) Checking or gate checking car seats even in car seat bags is an unsafe practice and results in a seat with an unknown history. Many people are

familiar with receiving scuffed or damaged luggage. Baggage handling practices are not appropriate for life-saving child safety devices as unseen damage can occur. Further, the checked car seat may be lost leaving the
(65) family without an appropriate child restraint at the destination.

COMPARATIVE QUESTIONS

1. Passage B emphasizes which of the following possibilities as a major safety concern that is NOT emphasized by Passage A?
   A. A child can become a projectile.
   B. A child's skeleton has not matured.
   C. A child could experience whiplash.
   D. A child could be suffocated due to negligence.

On this question, you will need to check out the choices without allowing yourself to jump to any one of them prematurely. Lines 46–47 discuss the possibility of a child becoming a projectile on a fast-moving airplane; there is no direct discussion of a child becoming a projectile in Passage A. So, the correct answer is **(A)**. (B) and (C) are discussed in Passage A. (D) is mentioned by neither passage.

2. Based on the information in the passages, a responsible parent would be most compliant with safety regulations if he or she:
   F. allowed a 30 pound child to ride with only a seatbelt on a plane.
   G. tightly held an infant across his or her torso while flying.
   H. allowed a relatively small two year old to forward-face on both a car and a plane.
   J. had a two year old child rear-face in the car and forward-face on a plane.

Lines 56–57 state that while on an airplane "within the limits of the car seat, parents may choose to rear or forward face their child." So, a parent would be compliant if he had a rear-facing child in the car and then had a forward-facing child on a plane. The correct answer is therefore **(J)**. Lines 48–49 state that children should be at least 40 pounds to safely be seated in an airplane seat, so (F) is incorrect. Lines 44–46 discuss the dangers of holding children without any supplemental restraints, making (G) incorrect. Lines 12–15 mention that major safety regulators advise parents to keep kids rear-facing until at least age 2 if not later, making (H) incorrect.

3. The fact that there are far more instances of children traveling in motor vehicles than instances of children traveling on airplanes best explains which of the following differences between the passages?
   A. The discussion of government regulatory bureaus in Passage A
   B. The greater specificity of the supporting data in Passage A
   C. The analysis of "lap babies" in Passage B
   D. The potential damage to transported car seats discussed in Passage B

Given that there are more instances of car seats in cars than in planes, it is reasonable to conclude that there would be far more data for statistics about car usage than plane usage. Passage A demonstrates quite a bit more specificity in its discussion of supporting data than does Passage B—in particular, the discussion about the number of deaths that have resulted in Sweden is more detailed than the more hypothetical thinking in Passage B. So, **(B)** is the correct choice. (A), (C), and (D) are all discussed, but the fact outlined in the question would not be strongly connected to them.

Now, practice your reading strategies with these four passages of gradually increasing difficulty. The first passage is a little easier than the average ACT passage. The second one is more typical of what you will find. The third one is more challenging than the average ACT Reading, and the last one much more difficult than what you will probably come across.

🔑 READING STRATEGY SUMMARY

- For most students, it makes sense to read the passage before going to the questions.
- When reading, focus on the big picture of what the passage is about.
- Don't hesitate to go back to the passage to clarify key details.
- When answering the questions,

  - Cover the answers,
  - Coast the question,
  - Create your own general idea,
  - Critically evaluate the answers.

- Skip around on the questions if needed—you don't have to do them in order.
- Determine what timing approach works best for you:

  - If doing all four passages, spend about 9 minutes a passage.
  - If reading three passages and going right to the questions on one passage, spend 10 minutes on the three passages you read and just 5 minutes on the one where you go right to the questions.
  - If you are going to just do three of the passages and guess on one of them, spend about 11–12 minutes on each passage you do.
  - If you know you're not a good reader, you can go right to the questions on every passage and spend about a minute a question.

Science

4

━━━━━━━━━━━━━━━━━━━━━━━━━━━━━━

⚷ WHAT ARE THE BASIC FACTS ABOUT THE ACT SCIENCE SECTION?

→ Comes at the end of the test
→ 35 minutes long
→ 6 or 7 passages total: 2 or 3 Data Representation, 3 Research Summaries, and 1 Conflicting Viewpoints
→ Questions generally become harder within a passage

Students typically have two major concerns about the ACT Science:

How much am I supposed to know?
How much am I supposed to read?

On most school science tests, you are expected to know quite a few facts in order to do well. But remember that the ACT is primarily a *thinking* test, not a knowledge test, so there is not much that you need to know ahead of time. Not every student will have taken physics, chemistry, anatomy, etc., so the ACT designs the science section to test your *overall skill level in analyzing scientific information*. The ACT makes things fair by occasionally expecting you to use background knowledge from *physical/earth science* and *biology*. Why? By the time you are a junior or senior in high school, you will certainly have taken at least these two very basic classes. Does this mean that you should go and reread your biology and physical science textbooks? No! It simply means that once in a while—typically 1–4 questions out of the 40 on the Science test—you will need to use simple background knowledge of facts like the following: photosynthesis, mitosis, kinetic energy, potential energy, density, pH, etc.

Knowing that *not necessarily all the information will be in front of you* will prevent you from panicking if there is a fact that you feel like you know, but you can't find it in the passage. The more science you take in school, the better prepared you will be, because you will be more comfortable with figuring out scientific information. Science classes help you do well on the ACT Science primarily by improving your *thought process*, and not as much by giving you concrete scientific facts that you need to know. To summarize, in about **90–95% of the Science questions the information will be in the passage, so you don't need to know much about the subject in order to do well.**

Since you don't need to know much about the subject, you might think that when you encounter a passage, you should read everything thoroughly because the information will be new to you. Or, you might think that it would waste your time to read the passage, and that you should just go to the questions. *To read or not to read—that is the question. . .*

- **Reading everything carefully before doing the questions is a problem** because you will end up spending *far too long* trying to completely understand the passage. Reading everything carefully makes perfect sense when preparing for a closed-book science test in school, but it will hurt you here given how quickly you need to go.
- **Going right to the questions is a problem** because you will get "tunnel vision" on the questions and won't have any sense of where to locate the information you need. When students go right to the questions, they often find that they don't see a graph or key piece of data that is *right in front of them.*

What is the solution? Think about it this way. . .

- **If you don't understand something in a MAP, you look at the KEY to clarify.**
- **If you don't understand something in the ACT Science GRAPHS, look at the READING to clarify.**

In looking at an unfamiliar map, it would be a complete waste of time to read the entire key before trying to figure out the map's overall organization. If you see a lot of blue on the map, it probably means that there is water! But if you find a weird symbol or strange line, you should take a look at the key or legend so you are not confused. Doing things this way ensures you *don't waste time* looking at unnecessary information, but it gives you the *flexibility* to clarify things that don't make sense.

Let's look at some examples to see how you can use this approach on the ACT Science to organize the passages in a quick yet thorough way.

TIP

The ACT Science assesses your ability to rapidly make sense of lots of information—a skill that will help you in most any job and many areas of study.

TYPES OF SOURCE MATERIAL ON THE ACT

What follows is a Data Representation Passage. There will be two or three of these on the Science test. *Don't read everything to start. Instead, look at the graphs first, and clarify any key terms that don't make sense by reading relevant parts of the passage.*

Data Representation

Apparent retrograde motion is a term used by astronomers to describe when the direction of an object's orbit appears to reverse itself. As viewed from Earth, all seven other planets in our solar system exhibit apparent retrograde motion at regular intervals. In Figure 1, the apparent path of Mars from November 2011 to June 2012 is illustrated relative to the Leo constellation, along with a star map of Leo.

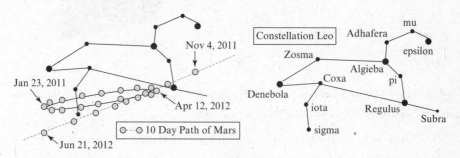

Figure 1

An early explanation for apparent retrograde motion involved the theory of *epicycles*, or smaller rotational paths within a planet's greater orbit. Using this idea, Ptolemy devised the geocentric planetary model shown in Figure 2, and Copernicus, the heliocentric model shown in Figure 3.

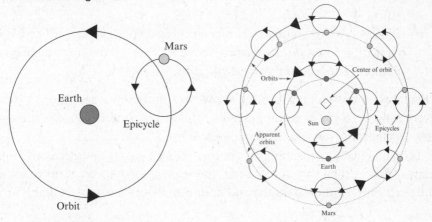

Figure 2   **Figure 3**

In reality, apparent retrograde is the result of each planet's distinct period of orbit. Because the Earth completes its orbit in a shorter timespan than the outer planets, each appears, at times, to reverse the direction of its general motion in the Earth's sky. An illustration of this is shown in Figure 4.

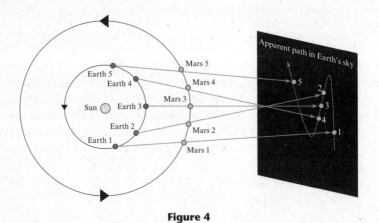

Figure 4

Organizing yourself on the above Data Representation should only take about 20–30 seconds. What should you have noticed?

- Figure 1 shows the path of Mars and how it mimics the constellation Leo.
- Figure 2 shows a planet going in an "epicycle" around Earth. This is a *key term* you may want to clarify. Typically when an unusual key term is given, the ACT Science will *italicize* it, making it easy to find. We look back at the reading and see that this refers to a smaller rotational path within a larger orbit.
- Figure 3 shows planets revolving around the sun while going in epicycles.
- Figure 4 is a little more confusing, and you may want to clarify what is happening based on the reading above it. It represents how the planets sometimes appear to reverse their orbits.

There was no need for background knowledge, and there was no need to read everything from the beginning. Look at the graphs, and if you don't understand something, use the reading to clear it up.

Let's practice organization on another science passage—a Research Summary. There will be three of these on the Science section. We want to maximize our general understanding and minimize the time we spend doing so.

Research Summary

A student is learning about the difference between series and parallel wiring in electrical circuits. In class the student learned that three properties of circuits—current, resistance, and voltage—are related through Ohm's Law; shown in Figure 1.

$$V = IR$$
Where,
$$V = Voltage, I = Current, R = Resistance$$

Figure 1

The student also knows that current describes the rate per second at which electric charge flows through a conductor, that resistance refers to the tendency of an electrical device to oppose the flow of electricity, and that voltage—the potential difference across two points of a circuit—is the driving force behind an electrical flow. Lastly, the student learned through research that current, resistance, and voltage interact differently in series and parallel circuits, though both remain governed by Ohm's Law, as illustrated in Figure 2.

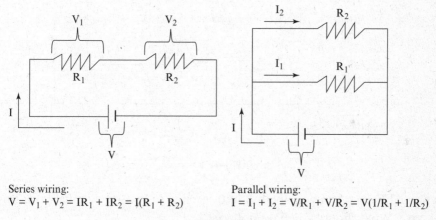

Series wiring:
$$V = V_1 + V_2 = IR_1 + IR_2 = I(R_1 + R_2)$$

Parallel wiring:
$$I = I_1 + I_2 = V/R_1 + V/R_2 = V(1/R_1 + 1/R_2)$$

Figure 2

Experiment 1

To observe the distinctions between series and parallel wiring firsthand, the student designed an experiment in which three different light bulbs were wired together and attached to a 12-V power source, first in series and then in parallel. Using a combination voltmeter-ammeter, the student measured and recorded data from each circuit. These results are shown in Table 1.

Table 1

Wired in Series		Wired in Parallel	
Bulb Resistance (Ω)	Voltage (V)	1/Bulb Resistance (1/Ω)	Current (A)
4	3.99	0.33	4
3	5.32	0.25	3
2	2.66	0.50	6

Experiment 2

Using the same materials, the student designed a third circuit that combines series and parallel wiring. Based on the results of Experiment 1, the student made several predictions about its properties. The circuit and these predictions are illustrated in Figure 3.

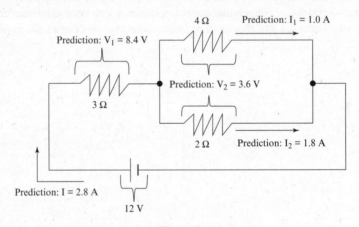

Figure 3

It should have taken you about 30–40 seconds to become familiar with this passage. What should you have noticed?

- Figure 1 gives an equation about Voltage, Current, and Resistance. We can assume that this is what the passage will discuss.
- Figure 2 shows series wiring on the left and parallel wiring on the right. If we need to further clear this up in the questions, we can do so by reading material that comes before. In the initial organization, knowing what they are generally doing is fine.
- Table 1 informs us that Experiment 1 involves comparing the effects of parallel and series wiring.
- Figure 3 demonstrates that Experiment 2 is concerned with predicting the effects of parallel and series wiring.

> It is not essential that you have a 100% understanding of the passage before the questions because as long as you are generally organized, you can gradually build your understanding of the passage in the questions as you go.

Now, let's talk about the Conflicting Viewpoints Passage. There will be just one of these on the Science test. It involves quite a bit more reading than any of the other passages because it often does not have *any* graphs, just paragraphs. When it does have graphs, as this one does, the graphs are typically far less helpful in putting together the overall idea of what's going on in the passage. So, *on the Conflicting Viewpoints Passage, be sure that you actually read the passage before going to the questions. However, you can spend <u>more time on the topic sentences of the paragraphs</u> because these are more important than the other sentences in the passage since they typically state the position of each scientist.* Read the first sentence of each paragraph very, very slowly, and read the rest of each paragraph at a normal pace. It should generally take you about 1–1.5 minutes to read over the material for the Conflicting Viewpoints. Here's one for practice.

Conflicting Viewpoints

Two biologists are studying evolutionary divergence among populations of *Ameerega cainarachi*, a poison dart frog endemic to western Amazonia. Despite belonging to the same species, the *haplotype* (a combination of alleles for different genes that are found close together on the same chromosome and are usually inherited together) of cytochrome b alleles can differ between neighboring populations of *A. cainarachi* in excess of 12%. This indicates an influence of genetic partitioning (i.e., the division of the species into different genotypes). A map summarizing the relative locations of the populations studied by the first biologist is shown in Figure 1, and that by the second biologist is shown in Figure 2. Biologist 1 and Biologist 2 provide different theories as to why there is this haplotypic divergence among the populations of the *Ameerega cainarachi* and the likely genetic partitioning that results.

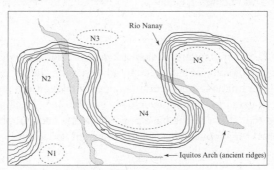

Figure 1

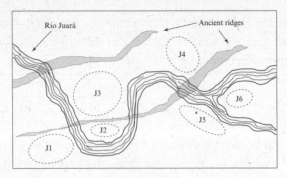

Figure 2

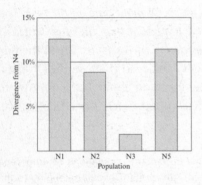

Figure 3

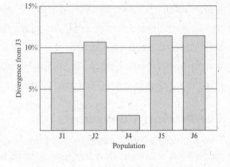

Figure 4

Biologist 1

Based on his observations, Biologist 1 supports the "riverine barrier" hypothesis, which claims that dispersion across opposite riverbanks is responsible for diversification in the phylogeographic structure of *A. cainarachi* populations. Biologist 1 contends that these rivers form an extremely difficult obstacle for a frog species to bypass, given their width, depth, and water speed. Using the N4 community as a standard for comparison, Biologist 1 graphed his findings in Figure 3.

Biologist 2

Using population J3 as her standard, Biologist 2 graphed her observations in Figure 4. Based on these results, Biologist 2 decided to advocate the "ridge" hypothesis, which postulates that ancient ridges—now eroded—once partitioned various populations of *A. cainarachi* for an extended period, eventually causing their haplotypic divergence. Biologist 2 argues that these ridges have posed a nearly impenetrable barrier to the exchange of different frog populations, given their height and width.

It should have taken you about 60–90 seconds to read this over and become familiar with the general ideas presented. What should you have gotten out of it?

- Understand from the introduction that the scientists are exploring the possible origins of different characteristics and genetic partitioning among dart frog populations.
- See that Biologist 1 argues that having rivers run through the frog populations causes their genetic variation.
- See that Biologist 2 argues that ancient ridges were responsible for separating frog populations and causing their genetic diversity.

Getting Organized	
Here is a general summary of how to get organized on the different types of passages you will face:	
Simple Graphs—typically a couple of straightforward graphs	Spend about 15–30 seconds getting organized, briefly looking at relevant parts of the passage to clarify unknown terms/concepts
Complex Graphs—may have multiple axes and labels, lots of information to process	Spend about 30–60 seconds getting organized, absorbing where things can be located in the passage, and quickly reading to clear up puzzling information in the graphs
Conflicting Viewpoints—reading-heavy passage with few, if any, graphs	Spend about 60–90 seconds reading through the passage, giving more emphasis to the topic sentences of each paragraph

🔑 STRATEGIES FOR READING SCIENCE PASSAGES

After getting organized on the passage, you can move into the questions. The ACT Science questions can be quite wordy and intimidating, so here are some strategies you can use to ensure you *don't waste time and don't make any careless mistakes* in reading the questions.

> **TIP**
>
> Science Strategy Paradox: The *more slowly* you read the questions, the *more quickly* you will finish the test and the better you will do!

Question Strategy 1: COAST the questions!

If there is only one section on which you coast (underline the question and circle key words), this is the one where it can help you the most. Why? Because the questions often contain *quite a bit of unnecessary information* about assumptions of the experiment that you can ignore. Coasting the question can help you focus on what is being asked, ignoring extra information along the way. There is only time to do the questions *one time well* on the Science, and coasting can make this happen. If you end up reading the questions too quickly, you will likely get intimidated and end up wasting a ton of time rereading the question and overthinking it. Go *slowly* one time through in order to go more *quickly* on the questions. Here is an example of what a **coasted science question** will look like:

According to Figure 1, as the pressure of the oxygen increases, the volume of the container:

Question Strategy 2: POINT as you go!

This is probably the most important strategy to breaking down the questions on the Science Reasoning. As you read the question, point to the information in the passage as it is given to you. If you are right handed, you should *roller coaster with your right hand*, and *point to key info with your left hand*.

Here is another way to think about this . . . If someone is giving you directions to his house, it will make a lot more sense for you to have the map out and *follow along with what he is saying* as opposed to trying to memorize the directions, and then look at the map. This is exactly what you want to do on the Science questions, but most people instinctively don't do this. Because they feel such pressure to finish, they try to read the questions quickly, memorizing tidbits of information, but then when they go to answer the question, they are totally lost.

To what should you point as you go? Pretend you have an ACT Science Question like this:

Table 1

Substance	Density (pounds per cubic foot)	Specific Heat
Aluminum	164	0.24
Ether	46	0.5
Lead	710	0.03
Steel	487	0.12

According to the information in Table 1, as the density of the substances increases, what happens to the specific heat of the substances?

Rather than trying to remember all of this and *then* look back at the passage, point to three things as you read the question.

1. Point to "Table 1."
2. Then point to the column with "Density."
3. Then point to the column with "Specific Heat."

Although pointing as you go will take a bit longer the first time through, it will save you time in the long run. Why? Because it is far better to read the question once and perfectly than it is to do it quickly and have to read it over and over again.

Question Strategy 3: WRITE as you go!

On some of the more complex questions, it will be helpful to write things down in shorthand to help you (1) focus on what the question is asking as well as to (2) not get things backwards. Consider a complex question like the following:

In Experiment 2, in which the scientist is determining the relationship between the temperature of the gases and their volumes, is the hypothesis that as the temperature increases the volume increases correct?

All you need to focus on is determining if there is a direct, positive link between temperature and volume. As you read the question, you can write something like this:

$$T\uparrow V\uparrow$$

That shorthand symbolizes what you need to do. It will also ensure that you don't get the directions mixed up, which will definitely cause you to miss the problem.

Question Strategy 4: The questions get HARDER within a passage!

Within a passage, the questions gradually go from ones that are relatively easy to ones that are much more difficult. On the earlier and easier questions, you simply have to FIND the answer—look at some information from a chart and you are good to go. On later questions, however, you will need to THINK quite a bit more. You may need to do things like reading parts of the passage, thinking about the applications of an experiment, or really breaking down the experimental procedure. **When you go to a new passage, the find-to-think pattern starts over.** (There is no consistent order of difficulty on the *passages*— just on the questions within a passage. The passages are in a random order of difficulty.) Due to this pattern, there are three things you need to do:

- **Don't OVERTHINK the EARLY questions.** You will be tempted to make the earlier questions in a passage seem quite a bit more difficult than they are. Don't let the tough wording intimidate you.
- **Don't UNDERTHINK the LATER questions.** At first glance, you may think you can answer these questions by matching up information from the graphs in the passage. If it seems too easy to be true, it probably is. You are very likely going to need to spend more time putting all of the information together to answer these questions by reading bits of the passage and thinking through the experiment in a more critical manner.
- **Manage your TIME and LET HARD QUESTIONS GO.** Your pace on the Science passages should be about **9 minutes for every 10 questions.** It is possible that there could be as few as 5 questions in a passage or as many as 8 questions in a passage. Also, there could be 6 or 7 passages. What is certain, however, is that you will have 35 minutes and 40 questions. So, the simplest thing to do is to take a little less than 9 minutes for every 10 questions. (Alternatives: If you want to quickly check how many passages there are by looking at the end of the test, you could take approximately

5 minutes per passage if there are 7 passages and approximately *6 minutes per passage if there are 6 passages.* For some students, it may be worth the time to check the end of the test so they can pace themselves this way.) If you find yourself falling behind the pace, you should <u>guess on the last question</u> of the passage. It is far more likely that the last question will be more difficult, so why waste your time trying to figure out a super-tough question when there will be 2 or 3 easy questions on the next passage that you can get in the same amount of time? Don't let your pursuit of perfection stand in the way of doing well. On the Science test, you must be comfortable letting some of the tough questions go so that you can fight for every possible point.

It makes sense for the ACT Science to have this "find-to-think" pattern because when you first take a look at a complex science passage, you will develop a greater understanding of what is happening in it as you do a couple of questions. *While there will be exceptions to this once in a while,* you can generally count on it being a general pattern that the ACT has consistently done on the Science. Since that general pattern is there, make sure you take advantage of it!

To summarize, here are the ways that you can **WASTE TIME** on the ACT Science and ways you can **SAVE TIME** to do things more effectively:

Science Time Wasters	Better Approaches
Reading more of the passage than necessary	Look at graphs first, then read as needed.
Getting stuck because you didn't see a figure that was right in front of you	Allow time to get organized before going into the questions.
Overthinking early questions on a passage	Know that the first questions within a passage are usually straightforward.
Rereading questions	Read the questions one time well.
Doing more questions than you should	Pick your battles. Guess on the last question of each passage if needed.
Doing more passages than you should	Skip an entire passage if need be. If you're a poor reader, don't do the conflicting viewpoints.
Double-checking	There is no time to double-check. Let things go and keep moving so you can give most of the questions a good shot.

Now, let's put all of these strategies together by going through a Data Representation Passage, a Research Summary, and a Conflicting Viewpoints.

First, let's look at a Data Representation Passage. There will be two or three of these passages on the ACT Science. This particular passage has several complex graphs and charts, so you should spend about 30–40 seconds organizing yourself before going to the questions. Don't get bogged down in all the details. Instead, look at the labels/axes of the different graphs and charts to determine the general idea of what is being presented.

PRACTICE SCIENCE QUESTIONS

Data Representation

Over the course of several million years, the three main varieties of rock undergo a series of dynamic transformations described as the rock cycle. A general outline of the cycle is illustrated in Figure 1.

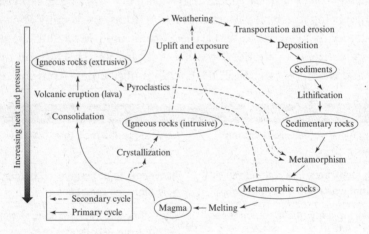

Figure 1

Within each main group, geologists often classify rocks more specifically on the basis of their physical properties and chemical compositions. A pair of igneous rocks can often possess the same mineral composition, but differ in texture. The classification of igneous rocks is summarized in Figure 2. Sedimentary rocks are also distinguished by composition and texture. An example of sedimentary rock classification is shown in Table 1.

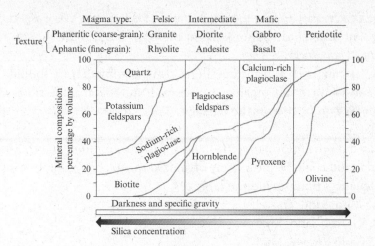

Magma type:	Felsic	Intermediate	Mafic	
Texture { Phaneritic (coarse-grain):	Granite	Diorite	Gabbro	Peridotite
Aphantic (fine-grain):	Rhyolite	Andesite	Basalt	

Figure 2

Table 1

Detrital (particulates of preexisting rock)			Chemical (minerals extracted from solution)		
Sediment Type	Properties	Name	Texture	Composition	Name
Gravel (>2 mm)	Rounded	Conglomerate	Crystalline	Calcite ($CaCO_3$)	Limestone
	Angular	Breccia		Gypsum ($CaSO_4 \cdot 2H_2O$)	Rock Gypsum
Sand (1/16–2 mm)	Quartz sand	Sandstone		Halite (NaCl)	Rock salt
	Quartz, >25% feldspar	Akrose	Clastic	Calcium Carbonate ($CaCO^3$) shells	Limestone (chalk and coquina)
Mud (<1/16 mm)	Silt	Siltstone	Typically Crystalline	Altered SiO_2 shells	Chert
	Clay	Shale		C altered from plant remains	Coal

What should you have gathered from your organization of this passage?

- Figure 1 outlines the types of changes that occur throughout the rock cycle.
- Figure 2 shows how several different rock properties are associated with one another: magma type, texture, mineral composition, darkness/specific gravity, and silica concentration.
- Table 1 shows how sedimentary rocks can be classified in a variety of ways: texture, composition, etc.

It would be very easy to take too much time in reading over every aspect of this passage, but as long as you understand the general organization, you will be ready for the question.

Now, let's take a look at the questions, remembering that we should **Coast, Point, and Write** to stay organized as we read, and that the questions will **get harder as we go further in the passage**.

1. Based on the information in Table 1, particulates from Gravel, Sand, and Mud could be most likely organized in which of the following sequences from smallest to largest?
    A. Mud, Sand, Gravel
    B. Gravel, Sand, Mud
    C. Sand, Gravel, Mud
    D. Mud, Gravel, Sand

The correct answer is (A). Don't overthink this question, given how early it is. We see particle size on the far left of Table 1, and the lengths of the typical particle sizes are given in millimeters. Gravel has a typical size of greater than 2 mm, Sand is between $\frac{1}{16}$ and 2 mm, and Mud is less than $\frac{1}{16}$ mm. So, putting these in order from *smallest to largest*, Mud would be smallest, then Sand, then Gravel.

2. Based on Figure 2, a rock that is coarse-grained, darkly colored, and has a relatively low silica concentration would most likely be primarily constituted of which of the following minerals?
    F. Potassium feldspars
    G. Biotite
    H. Hornblende
    J. Olivine

The correct answer is (J). We should point up to Figure 2 as we read this question, and save ourselves time by pointing to the characteristics of the rock mentioned. The rock mentioned would be to the far right of the figure, which is easy to see given its dark coloration and low silica concentration. Olivine would be the only option that would make sense.

3. Using the information in Figure 2, how might a geologist distinguish between granite and basalt?

I. Texture
II. Mineral composition
III. Coloration

A. I only
B. II only
C. I and II only
D. I, II, and III

The correct answer is **(D)**. We see how the questions build upon one another, with what we saw in the previous question putting us in a better position to answer this question. Because of this, it doesn't make nearly as much sense to skip around on the questions in the Science section as it would on the other sections. Figure 2 shows many different ways that minerals can be distinguished, and granite and basalt can be distinguished by all of these properties, given their different placements in the figure. Relative to basalt, granite would have a coarser texture, more quartz composition, and lighter coloration.

4. Based on the information in Figure 1, which of the following types of rocks is most likely to be formed due to influences from the Earth's atmosphere?

F. Igneous
G. Metamorphic
H. Sedimentary
J. Cannot be determined with the given information

(H) is the correct answer. As you can see, this problem involves a bit more thinking than the previous questions in the passage. Toward the top of Figure 1, we see that "weathering" is mentioned, and this is connected via a few steps to sedimentary rocks. Igneous and metamorphic rocks are closer to magma, which means they are deeper within the earth, and less likely to be formed due to events on the Earth's surface.

5. An archaeologist is seeking out dinosaur fossils. Based on the information in the passage, in which type of rock would she have the greatest chance of locating them?
   A. Peridotite
   B. Rhyolite
   C. Shale
   D. Pyroclastics

(C) is the correct answer. This question involves quite a bit more thinking and analysis than the earlier questions. It would be reasonable to conclude that a fossil would be found in rock that is close to the Earth's surface. Sedimentary rocks are more influenced by factors on the surface of the Earth, based on Figure 1. Additionally, Table 1 indicates that shell and plant remains have been found in sedimentary rocks. Shale is the only one of these rocks that is sedimentary—the others either are igneous or are influenced by igneous activity—so it is most likely that a dinosaur fossil would be found in it.

All together, the previous passage should have taken you about 5 minutes to complete.

Now, let's do a Research Summary Passage. There will be three of these on the ACT Science test. This passage has simpler graphs/charts than the previous passage, so spend only about 15–30 seconds looking over things.

Research Summary

The *specific heat* of a substance is the amount of heat per unit mass required to raise the temperature by one degree Celsius. Specific heat is calculated by using the following equation:

$$Q = cm\Delta T$$

Q represents the heat added, c the specific heat, m the mass of the substance, and ΔT the change in temperature.

Substances with higher specific heats are better insulators, and substances with lower specific heats are better conductors. This is because it takes more heat to heat up a substance that is an insulator and less heat to heat up a substance that is a conductor.

Researchers predicted that metallic substances would have lower specific heats than certain nonmetallic substances. In order to test this prediction, they did two experiments using the following experimental setup:

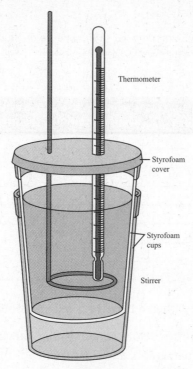

Figure 1

Stirrers of different substances were heated to a temperature of 50°C and subsequently added to water at a temperature of 20°C. The specific heats of the different substances were then calculated.

Study 1

Using the procedure outline above, researchers determined the specific heats for several metallic substances. The results are in Table 1 below.

Table 1

Metal	c in J/g °K (degrees Kelvin)	c in cal/g °C (degrees Celsius)
Aluminum	0.87	0.21
Copper	0.39	0.09
Gold	0.13	0.03
Silver	0.23	0.06

Study 2

Researchers did the same experimental procedure as in Study 1, while testing non-metallic substances. The results are in Table 2 below.

Table 2

Material	c in J/g °K (degrees Kelvin)	c in cal/g °C (degrees Celsius)
Brick	.9	0.22
Dry cement	1.55	0.37
Tar	1.47	0.35
Glass	.84	0.20
Solid plastic	1.67	0.4
Balsa wood	2.9	0.7
Rubber	2.01	0.48
Paper	1.4	0.33

What should you have gathered from your organization of this material?

- Notice from the introductory equation, the italicized "specific heat" in the introductory paragraph, and the drawing of the cup apparatus, that the studies involve determining specific heat.
- See from Table 1 that Study 1 involves figuring out the specific heats of different metals.
- See from Table 2 that Study 2 involves figuring out the specific heats of nonmetallic materials.

Now you are ready to attack the questions! **Coast, point, write**, and **don't overthink the early questions or underthink the later questions!**

1. Which of the substances in Table 1 would make the best conductor of heat?
   A. Aluminum
   B. Copper
   C. Gold
   D. Silver

(C) is correct. Even though this is an earlier/easier question, it requires us to briefly look over the reading to clarify how specific heat is related to conductivity. The second paragraph of the passage states that substances with lower specific heats are better conductors. So, we need to find the option with the lowest specific heat, which is gold. Although it would be nice if we could know ahead of time the exact extent to which we will need to refer to the reading, it is simply not possible. Be prepared to go back to it as a resource when you need clarification of table data.

2. If a piece of jewelry is a mixture of silver and gold, a scientist measuring its specific heat, measured in "c in cal/g °C", would most likely find it to be in which of the following ranges?
   F. 0.03–0.06
   G. 0.06–0.09
   H. 0.09–0.21
   J. 0.13–0.23

(F) is the correct answer. If something is a mixture of silver and gold, it would most likely have a specific heat somewhere between the specific heats of silver and gold. We can point back to Table 1 and see that the specific heat of gold (be sure you measure it in the right units!) is 0.03 and that of silver is 0.06. (F) puts this in the correct range. It would be easy to make a careless error on this question and look at the specific heat measurement in c in J/g °K. Coasting the question and pointing as you go will ensure that you don't make a simple careless error.

3. The results for which of the following nonmetallic substances is an exception to the prediction posed by the researchers?
   A. Tar
   B. Glass
   C. Rubber
   D. Paper

(B) is correct. Using common sense, where would the prediction posed by the researchers be found? Most likely in the introduction to the whole passage, since scientists like to make a prediction before they conduct experiments. Paragraph 3 states: "Researchers predicted that metallic substances would have lower specific heats than certain nonmetallic substances." So, if a nonmetallic substance DOES HAVE a lower specific heat than a metallic substance, this would pose a problem for the prediction by the researchers. According to Table 2, glass has a specific heat of 0.84 J/g °K. If we look at Table 1, we see that this is *lower* than the specific heat of aluminum, which is 0.87 J/g °K. So, glass would pose a problem for the researchers. All of the other options have specific heats *higher* than the metals in Table 1, so they would give evidence in support of the prediction.

4. Based on the information in Table 2, approximately how many calories would be required to raise the temperature of 2 grams of rubber by 1 degree Celsius?
   F. 0.5
   G. 1
   H. 2
   J. 4

(G) is the correct answer. We are moving into later questions, so more thinking will be needed. The specific heat of rubber using the calories measure is 0.48, and if we're careless, we will pick (F). The question asks how many calories would be required to raise 2 grams of rubber, not 1. In order to figure out exactly what the specific heat measurement means, go back to its definition in the passage. Fortunately, it's easy to find because "specific heat" is italicized: "The *specific heat* of a substance is the amount of heat per unit mass required to raise the temperature by one degree Celsius." To raise 1 gram of rubber by 1 degree Celsius takes 0.48 calories. To raise TWO grams would be double this, which is closest to answer choice (G), 1.

5. An architect wishes to make a house that will save on the energy costs for the owners by keeping the internal temperature constant, independent of the outside weather. Which of the following materials would be best to use for the walls of the house?
   A. Brick
   B. Cement
   C. Glass
   D. Balsa wood

(D) is correct. The question asks us to apply information from the passage to a real-world situation. Something that would keep the internal temperature constant would be a good *insulator*. Therefore, we should figure out which of these materials would make the best insulator by determining how specific heat relates to the quality of insulation. The second paragraph states that "substances with higher specific heats are better insulators." So, we just need to look at Table 2 to see which of the options has the highest specific heat. Balsa wood has the highest specific heat and would be the correct answer.

6. Researchers wished to test three liquids to see what their specific heats would be. They wish to make the experimental setup as much like the one in the study, to the extent reasonably possible. Which of the following parts of the experimental design would most need to be changed somehow in order to test a liquid?

F. Thermometer

G. Styrofoam cup

H. Styrofoam cover

J. Stirrer

(J) is correct. Often on later questions, we will need to think about the experimental procedure. We cannot simply locate the information in a table—we need to *think* our way through it. The experiment is designed to test the specific heats of different *solid substances* by placing a stirrer made of a given substance into the apparatus. If we were to test the specific heats of *liquids*, however, we could not put a solid stirrer of a liquid into another liquid to test it. So, it would be most critical to change the stirrer part of the procedure in order to conduct this test on liquids. Perhaps the liquids could be placed in a small container so that they wouldn't dissolve or disperse throughout the experimental apparatus.

TIP

The Conflicting Viewpoints Passage is the one Science passage that will definitely require a good bit of reading.

All together, the previous passage should have taken you about 5 to 6 minutes to complete.

Finally, let's do a Conflicting Viewpoints Passage. There will be just one of these on the Science test. Allow a bit more time to do the Conflicting Viewpoints—about 6 minutes or so. You can make up for the extra minute spent here by finishing an easy Data Representation or Research Summary Passage ahead of the pace. Sometimes there are graphs on the Conflicting Viewpoints, sometimes there aren't any. When you do have graphs, they are generally not nearly as useful in helping you put together the overall gist of the passage as they are on the Data Representation and Research Summary passages. So, there is no shortcut to actually reading the material. Read all of the material before doing the questions, but be sure to *pay closer attention to the TOPIC SEN-TENCES of each paragraph*, since scientists typically state their positions quite clearly at the beginning of each paragraph. In other words, read everything, but give more attention to the most important material (i.e., the beginning of each paragraph). Allow about 1–1.5 minutes to read things over before going to the questions.

Conflicting Viewpoints

Though geologists have more or less universally accepted the theories of plate tectonics and continental drift, the driving mechanism responsible for the movement of the plates remains something of a mystery. In general, scientists agree that continental drift is the result of a convective heat system, but the exact nature of that system is a point of contention. The basic tenets of these theories are illustrated in Figure 1.

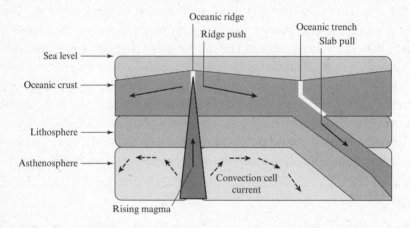

Figure 1

Theory 1

The convection cells responsible for continental drift must involve the Earth's entire mantle. Theories that limit convection to the outermost portions of the mantle cannot identify a suitable heat source for the convective current; only the extreme thermal energy concentrated around the Earth's core could exert a force of sufficient magnitude to drive the processes of plate tectonics. Rising from superheated mantle plumes at the core-mantle boundary, the convective energy approaches the crust through volcanic ridges and is subsequently conducted through the asthenosphere until recirculating to the mantle via subductive trenches. Although the heat-transfer mechanism behind asthenosphere-mantle convection remains, for now, elusive, there can be no doubt that as our knowledge of the inner Earth continues to grow, the answer will be forthcoming. An illustration of this theory is shown in Figure 2.

Theory 2

The convection cells that drive the motion of tectonic plates are necessarily isolated in the asthenospere, where lateral gradients of mineral density and thermal energy can account for the convection circuits in their entirety. Each cell begins by approaching the crust beneath an oceanic ridge, where rising magma and ultradense mineral layers combine to produce a thermally powered convective force, and a gravity-driven "ridge push." After dispersing across the upper asthenosphere along density and heat gradients, the cells re-circulate into the lower asthenosphere at oceanic trenches, where convective descent works in tandem with gravity-driven "slab pull" to complete the cell. An illustration of this theory is shown in Figure 3.

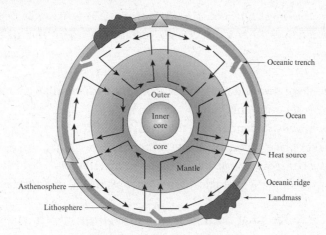

Figure 2

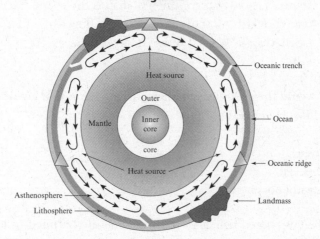

Figure 3

What should you have gathered from your reading?

- Understand from the introduction that geologists are debating *how* continental drift takes place.
- Understand that Theory 1 argues that continental drift is a convection process that involves the mantle of the Earth.

- Understand that Theory 2 argues that the convection from continental drift originates in the asthenosphere and doesn't involve as much circulation from the inner Earth.
- See that Theory 1 and Theory 2 differ in how deeply they believe the circulation from the Earth's convection goes within the Earth.

Now, let's do the questions, **coasting**, **pointing**, and **writing** as needed! The questions generally get harder as you go, just as they do on the other Science passage types.

1. Both geologists would agree on which of the following with respect to the cause of continental drift?
   A. It is heavily dependent on the Earth's mantle.
   B. It takes place primarily in the asthenosphere.
   C. It is a consequence of a convective heat system.
   D. It is no longer a geological phenomenon in the present day.

(C) is correct. To see what both geologists would agree with, take a look at the introductory paragraph to the whole passage. The second sentence states: "In general, scientists agree that continental drift is the result of a convective heat system." Don't overthink this question, given how early it is. (A) is what only Theory 1 believes. (B) is what only Theory 2 believes. (D) is believed by neither geologist.

2. Where would the geologists predict with precision that a volcano would most likely occur?
   A. An oceanic ridge
   B. A large landmass
   C. The ocean
   D. The asthenosphere

(A) is correct. The shared beliefs of both theories are outlined in Figure 1. A volcano will be formed from rising magma from deep within the Earth eventually leading to the surface. The rising magma, as labeled in the figure, eventually rises through an oceanic ridge. So, this would be the most likely spot for a volcano. The other options could very well have volcanos, but they are too imprecise to give us a precise idea of where a volcano would occur.

3. What would most likely allow scientists to make a conclusive determination as to which theory is correct?
   A. Observation of the severity and frequency of earthquakes in the lithosphere
   B. Data on the relative intensity of volcanic activity in the Earth's oceans
   C. An astronomical study of the continental drift patterns on the surface of Mars
   D. None of the above

(D) is correct. The theories disagree on what is going on deep within the Earth—Theory 1 believes there is heat convection on a much greater scale than does Theory 2. (A), (B), and (C) would all give us information about geological activity close to the Earth's surface and would not provide any clarification of which of the two theories is correct.

4. What does Theory 2 put forth as an additional factor that would allow convection to take place that Theory 1 does not consider?
   A. Convective heat
   B. Slab pull
   C. The lower asthenosphere
   D. Heat beneath the lithosphere

(B) is correct. The second-to-last sentence of Theory 2 states that slab pull works to complete the convective cell. Theory 1 considers all the other options, which you can quickly tell from looking at Figure 2.

5. Increased scientific knowledge about the interactions between which two layers of the Earth would be of most interest to the geologist in Theory 1?
   A. Lithosphere and asthenosphere
   B. Asthenosphere and mantle
   C. Mantle and outer core
   D. Outer core and inner core

(B) is correct. Theory 1 states in the second-to-last sentence that "although the heat-transfer mechanism behind asthenosphere-mantle convection remains, for now, elusive, there can be no doubt that as our knowledge of the inner Earth continues to grow, the answer will be forthcoming." So, clear knowledge about if and how heat is transferred between these two layers would potentially give credibility and explanatory value to Theory 1. The other options would provide explanations of some interest, but they would not be as critical to explaining the heat transfer mechanisms behind Theory 1.

6. Scientists hypothesize that nuclear fission is a major source of the heat that is created in the Earth's core. If nuclear fission with the Earth were to suddenly come to a complete stop, which theory would argue that continental drift would be more immediately impacted?
   A. Theory 1
   B. Theory 2
   C. Both would argue for an identical impact.
   D. Both would agree that such an event would have no impact on continental drift.

(A) is correct. From Figures 2 and 3, we can see that the convection in Theory 1 is directly impacted by the heat in the core of the Earth, while the convection in Theory 2 is much more indirectly impacted. Theory 1 would thus argue that continental drift would be more immediately impacted because the convection process that causes it would come to a halt. Theory 2 would argue that the convection process influencing continental drift would likely continue for a bit more time, and even if it came to a stop, other factors like slab pull would still contribute to continental drift.

7. How does Theory 2 primarily address the principal objection to its viewpoint that Theory 1 would have?
   A. Arguing that convection takes place within the upper asthenosphere
   B. Arguing that gravity-driven slab pull contributes to convective descent
   C. Arguing that magma and ultradense mineral layers provide a heat source
   D. Arguing that the inner core of the Earth provides the only source of convective heat

(C) is correct. Theory 1 states that "only the extreme thermal energy concentrated around the Earth's core could exert a force of sufficient magnitude to drive the processes of plate tectonics." In other words, only heat from the Earth's center is hot enough to have this kind of impact. Theory 2 responds to this objection by stating that "lateral gradients of mineral density and thermal energy can account for the convection circuits in their entirety." In other words, there is enough heat closer to the Earth's surface to contribute to continental drift.

🔑 SCIENCE STRATEGY SUMMARY

- The ACT Science is a 35-minute test with six or seven passages.
- Virtually everything you need to figure out the questions will be right in front of you.
- Spend about 9 minutes for every 10 questions, and guess on the last question of each passage, if needed, to save time.
- Look at the graphs first, then use the reading as needed (except on the Conflicting Viewpoints).
- Really understand the questions by coasting, pointing, and writing.
- Don't overthink the early questions within a passage and don't underthink the later questions within a passage, since the questions gradually become more difficult within a passage.

Writing

5

WHAT ARE THE BASIC FACTS ABOUT THE ACT WRITING TEST?

→ It is an optional part of the test, although many colleges do require it. (Go to *www.actstudent.org* to see if your college does.)
→ It is one essay for which you have 40 minutes to respond.
→ The prompt is a general topic, typically something related to current events or broad ethical issues.
→ Like the rest of the test, it is more an evaluation of skill than knowledge. You don't need to have particular background knowledge to do well.
→ Your essay is graded by 2 ACT-trained graders who each score it from 1 to 6 along four different domains: *Ideas and Analysis, Development and Support, Organization, and Language Use.* The two graders' scores are added together to give you scores along each of these four domains. Then, your total score is curved along the traditional 1–36 ACT scale. This 1–36 score will be reported, but <u>will not</u> affect your multiple-choice composite score.
→ The essay comes at the very end of the ACT, and you have a 5-minute break before you start.
→ You will have a page on which to prewrite—this page will not be scored. You will have about 3 pages on which to write your actual essay.
→ Make sure you respond in English, don't skip lines, write legibly, and use a number 2 pencil.

HOW IS THE NEW ACT ESSAY DIFFERENT FROM THE PREVIOUS ACT ESSAY?

	Old ACT Essay	New ACT Essay
Time	30 minutes	40 minutes
Topic	Typically a school-related topic	Topics related to current events, ethics, and general interest
Format	Brief background information followed by a prompt	More in-depth background and prewriting information with three points of view to consider
Scoring	Doesn't affect the overall ACT composite score. Scored between 2 and 12. Graders give an overall score with no subcategories.	Still doesn't affect the composite score. More intricate score reporting, with four different evaluation domains. Score will be curved like the other sections, with a scaled score between 1 and 36.

SAMPLE ACT WRITING PROMPT

Here is an example of a prompt, followed by a top-scoring essay and a scoring rubric.

Virtual Reality

Virtual reality—computer-based technology that enables users to visualize and experience artificial, three-dimensional worlds—is advancing at an astonishing pace. Immersive visualization technology is already well-established in the realms of personal entertainment and video gaming. Entrepreneurs are hoping to expand the reach of virtual reality to far more fields. Students could learn through hands-on programs instead of classroom instruction; thrill-seekers could experience space flight and deep-sea exploration from the comfort of their homes; surgeons could virtually operate on patients in far-away countries. The potential impact of the advancement of virtual reality technology requires thorough consideration.

Read and carefully evaluate these points of view. Each puts forth a specific way of thinking about the advancement of virtual reality.

Viewpoint One	Viewpoint Two	Viewpoint Three
Widespread virtual reality use will cause people to live in fantasy rather than reality. Personal relationships will be a major casualty as people immerse themselves in addictive entertainment.	Virtual reality is coming, whether we like it or not. So, it is best to prepare for its widespread implementation instead of fighting against the inevitable.	Virtual reality will be a great equalizer across humanity. No matter if people are rich or poor, all will have access to the same intellectual opportunities since "virtual scarcity" is impossible.

ESSAY ASSIGNMENT

Compose a focused essay in which you consider multiple viewpoints on the advancement of virtual reality. In your response, be certain to

- examine and assess the viewpoints provided
- express and develop your own point of view on the topic
- analyze the connections between your point of view and those provided

Your viewpoint may completely agree, somewhat agree, or not agree at all with any of those presented. No matter your perspective, provide clear, logical arguments supported by detailed examples to make your case.

Planning Your Response

Your prewriting notes on this page will not be considered in your score.

Use the following space to brainstorm ideas and map out your response. You may want to think about the following as you analyze the given prompt:
Strengths and weaknesses of the three viewpoints

- What good points do they make, and what potential objections do they ignore?
- Why might they be convincing to readers, and why might their perspectives fall short?

Your previous experience, background knowledge, and personal values

- What is your viewpoint on this topic, and what are its pros and cons?
- How will you craft an argument in support of your point of view?

Top-Scoring Sample Student Response

Graded by one reader as 6/6 for all four domains: Ideas and Analysis, Development and Support, Organization, and Language Use

Human resource departments have their work cut out for them. How can you really be sure that you are hiring the right person for the job? How can you be absolutely, without-a-doubt certain of the applicants' abilities before seeing them on the job? New employees almost always have a brief period of training and becoming comfortable with company values, but this period can quickly become burdensome and expensive when the new hire has to be taught the basics as well. Virtual reality technology can revolutionize the way students become professionals and enter their specific fields of work.

Imagine the mechanic who comes to his very first day of work already having changed a thousand oil filters, rebuilt ten engines, and replaced fifty tires. How about the airplane pilot who has successfully landed one hundred planes in distress before ever stepping foot in a cockpit? And wouldn't you prefer to know that the local hospital only hires surgeons who have perfected their skills virtually before touching a patient? For me, this last example is particularly relevant. As I enter college with hopes of earning my BSN, I know that beyond my general curriculum and specialized coursework lies hours of clinical study. Virtual reality technology could not only make my education more comprehensive but it could produce a more qualified nurse by graduation—not to mention the confidence I could take to the job market having encountered hundreds of situations in life-like capacities beforehand.

The implications of three-dimensional virtual realms hardly end there. Want to learn a language? The French classroom is hardly effective when compared to an immersion experience in France from your own living room, where you can converse with natives. Interested in astronomy? Go ahead and sit inside a virtual meteor shower. Virtual reality has endless implications for the future. The ways students are educated, the ways companies hire, and the possibilities for sharing knowledge are just some of the many paradigms that could be positively impacted by advancements in immersive visualization. While Viewpoint Three ignores the factors that could influence who has access to virtual reality and how those realms are controlled, it does coincide with my own argument that virtual reality can offer unprecedented intellectual and experiential opportunities.

As with all great change, virtual technology poses some serious challenges. I can easily understand the hesitation, like that expressed in Viewpoint One, surrounding a development that could quickly become an escape from reality. If a virtual world offers more fun and less risk, it could potentially become all-consuming and eventually deter actual social interaction. For instance, if your favorite band can be seen "live" from your own home, is there still appeal to pay for pricey tickets, navigate through hours of traffic, and see it in person? Or, if you embark on an African safari without the airline tickets and suffocating heat, would you venture to travel anymore at all? Concepts of reality become blurry when experience itself becomes artificial. A particularly farsighted critic might propose a future society that doesn't step foot outside their own doors.

Yet, this sort of apprehension accompanies every advancement, and has since long before the digital age. Instead, it seems more beneficial to deliberate on the possibilities that arise when virtual reality is complementary to, rather than a replacement of, our real experiences. I am in agreement with the second perspective in finding it useless to refute the inevitable. We are far from a civilization without social aspects, and if technology has shown us anything over the last decade, it's that it can be used to promote social connections. Despite the obstacles that accompany any far-reaching technology, virtual reality proffers an unparalleled opportunity to improve education, career training, and erudition.

Evaluation Notes

Why did this essay receive a perfect score?

- It has an excellent introduction, hooking the reader's interest by taking an unconventional approach to the prompt.
- It has a clear thesis, arguing that "virtual reality technology can revolutionize the way students become professionals and enter their specific fields of work."
- It provides an excellent context for discussion, showing the relevance of the topic to the narrator's chosen field of nursing.
- It examines all three viewpoints, not just explicitly mentioning them but considering parts of the perspectives with which the author agrees and disagrees.
- It relates each viewpoint to the author's point of view, considering the pros and the cons of the implications of each viewpoint.
- It acknowledges the complexity of the topic, especially in the analysis found in the essay's final paragraph.
- It provides specific evidence and support with creatively chosen personal and real-world examples.
- It has excellent organization and transitions: the paragraphs and ideas flow logically from one to the next.
- It has excellent wording and sentence variety, using precise vocabulary to convey the ideas and a mixture of sentence lengths and types to help maintain the reader's interest.
- It has virtually no grammar and spelling issues. Although it's not perfect, for a 40-minute essay written by a high school student, it is very solid.

You can use this generic rubric to evaluate your ACT Essays as you practice.

ACT WRITING RUBRIC

Ideas and Analysis: Considers multiple perspectives. Develops a clear and sophisticated thesis. Provides a useful context for analyzing the issue. Analyzes the implications, complexities, and underlying assumptions of different viewpoints.						
6: Excellent	5: Skillful	4: Adequate	3: Fair	2: Weak	1: Poor	____ /6

Development and Support: Provides an insightful and well-supported argument, placing the issue in a broad context. Uses reasoning and illustration to express the significance of the issue. Demonstrates an understanding of the complexity of the topic.						
6: Excellent	5: Skillful	4: Adequate	3: Fair	2: Weak	1: Poor	____ /6

Organization: Shows a skillful overall organizational approach. Has a clear, sustained position, accompanied by a logical sequence of ideas that builds the writer's argument. Provides clear and logical transitions between sentences and paragraphs.						
6: Excellent	5: Skillful	4: Adequate	3: Fair	2: Weak	1: Poor	____ /6

Language Use: The essay's language is well-suited to the argument. Vocabulary choice is precise and appropriate. Sentence structure is clear and varied. Tone, voice, and style are effective. Grammar, usage, and mechanics issues are minimized and do not interfere with the reader's understanding.						
6: Excellent	5: Skillful	4: Adequate	3: Fair	2: Weak	1: Poor	____ /6

	Essay Raw Score: ____ /24

Multiply your Essay Raw Score by 1.5 to get your approximate ACT Writing Scaled Score:

Essay Raw Score: _____ × 1.5 = _____ out of 36 possible points.

ACT Writing Scaled Score: ____ /36

Now that we have a general idea of what the ACT Writing is like, let's address four <u>ACT Writing Myths</u>. Many of these myths result from things we have been told that we must do for certain school essays—the ACT Writing is different from school essays and requires a different approach.

Myth	Reality
"I have to write a 5 paragraph essay."	Your essay is evaluated in a big picture way—the graders are not looking for a cookie-cutter formula. Although 5 paragraphs is fine, you don't have to confine yourself to this structure.
"I have to agree or disagree with one of the viewpoints."	You need to have a *position*—you don't have to completely agree or disagree with any one of the viewpoints. As long as you have a clear thesis and you defend your stance, you will be fine.
"I can't write using 'I,' 'you,' and personal examples."	You can absolutely use personal examples and observations—the prompts don't require particular background knowledge and are designed so you *can* use whatever you have observed or can imagine.
"I can't make any mistakes when I write. I need to be sure to edit my essay significantly."	The graders realize that your essay is a first draft and does not need to be perfect. The essays are graded more *positively than negatively*, meaning they are looking for reasons to give you points, not just to take points away. Don't let a fear of making mistakes hold you back from writing an in-depth response!

ACT ESSAY STRATEGIES

1. **Know the directions and format ahead of time.** The general format of the prompt will not change from test date to test date, although the topics will. Review the sample essays so you are comfortable with the overall structure of the new ACT Essay assignment. You do not want to waste time reading directions on test day.

2. **Manage your time well.** You have only 40 minutes to respond, so try not to spend more than 5 minutes prewriting. Spend at least 30 minutes actually writing your essay. The graders are not expecting absolute perfection, so you are generally better off continuing to develop your body paragraphs than spending several minutes at the end editing. Make your introduction and conclusion appropriately sized for a 3-page essay.

3. **Practice a full essay at least once—preferably more—before test day.** This is a very unusual sort of essay assignment—it is likely quite a bit different from essays you have written for school. Students typically make vast improvements after even just a little bit of practice with this type of essay prompt. Students who go into the ACT having never tried an essay like this often finish way too early or run out of time. Although practicing an essay is probably not the most enjoyable way to spend 40 minutes of your time, it will be a worthwhile investment.

4. **Create your thesis later if you cannot decide on your position.** Crafting a precise, analytical thesis is one of the greatest challenges of an essay like this. Even after a few minutes of prewriting, you still may not be sure of your stance—taking a stance when you are not sure where you are headed may limit you. If you are having trouble coming up with a thesis for your introductory paragraph, try one of two things:

- Use your introductory paragraph as a general "hook" about the topic, and put your thesis in your final paragraph.
- Leave a few lines blank at the beginning of your response, write your body paragraphs, and in the final 5 minutes come back and write your intro with the thesis statement.

Doing this will allow you to jump into your body paragraphs, which are typically far easier to start than a comprehensive thesis statement.

5. **Rely on the prompt and prewriting notes for brainstorming.** The ACT Essay will give you <u>plenty</u> of food for thought. You will have a broad introduction to the topic, three points of view, and a prewriting outline. Use this very specific guidance to spur your imagination and memory.

6. **Draw upon anything you know well for examples.** Do not limit yourself to "scholarly" or "sophisticated" examples—you can use anything you know well that is related to the topic. What hobbies do you have? What television shows and movies could be relevant? How about books or magazines you have read for fun? Have any of your friends or family had applicable experiences? If you can't remember anything that could be incorporated, use your imagination to create hypothetical scenarios.

7. **Minimize errors, but don't be a perfectionist.** For typical papers in school, you will have plenty of time to revise and edit your work. On the ACT Essay, time management is of the essence. Try your best to avoid spelling and grammar issues as you write, but don't spend more than a couple of minutes editing your essay when you are complete. Your time will be much better spent further developing your argument and examples.

8. **Write legibly.** ACT Essay graders will be evaluating countless responses—make it as easy as possible for them to give you a top score by making your handwriting readable.

9. **Explicitly mention each viewpoint.** The essay prompt requires you to analyze each of the three points of view. The graders will easily see that you have done this if you explicitly mention each viewpoint—say "Viewpoint One," "Viewpoint Two," and "Viewpoint Three" at least once in your response.

10. **Write as much high-quality material as you possibly can.** You will have a 5-minute break before the essay—take this time to recharge by walking around a bit and having a small snack. The essay comes at the end of the test, and you will likely be quite fatigued by this time. If you make a concerted effort to write all the way up until when time is called, you will almost certainly do far better than if you finish early and put your head down. Based on the released sample prompts and scores from ACT, *longer essays almost always score higher than shorter ones*. Quantity alone is not enough, but if you use all the available pages to write plenty of high-quality analytical writing, you will have a much better chance of doing well than if you are too brief.

FULL ESSAY SAMPLES AND EVALUATIONS

Having examined the fundamentals of a solid ACT Essay, let's put it all together by looking at 6 essays of different scoring levels, all of which respond to the same prompt. As you look through these, think about how the essays vary in the level of these big-picture writing qualities: Ideas and Analysis, Development and Support, Organization, and Language Use.

Cost of Education

The cost of a college education continues to grow. This trend is highly unlikely to stop anytime in the near future—colleges continue to charge more, and more than enough students are willing to pay the higher tuition. With education clearly benefitting both students (who are generally able to find more career opportunities with more education) and society as a whole (which is more prosperous as it has a better-educated workforce), the question becomes who should bear a greater responsibility in funding college education: students, their families, businesses, the government, or someone else? With different societies approaching this important topic in diverse ways, college education funding is a worthy topic for consideration.

Read and carefully evaluate these points of view. Each puts forth a specific way of thinking about college education funding.

Viewpoint One	Viewpoint Two	Viewpoint Three
Students should be the primary sources of their college educational funding. They have the most incentive to make sure the money doesn't go to waste.	Not everyone is in a position to afford a college education. To level the playing field for a diverse population, government should play the largest role in funding college.	The problem of ever-increasing college prices will never be solved from within the current system. Revolutionary changes from innovators outside the educational system are needed.

ESSAY ASSIGNMENT

Compose a focused essay in which you consider multiple viewpoints on how college should be funded. In your response, be certain to

- examine and assess the viewpoints provided
- express and develop your own point of view on the topic
- analyze the connections between your point of view and those provided

Your viewpoint may completely agree, somewhat agree, or not agree at all with any of those presented. No matter your perspective, provide clear, logical arguments supported by detailed examples to make your case.

Planning Your Response

Your prewriting notes on this page will not be considered in your score.

Use the following space to brainstorm ideas and map out your response. You may want to think about the following as you analyze the given prompt:
Strengths and weaknesses of the three viewpoints

- What good points do they make, and what potential objections do they ignore?
- Why might they be convincing to readers, and why might their perspectives fall short?

Your previous experience, background knowledge, and personal values

- What is your viewpoint on this topic, and what are its pros and cons?
- How will you craft an argument in support of your point of view?

Score of 1 in every category: Ideas and Analysis, Development and Support, Organization, and Language Use

College education continues to get more expensive and that isn't stopping anytime soon. It is totally ridiculus to expect students to pay for it. Most students won't even be able to go to college because of how much it cost. And that isn't fair. Then they will end up only working in low skilled jobs and never be able to make money or save for their own kids to go to college too. I think how much colleges charge is greedy. Since education is important for students and businesses and the government, it shouldn't just be up to the student to pay this outrageous prices. But maybe online colleges will help take down the bill.

Comments

This essay is extremely brief and doesn't address the points of view. Instead of analysis, it has simple assertions, like "that isn't fair." It fails to answer the question of who should be responsible for paying for college. The grammar and spelling are poor.

Score of 2 in every category: Ideas and Analysis, Development and Support, Organization, and Language Use

Ever since I was little, we been saving for college. I had a lemonade stand when I was eight and all the money went into my bank. Every birthday I prayed that nobody would give me money cause it always went to the bank. For Christmas my dad would put $100 in my college fund. College College College. Sometimes, I hated it. But now I'm 17 and applying to college and I have almost all the money I need from years and years of sacrifice.

It feels good to be able to pay by myself. Through my own sweat and blood. I didn't have cool shoes or new toys to brag about after every holiday but now I have something to brag about. I'm going to college and I won't have to go broke with loans or rely on other people to get where I want to go. It feels good to do it yourself. I think every student should save up like this—it makes it even more of an accomplishment.

Comments

The writer is able to incorporate more interesting examples than the writer of the first essay but fails to address the points of view. The essay has very simple sentence structure, virtually no analysis, and issues with comma usage. With only two body paragraphs, there is simply not enough here to present a solid argument.

Score of 3 in every category: Ideas and Analysis, Development and Support, Organization, and Language Use

The cost of college should vary from individual to individual to make it fair. Every student comes from a different background and their financial flexibility might depend on their parents jobs, their race, their familys medical history, and so on. The point is charging the same price for education doesn't make any sense when the students are all individuals with differing experience.

Take for instance, a student whose parents bring in six-figures and have had the luxury to put up the money for college versus a student whose mom is single and working two jobs to afford a house and food but has never been able to save extra money. Why should education, something that everyone needs, cost the same for them two students? If it does then it goes against democracy. Everyone is supposed to have a chance to move up in their lives, but if a child cannot go to college then they can't get a high paying job and so the cycle will just repeat itself. The way to approach the cost of college is to evaluate every prospective student and decide based on circumstances.

Obviously it is expensive to operate a university. From the buildings to the busses to the dorms to the professors, there are a lot of money involved. So, it cant be free. But the current costs are just outrageous and education has became all about getting as many students to attend so colleges can keep making money. Likewise the jobs out there are demanding more and more education. If everyone needs to go to college, then the government needs to find a way to make it possible for everyone without making the colleges go bankrupt. The way to do that is to charge based on situation rather than just a set price for everybody.

Comments

This represents a solid improvement over the previous essay. The introductory paragraph does have a brief thesis statement: "The cost of college should vary from individual to individual to make it fair." There is analysis present, especially in the second paragraph with the author asking a rhetorical question and pointing out the inconsistency in having students of different means required to pay the same cost. The final paragraph addresses the potential objection to the thesis (i.e., acknowledging that it is expensive to operate universities). Despite these strengths, there are substantial weaknesses: poor grammar and punctuation, simple and repetitive sentence structure, and generally vague examples. Also, the writer does not explicitly address the points of view.

Score of 4 in every category: Ideas and Analysis, Development and Support, Organization, and Language Use

How one pays for education is a relevant and evolving topic. The first viewpoint puts college education on the shoulders of the student. The second saves it primarily for the government. And the third suggests a revolutionary change to the current system. I agree with the second viewpoint.

Viewpoint One ignores the fact that college is expensive, perhaps much too expensive for the average family. Viewpoint Three suggests that our current system is somehow failing and needs dramatic change. It is only the second perspective that accounts for a diverse population with separate needs, abilities, and assets. The United States retains its position at the top of the ladder in research and education opportunities. Despite the nation's income gap, a combination of personal and governmental financing has opened the way for the most inovative workforce in all the world. The current system is working and since the citizens are more educated, making more money, and contributing further to the economy, the relationship is harmonius.

To put the entire cost of college onto the student is unfair. Tuition rates in public universities are approaching $25,000 per year and that's before any additional expenses. This bill is simply too much for the average American family. Especially since many degrees are taking five or six years now, and worse, students are having to go to graduate school to get the jobs they want. Then, consider African American families or American-Indian families or immigrants that are historically underprivileged or underrepresented. Its certainly even harder for them to afford college for their children. Yet, that shouldn't stop them from attending—in fact, it is even more of a reason for the government to help provide them with the opportunities to succeed.

Although the government shouldn't have to pay everything, with constant rising college tuition costs, students should be able to pursue a degree with manageable expenses.

Comments

The response does explicitly address every point of view, but does so in a rather mechanical way by simply restating what the viewpoints said and making simplistic statements of approval or disapproval. The essay is mostly free of grammar and spelling errors, but does have some problems that are distracting. The writer does present some decent analysis and thoughtful examples: a clear case is made for keeping the status quo and considering the situations of those from less privileged backgrounds. To improve the essay, the writer could do more to consider objections, provide more in-depth examples, and write with more elevated word choice and stylistic variety.

Score of 5 in every category: Ideas and Analysis, Development and Support, Organization, and Language Use

Tommy graduated somewhere near the end of his class. He's not particularly bright, but his low grade point average had more to do with a lack of interest in academics. Tommy knew his parents worked hard for their four-bedroom house on Maple Drive, but that they had never had an opportunity to really save money. Even if they had somehow managed to save up for their three children to attend college, he couldn't bear to imagine another four or five years sitting in a classroom. When Tommy turned eighteen, he joined the United States Army. The Army paid for Tommy to get a degree in Criminal Justice while he served his country. In two years, Tommy will complete his time with the military and join a civilian police force.

Tommy is my older brother, and his story shows that students can fund their own education if they want it badly enough. Besides the military, there are tremendous options for students to borrow and lend for college. I'm filling out the FAFSA now, which is one opportunity for students from low income families to get federal funding for their education. Not to mention, students who don't want to risk taking out loans or who don't qualify for scholarships can work their way through college. Online colleges, adult colleges, and evening classes offer multiple options for the working student to gain an education and make money simultaneously. There is a way for everyone.

Graduating seniors are young adults with their own goals. As such, we should take responsibility and work towards those goals—that is the essence of the American Dream. We are not entitled to free handouts, but instead establish the limits of our own success through our actions. I agree with Viewpoint One because it emphasizes the student's role in determining his or her own destiny. While there are many students whose families cannot afford to pay for college—mine included—that does not justify putting the bill on someone else, or even on the government like the second viewpoint suggests.

This nation was built on the idea that we can all pursue our own happiness through the liberties offered by American democracy. Tommy serves as a prime example of what can be accomplished when one decides to take hold of their future. His is also a lesson that traditional college education isn't the goal of every student. Whether it be at a university, in the military, or via online platforms, students should empower themselves by working toward their particular education and/or training goals.

Comments

This thoughtful response is strongest when it comes to establishing a relevant context for discussion through the use of a personal example. The writer takes things a step beyond the formulaic response of the previous essay by crafting a structure that goes beyond the simple agreement or disagreement with each point of view. While there is not much to criticize in this essay, there is not enough of an argument to take it to the next level. The writer should continue her analysis and examples with more breadth and depth. In particular, there should be more consideration of objections. Further, the writer could elevate her vocabulary choice and have more sentence variety.

Score of 6 in every category: Ideas and Analysis, Development and Support, Organization, and Language Use

At every family gathering in my conscious memory, my grandfather tells the story about how his parents pulled him out of school at fourteen years old because it was time for him to start providing for the family. He had been left "playing in school" long enough; many of his friends had stopped attending a year or two earlier to work odd jobs, help on the family farm, learn their father's trade, or raise younger siblings. He could read and write and do simple math—what more did he want? My mother has a similar tale about college. She enrolled after high school and attended one year, but she still recites, "it simply isn't for everyone." Sure, she would have loved to get her degree, but her job at the bank paid well and only required a diploma and on-the-job training.

In previous generations, higher education was seen as optional, but not necessary—at times, even an impediment to success. However, that is not the case now. Today, even entry-level positions require a four-year degree, and even those students interested in trade schools or the military complement their training with education. A university-educated workforce benefits every facet of society. Since a college education is imperative in today's job market and is mutually beneficial for both student and society, it should be offered free of charge to everybody just like a K–12 education.

Some agree with viewpoint one, arguing that students should be responsible for funding their own college education, but this statement is, in itself, exclusive. Only a small percentage of students can afford the hundreds of thousands of dollars that go into a college education. Others urge these students, those who may not have the financial freedom to pay out their own pocket, to pursue scholarships, federal grants, and loans. Yet, this solution is far from realistic. Scholarships and grants aren't available to *everybody*—still, it is everybody that has a right to an education and a place in the workforce. Moreover, we can see the devastation of taking out overwhelming loans by looking at today's students entering the job market. Overburdened by the loans, they enter an unpromising market as quickly as possible just to find out that they don't make enough to cover their monthly minimum payments, pay rent, and buy basic necessities. In a recent NPR broadcast, the average student was reported to graduate with over $80,000 in debt—that hardly seems like an encouraging start for anybody. Those who may agree with viewpoint two might think government could take on the burden of university educa-tion funding, but with our national debt already at several trillion dollars, this too is an impractical option.

My argument is in accordance with viewpoint three which demands another look at the current system. Once upon a time, high school was unre-alistic for many. Now, it seems absurd to suggest otherwise. Even a generation or two ago, college seemed optional. However, it is time that the world started thinking about education as a right rather than a privilege. With an expand-ing global economy and the demand for educated workers at its highest, col-lege should be offered free of cost to every citizen.

Comments

This sophisticated response sustains the reader's attention throughout. It begins with an interesting and relevant personal anecdote about the author's family history to establish a broad context for discussion. It uses this to draw a contrast between the educational demands of previous generations and the current generation, making the case for greater access to university education. The author provides substantial analysis of opposing points of view, explicitly addressing each of the points of view. The essay uses elevated vocabulary and has varied sentence structure, demonstrating excellent writing skill.

Now that you have become familiar with the ACT Essay grading process, write a response to the following prompt. After you are done, you can use the six example responses to help you determine your likely score.

ACT-STYLE WRITING PRACTICE

College Admissions

Perhaps more than ever before, a good college education is the gateway to career success. Students who earn admission to top schools have access to excellent instruction from world-renowned professors. Outside of the classroom, students at elite universities can network with their classmates, brainstorming entrepreneurial ventures and building the foundation for professional referrals. Admission to respected colleges has become increasingly competitive—students want their investment of time, energy, and money in their education to be worthwhile. College admissions officials are powerful gatekeepers for ambitious students from around the world. Given the important decisions these officials will make, what criteria should they use for admission?

Read and carefully evaluate these points of view. Each puts forth a specific way of thinking about college admissions criteria.

Viewpoint One	Viewpoint Two	Viewpoint Three
Admission decisions should be based on the applicants' academic potential. Grades and test scores should be examined to ensure the brightest students are admitted.	People smarts are more important for career success than book smarts. College admissions should be primarily based on applicant's demonstrated interpersonal skills.	Elite schools are too focused on preserving prestige instead of empowering young people. Schools should focus on providing a world-class education to as many students as possible.

ESSAY ASSIGNMENT

Compose a focused essay in which you consider multiple viewpoints on what should influence college admissions decisions. In your response, be certain to

- examine and assess the viewpoints provided
- express and develop your own point of view on the topic
- analyze the connections between your point of view and those provided

Your viewpoint may completely agree, somewhat agree, or not agree at all with any of those presented. No matter your perspective, provide clear, logical arguments supported by detailed examples to make your case.

Planning Your Response

Your prewriting notes on this page will not be considered in your score.

Use the following space to brainstorm ideas and map out your response. You may want to think about the following as you analyze the given prompt:

Strengths and weaknesses of the three viewpoints

- What good points do they make, and what potential objections do they ignore?
- Why might they be convincing to readers, and why might their perspectives fall short?

Your previous experience, background knowledge, and personal values

- What is your viewpoint on this topic, and what are the pros and cons of this viewpoint?
- How will you craft an argument in support of your point of view?

Sample Response, Score of 1 across all categories

Next year, when I apply to college, I hope the best schools are using a different criteria than all them given. I think leadership is most important for success. I think colleges should look for the worlds next leaders and find them by how they intereact and do extra curricular activities or volunteer. In my opinion, it's these students that stand out and are different from others. They lead. They know how to talk and inspire and unite. You find these students by looking for those in sports or volunteer work or in the band and even on debate teams. My coach once said that he rather have one true leader than a bunch of allstars. That's because it was clear to him that the pathway to winning is through finding the kids willing to relate to others, willing to step out their comfort zone, willing to push others when they can't push anymore.

Colleges should be looking for leaders and admission officials should set criteria for high school involvement because that will help them find the leaders. I think its silly to want the smartest kids or the best and brightest only because if they cant lead then they don't change any outcomes.

Sample Response, Score of 2 across all categories

Whether or not you get into college should be decided by your grade point average. Other standards like tests and essays cannot show long term commitment or gauge a sense of the person applying. A student's GPA though is like a map of them. It reflects not only intelligene but focus and work ethic. I never understood how one test or one piece of writing can tell you much about a student. Yet, a four year record can tell you a bunch.

I'm not saying this because I have a high GPA, but because it makes sense to me. If colleges want students who are out to work hard and students want colleges who are going to help them seucceed then doesn't it make sense that colleges should evaluate their applicants by an academic record?

Perspective one says test scores are representative of someone's potential, but there are so many really smart people who suck on test days, or just go blank, or overthink on tests. Can you say the same about a GPA? Could it be a fluke? No.

Then people who think like Viewpoint two are going to say that grades don't matter but they do. They aren't just applicable to careers in the field but say something about your character too. You don't just get A's for being a genius you also get them for working hard, going to a tutor, and asking the teacher to help you when your stuck. And three says everyone should be admitted but I don't think college is for everyone.

Sample Response, Score of 3 across all categories

Admissions decisions have to be well-rounded like the job market itself. Diversity is met only through a wide variety of students and colleagues; without it, any company in a global workforce suffers. Tests are important sure, but so is the ability to communicate with customers, think of new ideas, and lead groups of people—and tests have very little to say about those things.

The college that helps itself in the long-run is the college that is willing to recruit from a wide variety of populations varying in race, economic status, and yes, even academic success. I personally think having lots of different people from lots of different places enriches the classroom experience. Diversity is what is needed.

For my senior project, my teacher divided the classroom into fours making sure to team the best students with the worst students. At first, this was more annoying than anything else. But we soon learned that it added to our assignments, that it stirred discussion, and it even opened us up to new friends. The students who might not have been the most intelligent in the class turned out to have different outlooks and valuable perspectives—don't you think this is even more important at the college level.

I think colleges really effect what you end up doing and who you end up becoming and how much you end up making. Elite univerisities build a foundation for a lifelong, rewarding career field, and more people deserve that option than just those with the highest test scores. It is time the university operated like the real workforce and looked for a group to meet a wide set of needs rather than fill a small niche. Imagine what the world would be like if everyone was the same and offered the same skill sets.

Sample Response, Score of 4 across all categories

In a time when college means the difference between employment and unemployment, success and failure, admissions criteria must be based on more than a student's grades and test scores. Out in the real world, it is not those who can memorize formulas, recite facts, and recall obscure vocabulary that do well. Success comes more often than not to the approachable problem-solver who is willing to network within his or her field, adapt to new work environments, and who can be counted on to come to work every day ready to debate the best way to carry out a company's mission. Since college is designed as a platform to ready students for their prospective fields, it should place value on those same skills that are necessary in the workforce.

Take, for instance, one of the most significant jobs there is: that of the President. While having a genius who knows the Periodic Table of Elements like the back of his or her hand and who can recite 17th Century Italian poetry at the slightest prompting has its perks, it is much more important that the Executive Chief Officer be personable, trustworthy, and diplomatic. Is there anyone out there who would argue that Steve Jobs might of been more affective if he was a tad less interpersonal? Survey after survey tells the same story: companies are looking for creative, adaptive employees that can relate to consumers, clients, etc. Being smart isn't all there is to success, far from it.

The counterargument is that grades are representative of a students' work ethic, that test scores say something about a student's ability to work under pressure and think outside of the box. Perspective One states that these standards measure an applicant's "academic potential." Yet, it is more likely that they reflect only a miniscule part of what that applicant has to offer. Grades and test scores don't always embody character. Not everyone can be great at school—but in a market where everyone needs a degree, that is not a sufficient reason to deny someone admision to a university. Perspective Three argues that we should try to help as many students as possible. While this seems slightly ideal, it is much better than denying loads of students just because they had an off year, or had a teacher they weren't fond of, or just didn't get why it was important to read Hawthorne's "Scarlet Letter."

Grades and test scores cannot accurately evaluate one's potential, so I agree with Viewpoint Two.

Sample Response, Score of 5 across all categories

I am terrible at standardized testing. Terrible. So, it is no surprise that I doubled my efforts in the classroom and had three, yes three, of my teachers look over my college application. It's not fair. That is what I would say. I'm an excellent student, fourth in a class of over four hundred. I'm not exactly sure what I want to do with my life, but I'm ambitious. And I've taken initiative, emailing professionals in careers that I am interested in, even shadowing a nurse practitioner for a week last summer. Name another seventeen-year old kid you know who will give up a week of summer to trot around a hospital and eat cafeteria food that's somehow worse than the cafeteria food we eat the other hundred days of the year. I play two varsity sports plus the clarinet. I'm President of Student Council and even on the Debate Team. So, it's just not fair—to put everything, my entire future, on the line for one measly test score. That's how I thought about it, until I had to choose next year's Student Council President.

It's a barely acknowledged tradition, but it was important to me. There was some dignity in it, some power. It would be me alone who decided—buh-bye democracy. The juniors with mediocre test scores must have been also contemplating their short-comings for college application time because we had 16 students apply this year. I'm pretty sure 16 is a record. My victory had risen over a close call with four other nominees, one of which didn't even attend the school any longer. But my passing down of the crown would have to be a close and careful examination of 16 prospective leaders. I was stoked! Then, I took a look at the applications.

12 of the 16 were Honor-Roll students; 14 had impressive community service experience; 9 had previous leadership positions; 4 had taken Pre-Calc with me that very year and earned a better grade; and, all 16 had responded to the generic application question with a certain heedfulness. How would I ever decide? After three days of staring blankly at the applications, I had eliminated five juniors. After a week, I had reconsidered two of them, placing their applications safely back in the pile. I decided that I would have to endeavor to get to know each and every applicant to truly decide who would be my best replacement. No problem, between classes and homework and the library and basketball practice and clarinet lessons and my brother's wedding—oh, I give up! I wish I could just give them some sort of test—just some way, flawed or not, to get a grip on this!

And that's when I realized that—fair or not—it was the only way. Just like our winter performance would be the test for hours spent with my clarinet, just like the conference game would be the test for the Lady Bulldogs, there had to be some way to quantify and measure the criteria for college admissions. Better yet, the "test" didn't have to be lousy or ineffective. In fact, testing, albeit an evil, is a necessary evil that can efficiently gauge critical thinking skills, diligence, and long-term potential. It can measure what you know, how you approach problems, and provide a startlingly accurate hypothesis of your work ethic in the future. Grades and test scores are accurate criteria for admission, supplying a necessary witness to your past successes and allowing the university to admit intelligent and hard-working students.

My perspective develops on that of Viewpoint One, arguing that academic potential as illustrated by grades and test scores allows admission decisions to be made fairly and precisely. It is hardly conceivable to offer rigorous education on any other basis, as Viewpoint Two advocates. The way to satisfy Viewpoint Three is to embrace Viewpoint One.

Sample Response, Score of 6 across all categories

"I am a good fit because . . . ." No. "You should accept me on the grounds that I am . . . ." That's not it either! How about: "My experience and interests align with your university in a way that fosters mutual benefit"? The admissions essay often feels like more erasing than writing, more crumbling of paper than not. It is fall of my senior year and here I am; with the rest of the world's slightly-better-than-average students, trying to cast myself onto paper, futilely attempting to convince some unknown admissions committee member to differentiate me among the other 78 essays she has just flipped monotonously through. And for what? Does that essay really make a difference? Did she already write me off based on my ACT score? Or perhaps, my B— in AP Chemistry doesn't scream college-ready. The fact is, college admission is more competitive and more consequential than ever before, and to evaluate applications in any way other than a holistic approach is to downplay the hours, and even years, that went into every submission.

Perhaps, the only "fair" way to choose is to leave it to raw numbers. Bring on the GPA's and standardized test scores, and scrunch every individual into a tiny box that tries desperately to ignore the nuance and circumstance. Survival of the fittest, you say. Advocates of Viewpoint One will certainly agree that this is the only sound way to guarantee that the best and the brightest go on to the most respectable universities and then, the highest-paying jobs. Yet, this perspective leaves a lot on the table. Let us consider Einstein who didn't read until he was seven years old, causing teachers to assume he was mentally handicapped, or Emily Dickinson who had fewer than a dozen poems published during her lifetime. If nothing else, these examples prove that potential is not so easily evaluated.

Still, admissions committees must have some standard of measurement, and it is hardly realistic to get to know every applicant personally. And even if you could, interpersonal skills, (like in Viewpoint two), alone cannot ensure success at the university level—being likable is great and all, but it hardly earns you an A in that first calculus course. Instead, admissions criteria should take a holistic approach to each application, evaluating an applicant on his or her fit within the university based on academic success, communication skills, and future goals while accounting for socio-economic and racial diversity, as well as the personal story told by the essay. Similar to the workforce, the classroom benefits most from a diverse and well-rounded assembly that is able to engage and question one another in a stimulating, innovating environment.

Every high school student struggling to define themselves via a transcript and 500 words or less is unique and looking for something different in a college experience. To equate a good college education with high career placement or high graduation rates is to simplify a journey of self-discovery, intellectual curiosity, and fulfillment. Generally speaking, there is no cookie-cutter student. Some will indeed look for the school with the most prestigious test scores; others will seek out small class sizes and invested professors; still many will search out the campus that feels most like home; and, of course, there will be those who follow the footsteps of their parents, excited to finally give breath to the dozens of stories they've heard growing up. And the fact remains, the university cannot accept everyone as proposed in the third viewpoint—to do so would be to sacrifice quality for quantity.

Therefore, the way forward—to a more rewarding college experience, a better educated workforce, and a happier citizenry—is through admissions criteria that is just as idiosyncratic as the applicants themselves.

Evaluate your response using the above responses for guidance. Here is the rubric.

Ideas and Analysis: Considers multiple perspectives. Develops a clear and sophisticated thesis. Provides a useful context for analyzing the issue. Analyzes the implications, complexities, and underlying assumptions of different viewpoints.						
6: Excellent	5: Skillful	4: Adequate	3: Fair	2: Weak	1: Poor	_____ /6
Development and Support: Provides an insightful and well-supported argument, placing the issue in a broad context. Uses reasoning and illustration to express the significance of the issue. Demonstrates an understanding of the complexity of the topic.						
6: Excellent	5: Skillful	4: Adequate	3: Fair	2: Weak	1: Poor	_____ /6
Organization: Shows a skillful overall organizational approach. Has a clear, sustained position, accompanied by a logical sequence of ideas that builds the writer's argument. Provides clear and logical transitions between sentences and paragraphs.						
6: Excellent	5: Skillful	4: Adequate	3: Fair	2: Weak	1: Poor	_____ /6
Language Use: The essay's language is well-suited to the argument. Vocabulary choice is precise and appropriate. Sentence structure is clear and varied. Tone, voice, and style are effective. Grammar, usage, and mechanics issues are minimized and do not interfere with the reader's understanding.						
6: Excellent	5: Skillful	4: Adequate	3: Fair	2: Weak	1: Poor	_____ /6
					Essay Raw Score:	_____ /24
Multiply your Essay Raw Score by 1.5 to get your approximate ACT Writing Scaled Score: Essay Raw Score: _____ × 1.5 = _____ out of 36 possible points.						
					ACT Writing Scaled Score:	_____ /36

⚷ WRITING STRATEGY SUMMARY

- The ACT Writing is a 40-minute 1 Essay Response that comes at the end of the whole ACT.
- The question will not require specific background knowledge, but it will require good writing and argumentation.
- The prompt will consistently have you develop a position on a topic of general interest, incorporating analysis of three points of view into your response.
- Your response should
  - take a clear position
  - address all three points of view
  - consider complexity and counterarguments
  - provide specific evidence and support
  - demonstrate logical reasoning
  - remain focused
  - have good transitions
  - have proper wording and sentence variety
  - have solid grammar and spelling

ANSWER SHEET—PRACTICE TEST 1

Test 1: English

1 Ⓐ Ⓑ Ⓒ Ⓓ   20 Ⓕ Ⓖ Ⓗ Ⓙ   39 Ⓐ Ⓑ Ⓒ Ⓓ   58 Ⓕ Ⓖ Ⓗ Ⓙ
2 Ⓕ Ⓖ Ⓗ Ⓙ   21 Ⓐ Ⓑ Ⓒ Ⓓ   40 Ⓕ Ⓖ Ⓗ Ⓙ   59 Ⓐ Ⓑ Ⓒ Ⓓ
3 Ⓐ Ⓑ Ⓒ Ⓓ   22 Ⓕ Ⓖ Ⓗ Ⓙ   41 Ⓐ Ⓑ Ⓒ Ⓓ   60 Ⓕ Ⓖ Ⓗ Ⓙ
4 Ⓕ Ⓖ Ⓗ Ⓙ   23 Ⓐ Ⓑ Ⓒ Ⓓ   42 Ⓕ Ⓖ Ⓗ Ⓙ   61 Ⓐ Ⓑ Ⓒ Ⓓ
5 Ⓐ Ⓑ Ⓒ Ⓓ   24 Ⓕ Ⓖ Ⓗ Ⓙ   43 Ⓐ Ⓑ Ⓒ Ⓓ   62 Ⓕ Ⓖ Ⓗ Ⓙ
6 Ⓕ Ⓖ Ⓗ Ⓙ   25 Ⓐ Ⓑ Ⓒ Ⓓ   44 Ⓕ Ⓖ Ⓗ Ⓙ   63 Ⓐ Ⓑ Ⓒ Ⓓ
7 Ⓐ Ⓑ Ⓒ Ⓓ   26 Ⓕ Ⓖ Ⓗ Ⓙ   45 Ⓐ Ⓑ Ⓒ Ⓓ   64 Ⓕ Ⓖ Ⓗ Ⓙ
8 Ⓕ Ⓖ Ⓗ Ⓙ   27 Ⓐ Ⓑ Ⓒ Ⓓ   46 Ⓕ Ⓖ Ⓗ Ⓙ   65 Ⓐ Ⓑ Ⓒ Ⓓ
9 Ⓐ Ⓑ Ⓒ Ⓓ   28 Ⓕ Ⓖ Ⓗ Ⓙ   47 Ⓐ Ⓑ Ⓒ Ⓓ   66 Ⓕ Ⓖ Ⓗ Ⓙ
10 Ⓕ Ⓖ Ⓗ Ⓙ   29 Ⓐ Ⓑ Ⓒ Ⓓ   48 Ⓕ Ⓖ Ⓗ Ⓙ   67 Ⓐ Ⓑ Ⓒ Ⓓ
11 Ⓐ Ⓑ Ⓒ Ⓓ   30 Ⓕ Ⓖ Ⓗ Ⓙ   49 Ⓐ Ⓑ Ⓒ Ⓓ   68 Ⓕ Ⓖ Ⓗ Ⓙ
12 Ⓕ Ⓖ Ⓗ Ⓙ   31 Ⓐ Ⓑ Ⓒ Ⓓ   50 Ⓕ Ⓖ Ⓗ Ⓙ   69 Ⓐ Ⓑ Ⓒ Ⓓ
13 Ⓐ Ⓑ Ⓒ Ⓓ   32 Ⓕ Ⓖ Ⓗ Ⓙ   51 Ⓐ Ⓑ Ⓒ Ⓓ   70 Ⓕ Ⓖ Ⓗ Ⓙ
14 Ⓕ Ⓖ Ⓗ Ⓙ   33 Ⓐ Ⓑ Ⓒ Ⓓ   52 Ⓕ Ⓖ Ⓗ Ⓙ   71 Ⓐ Ⓑ Ⓒ Ⓓ
15 Ⓐ Ⓑ Ⓒ Ⓓ   34 Ⓕ Ⓖ Ⓗ Ⓙ   53 Ⓐ Ⓑ Ⓒ Ⓓ   72 Ⓕ Ⓖ Ⓗ Ⓙ
16 Ⓕ Ⓖ Ⓗ Ⓙ   35 Ⓐ Ⓑ Ⓒ Ⓓ   54 Ⓕ Ⓖ Ⓗ Ⓙ   73 Ⓐ Ⓑ Ⓒ Ⓓ
17 Ⓐ Ⓑ Ⓒ Ⓓ   36 Ⓕ Ⓖ Ⓗ Ⓙ   55 Ⓐ Ⓑ Ⓒ Ⓓ   74 Ⓕ Ⓖ Ⓗ Ⓙ
18 Ⓕ Ⓖ Ⓗ Ⓙ   37 Ⓐ Ⓑ Ⓒ Ⓓ   56 Ⓕ Ⓖ Ⓗ Ⓙ   75 Ⓐ Ⓑ Ⓒ Ⓓ
19 Ⓐ Ⓑ Ⓒ Ⓓ   38 Ⓕ Ⓖ Ⓗ Ⓙ   57 Ⓐ Ⓑ Ⓒ Ⓓ

Test 2: Mathematics

1 Ⓐ Ⓑ Ⓒ Ⓓ Ⓔ   16 Ⓕ Ⓖ Ⓗ Ⓙ Ⓚ   31 Ⓐ Ⓑ Ⓒ Ⓓ Ⓔ   46 Ⓕ Ⓖ Ⓗ Ⓙ Ⓚ
2 Ⓕ Ⓖ Ⓗ Ⓙ Ⓚ   17 Ⓐ Ⓑ Ⓒ Ⓓ Ⓔ   32 Ⓕ Ⓖ Ⓗ Ⓙ Ⓚ   47 Ⓐ Ⓑ Ⓒ Ⓓ Ⓔ
3 Ⓐ Ⓑ Ⓒ Ⓓ Ⓔ   18 Ⓕ Ⓖ Ⓗ Ⓙ Ⓚ   33 Ⓐ Ⓑ Ⓒ Ⓓ Ⓔ   48 Ⓕ Ⓖ Ⓗ Ⓙ Ⓚ
4 Ⓕ Ⓖ Ⓗ Ⓙ Ⓚ   19 Ⓐ Ⓑ Ⓒ Ⓓ Ⓔ   34 Ⓕ Ⓖ Ⓗ Ⓙ Ⓚ   49 Ⓐ Ⓑ Ⓒ Ⓓ Ⓔ
5 Ⓐ Ⓑ Ⓒ Ⓓ Ⓔ   20 Ⓕ Ⓖ Ⓗ Ⓙ Ⓚ   35 Ⓐ Ⓑ Ⓒ Ⓓ Ⓔ   50 Ⓕ Ⓖ Ⓗ Ⓙ Ⓚ
6 Ⓕ Ⓖ Ⓗ Ⓙ Ⓚ   21 Ⓐ Ⓑ Ⓒ Ⓓ Ⓔ   36 Ⓕ Ⓖ Ⓗ Ⓙ Ⓚ   51 Ⓐ Ⓑ Ⓒ Ⓓ Ⓔ
7 Ⓐ Ⓑ Ⓒ Ⓓ Ⓔ   22 Ⓕ Ⓖ Ⓗ Ⓙ Ⓚ   37 Ⓐ Ⓑ Ⓒ Ⓓ Ⓔ   52 Ⓕ Ⓖ Ⓗ Ⓙ Ⓚ
8 Ⓕ Ⓖ Ⓗ Ⓙ Ⓚ   23 Ⓐ Ⓑ Ⓒ Ⓓ Ⓔ   38 Ⓕ Ⓖ Ⓗ Ⓙ Ⓚ   53 Ⓐ Ⓑ Ⓒ Ⓓ Ⓔ
9 Ⓐ Ⓑ Ⓒ Ⓓ Ⓔ   24 Ⓕ Ⓖ Ⓗ Ⓙ Ⓚ   39 Ⓐ Ⓑ Ⓒ Ⓓ Ⓔ   54 Ⓕ Ⓖ Ⓗ Ⓙ Ⓚ
10 Ⓕ Ⓖ Ⓗ Ⓙ Ⓚ   25 Ⓐ Ⓑ Ⓒ Ⓓ Ⓔ   40 Ⓕ Ⓖ Ⓗ Ⓙ Ⓚ   55 Ⓐ Ⓑ Ⓒ Ⓓ Ⓔ
11 Ⓐ Ⓑ Ⓒ Ⓓ Ⓔ   26 Ⓕ Ⓖ Ⓗ Ⓙ Ⓚ   41 Ⓐ Ⓑ Ⓒ Ⓓ Ⓔ   56 Ⓕ Ⓖ Ⓗ Ⓙ Ⓚ
12 Ⓕ Ⓖ Ⓗ Ⓙ Ⓚ   27 Ⓐ Ⓑ Ⓒ Ⓓ Ⓔ   42 Ⓕ Ⓖ Ⓗ Ⓙ Ⓚ   57 Ⓐ Ⓑ Ⓒ Ⓓ Ⓔ
13 Ⓐ Ⓑ Ⓒ Ⓓ Ⓔ   28 Ⓕ Ⓖ Ⓗ Ⓙ Ⓚ   43 Ⓐ Ⓑ Ⓒ Ⓓ Ⓔ   58 Ⓕ Ⓖ Ⓗ Ⓙ Ⓚ
14 Ⓕ Ⓖ Ⓗ Ⓙ Ⓚ   29 Ⓐ Ⓑ Ⓒ Ⓓ Ⓔ   44 Ⓕ Ⓖ Ⓗ Ⓙ Ⓚ   59 Ⓐ Ⓑ Ⓒ Ⓓ Ⓔ
15 Ⓐ Ⓑ Ⓒ Ⓓ Ⓔ   30 Ⓕ Ⓖ Ⓗ Ⓙ Ⓚ   45 Ⓐ Ⓑ Ⓒ Ⓓ Ⓔ   60 Ⓕ Ⓖ Ⓗ Ⓙ Ⓚ

Test 3: Reading

1 Ⓐ Ⓑ Ⓒ Ⓓ   11 Ⓐ Ⓑ Ⓒ Ⓓ   21 Ⓐ Ⓑ Ⓒ Ⓓ   31 Ⓐ Ⓑ Ⓒ Ⓓ
2 Ⓕ Ⓖ Ⓗ Ⓙ   12 Ⓕ Ⓖ Ⓗ Ⓙ   22 Ⓕ Ⓖ Ⓗ Ⓙ   32 Ⓕ Ⓖ Ⓗ Ⓙ
3 Ⓐ Ⓑ Ⓒ Ⓓ   13 Ⓐ Ⓑ Ⓒ Ⓓ   23 Ⓐ Ⓑ Ⓒ Ⓓ   33 Ⓐ Ⓑ Ⓒ Ⓓ
4 Ⓕ Ⓖ Ⓗ Ⓙ   14 Ⓕ Ⓖ Ⓗ Ⓙ   24 Ⓕ Ⓖ Ⓗ Ⓙ   34 Ⓕ Ⓖ Ⓗ Ⓙ
5 Ⓐ Ⓑ Ⓒ Ⓓ   15 Ⓐ Ⓑ Ⓒ Ⓓ   25 Ⓐ Ⓑ Ⓒ Ⓓ   35 Ⓐ Ⓑ Ⓒ Ⓓ
6 Ⓕ Ⓖ Ⓗ Ⓙ   16 Ⓕ Ⓖ Ⓗ Ⓙ   26 Ⓕ Ⓖ Ⓗ Ⓙ   36 Ⓕ Ⓖ Ⓗ Ⓙ
7 Ⓐ Ⓑ Ⓒ Ⓓ   17 Ⓐ Ⓑ Ⓒ Ⓓ   27 Ⓐ Ⓑ Ⓒ Ⓓ   37 Ⓐ Ⓑ Ⓒ Ⓓ
8 Ⓕ Ⓖ Ⓗ Ⓙ   18 Ⓕ Ⓖ Ⓗ Ⓙ   28 Ⓕ Ⓖ Ⓗ Ⓙ   38 Ⓕ Ⓖ Ⓗ Ⓙ
9 Ⓐ Ⓑ Ⓒ Ⓓ   19 Ⓐ Ⓑ Ⓒ Ⓓ   29 Ⓐ Ⓑ Ⓒ Ⓓ   39 Ⓐ Ⓑ Ⓒ Ⓓ
10 Ⓕ Ⓖ Ⓗ Ⓙ   20 Ⓕ Ⓖ Ⓗ Ⓙ   30 Ⓕ Ⓖ Ⓗ Ⓙ   40 Ⓕ Ⓖ Ⓗ Ⓙ

Test 4: Science

1 Ⓐ Ⓑ Ⓒ Ⓓ   11 Ⓐ Ⓑ Ⓒ Ⓓ   21 Ⓐ Ⓑ Ⓒ Ⓓ   31 Ⓐ Ⓑ Ⓒ Ⓓ
2 Ⓕ Ⓖ Ⓗ Ⓙ   12 Ⓕ Ⓖ Ⓗ Ⓙ   22 Ⓕ Ⓖ Ⓗ Ⓙ   32 Ⓕ Ⓖ Ⓗ Ⓙ
3 Ⓐ Ⓑ Ⓒ Ⓓ   13 Ⓐ Ⓑ Ⓒ Ⓓ   23 Ⓐ Ⓑ Ⓒ Ⓓ   33 Ⓐ Ⓑ Ⓒ Ⓓ
4 Ⓕ Ⓖ Ⓗ Ⓙ   14 Ⓕ Ⓖ Ⓗ Ⓙ   24 Ⓕ Ⓖ Ⓗ Ⓙ   34 Ⓕ Ⓖ Ⓗ Ⓙ
5 Ⓐ Ⓑ Ⓒ Ⓓ   15 Ⓐ Ⓑ Ⓒ Ⓓ   25 Ⓐ Ⓑ Ⓒ Ⓓ   35 Ⓐ Ⓑ Ⓒ Ⓓ
6 Ⓕ Ⓖ Ⓗ Ⓙ   16 Ⓕ Ⓖ Ⓗ Ⓙ   26 Ⓕ Ⓖ Ⓗ Ⓙ   36 Ⓕ Ⓖ Ⓗ Ⓙ
7 Ⓐ Ⓑ Ⓒ Ⓓ   17 Ⓐ Ⓑ Ⓒ Ⓓ   27 Ⓐ Ⓑ Ⓒ Ⓓ   37 Ⓐ Ⓑ Ⓒ Ⓓ
8 Ⓕ Ⓖ Ⓗ Ⓙ   18 Ⓕ Ⓖ Ⓗ Ⓙ   28 Ⓕ Ⓖ Ⓗ Ⓙ   38 Ⓕ Ⓖ Ⓗ Ⓙ
9 Ⓐ Ⓑ Ⓒ Ⓓ   19 Ⓐ Ⓑ Ⓒ Ⓓ   29 Ⓐ Ⓑ Ⓒ Ⓓ   39 Ⓐ Ⓑ Ⓒ Ⓓ
10 Ⓕ Ⓖ Ⓗ Ⓙ   20 Ⓕ Ⓖ Ⓗ Ⓙ   30 Ⓕ Ⓖ Ⓗ Ⓙ   40 Ⓕ Ⓖ Ⓗ Ⓙ

Practice Test 1

▬◤◤◤◤◤◤◤◤◤◤◤◤◤◤◤◤◤◤◤◤◤◤◤◤◤◤

ENGLISH TEST

Time—45 minutes
75 Questions

> **Directions:** In the passages that follow, you will find underlined words and phrases. In the accompanying questions, there are alternatives to the underlined wording. For most questions, choose the option that expresses the idea most effectively, conforms to the standards of conventional English, or has wording consistent with the tone and style of the passage. If you think the original underlined wording is best, pick "NO CHANGE." For some problems, you will need to read a question about the underlined portion and pick the best answer to the question. Other problems may ask about portions of the passage or the entire passage. These questions will be indicated by a numbered box.
>
> Choose the best answer to each question and fill in the matching circle on your answer sheet. Be sure to consider any relevant context surrounding the question in determining your answer.

PASSAGE I ▬▬▬▬▬▬▬▬▬▬▬▬▬▬▬▬▬▬▬▬▬▬

In our years, patent law has become more important than ever before. If
  1

individuals and businesses are going to be willing to invest all of the time and
  2

resources necessary to invent something new there has to be adequate
  3

compensation for their hard work. A patent provides inventors with the

legal protection to ensure that no one will be able to steal an inventor's
  4

creative origin for a certain period of time. That way, inventors have a
  5

tremendous incentive to create stuff, knowing that a great deal of money can be
  6

made if they prove popular. 7 What kind of person helps the patent system

work effectively? Someone like African-American inventor Lewis Latimer does.

[1] Born in 1848 in Massachusetts, Lewis Latimer had been both the son of a
                                                                              8
runaway and that of a freed slave. [2] Despite widespread racial discrimination
8
in the United States at the time, Latimer was able to prove himself as a

capable young man with his service in the U.S. Navy at only age 15. [3]

After his naval service, he worked for a patent law firm where he mastered the

art of creating drawings for patents. 9 [4] Latimer was hired by two of the most

famous inventors of the time period—Alexander Graham Bell and Thomas
                                                          10
Edison—to create drawings of their works for the patent office. 11
      10

The power that Latimer had of observation that he developed as a
                                          12
draftsman contributed himself to the world of invention in two valuable ways.
                                          12
First, he was an inventor himself, patenting a better carbon filament system for

light bulbs and an innovative toilet system for train cars.

Second, he was able to serve as an expert witness in legal cases concerning
      13
patents for electrical light bulbs.

For those interested in being a part of all the innovation in the world today,

Latimer's example demonstrating the variety of ways that people can contribute:
                    14
as inventors, as patent facilitators, and as patent experts.

1. A. NO CHANGE
    B. high technology society
    C. world in which the use of technology is widespread
    D. times that value using technology in a popular fashion

2. F. NO CHANGE
    G. you
    H. one
    J. we

3. A. NO CHANGE
    B. something new; there
    C. something, new there
    D. something new, there

4. F. NO CHANGE
    G. insure
    H. assure
    J. reassure

5. A. NO CHANGE
    B. original creation
    C. creative origination
    D. creativity and origin

6. F. NO CHANGE
    G. things
    H. new and innovative products
    J. items

7. At this point in the paragraph, the writer is considering adding the
    following sentence:

    Patents cannot be made for laws of nature, physical phenomena and
    abstract ideas.

    Should the writer make this addition?
    A. Yes, because it provides additional details about the use of patents.
    B. Yes, because it addresses a question raised earlier in the passage.
    C. No, because it does not provide information on patent regulations.
    D. No, because it distracts from the focus of this paragraph.

8. F. NO CHANGE
    G. was the son of a runaway slave and also that of a freed slave
    H. was the son of a runaway slave and a freed slave
    J. were the son of slaves

9. The writer is considering deleting the words "patent" and "creating drawings for" from the preceding sentence. If the writer were to make these deletions, the essay would primarily lose:
   A. details that create a logical transition.
   B. specific descriptive material.
   C. in-depth literary analysis.
   D. an understatement of vital facts.

10. F. NO CHANGE
    G. period, Alexander Graham Bell and Thomas Edison to create
    H. period Alexander Graham Bell and Thomas Edison to create
    J. period, Alexander Graham Bell, and Thomas Edison, to create

11. What is the most logical and effective order of the sentences in the preceding paragraph?
    A. 1, 2, 3, 4
    B. 2, 1, 4, 3
    C. 4, 1, 3, 2
    D. 1, 3, 2, 4

12. F. NO CHANGE
    G. Latimer had a power of observation that contributed to the world of invention in two valuable ways that he developed as a draftsman.
    H. The powers that Latimer had helped him develop as a draftsman to contribute valuably in two ways to the invention world.
    J. Latimer's powers of observation that he developed as a draftsman helped him contribute to the world of invention in two valuable ways.

13. A. NO CHANGE
    B. However,
    C. In fact,
    D. Surprisingly,

14. F. NO CHANGE
    G. demonstrates
    H. had been demonstrating
    J. has been demonstrated

15. If the author had been assigned to write an essay discussing the life and contributions of an American inventor, would this essay fulfill the author's goal?
    A. Yes, because it discusses the biography and inventions of Lewis Latimer.
    B. Yes, because it details the lives of Alexander Graham Bell and Thomas Edison.
    C. No, because it focuses on many inventors rather than just one.
    D. No, because it primarily discusses patent law and patent expertise.

Passage II

In today's competitive job market, <u>you</u> cannot expect to find a job simply by
16
answering want ads. It is like the old <u>saying: "it's not what you know its who you</u>
17
know" that is so applicable. To find a job, you must have <u>both great qualifications</u>
18
<u>or outstanding, excellent networking skills.</u>
18

      <u>Job seeking can be a very stressful, time-consuming activity; social media</u>
19
<u>can help ease this burden.</u> Understand that if you are to use this networking
19
strategy, there must be nothing negative that employers can find on social

media <u>network, be certain to erase any compromised</u> pictures or profane
20
postings. <u>For an added price,</u> many social media networks will allow you to have
21
premium access to additional networking opportunities.

      <u>Another strategy</u> is to leverage connections <u>within</u> your friends and family
22   23
and ask them to contact employers on your behalf. If you were an employer

and had limited time to seek out qualified candidates, <u>hearing from a trusted</u>
24
<u>third-party that someone would be a great employee would make your job</u>
24
<u>much easier.</u> Have your network spread the word about you, <u>and the</u>
24   25
<u>impact will be much more than if the information straight from you had come.</u>
25
      <u>Join a business group in order to maximize your potential job leads.</u>
26
You can become a member of your local Chamber of Commerce;

<u>a variety of meetings are provided as a result of it.</u> Trade shows and conferences
27

can be more <u>pricey and</u> the investment can pay off big time. If you want to make
        28

money, you need <u>after all</u> to spend it. If you want to go the extra mile, you
        29

might see if there is an unpaid internship that you might do so that an

employer can see your work firsthand without the upfront investment.

    If you have a good bit of time before you will enter the job market,

<u>spend quite a bit of time looking at online job ads and their requirements,</u>
                               30
so that when the time comes to find a good job, you will be able to do so.

16.　F.　NO CHANGE
　　　G.　one
　　　H.　he or she
　　　J.　they

17.　A.　NO CHANGE
　　　B.　saying, its not what you know, its
　　　C.　saying: "it's not what you know, it's
　　　D.　saying it's not what you know, it's

18.　F.　NO CHANGE
　　　G.　both great qualifications and excellent networking skills.
　　　H.　both great qualifications and also outstanding networking skills.
　　　J.　both qualifications that are great and networking skills that have excellence.

19.　The writer is considering replacing the sentence so that it provides a specific economic reason as to why certain job seekers would want to use social networking. Which choice would be most effective in accomplishing this?
　　　A.　NO CHANGE
　　　B.　One of the most effective networking techniques you can use to share your qualifications is to promote yourself on social media networks.
　　　C.　For younger job seekers, use of social networking is a free way to make connections with potential employers.
　　　D.　If you want to make lots of money in your career, you will need to find a job that pays you accordingly.

20. F. NO CHANGE
    G. network—be certain to erase any compromising
    H. network: be certain to compromise with any
    J. network; be certain to erase any compromised

21. The writer is considering deleting the underlined portion of the sentence, and beginning the sentence with "Many." Should this phrase be kept or deleted?
    A. Kept, because it provides a relevant detail that clarifies what comes later in the sentence.
    B. Kept, because it gives a specific explanation as to how media networks determine the costs of their services.
    C. Deleted, because it does not give a specific dollar amount that these services would cost.
    D. Deleted, because it is not consistent with the tone of the rest of the essay.

22. F. NO CHANGE
    G. A further networking
    H. Furthermore, it
    J. A subsequent stratagem

23. A. NO CHANGE
    B. throughout
    C. among
    D. between

24. Which choice would follow most logically from the first part of this sentence and fit the context of the paragraph as a whole?
    F. NO CHANGE
    G. you would want to save yourself time by hiring from within your company rather than from outside your company.
    H. you would want to remove negative feedback about your company online to help you hire top candidates.
    J. it would make sense to have networking events to enable your business to cast a wide net.

25. A. NO CHANGE
    B. and it will have much more of an impact than if the information came straight from you.
    C. and much more an impact will be had then if the information had come straight from you.
    D. and there will be more of an impact then if the information came straight from you.

26. Which choice would best introduce this paragraph and provide a transition from the preceding paragraph?
    F. NO CHANGE
    G. If your network of friends and family won't be much help in gaining access to potential employers, you will need to take more initiative.
    H. Your network of friends and family can lead you to excellent business opportunities.
    J. While it may seem easy to wait for your friends to employ you in their businesses, you will be better off finding one yourself.

27. A. NO CHANGE
    B. which provides a variety of meetings to the public.
    C. many networking opportunities are provided by them.
    D. it will typically offer a variety of networking meetings.

28. F. NO CHANGE
    G. pricey, consequently
    H. pricey, but
    J. pricey with

29. The best placement in this sentence for the underlined portion would be:
    A. where it is now.
    B. before the word "if" (adjusting capitalization accordingly and putting a comma after the phrase)
    C. after the word "make"
    D. after the word "spend"

30. Which phrase, if inserted here, would be most consistent with the topic of the essay as a whole?
    A. NO CHANGE
    B. be sure to get the best education possible
    C. do not wait to begin building your network of contacts
    D. read the latest publications on developments in technology

PASSAGE III

When most people think of *Pi*, i.e., the number 3.14..., they groan as they

                                                31

think of: trigonometry, geometry, and physics problems. They become

        32

anxious as they try to remember the difference between area and

                                            33

circumference. Believe it or not, it is possible to have a great deal of

    33

fun with this all important number that represents <u>a fact that all math</u>

34

<u>students should memorize.</u>

34

      My math <u>teacher Mr. Wigram, has</u> the <u>annual tradition</u> of celebrating

35   36

"Pi Day" on March 14th of each year – yes, it's 3/14 on the calendar.

Pi day is the most <u>multifaceted</u> learning experience I have ever had.

37

Everyone brings in pies, like apple, cherry, and coconut cream.

<u>We calculate</u> various mathematical properties of the pies, such as

38

volume, surface area, and circumference. 39 In addition to the culinary

aspects of Pi Day, we can also earn extra credit for dressing up like an

ancient Greek scholar. (I have a great costume of the ancient Greek

mathematician Archimedes I will use this year.)

      The fun with Pi isn't limited to Mr. Wigram's class. The Massachusetts

Institute of Technology, a world-renowned university, emphasizes

math and science in its fields of study. They now let students know of

whether they were accepted via e-mail on March 14th, but they take it

a step further by making it to the exact minute and second that correspond

to the numbers in pi. If you don't find that interesting or entertaining, 40

you should not be going to M.I.T.

      The best idea I have heard is a joke products company <u>that provided for</u>

41

<u>creation of</u> a fake A.T.M. receipt that said the account balance after a cash

41

withdrawal was $314,159.27. <u>Why did it cost so much?</u> When
42

in a social setting, a single person could use the fake ATM receipt if a

potential date wanted <u>his or her</u> contact information. If the potential date
43

looked at the other side of the ATM receipt, he or she might be really

interested in going out! 44

    If you still don't believe in the fun of Pi and Pi Day, do not worry. The

next day after Pi day, March 15th, is the Ides of March, and you will have

quite a bit of fun <u>in your English class with all the Julius Caesar associations.</u>
45

31. Which of the following alternatives to the underlined portion would NOT
be acceptable?
A. , which is the number 3.14...,
B. , also known as the number 3.14...,
C. –the number 3.14...—
D. –whom is known as 3.14...--

32. F. NO CHANGE
G. think of, trigonometry,
H. think of trigonometry,
J. think of; trigonometry,

33. A. NO CHANGE
B. the difference of area or circumference.
C. how differently area and circumference can be.
D. the difference within area and circumference.

34. Given that all of the choices are true, which one would provide the
most logical and specific concluding definition in this sentence and best
contribute to the paragraph as a whole?
F. NO CHANGE
G. the ratio of the circumference of a circle to its diameter.
H. one of the most critical mathematical terms.
J. 3.14.

35. A. NO CHANGE
    B. teacher, Mr. Wigram has
    C. teacher, Mr. Wigram, has
    D. teacher Mr. Wigram has

36. F. NO CHANGE
    G. tradition
    H. yearly ritual
    J. regular occurrence

37. Which of the following alternatives to the underlined portion would be LEAST acceptable?
    A. multipart
    B. complex
    C. difficult
    D. elaborate

38. F. NO CHANGE
    G. We have calculating
    H. We calculated
    J. We had been calculating

39. If the author wishes to insert a sentence at this point that focuses on the topic of the paragraph while introducing a lighter tone, which of these options would be most effective?
    A. The volume of the pies is calculated using the formula $V = \pi r^2 h$.
    B. If I could eat while learning in all my classes, I would never have any trouble staying awake in school.
    C. My mother often throws pies at my Dad, which is hilarious to behold.
    D. Pies should be cooked at an oven temperature of 350°.

40. Which of the following true statements, if inserted here, would best express a limited degree of confidence on the part of the writer?
    F. I suppose
    G. undoubtedly
    H. I disagree that
    J. I know

41. A. NO CHANGE
    B. that made
    C. who created
    D. which manufactured in its factories

42. Given that all of the choices are true, which of the following would provide the most effective transition within the paragraph?
    F. NO CHANGE
    G. That is a lot of money.
    H. What would be the use for this?
    J. It is no coincidence that these are the same digits in the number Pi.

43. A. NO CHANGE
    B. their
    C. they're
    D. its

44. If the writer wished to emphasize one of the words in the preceding sentence by italicizing it, which of these words would be the most logical choice?
    F. date
    G. of
    H. she
    J. really

45. The writer is considering deleting the underlined phrase in this sentence. Should the phrase be kept or deleted?
    A. Kept, because it clarifies what exactly will be enjoyable about celebrating that particular date.
    B. Kept, because it summarizes the primary argument of the passage as a whole.
    C. Deleted, because it speaks about English Class instead of maintaining the mathematical focus.
    D. Deleted, because it is written in a much more casual tone than the rest of the essay.

PASSAGE IV

Hammerhead sharks or *Sphyrnidae sphyrna* are native to the Coco Islands
                                          46
near Costa Rica. They are named for the odd but fascinating shape of their

heads. Their heads are flat and horizontally extended in a manner called
      47
cephalofoil. Hammerheads can grow up to 20 feet long and be of a weight
                                                        48
that is up to 1,000 pounds.
      48

The hammerheads unique head shape is an evolutionary anomaly, since
      49   50
other species of shark have torpedo-shaped snouts. Original, they thought
                    51
that the shape of their heads gave them increased maneuverability, but it

was later discovered that their ability to make sharp turns without losing
                    52
stability comes more from the placement of their vertebrae. The positioning

of their eyes gives them very good binocular vision and a wide range in the
                    53
vertical plane, meaning they can see what is below and above them continuously.
                    54

Even though they have great vision, hammerheads are rather impaired

when compared to other sharks. They are the most negatively buoyant and

also have very small mouths proportionally to other species. Because of
                    55
the small extent of their mouths, hammerheads often feed from the

ocean floor and in schools, one of the very few species of shark to do so.
                    56
Despite their limited range, hammerhead sharks eat a variety of foods

including squid, octopuses, crustaceans, stingrays, fish, other sharks, and

sometimes their own young.

Besides having their distinctive heads, hammerhead sharks are one of the

few species of animal known to have skin that tans from lengthy sun

exposure. Sharks' increased melanin production is usually attributed to
                57
their lack of hair which in most animals would be enough to protect

them from the sun.

[1] Not much is known about hammerhead sharks before the

Tertiary Period. [2] Researchers <u>believes</u> they may have developed from
                                  58
carcharhinid sharks which evolved in the mid-Tertiary Period. [3]

As their bones are not mineralized, they very rarely fossilize. [4] This link

was made because of the resemblances <u>by the teeth with</u> the two types
                                       59
of sharks. 60

46. F. NO CHANGE
    G. sharks; or *Sphyrnidae sphyrna* are
    H. sharks, or *Sphyrnidae sphyrna*, are
    J. sharks—or *Sphyrnidae sphyrna*, are

47. A. NO CHANGE
    B. Whose
    C. Its'
    D. They're

48. F. NO CHANGE
    G. weigh up to 1,000 pounds.
    H. sometimes can go up to 1,000 pounds in weight.
    J. be 1,000 pounds at their maximum size.

49. A. NO CHANGE
    B. The hammerhead's uniquely
    C. The hammerheads' uniquely
    D. The hammerhead's unique

50. Which of the following alternatives to the underlined portion would be
    LEAST acceptable?
    F. anomaly;
    G. anomaly, because
    H. anomaly—
    J. anomaly, once

51. A. NO CHANGE
    B. Originally, they
    C. Originally, researchers
    D. Original, researchers

52. F. NO CHANGE
    G. cutting
    H. piercing
    J. intense

53. Given that all the choices are true, which one provides the most specific description of the range of shark vision?
    A. NO CHANGE
    B. the ability to see quite a bit
    C. 360 degree sight
    D. capacity to see all around

54. The best placement for the underlined portion would be:
    F. where it is now.
    G. before the word "vertical."
    H. before the word "plane."
    J. before the word "is."

55. A. NO CHANGE
    B. to those of other species
    C. to that of other species.
    D. to the species.

56. The writer is considering moving the underlined phrase so that it comes after the word "floor" in the sentence. If the writer were to do this, would the meaning of the sentence change?
    F. Yes, because it would no longer discuss what makes hammerheads unique among other sharks.
    G. Yes, because it would imply that the unique characteristic of sharks was its feeding on the ocean floor.
    H. No, because it still explains what makes hammerheads unique.
    J. No, because it provides a detail that is not essential to the sentence.

57. A. NO CHANGE
    B. Shark's
    C. A shark's
    D. Sharks

58. F. NO CHANGE
    G. will believe
    H. had believed
    J. believe

59. A. NO CHANGE
     B. in the teeth of
     C. within the teeth between
     D. of the teeth on

60. Which of the following sequences of sentences will make this paragraph most logical?
     A. 1, 2, 3, 4
     B. 2, 1, 3, 4
     C. 1, 3, 2, 4
     D. 4, 1, 3, 2

Passage V

With a yawn, I wake up with sand scratching between my toes. The plastic

bars of a beach chair are awkwardly pushing into pressure points on my back
                              61
creating knots I know will later make me regret my lengthy nap. As I shift to a

more comfortable position, I open my eyes, surprised at how dark it is.

Despite this, until I take off my black, UVA UVB protection aviators. I blink
62
stupidly in the sunlight and put my sunglasses back on. 63 Standing up,

stretching, and looking out to sea, it takes me a second to distinguishing the
                                                         64
ocean from the sky. The blues so closely resemble each other.
64
     [1] Trudging to the sand to the water, the humid air makes me feel more like
                  65
I'm swimming than walking. [2] I can already feel the perspiration sliding

down the center of my back. I pause at the shoreline, debating if the
         66
refreshing water is really worth the hypothermia. [3] 67 Losing my inhibitions,

I strip off my sweat soaked t-shirt and dive into the blue green water. [4] The
                                                          68
cold ocean revives me after my long cat nap on the beach. [5] Coming back

up I hear children playing, one crying because his sand creation was

destroyed, another chasing their sister with a piece of seaweed. 69

Heading back to my wonderfully comfortable beach chair, <u>the sand, I can feel,</u>
70

<u>begins to stick to my wet feet</u>, giving the illusion of my turning into a sand
70

monster. I make a mental note of the young boy with the ninja turtle swim trunks

who <u>has seeming</u> the most easily frightened in case I get bored later. Sighing, I
71

sit in my chair again and turn my face to the sun. I can almost feel the melanin

screaming <u>in protest to</u> the scorching rays. In my head I hear my mother and
72

dermatologist warning me about the dangers of over sun exposure. <u>Heeding</u>
73

<u>the voices in my head I reposition</u> my chair beneath the beach umbrella.
73

<u>Laying my head back</u> into the nylon strap I take a deep breath and drift
74

back off to sleep. 75

61. A. NO CHANGE
     B. awkward in their pushing into
     C. awkward
     D. awkwardly into

62. F. NO CHANGE
     G. That is,
     H. As a result,
     J. What is more,

63. In the preceding sentence, the word "stupidly" can logically be placed in
     all of the following places EXCEPT:
     A. Where it is now
     B. At the beginning of the sentence, followed with a comma
     C. After the word "I"
     D. After the word "the"

64. **F.** NO CHANGE
    G. to distinguish the ocean from
    H. for distinguishing the ocean of
    J. for distinguish the ocean on

65. **A.** NO CHANGE
    B. within
    C. of
    D. through

66. **F.** NO·CHANGE
    G. my back center part.
    H. the central portion of my back side.
    J. OMIT the underlined portion

67. The writer wants to insert a sentence here to provide a transition between the sentence before and after. Which of these choices would most effectively do so?
    A. Hypothermia is a serious medical condition that results from overexposure to cold temperatures.
    B. A sudden wave makes my decision for me as it soaks me up to my knees, raising goose bumps.
    C. The waves rhythmically undulate, making me feel like a nap is in order.
    D. I am confident that nothing could persuade me to make the jump into the cold ocean.

68. Which of the following alternatives to the underlined portion would NOT be acceptable?
    F. blue and green water
    G. blue-green water
    H. blue green, water
    J. green and blue water

69. The writer wants to insert the following sentence into the preceding paragraph:

    "Oh to be young again."

    Where is the most logical and effective placement of this sentence?
    A. After Sentence 1
    B. After Sentence 2
    C. After Sentence 4
    D. After Sentence 5

70. **F.** NO CHANGE
    G. I can feel the sand beginning to stick to my wet feet
    H. feeling the sand to my feet sticking
    J. I feel sand beginning to wetly stick to my feet

71. **A.** NO CHANGE
    B. have seemed
    C. seeming
    D. seems

72. **F.** NO CHANGE
    G. in protest in
    H. for protesting about
    J. for protesting over

73. **A.** NO CHANGE
    B. Heeding the voices, in my head I reposition
    C. Heeding the voices in my head, I reposition
    D. Heeding, the voices in my head, I reposition

74. **F.** NO CHANGE
    G. Lain my head back
    H. Lieing my head back
    J. Lying my back head

75. If the writer had been assigned to provide a comprehensive summary of the events that took place on her week-long warm-climate vacation, would this essay successfully fulfill the assignment?
    A. Yes, because it focuses on her time spent on an ocean and beach-themed vacation.
    B. Yes, because it highlights the feelings of relaxation that she felt during a trip.
    C. No, because we cannot reasonably conclude that this took place when it was warm outside.
    D. No, because the events of the essay take place during a short period of time, not a week.

If there is still time remaining, you may review your answers.

MATH TEST

Time—60 minutes
60 Questions

Directions: Determine the answer to each question, and then fill in the matching oval on your answer sheet. Do not spend too much time on any one problem. Solve as many as possible, then come back to ones that you have skipped. You are allowed to use a calculator on this section, but several of the problems are best completed without a calculator.

Unless stated otherwise, assume that drawings are NOT necessarily to scale, geometric figures are in a two-dimensional plane, "lines" are straight lines, and "average" means the arithmetic mean.

1. Andy wants to read several books from the required summer reading list. He must read one each from fiction, nonfiction, science, and history. There are 15 fiction, 12 nonfiction, 5 science, and 21 history books listed. How many different summer reading programs could he select?
   A. 53
   B. 265
   C. 8910
   D. 18,900
   E. 32,760

2. A person walked 3 miles to the east, then turned north and walked 10 miles, then turned west and walked 6 miles, and finally turned south and walked 16 miles. Approximately how far is the person from his starting point in miles?
   F. 3.4
   G. 6.7
   H. 9.2
   J. 12.8
   K. 22.0

3. A 12-ounce soft drink has 41 grams of sugar, which is 14% of the normal daily allowance for sugar. Approximately how many grams of sugar are recommended in the normal diet?
   A. 5.74
   B. 69
   C. 293
   D. 574
   E. 861

4. What is: $\dfrac{\frac{3}{4}+\frac{2}{3}}{\frac{5}{6}-\frac{1}{4}} =$

   F. $\dfrac{17}{7}$

   G. $\dfrac{5}{6}$

   H. $\dfrac{5}{14}$

   J. $\dfrac{2}{3}$

   K. $\dfrac{7}{15}$

5. The expression $(5x^3)^{-\frac{2}{3}}$ is equivalent to which of the following?

   A. $5x^2$

   B. $\dfrac{5}{3x^2}$

   C. $\dfrac{\sqrt[3]{25}}{x^2}$

   D. $\dfrac{1}{x^2\sqrt[3]{25}}$

   E. $\dfrac{1}{x^2\sqrt[3]{5}}$

6. The figure below is composed of two parallel lines and a transversal. Which of these expressions MUST add up to 360°?

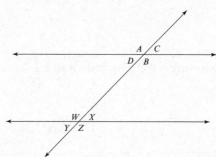

   F. $A + B + Y + X$
   G. $W + X + A + B$
   H. $A + B + C + W$
   J. $Z + X + D + C$
   K. $C + D + X + Y$

7. A mass mailing to potential Yearbook Advertisers is to be completed. Each letter requires an envelope, an information sheet, a return card, and a stamp. The following information is available:

   Envelopes: Box of 100, cost: $5.00
   Information sheet: $15.00 for 50 sheets
   Return Cards: Box of 200, Cost: $10.00
   Stamps: $0.44 each

   The Editor intends to mail 1,500 letters. What should be the budget for this mailing (in dollars), given that materials must be purchased in the whole units shown above?
   A. $30.44
   B. $660
   C. $1,205
   D. $1,260
   E. $1,265

8. If a clock chimes every hour the same number of times as the hour it is (e.g., at 3 P.M. it chimes 3 times) and once for every 15-minute increment between hours (e.g., at 3:15, 3:30, and 3:45), what will the total number of chimes be between 5:10 and 7:35 P.M.?
   F. 3
   G. 15
   H. 18
   J. 21
   K. 45

9. Which of the following could NOT be the sides of an isosceles triangle?
   A. 2, 2, 3
   B. 2, 3, 4
   C. 4, 12, 12
   D. 5, 5, 5
   E. 10, 10, 1

10. Which of the following is NOT equivalent to $2\frac{3}{8}$?

    F. 2.375

    G. $2 + \frac{3}{8}$

    H. $2 \times \frac{3}{8}$

    J. 2.375000

    K. $\frac{19}{8}$

11. Assume the following conditions:

    - a B is always an A.
    - a C is always a B.
    - a D is always an A.

    Which of the following *must* be true?
    A. an A is always a D
    B. a B is always a C
    C. a D is always a B
    D. a C is always an A
    E. a C is always a D

12. Jennifer is competing in a marathon, which is a 26.2-mile race. If Jennifer runs the first half of the race at 8 mph and the second half of the race at 6 mph, approximately how many hours does it take for her to complete the race?
    F. 2.62
    G. 3.74
    H. 3.82
    J. 4.12
    K. 14

13. Patricia makes $20,000 a year in her first year in a job, which was the year 2010. The following year, her salary increased by 10%, with another 10% increase on her salary the year after that. After two years of working in the job, what would her salary be?
    A. $2,000
    B. $4,000
    C. $22,000
    D. $24,000
    E. $24,200

14. If a and b are the smaller legs of a triangle and c is the length of the longest side, what must be true about a, b, and c?
    F. $a^2 + b^2 = c^2$
    G. $a + b > c$
    H. $a + b < c$
    J. $a = c$
    K. $a + b = c$

206 • Pass Key to the ACT

15. What is the *y*-coordinate of the midpoint of the line formed by (2, 8)
    and (–15, 8)?
    A. –7
    B. 8
    C. 10
    D. 13
    E. 18

16. What is the product of the least common multiple of 10 and 8 and the
    greatest common factor of 10 and 8?
    F. 16
    G. 20
    H. 40
    J. 60
    K. 80

17. A ball that is thrown down from a tall building falls a distance according
    to the following formula:

    $$x(t) = 8t + \frac{1}{2}(10)t^2$$

    (*x* is computed in meters.)

    How far has the ball fallen after 6 seconds?

    A. 108
    B. 180
    C. 228
    D. 948
    E. 1,848

18. When Isaac became married, he weighed much less than he does today.
    His ring finger has a diameter of 1.25 inches, while it had a diameter
    of just 1 inch when he was married. Assuming his ring is perfectly
    circular and fits his finger perfectly, by what percentage has Isaac's ring
    circumference increased from when he became married to the present day?
    F. 20%
    G. 25%
    H. 28%
    J. 30%
    K. 33%

19. Which of the following is the sum of two prime numbers?
    I. 2
    II. 9
    III. 11
    A. I only
    B. II only
    C. III only
    D. I and II only
    E. I, II, and III

20. A boat traveled 10 miles per hour for three hours due east. It then turned north, increased its speed to 20 miles per hour for two hours. How far, in miles, is the boat from its starting point after five hours?
    F. 5
    G. 30
    H. 50
    J. 70
    K. 150

21. What is the mean number of points scored per game by the team in the games listed in the table below?

Game Date	Total Points Scored
November 5	46
November 18	72
November 26	84
December 6	51
December 12	67

    A. 48
    B. 52
    C. 58
    D. 62
    E. 64

22. Terri opened a fast food restaurant. The initial cost to open the restaurant is $800,000. She has to pay daily operational costs of $250 and labor costs of $400. What expression represents her total cost if she has had the restaurant open for "D" days?
    F. $800,000 + 150D$
    G. $800,000 + 650D$
    H. $800,000 - 650D$
    J. $650 + 800,000D$
    K. $800,000 - 150D$

23. The volume of a sphere is calculated using the formula $\frac{4}{3}\pi r^3$, in which the r represents the radius of the sphere. What fraction of the volume of a sphere of radius x would a cube with a side length of x be?

   A. $\dfrac{\pi}{\frac{4}{3}}$

   B. $\dfrac{3}{4}\pi$

   C. $\dfrac{4}{\sqrt[3]{\pi}}$

   D. $\dfrac{1}{\frac{4}{3}\pi}$

   E. $\dfrac{3}{2\pi}$

24. In a box, there are 4 red balls, 8 yellow balls, and 12 purple balls. If a ball is randomly selected from this box, what is the probability that it will be yellow?

   F. $\dfrac{1}{5}$

   G. $\dfrac{1}{4}$

   H. $\dfrac{1}{3}$

   J. $\dfrac{1}{2}$

   K. 1

25. A novel has 400 pages and Veronica wants to estimate how long it will take her to complete it. She reads 250 words per minute. She counted the words on one quarter of a typical page and found that there were approximately 200 words per page. To the nearest minute, how long will it take Veronica to read the book?

   A. 225
   B. 320
   C. 400
   D. 450
   E. 850

26. A virus is spreading throughout the population of a town, and the number of people who have the virus doubles every 3 days. If there are 1,000 people in the town, and 10 people have the virus on January 1st, what is the earliest date at which the entire town would be infected with the virus, given that there are 365 days in a year, and 31 days in the month of January?
    F. January 10th
    G. January 21st
    H. January 31st
    J. February 10th
    K. In approximately three years

27. Which of these vowels does NOT have a vertical axis of symmetry?
    A. A
    B. E
    C. I
    D. O
    E. U

28. Mr. Cleary's class and Ms. Ntuala's class go to use the computer lab. There are 20 computers available, two of which do not work. Mr. Cleary's class has 14 kids, and Ms. Ntuala's class has 12 kids. If every student must use a computer and there can only be 2 students on a computer at most, what is the maximum number of students who can have a computer to themselves?
    F. 2
    G. 6
    H. 10
    J. 14
    K. 20

29. What is the slope of a line perpendicular to a line with the equation $-6x + 2y = -4$?
    A. -3
    B. $-\dfrac{1}{2}$
    C. $-\dfrac{1}{3}$
    D. 3
    E. 12

30. Dylan has to bake a cake at 350°F in the oven. The oven dial is set to degrees Celsius. The formula for conversion from degrees Celsius (C) to degrees Fahrenheit (F) is $F = \frac{9}{5}C + 32$. To what approximate temperature in Celsius should Dylan set the oven?

    F. 7
    G. 177
    H. 382
    J. 572
    K. 662

31. What is the equation for the circle depicted below?

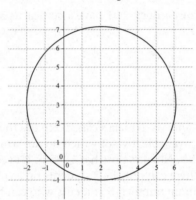

    A. $(x - 2)^2 + (y - 3)^2 = 16$
    B. $(x + 2)^2 + (y + 3)^2 = 16$
    C. $(x - 2)^2 - (y - 3)^2 = 16$
    D. $(x - 2)^2 + (y - 3)^2 = 64$
    E. $(x + 2)^2 + (y - 3)^2 = 16$

32. If m is an even integer, which of the following must be even?

    F. $m^2 + 1$
    G. $m^{-2} - 4$
    H. $m^3 + 1$
    J. $m^4 + 3$
    K. $m^6 - 2$

33. If $\log_3 x = 4$, $x = ?$

    A. 1
    B. 12
    C. 64
    D. 81
    E. 243

34. At what point in the *x-y*-coordinate plane do these two lines intersect?

Line One: $y = 2x + 4$
Line Two: $y = -3x - 5$

F. $(\frac{9}{5}, -\frac{2}{5})$

G. $(-\frac{9}{5}, \frac{2}{5})$

H. $(\frac{2}{5}, -\frac{9}{5})$

J. $(\frac{5}{9}, -\frac{5}{2})$

K. $(6, 12)$

35. Consider a point with coordinates (a, b), where a and b are both positive integers. In which quadrant will the point $(-5a, -7b)$ fall?
A. First
B. Second
C. Third
D. Fourth
E. Cannot be determined with the given information.

36. A washing machine has a normal cycle that lasts 45 minutes and a whites cycle that lasts 70 minutes. What fraction of the length of the whites cycle is the length of the normal cycle?

F. $\dfrac{1}{7}$

G. $\dfrac{1}{3}$

H. $\dfrac{9}{14}$

J. $\dfrac{2}{3}$

K. $\dfrac{14}{9}$

37. Which of the following expressions would give the measure of angle *A*?

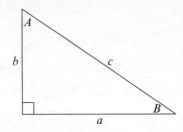

 A. sin *A*
 B. cos *C*
 C. $\tan^{-1} B$
 D. arcsin $\dfrac{c}{a}$
 E. arccos $\dfrac{b}{c}$

38. Zoey is laying bricks for her patio. The salesman wants to sell Zoey as many bricks as possible to cover her patio with a thickness of one brick, while not having any extra bricks. The patio area is a rectangle with dimensions 12 feet by 10 feet, and each individual brick is 4 inches by 6 inches by 2 inches. What would be the greatest number of bricks the salesman could sell to meet his sales criteria?
 F. 5,760
 G. 2,880
 H. 2,160
 J. 1,440
 K. 120

39. A teacher can grade 20 papers during an uninterrupted planning period and 10 papers for each hour he spends at home grading. What function models the number of papers he can grade given that he has 2 uninterrupted planning periods and *x* full hours devoted to grading at home?
 A. $20 + 2x$
 B. $20x + 10$
 C. $40x + 10$
 D. $40 + 10x$
 E. $80 + 20x$

40. If Wayne considers the letter "Y" to be a vowel but Kristen does not, thinking that there are only 5 vowels, by what percent is the probability that a randomly selected letter out of the 26 letter alphabet will be a vowel greater in Wayne's opinion than in Kristen's opinion?
   F. 5%
   G. 6%
   H. 20%
   J. 30%
   K. 32%

Questions 41–44 deal with the Rubik's cube, pictured below.

This Rubik's cube has sides of 6 different colors—red, green, white, yellow, blue, and orange. The objective is to twist the smaller cubes (which are of equal volume and fully fill the larger Rubik's cube) such that the large cube has sides of uniform color all around (i.e., one side is completely red, another completely blue, etc.).

41. How many smaller cubes are within the Rubik's cube, assuming the inside of the cube is hollow (i.e., there is no middle cube)?
   A. 9
   B. 26
   C. 27
   D. 54
   E. 81

42. In a completely solved Rubik's cube, what are the odds that if someone randomly touches a side that the side will be orange?

 F. $\dfrac{1}{12}$

 G. $\dfrac{1}{9}$

 H. $\dfrac{1}{8}$

 J. $\dfrac{1}{6}$

 K. $\dfrac{1}{4}$

43. If each smaller cube has a side length of 1 cm., what is the surface area in square centimeters of the large Rubik's cube when it is in cubical (not twisted at all) form?
 A. 9
 B. 27
 C. 54
 D. 108
 E. 162

44. If the sides of the entire Rubik's cube are of length 3 cm, what is the distance from one corner of an entire Rubik's cube to the corner of the entire Rubik's cube that is farthest away from it?

 F. $3\sqrt{2}$

 G. $3\sqrt{3}$

 H. 3

 J. 9

 K. $6\sqrt{3}$

45. What is the 5th term in a series in which the first term is 2 and each subsequent term is –2 multiplied by the preceding term?
 A. –16
 B. 32
 C. –32
 D. 64
 E. –64

46. If five sixths of y is added to one third of y, what is the end result as a fraction of y?

    F. $\dfrac{1}{24}$

    G. $\dfrac{1}{3}$

    H. $\dfrac{2}{3}$

    J. $\dfrac{7}{6}$

    K. $\dfrac{8}{3}$

47. In a right triangle with sides a, b, and c, where c is the hypotenuse, what is the cosine of angle A?

    A. $\dfrac{b}{c}$

    B. $\dfrac{c}{a}$

    C. $\dfrac{a}{b}$

    D. $\sqrt{a^2 + b^2}$

    E. $\dfrac{\sqrt{a^2 + b^2}}{b}$

48. A "perfect number" is defined as a positive integer that is equal to the sum of its distinct proper factors, which are the factors of the number other than the number itself. Which of the following is NOT a perfect number?
    F.   6
    G.   28
    H.   44
    J.   496
    K.   8,128

49. What is the vertex of the parabola given by the equation: $y = 2x^2 - 3$?
    A. $(0, 0)$
    B. $(0, -3)$
    C. $(-3, 2)$
    D. $(-2, 3)$
    E. $(4, 3)$

50. If point *x* is originally on the *y*-axis and has a positive value for its *y*-coordinate, where will the *y*-coordinate be if the point is rotated counterclockwise 200 degrees about the origin?
    F. 1st quadrant
    G. 2nd quadrant
    H. 3rd quadrant
    J. 4th quadrant
    K. 2nd and 3rd quadrant

51. If we take sin *x* and change it to 3 sin 2*x*, what will happen to the domain and range of the function?
    A. Domain and range remain the same
    B. Domain is double; range remains the same
    C. Domain is tripled; range is doubled
    D. Domain is the same; range is doubled
    E. Domain is the same; range is tripled

52. On a 100-question multiple-choice test, Hannah gets 1 full point for a correct answer, 0 points if she leaves the question blank, and –1/4 points for an incorrect answer. Hannah already has scored exactly 50 correct answers out of 60, and out of those first 60, she answered every question. What is the greatest number of questions she can omit on the remaining questions and still have a score of at least 70 on the test?
    F. 16
    G. 17
    H. 18
    J. 19
    K. 20

53. A portion of a regular polygon can be seen beneath a rectangle. If angles *B* and *C* are 12° and 18°, respectively, how many sides will the shape have?

    A. 10
    B. 11
    C. 12
    D. 13
    E. 14

54. $\dfrac{1}{20^{30}} - \dfrac{1}{20^{31}} = ?$

   F. $\dfrac{1}{20^{30}}$

   G. $\dfrac{1}{20^{31}}$

   H. $\dfrac{19}{20^{30}}$

   J. $\dfrac{19}{20^{31}}$

   K. $\dfrac{20}{20^{31}}$

55. If $f[x] = 3\begin{vmatrix} x & 2x \\ 4 & x^2 \end{vmatrix}$, what is the value of $f[2]$?

   A. $\begin{vmatrix} 2 & 4 \\ 4 & 4 \end{vmatrix}$

   B. $\begin{vmatrix} 6 & 12 \\ 12 & 12 \end{vmatrix}$

   C. $\begin{vmatrix} 6 & 4 \\ 18 & 9 \end{vmatrix}$

   D. $\begin{vmatrix} 12 & 6 \\ 4 & 8 \end{vmatrix}$

   E. $\begin{vmatrix} 4 & 8 \\ 4 & 16 \end{vmatrix}$

56. In the figure below, what is the percentage of the total area of the circle that the equilateral triangle occupies to the nearest whole number?

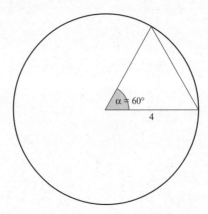

F. 14
G. 17
H. 18
J. 20
K. 22

57. The smallest possible period of this graph is closest to which of the following integers?

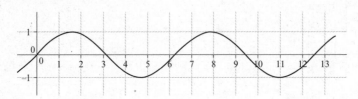

A. 1
B. 2
C. 3
D. 6
E. 13

58. Jayden is creating a scanning programming that will measure the heights of potential riders for a thrilling roller coaster. The ride is designed such that people who are greater than 48 inches tall are allowed to ride, along with people who are less than 78 inches. Jayden is programming a computer so that it will scan the heights of potential riders to determine if they are able to ride, and if not, the machine will buzz so that a ride operator will be able to deny them boarding. Which of the following inequalities will correctly give the full range of heights that are NOT allowed to ride the roller coaster?

   F. 48 < height < 78

   G. height < 48 or height < 78

   H. $|\text{height} - 63| \leq 15$

   J. $15 < |\text{height} - 63|$

   K. height < 78 and height > 48

59. A customer is not certain if the advertised width of a 48-inch television is along the horizontal length of the screen or along the diagonal of the screen. If the ratio of the length to the height of the television screen is 5 to 3, how much shorter, to the nearest inch, will the horizontal length of the television screen be if the measure is made along the diagonal of the television screen rather than along the horizontal length?

   A. 3
   B. 5
   C. 6
   D. 7
   E. 10

60. If each letter of the alphabet is assigned a numerical value of its place in the alphabet (e.g., D is assigned the value 4), what is the sum of the individual numbers that would correspond to the letters in the word CAFE?

   F. 8
   G. 15
   H. 16
   J. 19
   K. 24

If there is still time remaining, you may review your answers.

READING TEST

Time—35 minutes
40 Questions

> **Directions:** There are several reading selections in this section, each of which is followed by questions. After you read a passage, determine the best answer to each question and fill in the matching oval on your answer sheet. Refer back to the passages as often as you need.

PASSAGE I

Prose Fiction—*Cooking*

Don't mistake me—I'm not interested in waiting for the pot to boil. It's not the eating that ensnares me either. Not really. It's about the act itself; creative, transformative, the alchemy of the thing. Cooking is my ritual,
Line meditation, and prayer. I have my own holy oils, and pure, simmering waters
(5) where I give the dried grains their ablution; for my incense, the ecstasy of savory, unwonted spices. Like the ecstasies of shaman mystics in Peru, there are times when cooking can transport me, mentally, spiritually, through time and space.

With one hand on the knife, I pass a blade through the snowy bulb of an
(10) onion. The smell is of young sugar, the sound is crisp and gentle. Inside, the rings grow from the center with staggering geometry, and the flesh is gossamer pale; perfect almost to a fault. At once I am nine again, standing on the seat of a chair in my mother's impeccable kitchen. The color is white. Morning sunlight reflects from the cold water of a birdbath outside the window,
(15) and scatters across our plaster ceiling. Errant flecks dance in circles on tiles of polished porcelain. My mother is making quiche. I gaze into her steel mixing bowl, where golden yolks and pale cream amalgamize, becoming sleek and silken, constellated by chips of glittering onion.

"Reni, I have told you twice to stop," she says, laying her hand across my
(20) wrist as I try to sink my fingers in the bowl. Her words are sharp and precise, as if each one were clipped by a pair of silver scissors. By comparison, my own sound heavy and sluggish—I learned my words at school, among friends and teachers in a suburb of Indianapolis, USA, and know only a mouthful of my mother's Hindi. But her movements in the kitchen are as honed and
(25) meticulous as her English. She calculates her proportions to unfathomable fractions, stirring them in with mechanical consistency of motion. The odor of my fresh-cut onion starts to fade. I watch her turn away from me, and pour the contents of the bowl into a piecrust on the counter, where her American recipes lay, neatly spaced, in a trim mosaic of index cards. Appraisingly, her
(30) eyes slide over their instructions once more before she slides her quiche into

the oven, baking at four hundred twenty-five degrees Fahrenheit for twenty-nine and one half minutes.

The oven door snaps shut, and I am standing once again, aged twenty six years, beside my cutting board. The onion lies before me, minced into (35) fine, uniform fragments of one eighth of an inch. But I will not make quiche tonight. On the stove, my cream base boils over, expelling tiny, wan bubbles onto the pan's perimeter.

They hiss at me, sliding into the blue gas flame beneath. With a wooden spoon, I soothe the mixture, and it settles to gentle simmer. Reaching to a (40) shelf, I slide my index finger past a pantheon of stout, glass columns—coriander, cardamom, cayenne, cloves, cumin, cinnamon, mace, nutmeg—three jars deep, they span nearly the whole length of the cabinet. Emptying a bit of black cardamom into one palm, I scatter it over the pan. The texture is strong and coarse; the smell is of smoke and peppermint, faintly medicinal.

(45)   I reach for another jar, but a man's hand beats me to it—I am fifteen years old, raised mostly in Indiana, and visiting my father's house outside Calcutta, India. Flaking red and yellow stains embellish the stovetop and the table. He smiles at me because we can scarcely talk. His English is sparse, circuitous, and unpredictable. But he smiles, and hands me two unlabeled jars, keeping (50) two more for himself, and together we shake them, raining down a savory, polychrome flurry of dust into the pan below. He dips his finger in, licks it, and frowns. It's not that my father doesn't know how to cook. He does. But his dishes are guided by the subtler faculties—the tactile sensation of a thickening curry, the aromatic shifts as his naan nears fully baked. I lean over the (55) stove and inhale the dense, flavorsome steam.

I breathe out, and my base is below me, not quite ready, but not burning either. The spice cabinet is closed. Tonight I will not make masala either. All the ingredients I need are laid before me. My right hand counts out their proportions with surgical precision, while my left scoops them up in fistfuls, (60) letting the excess fall between its fingers. Together they'll prepare my meal. And with the heat of blue flames rising from the stove, words from the Aitareya Upanishad begin to take shape in my mind, "Here are the worlds and their guardians. Let me now bring forth food for them."

1. Based on the passage as a whole, the author most likely uses the quotation in lines 62–63 to illustrate what about her thoughts on the cooking process?
   A. How cooking can be used to make religious sacrifices to the gods
   B. How cooking is a key part of her religious rituals
   C. How cooking helps her mystically connect to the universe
   D. How cooking provides sustenance to the guardians of the world

2. Which of the following most accurately describes the differences in approach of the narrator's mother and father, respectively, to cooking?
   F. Sensual, ambitious
   G. Rational, intuitive
   H. Intellectual, precise
   J. Passionate, rigid

3. In the context of the third paragraph (lines 19–32), the language in lines 30–32 most evokes which of the following about the narrator's mother?
   A. Her precision
   B. Her happiness
   C. Her short temperedness
   D. Her love of cooking

4. It can reasonably be inferred from the last paragraph (lines 56–63) that the narrator as an adult has a personality most like:
   F. neither her mother's nor her father's.
   G. her mother's.
   H. her father's.
   J. a synthesis of both

5. In the third paragraph (lines 19–32), the narrator suggests that her mother most embraces which of the following?
   A. Her Hindu faith
   B. American culture
   C. Her use of scissors
   D. Mathematical calculation

6. Which of the author's senses is more significantly used to cause the second major flashback than the first flashback?
   F. Sight
   G. Smell
   H. Taste
   J. Touch

7. Which of the following would NOT be a logical possible explanation for the different paths of the narrator's parents?
   A. The mother returned to India to immerse herself in the Hindi language.
   B. The mother and father divorced amicably.
   C. The mother wished to immigrate to the United States, while the father wished to remain in India.
   D. The mother died when the child was in early adolescence.

8. On which of the following matters would the narrator's mother and father be most likely to strongly disagree?
   F. Global politics
   G. Culinary sanitation
   H. English curricula
   J. Architectural aesthetics

9. The fifth paragraph (lines 45–55) suggests that if the father of the narrator were to teach her how to perform a task, how might he do so?
   A. Lecture
   B. Use of a written manual
   C. Hands-on demonstration
   D. Multimedia presentation

10. The narrator has likely NOT been to which of the following place(s)?
    F. Indiana
    G. Peru
    H. Calcutta
    J. All of the above

PASSAGE II

Social Science—*"The Origin of the Noodle"*

Try to imagine a world without noodles—no pasta, no pad thai, no stroganoff, at least not in the way we think of them now—and you may begin to realize just how ubiquitous this starchy foodstuff has become, even among the
Line most distant cooking cultures of the world. Despite the noodle's relatively
(5) complex process of production, discoveries in anthropology and archaeology have proven it to be a surprisingly ancient food, dating back at least to 4000 B.C. Not surprisingly, however, given the noodle's widespread appeal and integral status in more than a few culinary traditions, the claim to its invention is often a hotly contested subject.
(10)   While the actual number of ingredients needed to make a noodle is modest, creating a batch of noodles of uniform pliability, texture and form is no small task. In general, noodles are made first by grinding grain into a flour, then mixing it with salt and water to produce a dough. Sometimes a mixture of several grains is used in order to achieve a particular constitution, and
(15) eggs can also be added for the same purpose. The dough is then rigorously kneaded by methods that have ranged from bouncing up and down on a bamboo rod, to simply stomping it underfoot, until it reaches the desired consistency and length. The dough is then sliced to create the individual noodles. As we all know, the finished product comes in all shapes, sizes, and
(20) compositions. But from the stout, yellow egg noodles of Italian pasta, to the

narrow, nearly diaphanous rice noodles of southeast Asia, all of them share the vital, sating role in the dishes in which they are used, and the laborious history of their manufacture.

(25) The complexity involved in creating noodles by hand—relative to the preparations of other foodstuffs of antiquity—seems to mark a certain degree of sophistication for the culinary art and technology of the culture in which a noodle is produced. And this, perhaps, is why so many peoples have laid claim to its origination. Historically, both Italy and the Middle East have particularly contended for the title. To many people the world over, Italian cook-

(30) ing is nearly synonymous with the pasta noodle, but surprisingly the oldest recorded use of noodles in Italy only dates back to the 8th century, during the Arab conquest of Sicily. This fact, in tandem with appearance of wheat flour in the Middle East around 5,000 B.C., has led some to favor the Arab world as the more likely candidate to have first created noodles. However, recent evidence

(35) has cast some doubt on this speculation, when the oldest known bowl of noodles was discovered in northwestern China.

In 2005, a sealed bowl was unearthed from beneath ten feet of soil at the Laija archeological, and found to contain a lump of miraculously well-preserved noodles. After examination, scientists estimated them to be ap-

(40) proximately 4,000 years old. It was also determined that the noodles were composed not of the wheat flour known at that time throughout the Middle East, but instead of two types of millet grain, which was widely cultivated throughout China as far back as 7,000 years ago.

One of the most revealing aspects of the find, however, as Archaeochemist

(45) Patrick McGovern at the University of Pennsylvania's Museum of Archaeology and Anthropology in Philadelphia points out, is the degree of skill required to fashion long, thin noodles like those found at Laija.

"This shows a fairly high level of food processing and culinary sophistication," he said.

(50) Thus, while those discovered at Laija may for the moment be the oldest empirical evidence of noodles, the deftness demanded for their creation seems to suggest that—even 4,000 years ago—the culinary artisans of China were already well-acquainted with the nuances of noodle-making.

Although the Laija discovery makes China home to the oldest known

(55) noodles, the origin of the noodle itself remains elusive, concealed in one of the many unlit corridors of antiquity. As such, there's no way to be certain that an even older noodle artifact may soon come to light elsewhere. But whether or not the details of the noodle's invention are ever truly settled, the continued rivalry to be named its birthplace stands as testimony to the

(60) noodle's persistent and pervasive place as a staple food for any culture that noodles have slipped into throughout their long and tangled history.

11. The main purpose of the passage can best be described as an effort to:
    A. explain how noodles are created in a variety of international cuisine.
    B. illustrate the historical controversy surrounding the question of the noodle's origin.
    C. describe the controversy over the proper use of noodles in different foods.
    D. demonstrate how the Laija discovery has settled the debate over the origin of the noodle.

12. According to the passage, scientists have found archaeological evidence giving the greatest support to which of the following peoples in their quest to be named the originators of the noodle?
    F. The Chinese
    G. The Arabs
    H. The Italians
    J. The Middle Easterners

13. The main function of the last sentence of the third paragraph (lines 34–36) in relation to the passage as a whole is:
    A. to conclusively demonstrate that China is the true originator of the noodle.
    B. to provide a transition to a more specific investigation.
    C. to give evidence of scientific doubts about the Chinese origin of the noodle.
    D. to show the chronology of the origination of the noodle.

14. Which of the following is NOT given by the author as a reason for the controversy over the origin of the noodle?
    F. Its use in more than a few culinary traditions
    G. The exclusive right that some cultures have to use noodles in their cooking
    H. The desire to see one's culture as technologically sophisticated, being able to produce such a complex item
    J. Its widespread appeal

15. As it is used in line 51, the word "deftness" most nearly means:
    A. wisdom.
    B. skill.
    C. creativity.
    D. research.

16. It can reasonably be inferred from the last paragraph of the essay (lines 54–61) that the question of the origin of the noodle is:
    F. no longer up for debate.
    G. still unsettled.
    H. no longer of interest to historians.
    J. a cause for grave conflict.

17. The author uses lines 29–32 to demonstrate the contrast between:
   A. mistaken information and an accurate observation.
   B. a cultural observation and historical fact.
   C. correct use of pasta and incorrect use.
   D. the Middle East and Italy.

18. In the second paragraph (lines 10–23), the author primarily emphasizes which of the following about the noodle's production?
   F. The many and varied shapes and sizes of noodles in international cookery
   G. The types of ingredients used by different cultures to craft noodles
   H. The methods through which noodle dough is kneaded.
   J. The uniformity and diversity of its creation across cultures

19. Which of the following could most likely be one of the "foodstuffs of antiquity" in paragraph three (line 25)?
   A. Tropical Fruit Pie
   B. Roasted Chicken with Mushroom Sauce
   C. Simple Broth
   D. Turnip, Carrot, and Beef Stew

20. Which of the following would be most similar to the historical and international controversy about the origin of the noodle?
   F. Europeans and Asians debating who created the printing process
   G. Native Americans and the Chinese debating over the correct religion
   H. Modern Americans and Europeans debating over the definition of football
   J. Scandinavians and Spaniards debating over who discovered America

PASSAGE III

Humanities—*Flushing Out Formal Art*

Marcel Duchamp pushes the idea of modern art and the modern artist with a peculiar, somewhat paradoxical style of visual art called "ready-mades." By taking objects found in everyday life, ones that he himself did
Line not physically create with his own hands and calling these objects "art," he
(5) forces his audience to seriously examine their ideas regarding the nature of art, as well as what it means to be an artist.

In 1917, Duchamp stirred up controversy in the art world by submitting a piece titled *Fountain* to the Society of Independent Artists' annual exhibition. Although the Society had promised to exhibit all submissions, they refused to
(10) include *Fountain* in their display. *Fountain*, as it turned out, presented many of the board members with a dilemma—they could not decide whether or not it was a work of art. What Duchamp submitted was a Bedfordshire style

porcelain urinal that he had purchased at the J.L. Mott Iron Works in New York City. After rotating the urinal 90 degrees onto its back, he signed the
(15) edge with the name and date "R. Mutt 1917," and titled the work *Fountain*. Without having reached a consensus concerning whether *Fountain* was or was not a work of art, the board members hid the piece from view during the exhibition. Interestingly, Duchamp was a member of the board at that time, and, having disguised his identity with a pseudonym, managed to participate
(20) in the debate.

While the original *Fountain* was lost soon after the debacle, public interest compelled Duchamp to create a replica, which has since been displayed in art galleries and museums around the world. However, the issues raised by its first submission in 1917 regarding the boundaries of art and the art-
(25) ist are far from settled. In essence, Duchamp wants the viewer to mentally interpret *Fountain* not as a urinal that is out of place but as a fully formed and legitimate work of art. For instance, if viewers can manage to suspend their contextual perceptions—namely, that the object before them is a urinal—they might consider *Fountain* from a purely visual perspective. Frankly,
(30) *Fountain* looks quite a bit like other works of abstract art and sculpture. It has a graceful round form, a stark black and white contrast, and a repetition of circles. It is organically symmetrical, and full of depth. In space, the sculpture is oriented in a way other than it would have been mounted in a rest room, giving the viewer a new visual perspective on a familiar object.

(35) Further, while a urinal is generally associated with the filth of public restrooms, and the unpleasantries of excretion, *Fountain* is round, smooth, lustrous, and clean—all things that are often considered attractive or pleasing to look at. Visually, *Fountain* isn't jarring whatsoever. The aversions that many viewers of the work experience can be attributed to the sculpture's contextual
(40) background. By displaying *Fountain* in an art exhibit, Duchamp seeks to "recontextualize" the piece, and, perhaps, to reinvent our mental associations with what was before an essentially unpleasant object.

Readymades also challenge our notions regarding the role of the artist. According to Duchamp, the role of the artist is not necessarily to create with
(45) his hands, but rather with his mind. As such, the artist is free to bring our attention to objects that are beautiful but may be overlooked in everyday life. Duchamp made a urinal a piece of artwork by adding a comical title and removing it from its typical surroundings and circumstances. In doing so he transforms the urinal into a work of art without physically changing
(50) or creating it. What's more, by turning the urinal on its back and moving it out of the restroom, Duchamp destroys its functional significance, which, in turn, changes its meaning. That is, *Fountain* no longer serves its intended purpose, and the urinal is no longer a urinal. Instead, it's a ceramic sculpture cast in a mold.

(55) Alongside other modern artists of the early twentieth-century, Duchamp made the final push from artist as a creator to artist as a thinker. Instead of creating *Fountain* he "chose" *Fountain*. In doing so he illustrated how anything can be considered for its visual, aesthetic elements, and that the artist

need not create the object but simply choose it, take ownership over it, invest
(60) the object with ideas, and call it art. Truly, the emergence of readymades
constituted a sharp, conceptual break with traditional notions of art, and
pushed the expressive scope of modern art to a new level. Duchamp made
his work out of an immaterial material, and used it to say something about
change in the modern world.

21. Based on the passage, it is reasonable to infer that which of the following
played the most significant role in the popularity of Duchamp's *Fountain*?
A. Aesthetics
B. Familiarity
C. Craftsmanship
D. Controversy

22. It can reasonably be inferred that Duchamp most likely chose to use a
pseudonym due to which of the following reasons?
F. To avoid stifling the intellectual debate
G. Due to his artistic and creative modesty
H. His low status would not have allowed his opinions to be heard
otherwise
J. He was not confident as to whether his work was indeed art

23. Lines 29–34 most likely are intended to address what potential objection by
the reader?
A. That something so commonplace couldn't possibly be art
B. That such a work would be fine in a bathroom at home
C. That a toilet gives no evidence of human craftsmanship
D. That this work would have functioned better less as a sculpture and
more as a landscape

24. Which of the following would be a "contextual perception" of the urinal in
line 28 that Duchamp wanted his viewers to suspend?
F. The expected spatial orientation of the urinal
G. The expected coloration of the urinal
H. The expected presence of flowing water in the urinal
J. The expected use of circular shapes in the design of the urinal

25. A modern-day board in an area of the performing arts is facing a dilemma similar to that of the board with respect to Duchamp's *Fountain* discussed in the passage. Which of the following would be a possible dilemma for the modern day board as far as whether to permit a particular art performance to proceed?
    A. A pianist is not sure that she has had sufficient practice to skillfully perform a famous symphony.
    B. A composer wishes to have an orchestra play a song titled "Silence," in which no musicians play at all.
    C. A theater director would like to do a controversial musical that highlights issues about female oppression.
    D. A dancer wants to do a ballet that involves some extremely dangerous jumps and twirls.

26. It can reasonably be inferred from the passage that all of the following would have been possible reasons that the board was wary about displaying *The Fountain* EXCEPT:
    F. fear of the lessening of artistic standards.
    G. lack of space to display such a sculpture.
    H. reluctance to promote an unknown figure.
    J. the bitter ridicule that could likely ensue.

27. Based on the passage, if someone were to go see an exhibition on Duchamp's Readymades, could she expect to find the works titled or untitled?
    A. Titled, because it aids in Duchamp's aim to recontextualize visual objects
    B. Titled, because his titles would likely help a viewer understand the everyday use for the artwork
    C. Untitled, because as an artist, Duchamp was primarily concerned with visual expression, not verbal
    D. Untitled, because a title would prevent the viewer from full utilization of her imagination

28. Based on the passage, which aspect of artistry was apparently more valued in earlier times than in modern times?
    F. Training
    G. Intellect
    H. Craftsmanship
    J. Cultural awareness

29. The title of Duchamp's *Fountain* is best described as:
    A. skeptical.
    B. ironic.
    C. controversial.
    D. irrelevant.

30. The author suggests in lines 43–45 that someone who embraced Duchamp's aesthetic mindset, as opposed to someone who dismissed his approach, would be able to find artistic beauty in:

F. a grove of trees in the forest.

G. art museums and cultural centers.

H. an electronics store in a mall.

J. looking through a telescope pointed at the night sky.

PASSAGE IV

Natural Science—*Neuroscience*

PASSAGE A

Magnetic resonance imaging, positron emission tomography, and several other remarkable technologies emerged in the 20th Century to transform the way we study the human brain. But for all the headway that these mod-
Line ern modalities have helped neuroscientists achieve within the laboratory, it
(5) is at times baffling to realize how much of what we currently know about the mind is derived not from carefully controlled experimentation, but from traumatic accidents, and random chance.

Even above the eminent researchers themselves, there are few names in neuroscience more emblematic of the field than those of H.M., S.M., and
(10) Phineas Gage: three individuals whose unique misfortunes provided the groundwork for contemporary investigations into the structural and physiological nature of memory, personality, and fear. H.M., for instance, was involved in a bicycle accident at age seven, after which he began to suffer from increasingly frequent bilateral temporal lobe seizures. After ten years,
(15) the episodes became intractable, and H.M. underwent an experimental surgery to remove his medial temporal lobes—including both hippocampal regions—in an effort to eliminate the portions of his brain responsible for generating the seizures. In a sense, the surgery was a success. H.M. survived, and no longer suffered from epilepsy. However, while he retained all his
(20) memories leading up to the procedure, it was discovered afterward that he'd permanently lost the ability to form new ones. Whereas in the past this condition—referred to medically as "anterograde amnesia"—was typically associated with significant head trauma, in the case of H.M., the literally surgical precision with which scientists could pinpoint damage to his brain
(25) shed a revolutionary new light on the function of the hippocampus, and established its role in generating long-term memory.

The story of S.M. is equally curious, and involved another pair of mysterious structures situated just adjacent to the hippocampus. S.M. was born with a rare, genetic neuro-cutaneous condition known as Urbach-Wiethe disease.
(30) The symptoms caused by this condition vary immensely from person to

person, but in the case of S.M., it manifested as a sclerotic hardening and subsequent destruction of her amygdalae, a pair of almond-shaped nuclei located in the anteromedial temporal lobes. As a result, S.M. lost the ability to experience fear. Throughout her life, she encountered mortal dan-
(35) ger on multiple occasions, but was consistently incapable of exhibiting either the emotional or autonomic responses associated with a fear state, including accelerated heart rate, bronchodilation, and pupillary dilation. Physiologically, S.M. still retained the ability to respond to the epinephrine or "adrenaline" that normally facilitates these processes. Rather, her brain
(40) simply lacked the capacity to release these hormones in response to normal, stress-inducing emotional triggers.

PASSAGE B

The amygdala, acting as a sort of processing pit stop in the limbic system, has long been described as the "fear center" of the brain. Recent research utilizing positron emission tomography has helped to affirm this supposition,
(45) implicating a variety of anxiety disorders, panic disorder, as well as certain changes observed in post-traumatic stress disorder with increased glucose metabolism in the region of the amygdala. Given its direct neural connections to both the hypothalamus and the locus coeruleus, it is not surprising that pathologically enhanced activity and responsivity in the amygdala
(50) may be responsible for mediating the inappropriately strong hormonal stress responses to non-threatening cues and stimuli so often observed in patients suffering from these disorders.
It is well-established, for instance, that the locus coeruleus is the principal site of norepinephrine synthesis in the brain, and that the secretion of nor-
(55) epinephrine from this region in response to psychological or physiological stress further induces the release of epinephrine to the bloodstream via sympathetic innervation of the adrenal medulla. Similarly, the amygdala's projections to the hypothalamus may very well play a role in the stress-induced secretion of cortisol from the adrenal cortex. Specifically, it may do so by
(60) upregulating the pulsatile frequency with which corticotropin-releasing hormone is sent to the anterior pituitary gland, causing an increased secretion of adrenocorticotropic hormone to the bloodstream.
What we are just beginning to appreciate, however, is the function of the amygdala in another highly prevalent set of neuropsychiatric conditions—
(65) namely, addiction—the symptoms of which it may play just as great a role in perpetuating. Apart from fear, the amygdala is known to be involved in emotional learning via its connections to the hippocampus, and to other limbic structures throughout the brain. Of particular interest in addiction studies are the amygdala's projections to the ventral tegmental area: a
(70) mesolimbic circuit that, when stimulated by the anticipation of a reward, releases dopamine to the prefrontal cortex, inducing feelings of excitement, and euphoria. Preliminary investigations indicate that the activity of this anticipatory reward pathway is greatly increased among individuals suffer-

ing from addiction, while, paradoxically, the dopamine-related response to
(75) external substances—such as nicotine, amphetamine, and cocaine—is actually diminished.

Questions 31–33 are about Passage A.

31. Which of the following explanations would most logically explain why sci-
   entists have not been able to study many cases of patients like H.M., S.M.,
   and Phineas Gage?
   A. When compared to other areas of medical research, like the study of
      cancer and heart disease, scientists do not yet have the technology to
      study the brain in-depth.
   B. Given the resulting life-changing trauma that brain modifications like
      theirs will likely cause, such changes can only be ethically studied when
      they result from accidents.
   C. There has not been sustained government and university funding to
      support research endeavors into changes in the brain.
   D. While scientists are interested in physical processes, study of the emo-
      tional consequences of brain trauma does not fall under the broad
      umbrella of scientific inquiry.

32. It is reasonable to infer that the doctors who operated on H.M.
   F. were taken aback by his unprecedented development of anterograde
      amnesia.
   G. were aware of the possibility of complications from the surgery, but felt
      it was worth proceeding given his disease.
   H. decided to proceed with an experimental treatment because of the last-
      ing, negative effects that anterograde amnesia had on his day-to-day life.
   J. learned about a new condition, anterograde amnesia, as a result of the
      study of his unfortunate accident.

33. A significant difference between the cases of S.M. and H.M. is with respect
   to
   A. the inheritance of their conditions.
   B. the normalcy of their situations.
   C. the interest scientists have in their cases.
   D. whether scientists could pinpoint the components of their brains that
      caused their disorders.

Questions 34–37 are about Passage B.

34. Based on the passage, which represents a proper sequence of mental events?
    F. Sensation of external threat → hormone secretion from the locus coeruleus → processing by the amygdala
    G. Processing by the amygdala → sensation of external threat → hormone secretion from the locus coeruleus
    H. Sensation of external threat → processing by the amygdala → hormone secretion from the locus coeruleus
    J. Hormone secretion from the locus coeruleus → processing by the amygdala → sensation of external threat

35. As the term is used in line 63, "appreciate" most nearly means
    A. understand.
    B. regulate.
    C. praise.
    D. grow.

36. The author of the passage would most likely consider the label of "fear center" as applied to the amygdala as
    F. true and comprehensive.
    G. true but not comprehensive.
    H. of dubious validity.
    J. pioneering and final.

37. The author uses lines 72–76 to most strongly suggest that drug addicts typically experience
    A. greater internal rewards from using abusive substances while simultaneously finding increased external satisfaction.
    B. relatively minimal negative impact unless they are influenced by known stimulants like nicotine or cocaine.
    C. significantly increased craving for illegal substances along with an increased capability of acquiring them.
    D. increased desire for a substance coupled with less satisfaction as they use it more frequently.

Questions 38–40 are about both passages.

38. Which patient analyzed in Passage A would be most relevant to the focus of Passage B?
    F. H.M.
    G. Phineas Gage
    H. S.M.
    J. Urbach-Wiethe

39. Based on both passages, what would be the most helpful takeaway for a practicing psychiatrist about human hormone levels?
    A. Beware of overprescription.
    B. Balance is key.
    C. Let bygones be bygones.
    D. If it's natural, it's good.

40. The author of Passage B would most likely state that during a frightening car near-accident, patient S.M. would experience abnormally low levels of which of the following?

    I. Epinephrine
    II. Dopamine
    III. Cortisol

    F. I only
    G. II and III only
    H. I and III only
    J. All of the above

If there is still time remaining, you may review your answers.

SCIENCE TEST

Time—35 minutes
40 Questions

Directions: There are several passages in this section, each of which is followed by questions. After reviewing a passage, choose the best answer to each question and fill in the matching oval on your answer sheet. Refer back to the passages as often as you need. Calculators are NOT permitted on this test.

PASSAGE I

The autonomic nervous system—which regulates the bodily functions over which we have no direct control—is separated into two divisions: the sympathetic, and the parasympathetic. The neuronal pathways for these two divisions are illustrated in Figure 1.

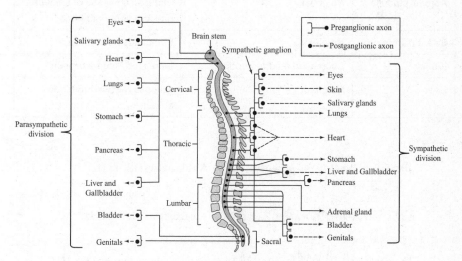

Figure 1

Due to the different, sometimes oppositional results of stimulation by the two divisions, the sympathetic division is often referred to as the "fight or flight" division, and the parasympathetic as the "resting and digesting" division. Their effects on target organs and systems are summarized in Table 1. Additionally, specific brain wave patterns can be associated with the regulation of the autonomic nervous system. Four common varieties of brain waves are shown in Figure 2.

Table 1

Target Structure	Parasympathetic Effects	Sympathetic Effects
Stomach	Increases gastric acid secretion, relaxes pyloric sphincter	Decreases gastric acid secretion, constricts pyloric sphincter
Lungs	Constricts bronchioles	Dilates bronchioles
Heart	Decreases and steadies rate of contraction	Increases rate and force of heartbeat
Salivary and lacrimal glands	Increases saliva and tear production	Inhibits glands; dry mouth and dry eyes
Iris	Constricts pupils	Dilates pupils
Ciliary muscle	Bulges lens for close vision	Flattens lens for distant vision
Adrenal medulla	No effect	Stimulates release of epinephrine and norepinephrine
Sweat glands	No effect	Stimulates perspiration
Kidney	Decreased fluid resorption	Increased fluid resorption
Liver	No effect	Glucose released to bloodstream

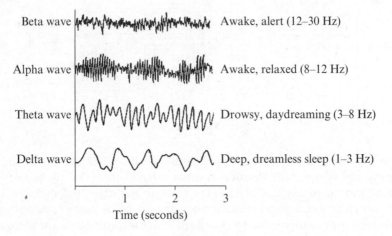

Beta wave — Awake, alert (12–30 Hz)

Alpha wave — Awake, relaxed (8–12 Hz)

Theta wave — Drowsy, daydreaming (3–8 Hz)

Delta wave — Deep, dreamless sleep (1–3 Hz)

Time (seconds)

Figure 2

1. According to Figure 1, which of the following parts of the spine would be farthest from the skull?
   A. Cervical
   B. Thoracic
   C. Lumbar
   D. Sacral

2. According to Table 1, parasympathetic effects on the human body would most likely be associated with
   F. expansion of both the bronchioles and pupils.
   G. expansion of the bronchioles and narrowing of the pupils.
   H. narrowing of the bronchioles and expansion of the pupils.
   J. narrowing of both the bronchioles and pupils.

3. According to the data in Figure 1, the brainstem does NOT appear to directly impact parasympathetic functioning in which of the following bodily parts?
   A. Stomach
   B. Bladder
   C. Lungs
   D. Liver and gallbladder

4. According to Figure 1, most of the systems in the body receive neuronal messages from the brain through the following sequence:
   F. 1. Preganglionic axons 2. Postganglionic axons.
   G. 1. Postganglionic axons 2. Preganglionic axons.
   H. Postganglionic axons alone.
   J. Preganglionic axons alone.

5. According to Figure 2, a researcher could best use which of the following characteristics of a wave to distinguish between delta waves and theta waves?
   A. Frequency
   B. Amplitude
   C. Whether the person is asleep
   D. Eye movements

6. Based on the information in Table 1, which structure in the body would be affected when the body sensed a threat from a predator, but would not be affected when the body was simply taking a nap?
   F. Salivary gland
   G. Kidney
   H. Adrenal gland
   J. Iris

PASSAGE II

Normal rain water has a pH value of between 5.6 and 7.0. *Acid rain* is rain water that has a pH value of under 5.6, with the possibility of going as low as 4.3. Acid rain is created due to the mixing of rain water with pollution by-products, such as carbon dioxide, carbon monoxide, hazardous air pollutants, lead, and a variety of other substances. Researchers conducted experiments to gauge the impact of acid rain on the environment.

Study 1

Researchers monitored the pH levels of rain water at different distances (radii) from a nonfiltered coal power plant. The distances from the power plant and pH recorded in rain water collected at those distances are in Figure 1.

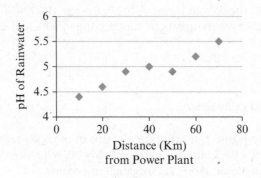

Figure 1

Study 2

Next, researchers did a study to determine the acidity that would be lethal to different species of animals. The animals are all able to survive in waters less acidic than the ones that kill them. The information is given in Figure 2 below.

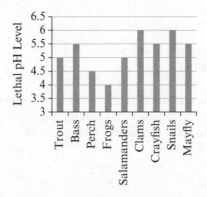

Figure 2

Study 3

Finally, researchers investigated the effects of acid rain on plant life. *Epicuticular Wax* is a protective coating that prevents pollutants from penetrating the inner membranes of tree leaves. Researchers theorized that, as the epicuticular wax coating on plants was reduced by acid rain, the trees would experience measurable harm due to a lack of protection from external pollutants. Researchers tested several tree leaves to determine the impact of exposure to 10" total of severe acid rain—pH of 4.3. The 10" of rain was gradually distributed over the leaf coatings in a period of 1 month, in order to closely replicate acid rain exposure process that leaves would undergo in the natural environment. The percentage decrease in the epicuticular wax coatings in the different plants over the month-long period is provided in Figure 3.

Percentage of Wax Lost Due to Acid Rain

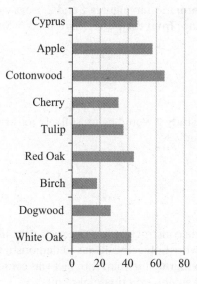

Figure 3

7. According to Figure 3, which of the following trees is most likely to be negatively impacted by acid rain?
   F. Birch
   G. Cherry
   H. Apple
   J. White oak

8. An unknown animal is alive when it is in water of pH 6.0, but dead when it is in water of pH 5.0. Which of the following could be the unknown animal?
   F. Clam
   G. Bass
   H. Frog
   J. Perch

9. A water sample with which of the following pH levels would NOT be considered acid rain?
   A. 5.8
   B. 5.5
   C. 5.0
   D. 4.5

10. According to the information in Figures 1 and 2, frogs would be unable to survive at what distance from the power plant used in Study 1?
    F. 10 km
    G. 40 km
    H. 70 km
    J. None of the above

11. Which animal from Study 2 would be most likely to survive under the acid rain conditions of Study 3?
    A. Bass
    B. Frog
    C. Clam
    D. Snail

12. Information about the construction of the experiment in Study 2 has been omitted. A scientist whose objective it was to demonstrate that acid rain was more harmful to marine life than it in fact was could have done which of the following to skew the experimental results?
    F. Use unhealthy animals as test subjects
    G. Expose the animals to acidic water at a higher rate than they would be exposed to it in the wild
    H. Pick animals with unusually high sensitivity to acid, omitting animals with high resistance to acid
    J. All of the above

13. Which of the following objectives would make the findings from Study 3 more useful to scientists in their effort to determine the effects of acid rain on the environment?
    I. A study that determines the relationship between percentage of leaf wax removed and life span of trees
    II. A study that determines the relationship between the life spans of animal life and exposure to pollutants
    III. A study that determines the relationship between acid rain and the presence of oxygen in lakes and streams
    A. I only
    B. II only
    C. II and III
    D. I, II, and III

Passage III

In the 1800s, astronomers and physicists were puzzled by the inconsistency between their observations of the orbit of the planet Mercury and what their calculations of the planetary orbit should be based on Newtonian physics. Based on the Newtonian theory of Universal Gravitation (published in the year 1687), Mercury's orbit should have been of greater diameter than it was. In an effort to explain this phenomenon, two major theoretical constructs were provided: the possibility of an unobserved planet, named "Vulcan," and the later theory of Relativity by Einstein in the 20th century.

Theory 1: Planet Vulcan

The inconsistency between the predicted orbit of Mercury and the actual orbit of Mercury can be explained without having to negate Newton's theory of Universal Gravitation. As long as there is an astronomical body that is between the Sun and Mercury, it will account for the shifted orbit of the planet. This planet, which we will call "Vulcan," is understandably difficult to observe. Given its proximity to the Sun, it will have a more rapid orbit (probably only a few days), making it impossible to fix a telescope on one point of the sky to observe it clearly. Furthermore, observations will be distorted due to the brightness of the nearby Sun—which will make any pitch-black telescopic observations of the planet impossible—and the relatively small size of the planet.

Theory 2: Relativity

The inconsistency between the predicted orbit of Mercury and the actual orbit of Mercury can be explained by the fact that the predicted orbit is incorrect. Even though Newtonian mechanics will correctly predict astronomical events with a great deal of accuracy, the relativistic nature of matter and time account for the shift in Mercury's orbit that astronomers have observed. The gravitation is mediated by the curvature of spacetime that results from the proximity of the

Sun and its large gravitation. As a consequence, Mercury's orbit is slightly shifted. Relativity can explain Mercury's orbit without recourse to an unobserved planetary body.

14. Besides postulating that there was a planet Vulcan, which of the following would NOT have been both (1) a plausible explanation for amateur astronomers in the 1800s as to why Mercury orbited as it did and (2) consistent with Newton's theory of Universal Gravitation?
   F. Mercury's perceived orbit was within the margin of observational error.
   G. An undiscovered asteroid belt was pulling Mercury in the direction predicted by Newton's theory.
   H. The relativistic nature of space and time.
   J. Demonstrating other observational errors in long-distance telescopic observation.

15. Even with clear and convincing evidence that Relativity was a superior theory in explaining the orbit of Mercury, a scientist in the year 1900 would most likely consider which of the following a major obstacle to overturning Newton's theory of Gravitation?
   A. It had evidently been considered accurate for over 200 years.
   B. It was inaccurate with respect to predicting Mercury's orbit.
   C. It did not take into account the relativistic nature of space and time.
   D. It was unable to anticipate astronomical observations of Vulcan.

16. Astronomers only noticed an inconsistency between their observations of Mercury and Newton's theoretical predictions; they did not observe any inconsistency when they made observations of the planet Jupiter and its orbiting moon Io. Which of the following qualities would a proponent of Theory 2 assert accounts for this difference?
   F. The brightness of the Sun
   G. The small size of the planet Vulcan
   H. The relatively large mass of the Sun
   J. The speed of Jupiter's orbit

17. Which of the following was NOT a potential obstacle to observation of the supposed planet Vulcan as postulated by Theory 1?
   A. Vulcan's rapid orbit
   B. Brightness of the Sun
   C. The orbit of Mercury
   D. Small size of the planet

18. A proponent of Theory 1 would assert that planets that are farther away from the Sun, when compared to planets close to the Sun, would make:
    F. more complete orbits in a given period of time.
    G. fewer complete orbits in a given period of time.
    H. the same number of orbits in a given period of time.
    J. we cannot make any inferences about this from the discussion of Theory 1.

19. When would a proponent of Theory 2 allow that Newton's theory of Universal Gravitation still be useful in predicting the movements of objects? When only a small amount of _____ is required?
    A. relativity
    B. precision
    C. observation
    D. proximity

20. An astronomer wishes to test the validity of Theory 1 but is primarily concerned about the interference to observation of the planet Vulcan due to the extreme brightness of the Sun. What would be the best time during the day for the astronomer to make an observation in search of the planet Vulcan?
    F. A meteor shower
    G. A solar eclipse
    H. The summer solstice
    J. The winter solstice

Passage IV

Nuclear decay is a process by which unstable chemical compounds become more stable. If, in the process of nuclear decay, a compound emits particles from its nucleus, that substance is said to be radioactive. There are four common types of radioactive particles.

1. In α-decay, the radioactive nucleus emits an α-alpha particle, which consists of two neutrons and two protons.
2. In β-decay, the nucleus attempts to become more stable by converting a neutron to a proton. When this occurs, the compound emits a β-particle, which is identical to an electron.
3. In positron-emission, the nucleus becomes more stable by converting a proton to a neutron. When this happens, a positron is emitted. A positron has the same mass as an electron, but an opposite charge.
4. γ-rays are often emitted from a radioactive nucleus alongside other radioactive particles.

Different radioactive particles are emitted from the nucleus with different amounts of energy. For the particles above, gamma rays have the highest energy, positrons and beta particles possess equal energy, and alpha particles have the least amount of energy. Sometimes, even after a decay event, the nucleus is still unstable. In such cases, the resulting compound is also radioactive and will undergo further radioactive decay. This process may repeat many times over many thousands of years and is referred to as a "decay chain." A graduate student is studying the decay chain of ^{222}Radon.

Experiment 1

The student knows the identity of the next several compounds that arise in the ^{222}Radon decay chain but does not know how they are formed. In order to determine what sort of decay is taking place, the student conducts an experiment that measures the energy of the radioactive particles being emitted in each step of the decay chain by passing the particles through a series of metal shields of increasing density. Alpha particles could not penetrate any of the shields, beta particles and positrons penetrated the first shield but not the second, and gamma rays were able to penetrate the first and second, but not the third. The student's findings are summarized in Figure 1.

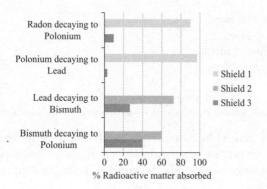

Figure 1

Experiment 2

The student had planned to continue his first experiment, but when he was about to test the newly formed polonium (decayed from bismuth), he discovered that nearly all of it had already decayed to form ^{214}Lead. Instead, the student decided to begin with a 10-g sample of lead decayed from polonium and determine its half-life by observing the sample's decay over time. The student then repeated the experiment using a 5-g sample of bismuth decayed from lead, and a 2.5-g sample of polonium decayed from bismuth. His observations are recorded in Tables 1, 2, and 3.

Table 1

Time Elapsed (min)	Mass Lead (g)
0	10.0
10	8.15
20	6.30
30	4.50

Table 2

Time Elapsed (min)	Mass Bismuth (g)
0	5.0
10	3.75
20	2.50
30	1.25

Table 3

Time Elapsed (microseconds)	Mass Polonium (g)
0	2.50
50	2.11
100	1.72
150	1.33

21. Based on the information in Table 1, which of the following represents the range in which the student would expect to find the half-life of lead?
   A. 0–10 minutes
   B. 10–20 minutes
   C. 20–30 minutes
   D. 30–40 minutes

22. Based on the information in Figure 1 and Tables 1, 2, and 3, which of the following substances has the smallest half-life?
   F. Lead
   G. Bismuth
   H. Polonium
   J. Half-lives are identical for all these substances.

23. Which of the following lists the shields in Figure 1 in decreasing order of the sizes of the openings that they each have through which particles can pass?
    A. 1, 2, 3
    B. 3, 2, 1
    C. 2, 1, 3
    D. 3, 1, 2

24. Which table(s) of results from Experiment 2 present(s) data that are internally inconsistent with the concept of exponential radioactive decay?
    F. Table 1
    G. Table 2
    H. Table 3
    J. All of the tables

25. Which step in the decay chain of ^{222}Radon most likely emits the greatest number of larger particles as a percentage of the total particles it emits?
    A. Radon to polonium
    B. Polonium to lead
    C. Lead to bismuth
    D. Bismuth to polonium

26. Lead 214 has an atomic mass of 214 and an atomic number of 82. If lead 214 experiences alpha particle decay, what will the new atomic mass and atomic number be?
    F. Mass: 212, Number: 80
    G. Mass: 210, Number: 80
    H. Mass: 210, Number: 82
    J. Mass: 214, Number: 78

27. The student wishes to find whether a beta particle or positron passed through shield 1 and is absorbed by shield 2. In order to test for this, he should use a device that measures which of the following?
    A. Mass
    B. Charge
    C. Velocity
    D. Acceleration

PASSAGE V

Physics students conducted experiments to determine the refraction indices of different substances. They used Snell's Law, which describes the properties of light that is refracted as it goes through one medium and the interface of another medium. Snell's Law is as follows:

$$\frac{\sin \theta_1}{\sin \theta_2} = \frac{v_1}{v_2} = \frac{n_2}{n_1}$$

in which the angles (θ) are the angles that the light is traveling with respect to its current medium, the velocity (v) is the speed at which the light is traveling, and the Refractive Index (n) is a constant value that determines the refraction of the light based on the makeup of the medium. Everything with a subscript of "1" refers to the light as it goes through the first substance, and everything with a subscript of "2" refers to the light as it goes through the other substance.

The Refractive Index (n) of a substance is determined by taking the velocity of light in a vacuum (c), and dividing it by the velocity of light in the medium (v). This is given in the following equation:

$$n = \frac{c}{v}$$

A graph of this phenomenon is provided below:

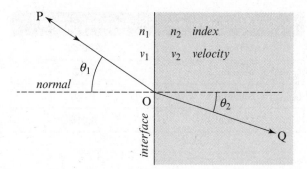

Experiment 1

A laser beam was shone through some known mediums at room temperature and standard atmospheric pressure. The angles of the light were measured using a highly precise electronic protractor, which enabled the Refractive Indexes to be recorded. The greater the light was bent, the greater the Refractive Index. The results of the experiment are in Table 1 below.

Table 1

Medium/Material	Refractive Index (n)
Vacuum	1.00000
Water	1.3330
Carbon dioxide	1.00045
Diamond	2.419
Cubic zirconia	2.16
Air	1.00028
Silicon	4.01
Human cornea	1.3375

Experiment 2

The procedure from Experiment 1 was repeated using four unknown substances. The refractive indexes are provided in the table below.

Table 2

Medium/Material Number	Refractive Index (n)
Material 1	1.00025
Material 2	2.17
Material 3	1.765
Material 4	4.015

28. Which of the materials in Experiment 2 is most likely Cubic Zirconia?
    F. Material 1
    G. Material 2
    H. Material 3
    J. Material 4

29. Light passing through which of the following mediums will be bent the least?
    A. Water
    B. Carbon dioxide
    C. Air
    D. Silicon

30. Which of the following expresses the velocity of light through a substance in terms of the speed of light in a vacuum and the refractive index of that substance?

 F. $v = \dfrac{c}{n}$

 G. $v = cn$

 H. $v = \dfrac{n}{c}$

 J. $v = cn^2$

31. According to the information in Table 1, light will travel most quickly through which substance, given that all other conditions are equal?
 A. Diamond
 B. Cubic zirconia
 C. Carbon dioxide
 D. Silicon

32. Based on the information in Table 1, it is most likely that the human eye is composed primarily of:
 F. carbon dioxide.
 G. water.
 H. silicon.
 J. air.

33. An optometrist is trying to determine the optimal material for a patient who has a cornea disorder to use in glasses lenses to see objects so that they will not be bent. Based on the information in Table 2, which of the following materials would be the best to use for the lenses of the glasses?
 A. Material 1
 B. Material 2
 C. Material 3
 D. Material 4

34. An unknown material is being tested for its Refractive Index. Is it possible that this material will have a Refractive Index of less than 1.0?
 F. Yes, as demonstrated by the information in Tables 1 and 2, some materials do have Refractive Indexes less than 1.0.
 G. Yes, if the angles through which the light is traveling through a medium are equivalent, the Refractive Index will be less than 1.0.
 H. No, nothing can have a Refractive Index less than 1.0, which is the Refractive Index of light in a vacuum.
 J. No, the Refractive Index of light through a wide variety of mediums remains constant.

PASSAGE VI

In 1869, a Russian-born chemist named Dmitri Mendeleev successfully designed the immediate predecessor to the modern periodic table of elements. Mendeleev was among the first to realize that when the elements are arranged in order of increasing atomic mass, certain chemical properties tend to repeat at regular intervals. As we now know that these "periodic trends" are the result of valence shell electrons, today the elements are arranged in order of atomic number rather than mass. However, Mendeleev's recognition of periodic law allowed him to predict with startling accuracy not merely the existence, but the chemical properties of then-undiscovered elements germanium, gallium, and scandium. Currently, the commonly acknowledged periodic trends are:

1. Electron affinity, which quantifies the amount of energy absorbed or emitted when an element acquires an additional electron in its valence shell. The magnitude of electron affinity increases (becomes more negative) from left to right across a period (with the exception of the noble gases) and decreases from top to bottom in a group.
2. Atomic radius, which is defined as the radial distance from the center of the atomic nucleus to the atom's outermost electron. Atomic radius decreases from left to right across a period and increases from top to bottom in a group.
3. Ionization energy, which quantifies the amount of energy required to remove one electron from a neutral element's valence shell. Ionization energy increases from left to right across a period and decreases from top to bottom in a group.
4. Electronegativity, which describes the degree of pull that an element exerts on shared electrons when it is involved in a chemical bond. Electronegativity increases from left to right across a period and decreases from top to bottom in a group.
5. Metallic character, which represents an element's likelihood to exhibit the physical, metallic properties of ductility, malleability, and heat/energy conduction. Metallic character decreases from left to right across a period and increases from top to bottom in a group.

A simple representation of the modern periodic table is shown in Figure 1.

Periodic Table of the Elements

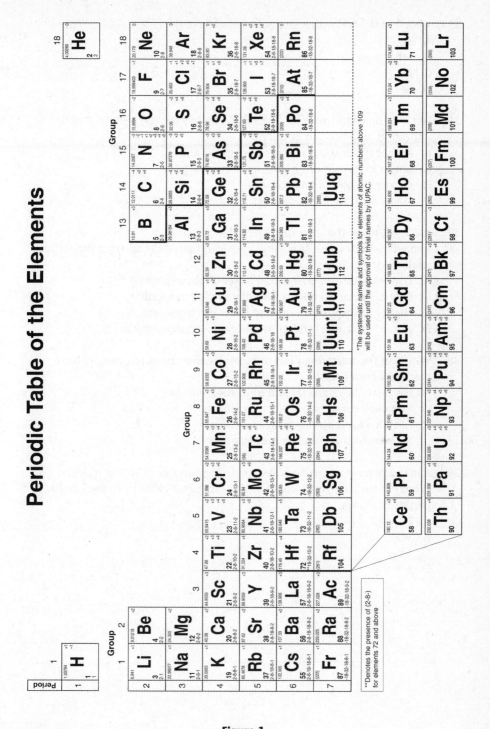

Figure 1

35. Which of the following elements would have the largest atomic radius?
    A. Ti
    B. Mn
    C. Zn
    D. Br

36. What is the relationship of Carbon (C) to Oxygen (O) with respect to ionization and electron affinity?
    F. Higher in ionization, lower in electron affinity
    G. Lower in ionization, higher in electron affinity
    H. Higher for both characteristics
    J. Lower for both characteristics

37. It is most likely that scientists were able to predict, prior to its discovery, that Scandium (Sc) had what properties relative to Selenium (Se)?
    A. Lower ionization energy and lower electronegativity
    B. Lower ionization energy and higher electronegativity
    C. Higher ionization energy and lower electronegativity
    D. Higher ionization energy and higher electronegativity

38. Which of the following pairs of periodic table characteristics are NOT positively correlated?
    F. Nonmetallic character and ionization energy
    G. Metallic character and electron affinity
    H. Atomic radius and metallic character
    J. Electron affinity and electronegativity

39. A manufacturer wishes to make a cooking pan that will heat quickly. Which of the following would likely be the best element to use for this purpose?
    A. N
    B. Al
    C. Cu
    D. F

40. An unknown elemental substance is found to have the following characteristics:

- Nonmetallic
- High electron affinity
- High ionization energy

Which of the following is most likely the unknown substance?
F. Fluorine
G. Oxygen
H. Nitrogen
J. Hydrogen

If there is still time remaining, you may review your answers.

WRITING TEST

Time: 40 Minutes

Foreign Aid

Poverty in third-world countries is a major global concern. With a significant economic gap between well-developed and developing countries, many argue that relatively prosperous countries should increase their help to impoverished nations. Foreign aid could take many forms—providing direct monetary contributions from the government, building health infrastructure, providing better educational opportunities, or promoting business investment. While many see a need to provide help to the needy, there are concerns about whether corruption and inefficiency will make aid efforts futile. With human fortunes and lives at stake, foreign aid is a critical current topic.

Read and carefully evaluate these points of view. Each puts forth a specific way of thinking about foreign aid.

Viewpoint One	Viewpoint Two	Viewpoint Three
True charity cannot be forced by mandatory government aid. Meaningful help for those in needy countries can only come from deeply passionate individuals who willingly sacrifice their time, money, and expertise.	How can people in developed countries have large homes and enormous meals when there are people in other countries who are homeless and starving? It is fundamentally immoral for there to be widespread inequality.	Governments in more developed countries need to put first things first—if their own citizens lack adequate education, healthcare, and nutrition, what business do they have taking care of people in distant lands?

ESSAY ASSIGNMENT

Compose a focused essay in which you consider multiple viewpoints on foreign aid. In your response, be certain to

- examine and assess the viewpoints provided
- express and develop your own point of view on the topic
- analyze the connections between your point of view and those provided

Your viewpoint may completely agree, somewhat agree, or not agree at all with any of those presented. No matter your perspective, provide clear, logical arguments supported by detailed examples to make your case.

Planning Your Response

Your prewriting notes on this page will not be considered in your score.

Use the following space to brainstorm ideas and map out your response. You may want to think about the following as you analyze the given prompt:

Strengths and weaknesses of the three viewpoints

- What good points do they make, and what potential objections do they ignore?
- Why might they be convincing to readers, and why might their perspectives fall short?

Your previous experience, background knowledge, and personal values

- What is your viewpoint on this topic, and what are the pros and cons of this viewpoint?
- How will you craft an argument in support of your point of view?

ANSWER KEY

English

1. B	16. F	31. D	46. H	61. A
2. F	17. C	32. H	47. A	62. G
3. D	18. G	33. A	48. G	63. D
4. F	19. C	34. G	49. D	64. G
5. B	20. G	35. C	50. J	65. D
6. H	21. A	36. G	51. C	66. F
7. D	22. F	37. C	52. F	67. B
8. H	23. C	38. F	53. C	68. H
9. B	24. F	39. B	54. F	69. D
10. F	25. B	40. F	55. B	70. G
11. A	26. G	41. B	56. G	71. D
12. J	27. D	42. H	57. A	72. F
13. A	28. H	43. A	58. J	73. C
14. G	29. B	44. J	59. B	74. F
15. A	30. C	45. A	60. C	75. D

Mathematics

1. D	13. E	25. B	37. E	49. B
2. G	14. G	26. G	38. H	50. J
3. C	15. B	27. B	39. D	51. E
4. F	16. K	28. H	40. H	52. G
5. D	17. C	29. C	41. B	53. C
6. F	18. G	30. G	42. J	54. D
7. E	19. B	31. A	43. C	55. B
8. J	20. H	32. K	44. G	56. F
9. B	21. E	33. D	45. B	57. D
10. H	22. G	34. G	46. J	58. J
11. D	23. D	35. C	47. A	59. D
12. H	24. H	36. H	48. H	60. G

Reading

1. C	9. C	17. B	25. B	33. B
2. G	10. G	18. J	26. G	34. F
3. A	11. B	19. C	27. A	35. B
4. J	12. F	20. F	28. H	36. G
5. B	13. B	21. D	29. B	37. C
6. J	14. G	22. F	30. H	38. F
7. A	15. B	23. A	31. C	39. B
8. G	16. G	24. F	32. H	40. H

Science

1. D	9. A	17. C	25. B	33. A
2. J	10. J	18. G	26. G	34. H
3. B	11. B	19. B	27. B	35. A
4. F	12. J	20. G	28. G	36. G
5. A	13. A	21. C	29. C	37. D
6. H	14. H	22. H	30. F	38. H
7. C	15. A	23. A	31. B	39. B
8. G	16. H	24. J	32. G	40. H

ACT SCORING GUIDE

(These norms are based on sampling classes of students, not on a nationwide sample.)

Calculate your overall composite score by adding the individual scores from each of the four sections and dividing by 4. You can round up.

Score	English	Math	Reading	Science	Score
36	75	60	40	40	36
35	74	58–59	38–39	38–39	35
34	72–73	56–57	36–37	36–37	34
33	71	54–55	35	35	33
32	70	52–53	34	34	32
31	69	50–51	33	33	31
30	68	49	32	32	30
29	66–67	48	31	31	29
28	65	46–47	29–30	30	28
27	63–64	44–45	27–28	29	27
26	61–62	42–43	26	28	26
25	59–60	40–41	25	26–27	25
24	57–58	38–39	23–24	24–25	24
23	55–56	36–37	22	23	23
22	53–54	34–35	21	21–22	22
21	50–52	32–33	20	20	21
20	47–49	30–31	18–19	18–19	20
19	44–46	28–29	17	16–17	19
18	42–43	25–27	16	15	18
17	40–41	22–24	15	14	17
16	37–39	19–21	14	12–13	16
15	35–36	16–18	13	11	15
14	33–34	12–15	12	10	14
13	30–32	9–11	10–11	9	13
12	28–29	7–8	8–9	8	12
11	25–27	6	7	7	11
10	23–24	5	6	6	10
9	20–22	4	5	5	9
8	17–19	3	–	4–5	8
7	14–16	–	4	3	7
6	12–13	2	–	–	6
5	9–11	–	3	2	5
4	6–8	1	2	–	4
3	4–5	–	1	1	3
2	2–3	–	–	–	2
1	0–1	0	0	0	1

ACT WRITING RUBRIC

<table>
<tr><td colspan="7">Ideas and Analysis: Considers multiple perspectives. Develops a clear and sophisticated thesis. Provides a useful context for analyzing the issue. Analyzes the implications, complexities, and underlying assumptions of different viewpoints.</td><td rowspan="2"></td></tr>
<tr><td>6: Excellent</td><td>5: Skillful</td><td>4: Adequate</td><td>3: Fair</td><td>2: Weak</td><td>1: Poor</td><td>_____ /6</td></tr>
</table>

<table>
<tr><td colspan="7">Development and Support: Provides an insightful and well-supported argument, placing the issue in a broad context. Uses reasoning and illustration to express the significance of the issue. Demonstrates an understanding of the complexity of the topic.</td><td rowspan="2"></td></tr>
<tr><td>6: Excellent</td><td>5: Skillful</td><td>4: Adequate</td><td>3: Fair</td><td>2: Weak</td><td>1: Poor</td><td>_____ /6</td></tr>
</table>

<table>
<tr><td colspan="7">Organization: Shows a skillful overall organizational approach. Has a clear, sustained position, accompanied by a logical sequence of ideas that builds the writer's argument. Provides clear and logical transitions between sentences and paragraphs.</td><td rowspan="2"></td></tr>
<tr><td>6: Excellent</td><td>5: Skillful</td><td>4: Adequate</td><td>3: Fair</td><td>2: Weak</td><td>1: Poor</td><td>_____ /6</td></tr>
</table>

<table>
<tr><td colspan="7">Language Use: The essay's language is well-suited to the argument. Vocabulary choice is precise and appropriate. Sentence structure is clear and varied. Tone, voice, and style are effective. Grammar, usage, and mechanics issues are minimized and do not interfere with the reader's understanding.</td><td rowspan="2"></td></tr>
<tr><td>6: Excellent</td><td>5: Skillful</td><td>4: Adequate</td><td>3: Fair</td><td>2: Weak</td><td>1: Poor</td><td>_____ /6</td></tr>
</table>

Essay Raw Score:	_____ /24

Multiply your Essay Raw Score by 1.5 to get your approximate ACT Writing Scaled Score:

Essay Raw Score: _____ × 1.5 = _____ out of 36 possible points.

ACT Writing Scaled Score:	_____ /36

ANSWER EXPLANATIONS

English

1. **(B)** strikes an appropriate balance between description and wordiness. (A) is not sufficiently descriptive and (C) and (D) are both too wordy.

2. **(F)** provides the necessary details to clarify what would otherwise be a vague pronoun. Pronouns are fine to use so long as we know that to which they are referring, which would not be the case here.

3. **(D)** places a comma after the introductory, dependent clause. An independent clause (complete sentence) then follows starting with "there has." (A) doesn't work because we need a pause here, (B) has a semicolon, which requires a complete sentence on either side of it, and (C) puts the comma in the wrong place.

4. **(F)** since "ensure" means to "make certain something will take place." "Insure" has to do with money, "assure" has more to do with *saying* than with *doing*, and "reassure" involves restoring confidence.

5. **(B)** gives the intended meaning—the inventor made an original creation. (A) and (C) would refer to the inventor's personal origin rather than something the inventor made. (D) also refers to the inventor's personal origin while shifting the intended meaning from something the inventor created to the creativity itself.

6. **(H)** provides relevant description to clarify what is being mentioned—based on the context, it is important to show that inventors don't merely want to create, but that they want to create items worthy of commercial success. (F), (G), and (J) are too vague.

7. **(D)** There is no need for this information because the focus of the paragraph is on the legal and economic reasons for a patent system. Although it is superficially relevant since it mentions patents, it doesn't discuss the aspect of patents on which the paragraph focuses.

8. **(H)** puts it in the appropriate past tense with the "was" making it singular, thereby agreeing with "Lewis Latimer." (F) is too wordy and uses the incorrect verb tense. (G) is too wordy, and (J) does not have correct subject-verb agreement since "were" is plural.

9. **(B)** If we took out these words, it would sound as though Latimer "worked for a law firm where he mastered the art of patents." This would be too vague—what does "the art of patents" entail? Leaving these words in provides specific description as to what exactly he learned.

10. **(F)** correctly provides a heavy pause on either side of the names, since they interrupt the flow of the sentence. Although commas could also work to make this separation if used in place of both dashes, there are too few commas in (G) and (H) and too many in (J).

11. **(A)** puts the events in the paragraph in correct chronological order, starting with Latimer's birth, then his youth, and finally his early career.

12. **(J)** places the phrases in the sentence in the most logical sequence. The other choices have the same information but do not have logical flows.

13. **(A)** "Second" provides the most logical introduction to the sentence since it is parallel to the format found in the previous sentence that begins with "First." The author is listing off two different ways that Latimer contributed to the world of invention.

14. **(G)** is correct with the tense (present) and subject-verb agreement (singular). It is also not unnecessarily wordy.

15. **(A)** The essay as a whole does indeed focus on the life and contributions of inventor Lewis Latimer. Although it mentions other inventors and mentions patent law/expertise, it does not *focus* on these items.

16. **(F)** since "you" is the wording used throughout the essay. The essay is more casual and conversational in tone.

17. **(C)** A colon works here to give a strong break before the clarifying quotation. (B) and (D) do not provide a needed quotation mark to begin the quote, and (A) lacks a needed comma and an apostrophe on the second "its."

18. **(G)** preserves the intended meaning while not being wordy. The other choices all use unnecessary words.

19. **(C)** is the only answer that gives "a specific economic reason" as to why people would use social networking. (A) and (B) are not sufficiently specific, and (D) focuses on economics but not on social networking.

20. **(G)** uses a dash that correctly gives a heavy pause between the two independent clauses in the sentence. (F) has a comma splice. (H) and (J) have appropriate punctuation, but their modifications of "compromise" change it to usages that incorrectly modify the intended meaning.

21. **(A)** If we did not have this introductory phrase, we would have no idea of the conditions under which social media networks will permit premium access. (B) is incorrect because it does not provide a specific explanation—it simply states the policy.

22. **(F)** is consistent with what immediately follows in the sentence, since leveraging connections among friends and family would indeed be a "strategy," not a "networking" as (G) states. (H) has an unclear pronoun, "it." (J) has far too formal a tone for this conversational essay.

23. **(C)** "Among" is appropriate to use when talking about three or more things—surely the average person has three or more friends or family members. "Between," as in (D), is used for comparing two items. "Within," as in (A), and "throughout," as in (B), are mostly used when discussing physical locations and would be inappropriate when mentioning connections with people.

24. **(F)** Earlier in the paragraph the author mentions how it is important to use the connections of friends and family in seeking employment. (F) provides the most direct and logical explanation as to why an employer would find these kinds of recommendations helpful. (G), (H), and (J) all provide logical strategies an employer would use, but they don't connect to the context of the rest of the paragraph.

25. **(B)** has logical word order and correctly uses "than" since the author is doing a comparison. "Then," as used in (C) and (D), is used for time. (A) inverts the word order in an awkward way.

26. **(G)** The previous paragraph focuses on the benefits of using friends and family to make job connections, and the current paragraph focuses on independent, individual tasks one can do to help land a job. (G) is the only option that successfully connects both of these themes in a comprehensive way.

27. **(D)** uses the pronoun "it" in reference to the "Chamber of Commerce," provides a complete sentence (which is necessary after a semicolon), and puts the words in a logical sequence. (A) has an inverted word order and does not use proper wording in saying "as a result of it," with the "it" referring to the Chamber of Commerce. (B) does not provide a complete sentence after the semicolon, and (C) uses passive voice.

28. **(H)** gives the correct logical transition between the two parts of the sentence, with the first part mentioning the expense of these shows, and the second part showing how the price can indeed be worthwhile.

29. **(B)** puts the phrase at the beginning of the sentence, where it provides a transition from the previous sentence, which focuses on how an investment in trade shows can pay off. The other options do not provide this transition and would interrupt the flow of the sentence.

30. **(C)** correctly encompasses the focus of the essay as a whole, which is how one should use networking to find a job. A quick skim of the topic sentences of each of the paragraphs of the essay should be enough to help you determine the essay's focus.

31. **(D)** The question asks which would NOT be acceptable, and (D) uses "whom," which we use with people, not with numbers.

32. **(H)** is the only answer that does not interrupt the phrase "think of trigonometry," which should not have any punctuation within it.

33. **(A)** uses the proper phrasing of "difference between," which is needed to convey the logical comparison of two different items. It is incorrect to say "difference of" when comparing two things, as in (B). (C) uses "differently," which is an adverb. It does not make sense to say "difference within," as in (D), since we are doing a comparison between two separate items rather than looking at the difference within one item.

34. **(G)** Stating "the ratio of the circumference of a circle to its diameter" provides the most logical and specific definition as the question demands. (F) and (H) are too vague, and (J) doesn't provide a definition.

35. **(C)** sets the name of the teacher off to the side by surrounding it with commas. It is necessary to do this because it is an appositive, with the description of "my math teacher" clear enough to narrow it down to one person, making it fine to surround the person's name with commas. The other answers do not provide needed pauses.

36. **(G)** keeps the sentence from being repetitive while maintaining the intended meaning. Later in the sentence it says the celebration is held "each year," making it unnecessary to say "annual," as in (F), or "yearly," as in (H). (J) changes the intended meaning because "Pi Day" is more of a tradition or celebration, not merely an "occurrence."

37. **(C)** We want what is LEAST acceptable as an alternative to "multifaceted," which means having many parts or facets. (C), "difficult," does not necessarily mean that something would have many parts. (A), "multipart"; (B), "complex"; and (D), "elaborate," all convey much more of a sense of having many parts.

38. **(F)** is the only choice that is in the present tense, as the rest of the paragraph is.

39. **(B)** both focuses on the topic of the paragraph *and* introduces a lighter tone. (A) deals with the topic of the paragraph, but is in a serious tone. (C) is a lighter tone, but is not relevant to the paragraph. (D) is irrelevant to the paragraph and has a serious tone.

40. **(F)** uses the word "suppose," which would indicate a limited degree of confidence, as the question demands. (G), "undoubtedly"; (H), "disagree"; and (J), "know," all indicate a *great deal* of confidence.

41. **(B)** is the most concise and grammatically correct option. (A) and (D) are too wordy, and (C) refers to a joke products company as a person by using "who."

42. **(H)** provides a logical transition between the previous sentence that discusses how a joke products company manufactures a fake ATM receipt with an extraordinarily large amount of money on it, and the following sentences that explain how someone could use the receipt to pretend to have far more money than one actually does in order to seduce a date.

43. **(A)** This refers to "a potential date," which would be a singular person, making "his or her" appropriate.

44. **(J)** It makes the most sense to add emphasis to an adjective, like "really," because the author can show the great degree to which one might be interested in going on a date.

45. **(A)** discusses why keeping this phrase would be correct. Even though the "Ides of March" is known by some people, it demands some clarification for general readership.

46. **(H)** places the scientific name for "Hammerhead sharks" in commas, appropriately moving this helpful but nonessential phrase out of the way. (F) and (G) do not isolate the phrase, and (J) is inconsistent in its punctuation—a dash on either side of the phrase would be fine, but a comma and a dash mixed together like this would not work.

47. **(A)** gives the correct possessive word, "their," referring to the plural "Hammerhead sharks."

48. **(G)** is the only option that is both parallel with the earlier phrasing in the sentence, "grow up to," and not too wordy.

49. **(D)** When referring to a species, we can use the singular form of the species name. So, we can say "The hammerhead" in order to refer to the species as a whole. Then, we need an apostrophe followed by an "s" to indicate possession since it is singular. (A) does not show possession, (B) uses the adverb "uniquely" instead of "unique," and (C) uses the plural form of "hammerhead" along with the adverb.

50. **(J)** The question seeks what is LEAST acceptable as an alternative. "Since" provides a more direct causal relationship, which (F), (G), and (H) would do. Using "once" would take away this direct causal relationship.

51. **(C)** is the only answer that both uses "originally" correctly (since we are referring to the way they *thought* and we must use an adverb) and clarifies the subject of the sentence by saying "researchers."

52. **(F)** Although these words are all similar in their dictionary definitions, "sharp" is the best fit for describing physical turns that an animal would make.

53. **(C)** gives a precise description of the range of a shark's vision, as the question demands. The other options are all too vague.

54. **(F)** places "continuously" at the end of the sentence, giving the logical meaning that hammerheads can see what is below and above them at the same time. It would be inappropriate to place it before "vertical" or "plane," as in (G) or (H), because we would have the adverb "continuously" describing nouns. It would be nonsensical to place it after "is" because that would indicate that there are objects that never move from above or beneath them.

55. **(B)** provides a logical comparison between the "small mouths" and "those," which stands in for *the mouths of other fish species*. We need to compare "mouths" to "mouths," not "mouths" to "species," which (A) and (D) would do. (C) is numerically incorrect, using the singular "that" instead of the plural "those."

56. **(G)** The sentence currently indicates that hammerheads are one of the few species to both feed from the ocean floor and in schools—if we moved this

phrase, it would indicate that they are only unique because of feeding off the ocean floor, with no uniqueness resulting from feeding in schools.

57. **(A)** since we are referring to plural sharks possessing "increased melanin production."

58. **(J)** is the only option that is in the present tense, as is the surrounding context, and is numerically in agreement with the plural subject, "Researchers."

59. **(B)** is the correct idiom to use. We need to follow "resemblances" with "in" rather than with a different preposition, like "by," "within," or "of."

60. **(C)** Sentence 3 needs to follow 1, since it explains why we don't know much about hammerhead sharks from the Tertiary Period. Sentence 4 needs to follow 2, since it elaborates on the evolutionary link between hammerheads and carcharhinid sharks.

61. **(A)** conveys the most logical meaning, namely that the plastic bars are pushing in an awkward way into the narrator's back. (B) is too wordy and uses awkward wording, (C) would literally say the plastic bars are pressure points, and (D) lacks a verb.

62. **(G)** gives an appropriate introduction to the sentence, which transitions from the previous sentence about how it seems very dark, to the current sentence, which explains how it becomes much brighter as a result of taking off the sunglasses. (F) would show contrast, (H) would show a direct cause-effect, and (J) is like the word "furthermore."

63. **(D)** We cannot use "stupidly," which is an adverb, in front of the noun, "sunlight." Only an adjective like "stupid" would be appropriately placed here. Don't neglect the "EXCEPT" in the question.

64. **(G)** We need to use the infinitive form of the verb, "to distinguish," and also need to use the correct idiomatic preposition, "from," since we would not say "distinguish of."

65. **(D)** uses the correct idiom, "trudging through," since the narrator is walking through the sand to the water.

66. **(F)** puts the words in the most logical order, unlike (G), which would change the meaning of the original phrase. (H) is too wordy, and (J) would remove the important clarifying information in this phrase.

67. **(B)** conveys the thought process that empowers the narrator to take the plunge into the water, providing a logical connection between the two sentences. (A), (C), and (D) all are contradicted by the fact that the narrator *does* jump in the water in the next sentence.

68. **(H)** unnecessarily separates descriptive adjectives from what they are describing (i.e., the water), and so would NOT work.

69. **(D)** is the best placement for this sentence because sentence 5 describes young children playing.

70. **(G)** We need to start this part of the sentence with "I," so that we clarify who is heading back to the wonderfully comfortable beach chair. (F) would indicate the "sand" is heading back. (H) lacks a subject. (J) has awkward phrasing by saying "wetly stick."

71. **(D)** puts the verb in the correct tense, present, and correct number, singular, so that it agrees with the subject "boy."

72. **(F)** uses the correct idiomatic expression, "in protest to."

73. **(C)** puts a comma after the introductory dependent clause, "Heeding the voices in my head." No other comma is necessary.

74. **(F)** uses the correct word option, "laying," which refers to the physical act of placing something. "Lying" would be to recline or to tell a lie, and "lieing" is not a word. "Lain" is the past participle (like "had lain").

75. **(D)** The question asks if the essay would provide a thorough explanation of the events that took place over a week, but the essay only focuses on a relatively short period of time spent sunbathing.

Mathematics

1. **(D)** Each book is an independent choice, so multiply the numbers together:

$$15 \times 12 \times 5 \times 21 = 18,900$$

2. **(G)** The path is sketched below:

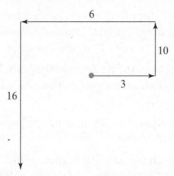

This makes for a net change of 3 miles to the west, and 6 miles to the south, as sketched below:

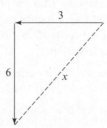

Then use the Pythagorean theorem to solve for the direct distance between the starting point and ending point:

$$3^2 + 6^2 = x^2$$

$$\sqrt{3^2 + 6^2} = x$$

$$6.7 \approx x$$

3. **(C)** 41 grams represents 14% of the normal daily sugar allowance, so we can make an expression to solve for the normal daily sugar allowance (x):

$$41 \text{ grams} = 0.14x$$

$$\frac{41}{0.14} \approx 293 \approx x$$

The fact that the soft drink is 12 ounces is irrelevant to solving this problem.

4. **(F)** The numerator is $\dfrac{3}{4} + \dfrac{2}{3} = \dfrac{9}{12} + \dfrac{8}{12} = \dfrac{17}{12}$.

The denominator is $\dfrac{5}{6} - \dfrac{1}{4} = \dfrac{10}{12} - \dfrac{3}{12} = \dfrac{7}{12}$.

Divide the numerator by the denominator to get the answer: $\dfrac{\frac{17}{12}}{\frac{7}{12}} = \dfrac{17}{7}$

5. **(D)** $(5x^3)^{-\frac{2}{3}} = \dfrac{1}{(5x^3)^{\frac{2}{3}}} = \dfrac{1}{5^{\frac{2}{3}} x^{\frac{6}{3}}} = \dfrac{1}{\sqrt[3]{25}x^2} = \dfrac{1}{x^2\sqrt[3]{25}}$

6. **(F)** Since the lines are parallel and are cut by a transversal, $A = B = W = Z$ and $C = D = Y = X$. (The big angles are all equal and the small angles are all equal.) Any one of the first set of angles will be supplementary to an angle from the second set, meaning for example that $A + C = 180°$. So, if we have two angles from the first set and two from the second set, they will add up to360°. $A + B + Y + X$ is the only one of the options that would do this.

7. **(E)** In order to have a total of 1,500 letters, the Editor will need a total of 15 boxes of envelopes, 30 information sheet sets, 8 boxes of return cards (since we cannot buy just 7.5 boxes), and 1,500 stamps. Multiply the units by their respective prices and then add the amounts to get the grand total for the budget:

$$15 \times \$5 + 30 \times \$15 + 8 \times \$10 + 1{,}500 \times \$0.44 = \$1{,}265.00$$

8. **(J)** The clock chimes 6 times at 6:00, 7 times at 7:00, and once each at 5:15, 5:30, 5:45, 6:15, 6:30, 6:45, 7:15, and 7:30 for 8 more times. $6 + 7 + 8 = 21$.

9. **(B)** At least two of the sides must be equivalent in order for a triangle to be isosceles. (B) is the only option that does not have at least two of the sides equal. An equilateral triangle is still isosceles, so (D) is not correct.

10. **(H)** $2 \times \dfrac{3}{8} = \dfrac{6}{8} = \dfrac{3}{4}$ which is NOT equivalent to $2\dfrac{3}{8}$.

11. **(D)** Visualize each of the conditions as a circle and put them within one another as the conditions dictate:

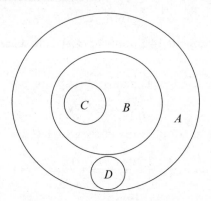

From this, we can see that C must always fall within A.

12. **(H)** Each half of the race will be 13.1 miles. Use the formula Distance = Rate × Time to determine the time for each half, which we will call T_1 and T_2.

Time for the first half: $D = RT$ so $13.1 = 8T_1$, making the time for the first half

$$\frac{13.1}{8} = 1.6375.$$

Time for the second half: $D = RT$ so $13.1 = 6T_2$, making the second half time

$$\frac{13.1}{6} = 2.183.$$

Then, add the times together to get the total time to complete the race:

$$1.6375 + 2.183 \approx 3.82.$$

13. **(E)** Multiply by 1.1 for each year where there was a 10% overall salary increase:

$$20,000 \times 1.1 \times 1.1 = 24,200$$

14. **(G)** This is simply a restatement of the Triangle Inequality Theorem, which states that the two shortest sides of a triangle must add up to more than the longest side.

15. **(B)** Don't worry about doing the x-coordinate—simply figure out the average of the y-coordinates.

$$\frac{8+8}{2} = 8$$

16. **(K)** The least common multiple of 10 and 8 is 40, and the greatest common factor of 10 and 8 is 2. So, the product of these two numbers would be 40 × 2 = 80.

17. **(C)** Just plug the 6 seconds in for t.

$$x(6) = 8 \cdot 6 + \frac{1}{2}(10)6^2 = 228$$

18. **(G)** Circumference = πD. The original circumference is $\pi \times 1 = \pi$. The new circumference is $\pi \times 1.25 = 125\pi$. The amount of the increase in circumference is $125\pi - \pi = 0.25\pi$. Determine the percent increase:

$$\frac{0.25\pi}{\pi} \times 100 = 25\%$$

19. **(B)** 2 is not the sum of two prime numbers, since 1 is not considered prime. 2 + 7 = 9 so 9 works. 11 has no two prime numbers that add together to make it.

20. **(H)** The boat will travel 10 × 3 = 30 miles to the east, and 20 × 2 = 40 miles to the north. You can then use the Pythagorean theorem to solve for the straight-line distance from its starting point:

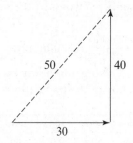

$30^2 + 40^2 = 50^2$ so 50 is the correct distance. This is also a multiple of the 3-4-5 special right triangle so if you see that, you can save yourself some time.

21. **(E)** The mean of a set of numbers is equal to the sum divided by how many numbers are in the set: $\frac{\text{Sum}}{\text{Number}}$ = Mean.

For this set, the mean can be calculated as follows:

$$\frac{46 + 72 + 84 + 51 + 67}{5} = \frac{320}{5} = 64$$

22. **(G)** Terri will have to pay $800,000 no matter how many days the restaurant is open, making this a fixed cost. Each day the restaurant is open, there will be $250 + $400 = $650 in costs. So, add the fixed cost of $800,000 together with $650 per day, and the expression is 800,000 + 650D.

23. **(D)** Divide the volume of the cube by the volume of the sphere. The cube uses x for its side length, and the sphere uses x for the radius:

$$\frac{x^3}{\left(\frac{4}{3}\right)\pi x^3}$$

The x^3 cancels from the top and bottom of the expression, leaving you with

$$\frac{1}{\frac{4}{3}\pi}.$$

24. **(H)** Calculate the probability by taking the number of yellow balls and dividing by the total number of balls of all colors:

$$\frac{8}{4+8+12} = \frac{8}{24} = \frac{1}{3}$$

25. **(B)** The total number of pages Veronica will read is

$$400 \text{ pages} \times 200 \text{ words per page} = 80,000 \text{ words}$$

Then, divide the total number of words by the number of pages Veronica can read per minute:

$$\frac{80,000}{250} = 320 \text{ minutes.}$$

26. **(G)** You can attack this in an organized way by writing out the values of the January dates and the values of the populations so you can see the pattern:

Date	1st	4th	7th	10th	13th	16th	19th	22nd
Population	10	20	40	80	160	320	640	1,280

Looking at this trend, it is clear that by January 21st the population in the town will exceed 1,000 people.

27. **(B)** A, I, O, and U can all be split right down the middle vertically:

E cannot.

28. **(H)** There are 18 computers that work, so the two classes must share 18 computers. You can think about it as two series of overlapping lines. The amount that they overlap will equal the amount that 14 + 12 is greater than 18:

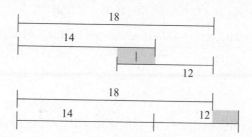

So, do 14 + 12 = 26 then do 26 – 18 = 8 to find the overlapping amount. Then, do 18 – 8 = 10 to find the number of computers that students will have to themselves. The 8 computers are used by pairs of students.

29. **(C)** Put the original equation in slope-intercept form to determine its slope:

$$-6x + 2y = -4$$
$$2y = 6x - 4$$
$$y = 3x - 2$$

So the slope of the original equation is 3. Find the *negative reciprocal* of 3 to determine the slope of a line perpendicular to this line, which is $-\dfrac{1}{3}$.

30. **(G)** Plug in 350° for F in the equation, and then solve for C.

$$350 = \frac{9}{5}C + 32$$

$$318 = \frac{9}{5}C$$

$$\frac{318}{\frac{9}{5}} \approx 177°C$$

31. **(A)** The center of the circle is (2, 3) and its radius is 4. So, plugging it into $(x - h)^2 + (y - k)^2 = r^2$, where (h, k) is the center point and r is the radius, the equation would be $(x - 2)^2 + (y - 3)^2 = 16$.

32. **(K)** You can plug in an even integer like 4 for m and try it out in each of the choices:

   F. $4^2 + 1 = 17$

   G. $4^{-2} - 4 = -3\dfrac{15}{16}$

   H. $4^3 + 1 = 65$

   J. $4^4 + 3 = 259$

   K. $4^6 - 2 = 4,094$

As we can see, 4,094 is the only one of these that is an even number. Since the question asks for what *must* be even, just one case where a choice is wrong would make it completely wrong.

33. **(D)** Another way of expressing this is $3^4 = x$. $3^4 = 81$.

34. **(G)** Set the equations equal to one another and solve for x:
$$2x + 4 = -3x - 5$$
$$5x = -9$$
$$x = -\frac{9}{5}$$

You can stop there because (G) is the only choice that has $-\frac{9}{5}$ as its x value.

35. **(C)** You can plug in numbers on this. For example, we can make $a = 2$ and $b = 2$. This would make $(-5a, -7b) = (-5 \times 2, -7 \times 2) = (-10, -14)$, which would be in the third quadrant.

36. **(H)** Take the 45 minutes for the wash cycle and divide it by the 70 minutes for the whites cycle:
$$\frac{45}{70} = \frac{9 \times 5}{14 \times 5} = \frac{9}{14}$$

37. **(E)** The cosine of angle A equals the adjacent side b divided by the hypotenuse c:
$$\cos A = \frac{b}{c}$$
So, to get the value of angle A, take the arccos of both sides (which is the inverse of the cosine function), which will get angle A by itself:
$$A = \arccos\left(\frac{b}{c}\right)$$

38. **(H)** To maximize the number of bricks sold, the smallest face of each brick should be used to cover the patio. The smallest face is 4 inches × 2 inches = 8 square inches in area. The area of the entire patio is given converting each of the patio dimensions to inches by multiplying the 12 feet by 12 inches and the 10 feet by 12 inches, making the patio 144 × 120 inches = 17,280 square inches. Then, divide the patio area by the brick area:
$$\frac{17,280}{8} = 2,160.$$

39. **(D)** Since there are two planning periods, the teacher will grade 40 papers then. The teacher will grade 10 papers for every x hour spent at home. So, the expression would be $40 + 10x$.

40. **(H)** Wayne believes the probability to be $\frac{6}{26}$ and Kristen believes it to be $\frac{5}{26}$.

$$\frac{6}{26} - \frac{5}{26} = \frac{1}{26}$$

$\dfrac{\frac{1}{26}}{\frac{5}{26}}$ = 0.2, which equates to a 20% higher amount

41. **(B)** The cube is 3 × 3 × 3 in its dimensions, so it has 27 cubes all together. However, the middle cube is empty, so 27 – 1 = 26 total smaller cubes.

42. **(J)** Each of the six sides will be a different color, with one full side being completely orange. So, the odds are $\frac{1}{6}$ that one side will be orange.

43. **(C)** The surface area of each side of the cube is 3 × 3 = 9, and there are 6 sides all together, so the surface area of the entire cube will be 9 × 6 = 54 square centimeters.

44. **(G)** Solve this in a couple of steps. First, find out what the hypotenuse is along one of the faces of the cube:

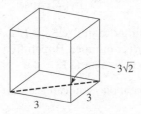

Then, you can make a right triangle that will enable you to solve for the distance between the two opposite corners:

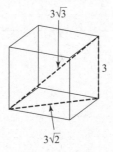

The Pythagorean theorem allowed us to make this calculation: $32 + \left(3\sqrt{2}\right)^2 = \left(3\sqrt{3}\right)^2$. So the distance between opposite corners would be $3\sqrt{3}$.

45. **(B)** Write it out in an organized way and multiply each term by –2 to get the next term:

Term Itself	2	–4	8	–16	32
Term Number	1st	2nd	3rd	4th	5th

So, 32 would be the correct answer.

46. **(J)** Turn it into an algebraic expression and then simplify:

$$\frac{5}{6}y + \frac{1}{3}y = \frac{5}{6}y + \frac{2}{6}y = \frac{7}{6}y$$

47. **(A)** Draw this out to visualize it, with the letters of the sides and angles being opposite of one another:

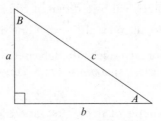

The cosine of angle A will be the $\dfrac{\text{adjacent}}{\text{hypotenuse}} = \dfrac{b}{c}$.

48. **(H)** The factors of 44 other than itself are 1, 2, 4, 11, and 22. They add up to 40, so 44 is not a perfect number. Hopefully you figured this out without having to try to factor choices J and K!

49. **(B)** If you graph the parabola, you can see that its vertex is its very lowest point:

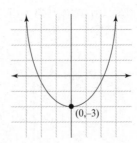

So, (0, –3) is the vertex.

50. **(J)** Draw a picture to visualize what happens:

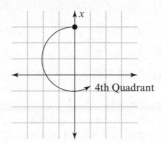

200 degrees of counterclockwise rotation will take it to the other side of the *y*-axis, since 360 degrees would be a full rotation.

51. **(E)** The original sine function will look like this:

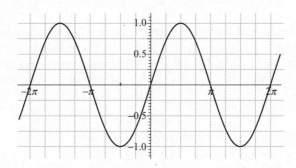

The modified sine function will look like this:

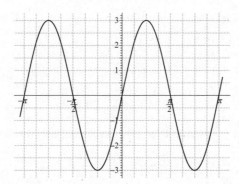

The "2" impacts the *frequency* of the function, with the sine function hitting the *x*-axis twice as often. The domain (*x* values) of the function will continue to be from positive to negative infinity. The "3" impacts the *amplitude* of the function, with the sine function *tripling* its *range* (*y* values).

52. **(G)** We know that out of the first 60 questions, Hannah has already gotten 50 questions right and 10 questions wrong. This means that her score would be $50 - \frac{1}{4} \times 10 = 47.5$ up to that point. So, she needs to get at least 22.5 more points in order to get a 70. She wants to omit as many questions as possible, so we should assume that out of the remaining questions, she should not miss any because these would not count toward her goal score nor would they count toward the number of questions omitted. Since she cannot answer any partial questions, she should get 23 of the remaining 40 questions right in order to get at least a 70. This would leave 17 questions omitted.

53. **(C)** We can determine the outer angle of the triangle since there are 180° in a triangle, and $180 - 12 - 18 = 150$

The total number of degrees in a regular polygon is determined by the formula $(n - 2)180 = $ *total degrees* where n represents the number of sides. The total number of degrees would be equal to $150 \times n$ in this case because each of the outer angles would be identical. So, we can set up the following expression and solve for n:

$$(n - 2)180 = 150n$$
$$180n - 360 = 150n$$
$$30n = 360$$
$$n = 12$$

54. **(D)** To subtract these from one another, put them in terms of a least common denominator. By multiplying $\frac{1}{20^{30}}$ by $\frac{20}{20}$, both parts will have a denominator of 20^{31}. We should express both parts with a common denominator and then simplify. Here is how we can simplify $\frac{1}{20^{30}}$.

$$\frac{1}{20^{30}} \times \frac{20}{20} = \frac{20}{20^{31}}$$

Now, subtract $\frac{1}{20^{31}}$ from this now that they have the same denominator:

$$\frac{20}{20^{31}} - \frac{1}{20^{31}} = \frac{19}{20^{31}}$$

55. **(B)** When multiplying a matrix by a number, multiply each cell of the matrix by the number for your result:

Take $3\begin{vmatrix} x & 2x \\ 4 & x^2 \end{vmatrix}$ and plug in 2 for x: $3\begin{vmatrix} 2 & 4 \\ 4 & 4 \end{vmatrix}$

Then multiply each cell by 3: $\begin{vmatrix} 3\times2 & 3\times4 \\ 3\times4 & 3\times4 \end{vmatrix} = \begin{vmatrix} 6 & 12 \\ 12 & 12 \end{vmatrix}$.

56. **(F)** We need to determine the area of the triangle and then divide it by the area of the whole circle. First, let's determine the area of the triangle. The base of the triangle is labeled as 4. What is the height? Figure it out by realizing that this is an equilateral triangle, with all the sides and angles equal. This allows us to see what the height would be using either the Pythagorean theorem or using the properties of a 30-60-90 triangle.

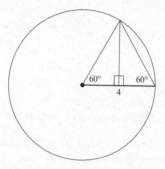

Let's take a closer look at one of the 30-60-90 triangles that makes up half of this equilateral triangle to determine what the height would be.

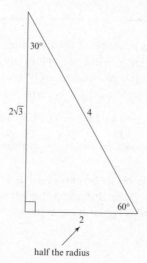

The height of the triangle is $2\sqrt{3}$ and the base of the triangle is 4, so the area is:

$$\frac{1}{2} \text{ Base} \times \text{Height} = \frac{1}{2} \times 4 \times 2\sqrt{3} = 4\sqrt{3}$$

The area of the circle as a whole is $\pi r^2 = \pi 4^2 = 16\pi$.

So, compute the percent the triangle's area is of the circle's area as follows:

$$\frac{4\sqrt{3}}{16\pi} \times 100 = 13.8\% \approx 14\%$$

57. **(D)** The period of a function corresponds to how long it takes to go through a full cycle without repeating. The smallest possible period of this function can be seen in the graph below:

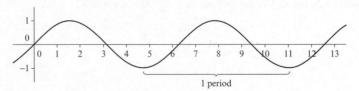

The function repeats about every 6 units. It also repeats about every 12 units, 24 units, etc., but the smallest possible period is 6 units.

58. **(J)** One way to solve this is to plug in points that would work within this range (i.e., values greater than 78 and less than 48), and gradually eliminate the choices. Another way is to think that the answers will be greater than 78 and less than 48 and put this on a number line:

In order to express this in terms of the absolute value, we must shift all the possible points to the left so that the values are symmetrical about zero. If we subtract 63 from all the values, the numbers would shift to the left so all the values would be symmetrical about zero:

$$48 - 63 = -15 \qquad 78 - 63 = 15$$

The set of values can therefore be expressed as $15 < |\text{height} - 63|$ since all of the height values have been shifted to the left 63 units, and the difference between the height and 63 must have an absolute value of greater than 15.

59. **(D)** Start by drawing a picture of the screen configuration to see what the different ratios would be.

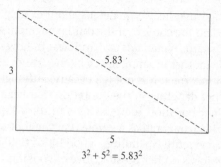

$$3^2 + 5^2 = 5.83^2$$

We can then set up a proportion to solve for what the horizontal length would be if the width is considered along the diagonal instead of along the bottom:

$$\frac{\text{horizontal length}}{\text{distance along diagonal}} = \frac{x}{48} = \frac{5}{5.83}$$

Cross-multiply to solve for x: $5.83x = 5 \times 48$ so $x = 41.16$.

Then, subtract 41.16 (the horizontal length if the 48 corresponds to the diagonal) from 48 (the horizontal length if the 48 corresponds to the width along the bottom of the TV).

$$48 - 41.16 \approx 7$$

60. **(G)** Carefully write this out:

Letter	C	A	F	E
Numerical Value	3	1	6	5

$$3 + 1 + 6 + 5 = 15$$

Reading

1. **(C)** This quotation connects the last paragraph to the first paragraph, where in lines 6–8 the narrator states "Like the ecstasies of shaman mystics in Peru, there are times when cooking can transport me, mentally, spiritually, through time and space." There is no evidence that she is making an *actual* religious sacrifice as in (A), doing an *actual* religious ritual, as in (B), or giving *real* food to the gods, as in (D). The metaphorical language instead implies that she is mystically connecting to the universe.

2. **(G)** Be sure that the first adjective applies to the mother and the second adjective to the father. The third paragraph (lines 19–32) clearly illustrates that the mother is very rational and precise in her approach, given her language and her movements. The fifth paragraph clearly illustrates that the father is

very sensual and intuitive in his approach, given how he doesn't follow a precise recipe but goes with his instincts. (G) is the only answer that correctly describes how the mother and father, respectively, approach cooking.

3. **(A)** This language gives us *precise* details about exactly how the quiche will be cooked. Based on the context of the third paragraph, we see that the narrator's mother is "sharp," "meticulous," and neat in how she cooks. While it is possible that the mother is happy in the kitchen, lines 29–32 do not speak to this, making (B) incorrect. It is not (C) because although the mother is short tempered with her daughter in the quotation that begins the paragraph, we do not see evidence of short temperedness in these lines. Finally, while we can infer from this paragraph as a whole that the mother might enjoy cooking, since she is evidently spending a good bit of time doing it, the lines in question do not focus on her possible love of cooking.

4. **(J)** This sentence from lines 58–60 clearly illustrates how the narrator is a synthesis of both her mother's precise personality, as portrayed in the third paragraph, and her father's more intuitive personality, as portrayed in the fifth paragraph: "My right hand counts out their proportions with surgical precision, while my left scoops them up in fistfuls, letting the excess fall between its fingers." Her right hand represents her mother's influence and her left hand represents her father's influence.

5. **(B)** There is ample evidence in this paragraph that the mother embraces American culture: She has chosen to live in Indianapolis, USA; she speaks English meticulously, and she neatly organizes her American recipes. There is no direct evidence that she actively practices Hinduism, as in (A). The reference to scissors in line 21 is metaphorical, making (C) incorrect. While she does calculate her proportions carefully, this is more as a means to the end of embracing American culture, making (D) a persuasive but ultimately incorrect choice.

6. **(J)** The first major flashback begins in lines 9–10, where smell evokes memories of the narrator's mother. Line 33 does not begin a flashback, but rather brings the narrator back to the present day. The *second* major flashback starts in line 45—reaching for a jar helps the narrator remember time spent with her father. *Touch* is the sensation that helps to bring about this association.

7. **(A)** Be sure that you notice the NOT in the question. The third paragraph discusses how the narrator's mother lives in Indianapolis and has learned to speak English precisely. Her mother is evidently doing all she can to embrace American culture. So, it would be illogical to conclude that the mother has returned to India to immerse herself in the Hindi language. (B) would be possible, since the mother and father live in very different cities. (C) could work, since the mother lives in Indianapolis and the dad lives in Calcutta. (D) could also work, since the narrator's flashback to her mom starts by saying that she was "nine again" (line 12). Her flashback to her father happens when she is a teenager (line 45).

8. **(G)** In lines 19–20, the narrator's mother scolds the narrator for trying to sink her fingers into the bowl. The narrator's father, on the other hand, has no problem dipping his finger into food in order to taste it (lines 51–52). So, we have direct evidence that the mother and father had different attitudes about culinary sanitation. Whereas it is possible that the mother and father have different attitudes about politics, English curricula, and architectural aesthetics, we do not find direct evidence of diverging views, as we do when it comes to keeping clean in the kitchen.

9. **(C)** The narrator's father is unable to speak the narrator's primary language—English. We can see this in lines 47–48: "He smiles at me because we can scarcely talk." Since the narrator and her father cannot communicate linguistically, the father uses hands-on techniques to demonstrate cooking techniques to his daughter, as seen throughout the fifth paragraph (lines 45–49). Lacking linguistic communication, a lecture (A) and a written manual (B) would not make sense to use. Although a multimedia presentation (D) could be more helpful than written or spoken presentations, there is no evidence that the narrator's father has access to the technology that would be required to do this.

10. **(G)** Be sure you notice the NOT in this question. Lines 45–46 mentions that the narrator has been raised in Indiana, making (F) incorrect. She has visited her father's house in Calcutta based on line 46, making (H) incorrect. The only mention of Peru is in line 10 where it is used to express a metaphorical analogy between religious practices and the art of cooking, making (G) correct. Since the narrator *has* evidently been to two of the places in the choices, (J) would be wrong.

11. **(B)** The key thing to focus on in reading this question is what is the "main purpose." We must consider why the author wrote this piece, and illustration of the controversy of the noodle's origin is the main purpose we find. We see this because throughout the text, China, Italy, and the Middle East are all presented as making claims to be the originators of the noodle. (A) and (C) give information that is mentioned in the passage, but they do not discuss the main purpose. (D) also gives information that is in the passage, but the Laija discovery did not settle the controversy conclusively.

12. **(F)** According to lines 50–53, China has the oldest known evidence of noodle making but also cements this finding by arguing that the skill that was demonstrated in the particular noodle's creation could only exist with a long familiarity on the part of the Chinese in making them.

13. **(B)** The transition is to lines 37–53 where there is an in-depth investigation into the archaeological discovery at Laija in China. It is not (A) because there is no conclusive establishment that China is the originator of the noodle in this section, nor in any part of the text. If it had been (C), we would find much more specific scientific information, but this section is way too vague. If it had been (D), we would find further discussion of the events leading into the noodles' creation.

14. **(G)** Be sure you didn't neglect the NOT in the question. The answer is not (F) because a number of cultures that use noodles are mentioned, such as Chinese and Middle Eastern. The answer is not (H) because the complex process of production is discussed in line 5. The answer is not (J) because in line 7, the author mentions the noodle's widespread appeal. This leaves us with (G) through process of elimination.

15. **(B)** "Skill" makes the most sense here because we are discussing how the noodles are made. No one is inventing a noodle, researching its creation, or studying the noodle.

16. **(G)** In lines 57–61, the author leaves the question of the noodle's origin open, while acknowledging the interest in the question itself. "Unsettled" simply means that it has not been decided.

17. **(B)** Be sure to focus on the use of this sentence rather than just summarizing what it means. The contrast is between the cultural observation that Italy is widely assumed to be the originator of the noodle and the historical fact that Italy has not had the noodle all that long relative to other countries. (C) and (D) try to trap us with specific information that was in the passage. (A) seems persuasive, but the first part where it states that it is "mistaken information" is not the case here. The author is merely observing that people may be mistaken, which is different from presenting mistaken information himself. Additionally, the second part is not quite fitting for what we have here—the author is not making an accurate observation because the author could not have personally observed this, as it took place so far in the past.

18. **(J)** Focus on what the question is asking: the "primary" emphasis on what aspect of the noodle's production. J is correct because we see information about how the production of the noodle is "uniform," i.e., similar, while having different implementations across cultures. The other answers give us relevant information but do not give us the primary emphasis.

19. **(C)** The implication based on the context is that most of the food served long ago was fairly simple to prepare. That's why the author mentions the relative complexity of the noodle's creation compared to the other foods of the times. So, we pick the food that would be the easiest to prepare, which would clearly be the simple broth.

20. **(F)** The theme of the passage is that people of different cultures dispute the origin of a very useful and popular item, the noodle, because they all wish to take credit for this. (G) doesn't work because religion is not a technical invention, (H) doesn't work because football is a game not a manufactured item, and (J) doesn't work because it is an exploratory discovery rather than a human creation.

21. **(D)** This can be most directly seen in lines 7–8, where it states that "Duchamp stirred up controversy in the art world by submitting a piece . . ." Throughout the passage, the art board members, art observers, and the author himself all demonstrate interest in the question of whether a

toilet bowl can be considered art. While the toilet may have some aesthetic merits (A), is familiar to art lovers (B), and can be well crafted (C), controversy is clearly the primary attribute that made this a famous art work.

22. **(F)** As discussed in the second paragraph, Duchamp used a pseudonym to maintain his anonymity while contributing to the discussion about whether to display the *Fountain* at an original exhibition. Had the other members of the board known that he was the one making comments, it is reasonable to infer that the board members would have been influenced in some way by this. In all likelihood, they may not have made a decision based on the merits of the art, but on the reputation of the artist. Throughout the essay, Duchamp is portrayed as a confident and well-renowned artist, making the other options incorrect.

23. **(A)** These lines serve to expand upon the statement in line 29, "they might consider *Fountain* from a purely visual perspective." The artwork is a urinal, so it would be natural for an observer to question its artistic merits. Lines 29–34 go on to explain how the commonplace urinal can be seen in an artistic, visual way. (B) is true, but there is no evidence that a reader would likely have this objection. (C) not only is untrue but lacks any evidence of this being a likely objection. (D) would not be a reasonable objection because *Fountain* simply is presented as a work of art, not as the particular art form—a landscape.

24. **(F)** The only major difference between the *Fountain* and a typical urinal is that the artwork is placed on the floor facing upwards rather than its typical orientation on a restroom wall. So, the contextual suspension needed would be to ignore this "spatial orientation." The urinal in the artwork will still be white, making (G) incorrect. It will also still have water present, making (H) incorrect. It will also continue to have circular shapes in its design, making (J) incorrect.

25. **(B)** The nature of the dilemma faced by the board with respect to Duchamp's *Fountain* was whether so commonplace an object could be considered "art." (B) is the only choice that is analogous to this dilemma, since it would be counterintuitive to consider something "music" if there is no music being played. (A) focuses on the skill of the artist rather than whether something can be considered art. (C) includes controversy but not the type of controversy that the essay portrays. (D) is far from what is given in the essay as there is no element of danger in the artwork of Duchamp.

26. **(G)** Be sure you notice the EXCEPT in the question. The artwork would not take up much space at all, since it is a common urinal. So, a concern about the lack of space would be unwarranted. It is not (F) because it would be reasonable to be concerned that a urinal would lower artistic standards. Since Duchamp used a fake name when he submitted the artwork, it would be reasonable for the board to be reluctant to promote an unknown figure, as in (H). It would also be reasonable to be fearful of public ridicule that could result from such a controversial display, as in (J).

27. **(A)** Since Duchamp did indeed give the artwork a title, as discussed in line 15, a museum goer could most reasonably expect to find the artwork titled, making (C) and (D) incorrect. The type of title Duchamp uses is very telling because he takes a commonplace object—a urinal—and recontextualizes it with an artistic title, *Fountain*.

28. **(H)** Lines 55–56 point to craftsmanship as having less importance, since many modern artists were moving from the "artist as a creator to artist as a thinker." Skillfully crafting works of art became less important, while thinking in creative ways became more important. "Training," as in (F) is too vague—what type of training would this be? "Intellect," as in (G), and "cultural awareness," as in (J), took on more importance in *modern* times, based on the passage.

29. **(B)** This is an "ironic" name for the artwork because it is a commonplace restroom urinal—not something that people would typically consider to be a fountain. It is not (A) because no skepticism is expressed by naming it this, although many art observers could very well be skeptical that this is a form of art. It is not (C) because the title itself is not very controversial, although the art itself is. Even though some might find the title to be controversial, it is more aptly described as ironic. (D) is incorrect, since the title is at least somewhat relevant because water shoots out of the urinal like a fountain.

30. **(H)** Duchamp was able to find artistic merit in everyday, manmade objects. (H) is the only choice that involves looking at such objects. (F) and (J) involve observation of nature, and (G) involves observation of more "standard" art.

31. **(B)** Lines 10–12 refer to these three persons, stating that their "unique misfortunes provided the groundwork for contemporary investigations into the structural and physiological nature of memory, personality, and fear." They all experienced traumatic brain injuries or surgeries, things that no one would volunteer to undergo, or that no ethical doctor would willingly cause. So, this choice is the best option since it gives a logical rationale for the lack of many cases like theirs, even though more such cases would likely give further insight into the human mind. It is not choice (A) because there is no indication in the passage that scientists have not had the technology to study the brain. Choice (C) is incorrect because there is no mention of the presence of a lack of funding. It is not choice (D) because the scientists in the passage do demonstrate an interest in studying human emotions.

32. **(G)** Lines 15–17 state that H.M. had life-altering seizures that became "intractable," so he "underwent an experimental surgery to remove his medial temporal lobes." It is thus reasonable to infer that H.M. underwent the surgery because his condition was extremely severe, and also that the scientists were not certain as to what the results would be, including negative complications, since it was an experimental procedure. It is not (F), because the passage indicates that head trauma was associated with this condition. It is not (H) because the amnesia came after the surgery. It is not (J) because this

condition had been previously documented, although its precise cause was unclear.

33. **(A)** According to the passage, H.M. developed his condition from a chain of events stemming from a bike accident, whereas S.M. inherited her condition genetically. It is not choice (B) because both conditions were abnormal. It is not choice (C) because scientists are interested in both of their situations. It is not choice (D) because scientists were able to pinpoint the brain components that contributed to the conditions for both of the patients.

34. **(H)** Lines 47–52 indicate that when a dangerous sensory stimulus is present, the amygdala acts as a processing center for fear, causing the secretion of hormones from the locus coeruleus and other bodily glands. The other options all confuse the sequence by which this process occurs.

35. **(A)** "Understand" is the only option that appropriately means that scientists are developing a better "appreciation" of how the amygdala functions.

36. **(G)** The author would agree that this statement is factual, since he states that recent positron emission tomography research has given supporting evidence. The author would say that this label is not comprehensive, however, because the author mentions other parts of the body, like the hypothalamus and the locus coeruleus, that are associated with fear. Moreover, the author places the term "fear center" in quotation marks, which typically means that the writer is dissociating himself or herself from a given idea. Choices (F) and (J) are too extreme in the positive direction, and choice (H) is too extreme in the negative direction.

37. **(D)** The addicts experience greater desire for the substances because "the activity of this anticipatory reward pathway is greatly increased." Also, they experience less satisfaction as they use it more frequently because they do not receive as much dopamine when using the drugs. It is not choice (A) because they receive diminished internal rewards from the substances. It is not choice (B) because the author indicates that their dopamine levels go down. It is not choice (C) because the author does not state that there is any increase in the abusers' capability to acquire the substances.

38. **(H)** S.M. would be most interesting to the author of Passage B because her amygdalae were destroyed, and the amygdala is the focus of Passage B. It is not choice (F) because H.M. had a condition resulting from the removal of his medial temporal lobes. It is not choice (G) because the author only mentions Phineas Gage in passing and does not analyze him. It is not(J) because this is the name of a disease, not a patient analyzed in the passage.

39. **(B)** The brain traumas of H.M. and S.M. in Passage A resulted in highly unbalanced brains, and Passage B associates panic disorders and addiction with a lack of chemical balance in the brain. It is not choice (A) because the authors do not express concern with the overprescription of drugs. It is not choice (C) because the authors want to learn from past experience, not forget about them. It is not choice (D) because Passage A mentions that S.M.

naturally inherited her condition, and Passage B mentions the negative consequences of panic disorders, doing so without stipulating that their causes had to be nonnatural.

40. **(H)** Patient S.M. had a destroyed amygdala, which the author of Passage B states is associated with the release of epinephrine and cortisol. The final paragraph of Passage B states that the amygdala is associated with the release of dopamine when there is an anticipated reward—a near car accident would most certainly not be an anticipated reward.

Science

1. **(D)** Simply look at which of these parts of the spine is lowest in the spinal column, which would make it the farthest from the skull. The Sacral is at the very bottom.

2. **(J)** Based on the information in Table 1, parasympathetic effects on the body will cause constriction of the bronchioles and constriction of the pupils. In other words, both the bronchioles and pupils would narrow.

3. **(B)** Be sure you notice the NOT in the question. There is no arrow connecting the brainstem to the bladder. There is an arrow connecting the sacral part of the spinal column to the bladder.

4. **(F)** Following the arrows of the neural pathways, we see that for every single bodily system, the preganglionic axons are triggered before the postganglionic axons are. It also helps that the prefixes of both words, *pre*ganglionic and *post*ganglionic give you a hint as to their likely order.

5. **(A)** Using a bit of background knowledge from physical science, we can recognize that the delta waves and the theta waves differ in how frequently they go through a complete cycle, with theta waves having a much greater frequency than delta waves. Their amplitude, or relative height, is about the same, making (B) incorrect. Although looking at someone's sleep state could be useful, it is not as precise as the frequency would be since it might be tough to distinguish whether someone is daydreaming or actually sleeping. So, (C) is incorrect. The subject's eyes would likely be closed in both situations, so (D) is incorrect.

6. **(H)** Based on the paragraph before Table 1, we would want something that would only use the "fight or flight" response, not the "resting and digesting" response. So, we would need something that has no parasympathetic effect, since this is associated with resting. The adrenal gland is the only option that has no parasympathetic effect.

7. **(C)** According to Figure 3, the apple tree has the highest percentage of its wax lost due to acid rain.

8. **(G)** Bass die at a pH of 5.5, so it is the only one of these animals that would be alive at a pH of 6.0 and dead at a pH of 5.0.

9. **(A)** According to the second sentence of the passage, acid rain is rain water that has a pH value between 4.3 and 5.6. So, water with a pH of 5.8 would NOT fall within the definition of acid rain, unlike the other options.

10. **(J)** This is an easy question to get things mixed around—*lower* pH indicates *higher* acidity. Since frogs are killed at a pH of 4.0, the pH at each of the given distances would be *greater* than the pH that would kill the frogs since the water would be *less* acidic. So, the frog would survive in all of the given distances from the power plant.

11. **(B)** According to the paragraph that accompanies Study 3, the researchers conducted their study to replicate acid rain that has a pH of 4.3. Based on Figure 2, frogs are the only animals listed that have a deadly pH level of less than 4—bass, clams, and snails would all die at this pH level.

12. **(J)** The scientist in question would want to show that acid rain would kill marine animals more than it actually did in the wild. Using unhealthy animals would certainly skew the results toward showing more harm, making (F) correct. Using unnaturally high levels of acid would skew the results, making (G) correct. Picking animals that have a greater tendency to die as a result of acid exposure would also skew the results, making (H) correct.

13. **(A)** The results of Study 3 only provide information about the percentage of wax lost due to acid rain exposure. We do not know the extent to which a loss of wax is harmful to trees, so any information that could clarify this would be helpful. Option I would clearly do so. Option II would focus on animals rather than trees, so it would be irrelevant. Option III focuses on lakes and streams instead of trees, so it too would be irrelevant.

14. **(H)** Don't neglect the NOT in the question. Based on the introductory paragraph, the relativistic nature of space and time would not have been a plausible explanation to amateur astronomers in the 1800s because the theory of Relativity was not established until the 20th century (i.e., the 1900s). All of the other options would have made sense given the widespread belief in Newtonian physics.

15. **(C)** Paraphrasing the question, which of these would be most likely to stand in the way of a scientist in the year 1900 finding a flaw with Newton's theory of Gravitation? (B) was a problem with Newton's theory. (C) would not have been relevant to a physicist of that time period. (D) is not supported by the passage, since there were no astronomical observations of Vulcan since it didn't exist. The fact that the theory had been in place for a long period of time would have likely made it more difficult for the average scientist to be confident in overturning a widely accepted theory.

16. **(F)** Theory 2 states that the gravitation that causes the apparent existence of an astronomical body between the Sun and Mercury is in fact "mediated by the curvature of spacetime that results from the proximity of the Sun and its large gravitation." In other words, the Sun's enormous size creates a curve

in spacetime that makes it seem like there must be a planet between the Sun and Mercury. Jupiter is not even close to as large as the Sun, so it is far less likely that an observer of Jupiter and its moon would be able to detect the curvature in spacetime that would result from Jupiter's gravitational field. The other options would have no impact on the inconsistency in this observation.

17. **(C)** Be sure you notice the NOT in the question. The author of Theory 1 mentions (A), (B), and (D) as being potential observational obstacles, but it does not mention (C).

18. **(G)** Theory 1 states that given the supposed planet Vulcan's "proximity to the Sun, it will have a more rapid orbit." We can therefore conclude that a planet *far* from the Sun would have *less* frequent orbits.

19. **(B)** Theory 2 states that "Even though Newtonian mechanics will correctly predict astronomical events with a great deal of accuracy, the relativistic nature of matter and time account for the shift in Mercury's orbit that astronomers have observed." In other words, if we do not require much *precision* in our observations, Newtonian mechanics will work for virtually any measurement we would conduct. The amount of observation (C) or proximity (D) would be irrelevant, and if we wanted to account for relativity (A), then the theory of Relativity would be needed, not Newtonian mechanics.

20. **(G)** One of the obstacles to the observation of the possible planet Vulcan cited by Theory 1 is the brightness of the Sun drowning out the possibility of seeing Vulcan. If the brightness of the Sun could be diminished, it would make it easier to observe Vulcan. A solar eclipse involves the moon covering the Sun, which would make it easier for observers on Earth to see objects that would otherwise be drowned out by the nearby light of the Sun. The other astronomical events would do nothing to diminish the overwhelming brightness of the Sun relative to the objects close to it.

21. **(C)** The mass of the lead starts at 10.0 grams, and would be at 5.0 grams somewhere between 20 and 30 minutes. The half-life is the time that has elapsed when half of the original amount would have decayed away.

22. **(H)** Based on Table 3, polonium will decrease most rapidly given that its time elapsed is measured in microseconds. So, polonium will have the smallest half-life.

23. **(A)** In the description of Experiment 1, it states that beta particles and positrons could penetrate the first shield but not the second, and that the gamma rays were only stopped by the third shield. A larger particle opening might stop a relatively large particle, like an alpha, but would allow smaller particles, like gamma rays, to pass through. So, we can conclude that if we were to list the shields in *decreasing* order of the sizes of their particle openings, it would be 1, 2, 3.

24. **(J)** With radioactive decay, there should be a consistent percent decrease of the substance—the simple arithmetic difference between the numbers should not be the same, since there will be an exponential rate of decay. Table 1 has the same arithmetic difference between 0–10 minutes and 10–20 minutes; Tables 2 and 3 have the same arithmetic difference within their entries. Therefore, all of the tables present data that is inconsistent with the concepts of exponential radioactive decay.

25. **(B)** In order to have the highest relative percent of large particles of the total number of particles, we need to have the step in the decay process that has the highest percent of its particles absorbed by Shield 1. Why? Because Shield 1 traps the large alpha particles but not the smaller types of particles. So, (B) makes sense since almost all of the radiated particles in this step are absorbed by Shield 1.

26. **(G)** As discussed toward the beginning of the passage, an alpha particle has two neutrons and two protons. Losing one of these would cause the atomic mass to decrease by 4 units, since protons and neutrons are each one atomic mass unit in size. It would also cause the atomic number to go down by 2, since only the loss of the two protons would decrease the atomic number. Thus, the atomic mass goes from 214 to 210, and the atomic number goes from 82 to 80.

27. **(B)** As particle fact #3 states, a "positron has the same mass as an electron, but an opposite charge." So, configuring a device to measure charge would best enable a scientist to detect if a particle were a positron or an electron.

28. **(G)** Look at the refractive index for cubic zirconia, and you find that it is 2.16. Material 2 in Table 2 has a refractive index of 2.17, making it the material most likely to be cubic zirconia.

29. **(C)** According to the experiment description in Experiment 1, the higher the Refractive Index, the more light will be bent. Air has the lowest refractive index, so it will bend light the least.

30. **(F)** Simply take the equation given for refractive index, $n = \dfrac{c}{v}$, and solve for v.

31. **(C)** Consider the provided equation that relates refractive index, light velocity in a medium, and the speed of light: $n = \dfrac{c}{v}$. Cross-multiply to isolate the v so we can see how c and n will affect v: $n = \dfrac{c}{v} \rightarrow v = \dfrac{c}{n}$. So, the lower the value of n, the higher the light velocity through a particular medium will be. According to Table 1, carbon dioxide has the lowest refractive index (n) of any of the given values, so light will travel most quickly through it.

32. **(G)** In Table 1, the human cornea, which is part of the eye, is said to have a refractive index of 1.3375. This is closest to the refractive index of water,

which is 1.3330. So, it is reasonable to conclude that the human eye is most likely composed primarily of water.

33. **(A)** In order to have a material that bends light very little, it would be helpful to have a material with a very low refractive index. Material 1 is the best fit because it has by far the lowest Refractive Index of any of the materials.

34. **(H)** Light is either bent or not bent—there is no other option. If the light is not bent at all by a material, the material will have a refractive index of 1. If it is bent even a little bit, it will have a refractive index greater than 1. Therefore, it is not possible for a material to have a refractive index less than 1. It is not (J) because, as we can see from the data, quite a few materials have Refractive Indexes that vary quite a bit from one another.

35. **(A)** According to Period Trend #2, "Atomic radius *decreases* from left to right across a period and *increases* from top to bottom in a group." So, Ti would have the *largest* atomic radius since it is the farthest to the left along its row.

36. **(J)** According to Trend #3, ionization energy increases from left to right. So, carbon will have a lower ionization energy than oxygen, since it is farther to the left. According to Trend #1, electron affinity increases from left to right. So, carbon will have a lower electron affinity than oxygen.

37. **(A)** Scandium is element number 23, and Selenium is element number 34, making Scandium farther to the left on the periodic row than Selenium. Based on Trend number 3, ionization energy increases from left to right across a period, so Scandium will have lower ionization energy than Selenium. Based on Trend number 4, electronegativity increases from left to right across a period, so Scandium will have lower electronegativity than Selenium.

38. **(G)** To be positively correlated, as one thing increases, the other will increase as well. Metallic character and electron affinity are NOT positively correlated because they have an opposite relationship.

39. **(C)** In order for something to heat quickly, it would need to conduct heat well. According to Trend #5, metallic character is associated with an element's likelihood of being a good conductor. The higher the metallic character, the better it will be at conducting heat and energy. "Metallic character decreases from left to right across a period and increases from top to bottom," so Cu would likely be the best conductor based on the given information.

40. **(F)** To fit all of these criteria, we need a substance that will be to the right of the periodic table. Fluorine would fit the criteria given how far to the right it is out of all the substances.

Sample Top-Scoring Writing Response

A century ago, it made sense for governments to focus solely on their own nations. Today, computers, airplanes, drones, virtual technologies, nuclear weapons, and other implications of globalization make it imprudent to consider national boundaries in the same way as previous generations. The world seems smaller than ever, and it is unreasonable to assume that by prioritizing its own citizens a country can avoid international and even intercontinental relationships. Individuals as well as governments will benefit from a more global approach to social and political issues. In the topic of foreign aid, developed countries have a duty to provide basic human rights like food, health, and liberty to as many of the world's citizens as possible.

The argument for the third perspective is cogent, but ignores the growing globalization of today's world. Education, healthcare, and nutrition are basic rights of all humans and since the workforce and social lives of people are no longer limited by geographical constraints like in the past, developed countries have a role in creating a worldwide higher quality of life. In the first viewpoint, aid is limited to a private or individual concern which severely narrows the possibilities for change. While individuals interested in humanitarian and philanthropic work can absolutely make a difference, there are events and circumstances that far outweigh the help that charitable individuals can give. For instance, when the 2013 typhoon hit the Philippines, devastating the infrastructure of the nation and leaving thousands homeless and without access to basic necessities, the help given by external governments was indispensable in saving lives and rebuilding homes and businesses.

It might seem easier to say that governments should work on their own nations first or that third-world problems are far too numerous to truly make a difference. Yet, the United States will surely never find itself in a situation where all of its citizens are happy and satisfied and completely healthy—so this line of thinking would never leave room for international aid. And while third-world poverty is overwhelming to say the least, that is what makes it all the more urgent to give as much help as possible. A campaign against poverty on the radio this week reported that over 20,000 people die every single day from hunger even though there is already enough food in the world to feed everybody. It went on to say that in places like Sub-Saharan Africa where hunger is an everyday anxiety, one in four persons is undernourished. My position is in agreement with the second perspective because I believe no person should ever have to die from hunger, whether that be in the United States or in Sub-Saharan Africa.

Every year, developed governments spend billions on defense and the building of nuclear bombs, millions on studying and protecting threatened animal and plant species, and thousands on unnecessary medical visits and tests. I recently heard of a federal research project that spent millions of dollars testing the effects of narcotics on various birds. My point is not that any of these things are undeserving of funding, but instead that they seem rather trivial when compared to the devastating statistics mentioned above. Of the trillions of dollars we spend here in the United States, foreign aid to put food in stomachs, distribute medical supplies, and provide education seems to me money well spent.

ANSWER SHEET—PRACTICE TEST 2

Test 1: English

1 Ⓐ Ⓑ Ⓒ Ⓓ   20 Ⓕ Ⓖ Ⓗ Ⓙ   39 Ⓐ Ⓑ Ⓒ Ⓓ   58 Ⓕ Ⓖ Ⓗ Ⓙ
2 Ⓕ Ⓖ Ⓗ Ⓙ   21 Ⓐ Ⓑ Ⓒ Ⓓ   40 Ⓕ Ⓖ Ⓗ Ⓙ   59 Ⓐ Ⓑ Ⓒ Ⓓ
3 Ⓐ Ⓑ Ⓒ Ⓓ   22 Ⓕ Ⓖ Ⓗ Ⓙ   41 Ⓐ Ⓑ Ⓒ Ⓓ   60 Ⓕ Ⓖ Ⓗ Ⓙ
4 Ⓕ Ⓖ Ⓗ Ⓙ   23 Ⓐ Ⓑ Ⓒ Ⓓ   42 Ⓕ Ⓖ Ⓗ Ⓙ   61 Ⓐ Ⓑ Ⓒ Ⓓ
5 Ⓐ Ⓑ Ⓒ Ⓓ   24 Ⓕ Ⓖ Ⓗ Ⓙ   43 Ⓐ Ⓑ Ⓒ Ⓓ   62 Ⓕ Ⓖ Ⓗ Ⓙ
6 Ⓕ Ⓖ Ⓗ Ⓙ   25 Ⓐ Ⓑ Ⓒ Ⓓ   44 Ⓕ Ⓖ Ⓗ Ⓙ   63 Ⓐ Ⓑ Ⓒ Ⓓ
7 Ⓐ Ⓑ Ⓒ Ⓓ   26 Ⓕ Ⓖ Ⓗ Ⓙ   45 Ⓐ Ⓑ Ⓒ Ⓓ   64 Ⓕ Ⓖ Ⓗ Ⓙ
8 Ⓕ Ⓖ Ⓗ Ⓙ   27 Ⓐ Ⓑ Ⓒ Ⓓ   46 Ⓕ Ⓖ Ⓗ Ⓙ   65 Ⓐ Ⓑ Ⓒ Ⓓ
9 Ⓐ Ⓑ Ⓒ Ⓓ   28 Ⓕ Ⓖ Ⓗ Ⓙ   47 Ⓐ Ⓑ Ⓒ Ⓓ   66 Ⓕ Ⓖ Ⓗ Ⓙ
10 Ⓕ Ⓖ Ⓗ Ⓙ   29 Ⓐ Ⓑ Ⓒ Ⓓ   48 Ⓕ Ⓖ Ⓗ Ⓙ   67 Ⓐ Ⓑ Ⓒ Ⓓ
11 Ⓐ Ⓑ Ⓒ Ⓓ   30 Ⓕ Ⓖ Ⓗ Ⓙ   49 Ⓐ Ⓑ Ⓒ Ⓓ   68 Ⓕ Ⓖ Ⓗ Ⓙ
12 Ⓕ Ⓖ Ⓗ Ⓙ   31 Ⓐ Ⓑ Ⓒ Ⓓ   50 Ⓕ Ⓖ Ⓗ Ⓙ   69 Ⓐ Ⓑ Ⓒ Ⓓ
13 Ⓐ Ⓑ Ⓒ Ⓓ   32 Ⓕ Ⓖ Ⓗ Ⓙ   51 Ⓐ Ⓑ Ⓒ Ⓓ   70 Ⓕ Ⓖ Ⓗ Ⓙ
14 Ⓕ Ⓖ Ⓗ Ⓙ   33 Ⓐ Ⓑ Ⓒ Ⓓ   52 Ⓕ Ⓖ Ⓗ Ⓙ   71 Ⓐ Ⓑ Ⓒ Ⓓ
15 Ⓐ Ⓑ Ⓒ Ⓓ   34 Ⓕ Ⓖ Ⓗ Ⓙ   53 Ⓐ Ⓑ Ⓒ Ⓓ   72 Ⓕ Ⓖ Ⓗ Ⓙ
16 Ⓕ Ⓖ Ⓗ Ⓙ   35 Ⓐ Ⓑ Ⓒ Ⓓ   54 Ⓕ Ⓖ Ⓗ Ⓙ   73 Ⓐ Ⓑ Ⓒ Ⓓ
17 Ⓐ Ⓑ Ⓒ Ⓓ   36 Ⓕ Ⓖ Ⓗ Ⓙ   55 Ⓐ Ⓑ Ⓒ Ⓓ   74 Ⓕ Ⓖ Ⓗ Ⓙ
18 Ⓕ Ⓖ Ⓗ Ⓙ   37 Ⓐ Ⓑ Ⓒ Ⓓ   56 Ⓕ Ⓖ Ⓗ Ⓙ   75 Ⓐ Ⓑ Ⓒ Ⓓ
19 Ⓐ Ⓑ Ⓒ Ⓓ   38 Ⓕ Ⓖ Ⓗ Ⓙ   57 Ⓐ Ⓑ Ⓒ Ⓓ

Test 2: Mathematics

1 Ⓐ Ⓑ Ⓒ Ⓓ Ⓔ   16 Ⓕ Ⓖ Ⓗ Ⓙ Ⓚ   31 Ⓐ Ⓑ Ⓒ Ⓓ Ⓔ   46 Ⓕ Ⓖ Ⓗ Ⓙ Ⓚ
2 Ⓕ Ⓖ Ⓗ Ⓙ Ⓚ   17 Ⓐ Ⓑ Ⓒ Ⓓ Ⓔ   32 Ⓕ Ⓖ Ⓗ Ⓙ Ⓚ   47 Ⓐ Ⓑ Ⓒ Ⓓ Ⓔ
3 Ⓐ Ⓑ Ⓒ Ⓓ Ⓔ   18 Ⓕ Ⓖ Ⓗ Ⓙ Ⓚ   33 Ⓐ Ⓑ Ⓒ Ⓓ Ⓔ   48 Ⓕ Ⓖ Ⓗ Ⓙ Ⓚ
4 Ⓕ Ⓖ Ⓗ Ⓙ Ⓚ   19 Ⓐ Ⓑ Ⓒ Ⓓ Ⓔ   34 Ⓕ Ⓖ Ⓗ Ⓙ Ⓚ   49 Ⓐ Ⓑ Ⓒ Ⓓ Ⓔ
5 Ⓐ Ⓑ Ⓒ Ⓓ Ⓔ   20 Ⓕ Ⓖ Ⓗ Ⓙ Ⓚ   35 Ⓐ Ⓑ Ⓒ Ⓓ Ⓔ   50 Ⓕ Ⓖ Ⓗ Ⓙ Ⓚ
6 Ⓕ Ⓖ Ⓗ Ⓙ Ⓚ   21 Ⓐ Ⓑ Ⓒ Ⓓ Ⓔ   36 Ⓕ Ⓖ Ⓗ Ⓙ Ⓚ   51 Ⓐ Ⓑ Ⓒ Ⓓ Ⓔ
7 Ⓐ Ⓑ Ⓒ Ⓓ Ⓔ   22 Ⓕ Ⓖ Ⓗ Ⓙ Ⓚ   37 Ⓐ Ⓑ Ⓒ Ⓓ Ⓔ   52 Ⓕ Ⓖ Ⓗ Ⓙ Ⓚ
8 Ⓕ Ⓖ Ⓗ Ⓙ Ⓚ   23 Ⓐ Ⓑ Ⓒ Ⓓ Ⓔ   38 Ⓕ Ⓖ Ⓗ Ⓙ Ⓚ   53 Ⓐ Ⓑ Ⓒ Ⓓ Ⓔ
9 Ⓐ Ⓑ Ⓒ Ⓓ Ⓔ   24 Ⓕ Ⓖ Ⓗ Ⓙ Ⓚ   39 Ⓐ Ⓑ Ⓒ Ⓓ Ⓔ   54 Ⓕ Ⓖ Ⓗ Ⓙ Ⓚ
10 Ⓕ Ⓖ Ⓗ Ⓙ Ⓚ   25 Ⓐ Ⓑ Ⓒ Ⓓ Ⓔ   40 Ⓕ Ⓖ Ⓗ Ⓙ Ⓚ   55 Ⓐ Ⓑ Ⓒ Ⓓ Ⓔ
11 Ⓐ Ⓑ Ⓒ Ⓓ Ⓔ   26 Ⓕ Ⓖ Ⓗ Ⓙ Ⓚ   41 Ⓐ Ⓑ Ⓒ Ⓓ Ⓔ   56 Ⓕ Ⓖ Ⓗ Ⓙ Ⓚ
12 Ⓕ Ⓖ Ⓗ Ⓙ Ⓚ   27 Ⓐ Ⓑ Ⓒ Ⓓ Ⓔ   42 Ⓕ Ⓖ Ⓗ Ⓙ Ⓚ   57 Ⓐ Ⓑ Ⓒ Ⓓ Ⓔ
13 Ⓐ Ⓑ Ⓒ Ⓓ Ⓔ   28 Ⓕ Ⓖ Ⓗ Ⓙ Ⓚ   43 Ⓐ Ⓑ Ⓒ Ⓓ Ⓔ   58 Ⓕ Ⓖ Ⓗ Ⓙ Ⓚ
14 Ⓕ Ⓖ Ⓗ Ⓙ Ⓚ   29 Ⓐ Ⓑ Ⓒ Ⓓ Ⓔ   44 Ⓕ Ⓖ Ⓗ Ⓙ Ⓚ   59 Ⓐ Ⓑ Ⓒ Ⓓ Ⓔ
15 Ⓐ Ⓑ Ⓒ Ⓓ Ⓔ   30 Ⓕ Ⓖ Ⓗ Ⓙ Ⓚ   45 Ⓐ Ⓑ Ⓒ Ⓓ Ⓔ   60 Ⓕ Ⓖ Ⓗ Ⓙ Ⓚ

Test 3: Reading

1 Ⓐ Ⓑ Ⓒ Ⓓ	11 Ⓐ Ⓑ Ⓒ Ⓓ	21 Ⓐ Ⓑ Ⓒ Ⓓ	31 Ⓐ Ⓑ Ⓒ Ⓓ
2 Ⓕ Ⓖ Ⓗ Ⓙ	12 Ⓕ Ⓖ Ⓗ Ⓙ	22 Ⓕ Ⓖ Ⓗ Ⓙ	32 Ⓕ Ⓖ Ⓗ Ⓙ
3 Ⓐ Ⓑ Ⓒ Ⓓ	13 Ⓐ Ⓑ Ⓒ Ⓓ	23 Ⓐ Ⓑ Ⓒ Ⓓ	33 Ⓐ Ⓑ Ⓒ Ⓓ
4 Ⓕ Ⓖ Ⓗ Ⓙ	14 Ⓕ Ⓖ Ⓗ Ⓙ	24 Ⓕ Ⓖ Ⓗ Ⓙ	34 Ⓕ Ⓖ Ⓗ Ⓙ
5 Ⓐ Ⓑ Ⓒ Ⓓ	15 Ⓐ Ⓑ Ⓒ Ⓓ	25 Ⓐ Ⓑ Ⓒ Ⓓ	35 Ⓐ Ⓑ Ⓒ Ⓓ
6 Ⓕ Ⓖ Ⓗ Ⓙ	16 Ⓕ Ⓖ Ⓗ Ⓙ	26 Ⓕ Ⓖ Ⓗ Ⓙ	36 Ⓕ Ⓖ Ⓗ Ⓙ
7 Ⓐ Ⓑ Ⓒ Ⓓ	17 Ⓐ Ⓑ Ⓒ Ⓓ	27 Ⓐ Ⓑ Ⓒ Ⓓ	37 Ⓐ Ⓑ Ⓒ Ⓓ
8 Ⓕ Ⓖ Ⓗ Ⓙ	18 Ⓕ Ⓖ Ⓗ Ⓙ	28 Ⓕ Ⓖ Ⓗ Ⓙ	38 Ⓕ Ⓖ Ⓗ Ⓙ
9 Ⓐ Ⓑ Ⓒ Ⓓ	19 Ⓐ Ⓑ Ⓒ Ⓓ	29 Ⓐ Ⓑ Ⓒ Ⓓ	39 Ⓐ Ⓑ Ⓒ Ⓓ
10 Ⓕ Ⓖ Ⓗ Ⓙ	20 Ⓕ Ⓖ Ⓗ Ⓙ	30 Ⓕ Ⓖ Ⓗ Ⓙ	40 Ⓕ Ⓖ Ⓗ Ⓙ

Test 4: Science

1 Ⓐ Ⓑ Ⓒ Ⓓ	11 Ⓐ Ⓑ Ⓒ Ⓓ	21 Ⓐ Ⓑ Ⓒ Ⓓ	31 Ⓐ Ⓑ Ⓒ Ⓓ
2 Ⓕ Ⓖ Ⓗ Ⓙ	12 Ⓕ Ⓖ Ⓗ Ⓙ	22 Ⓕ Ⓖ Ⓗ Ⓙ	32 Ⓕ Ⓖ Ⓗ Ⓙ
3 Ⓐ Ⓑ Ⓒ Ⓓ	13 Ⓐ Ⓑ Ⓒ Ⓓ	23 Ⓐ Ⓑ Ⓒ Ⓓ	33 Ⓐ Ⓑ Ⓒ Ⓓ
4 Ⓕ Ⓖ Ⓗ Ⓙ	14 Ⓕ Ⓖ Ⓗ Ⓙ	24 Ⓕ Ⓖ Ⓗ Ⓙ	34 Ⓕ Ⓖ Ⓗ Ⓙ
5 Ⓐ Ⓑ Ⓒ Ⓓ	15 Ⓐ Ⓑ Ⓒ Ⓓ	25 Ⓐ Ⓑ Ⓒ Ⓓ	35 Ⓐ Ⓑ Ⓒ Ⓓ
6 Ⓕ Ⓖ Ⓗ Ⓙ	16 Ⓕ Ⓖ Ⓗ Ⓙ	26 Ⓕ Ⓖ Ⓗ Ⓙ	36 Ⓕ Ⓖ Ⓗ Ⓙ
7 Ⓐ Ⓑ Ⓒ Ⓓ	17 Ⓐ Ⓑ Ⓒ Ⓓ	27 Ⓐ Ⓑ Ⓒ Ⓓ	37 Ⓐ Ⓑ Ⓒ Ⓓ
8 Ⓕ Ⓖ Ⓗ Ⓙ	18 Ⓕ Ⓖ Ⓗ Ⓙ	28 Ⓕ Ⓖ Ⓗ Ⓙ	38 Ⓕ Ⓖ Ⓗ Ⓙ
9 Ⓐ Ⓑ Ⓒ Ⓓ	19 Ⓐ Ⓑ Ⓒ Ⓓ	29 Ⓐ Ⓑ Ⓒ Ⓓ	39 Ⓐ Ⓑ Ⓒ Ⓓ
10 Ⓕ Ⓖ Ⓗ Ⓙ	20 Ⓕ Ⓖ Ⓗ Ⓙ	30 Ⓕ Ⓖ Ⓗ Ⓙ	40 Ⓕ Ⓖ Ⓗ Ⓙ

Practice Test 2

ENGLISH TEST

Time—45 minutes
75 Questions

Directions: In the passages that follow, you will find underlined words and phrases. In the accompanying questions, there are alternatives to the underlined wording. For most questions, choose the option that expresses the idea most effectively, conforms to the standards of conventional English, or has wording consistent with the tone and style of the passage. If you think the original underlined wording is best, pick "NO CHANGE." For some problems, you will need to read a question about the underlined portion and pick the best answer to the question. Other problems may ask about portions of the passage or the entire passage. These questions will be indicated by a numbered box.

Choose the best answer to each question and fill in the matching circle on your answer sheet. Be sure to consider any relevant context surrounding the question in determining your answer.

PASSAGE I

[1]

Since the beginning of time, people have needed a way to express their distress with those surrounding them. <u>With cavemen, this probably merely consisted of a sharp knock on the head with a club.</u> (1) However, <u>he is</u> (2) more concerned with expression and how we went from the clever innuendos, which require a high command of the English language, to primitive swear words. <u>Personally if someone wished to insult me,</u> (3) I'd much rather they say something intelligent than show off <u>their own idiocy and lack of originality.</u> (4)

[2]

Perhaps the earliest known spoken insult was "idiot." With its earliest

recorded usage <u>has been</u> in the 1300s, it has sadly transformed in definition
                  5

and no longer applies to how it is used today. In the arsenal of the American

teen, idiot is almost an endearing term among friends. <u>As a result</u> the
                                              6

original definition is <u>more sharply</u> than the dulled version used today.
                        7

In its origination, an "idiot" was a "person so mentally deficient as to

be incapable of ordinary reasoning." Following idiot in birth was "tattletale."

<u>It's</u> thought to be dated to 1481, but didn't take on the exact meaning
8

now associated with it until 1888.

[3]

With slavery as a popular institution, insults took a turn in the 1800s when

they centered on race. Offenses in this time mostly consisted of racial slurs.

In the 1900s, it was time for a fresh round of new words. "Nitwit," "dingbat,"

and "jerk" were all coined <u>among</u> 1909 and 1935.
                                                  9

[4]

The best and most innovative insults came from <u>the bard himself</u>. In 1591,
                                                  10

Shakespeare wrote "Thou lump of foul deformity!"[1] That was when the insult

---

[1]*Richard III.*

was at its apex—the golden age so to speak. There are masses of Shakespearian
          11
insults, others include: "You [sir] are as a candle, the better burnt out."

(*Henry IV*) and "Thou villainous dread-bolted blind-worm!"

[5]

In the 1950s insults started going downhill. Less new words were created,
                                              12
as most of them were versions of earlier ones. Insults like "wacko," "jerk

off," and "weirdo" were part of this trend. Also beginning in the 1950s and

through modern times, were the innovation of combining swear words
                        13
with others to create new insults.

[6]

The verbal insult has evolved a lot in the years since it has become

commonplace. It has gone from its pinnacle to its lowest of low. [14]

1.   The writer is considering deleting this sentence. Should the writer make
     this deletion?
     A. Yes, the information is irrelevant to the paragraph.
     B. Yes, the sentence is inconsistent with the tone of the rest of the essay.
     C. No, without the sentence, the following sentence would not make
        sense.
     D. No, this information is critical to the main point of the essay as a
        whole.

2.   F. NO CHANGE
     G. One is
     H. You are
     J. I am

3. A. NO CHANGE
    B. Personally, if someone wished to insult me,
    C. Personally, if someone wished to insult me
    D. Personally if someone wished to insult me

4. F. NO CHANGE
    G. their own lack of creativity
    H. the glaring presence of idiocy and complete and total lack
       of creativity
    J. OMIT the underlined portion

5. A. NO CHANGE
    B. had been
    C. was
    D. OMIT the underlined portion

6. F. NO CHANGE
    G. Consequently
    H. But
    J. Additionally

7. A. NO CHANGE
    B. sharper
    C. sharpest
    D. sharply

8. F. NO CHANGE
    G. Its
    H. The insult of "tattletale" was
    J. "Tattletale," in fact, was

9. A. NO CHANGE
    B. in
    C. between
    D. on

10. The writer is considering modifying the wording in this underlined portion, and changing it to:

    "William Shakespeare,"

    which is known to the readers as being the same person as "the bard" referred to here. Is this change in wording necessary?
    - F. Yes, because it clearly names the person who is being discussed.
    - G. Yes, because it would add an air of formality to the paragraph, making it consistent with the style of the surrounding sentences.
    - H. No, because it would be inconsistent with the tone of the remainder of the essay.
    - J. No, because it avoids unneeded repetition in the sentence that follows, because it uses a nickname for Shakespeare the readers would recognize.

11. A. NO CHANGE
    B. apex, the golden,
    C. apex: the golden,
    D. apex the golden,

12. F. NO CHANGE
    G. Much less
    H. Fewer
    J. Much fewer

13. A. NO CHANGE
    B. was
    C. has been
    D. are

14. The author wishes to put a sentence at this point that concludes the essay by maintaining its subject matter and tone. Which of the following best accomplishes this?
    - F. The insult is clearly one of the most important historical events in recent memory.
    - G. When wondering how best to express discontent with people, think W.W.T.B.S.—"What Would the Bard Say?"
    - H. We can only hope that it will return to its previous zenith of quality, instead of the garbage it has now become.
    - J. The world will be much better off if insults can become something we only study in history class instead of practice in daily life.

15. Which of the following represents the most logical arrangement of the paragraphs in the passage?
   A. As they are now
   B. 6, 2, 3, 4, 5, 1
   C. 1, 2, 4, 3, 5, 6
   D. 1, 3, 2, 4, 5, 6

PASSAGE II

The story of the Atlantic Green Sea Turtle is tragic, <u>and</u> not without
                                                                          16
hope. *Chelonia mydas* are a type of sea turtle completely unique to

<u>a few restricted and exclusive areas of the world</u>. They tend to cluster
                                                       17
around high-energy oceanic beaches, convergence zones in the pelasic habitat,

benthic feeding grounds, and other shallow protected waters. These areas are

unlike anywhere else in the world. 18 They only range from the mid-eastern

coast <u>of the U.S. to Texas</u> and Hawaii.
         19

With declining numbers tracked since 1981, the Atlantic Green Sea Turtles

<u>have only recently began</u> their climb back into a more consistent and
         20
healthy level of sustainability. They face <u>constantly</u> peril from natural disasters
                                              21
like hurricanes, which caused their numbers to decrease in 2004. However,

the biggest endangerment to *Chelonia mydas* is human activity. Their accidental

capture in gill nets, trawls, traps, and pots <u>(all used in commercial fishing)</u> has
                                                                   22
an overwhelming effect on the turtle's numbers. Fish consumption is

highly debated because of its unintentional, but devastating <u>affect</u> on

23

the environment.

<u>Humans have caused nothing but harm toward the precious sea turtle.</u>

24

Atlantic Green Sea Turtles were placed on the endangered species list, so

deliberate hunting and <u>harvesting of turtles is now illegal</u>. For the sea turtles

25

to be delisted, the 1991 Federal Recovery Plan requires that the following

<u>three criteria be met. First, Florida, must support</u> an average of 5,000 nests for

26

6 <u>following</u> years. Second, there must be at least 105 kilometers of nesting

27

beach that are able to sustain <u>at least</u> 50% of U.S. turtle nests. Finally,

28

there must be a drop in stage class mortality results and an increase in

individual foraging grounds.

<u>In addition to being listed in the Endangered Species Act, Atlantic Green</u>

29

<u>Sea Turtles are also listed in various other restrictive agreements.</u> These

29

agreements do everything from prohibit international trade of turtles, to

protect national and international habitat and nesting areas.

With sea turtle numbers on the rise, the problem seems to be decreasing.

But the struggle against human interference is <u>going to last a long, long time.</u>

30

Groups like STRP (Sea Turtle Restoration Project) must constantly bring suit

against commercial fisherman in order to see that the EPA guidelines are

upheld and *Chelonia mydas* are protected.

16. F. NO CHANGE
    G. because it is
    H. but
    J. thus

17. A. NO CHANGE
    B. a few exclusive, unique areas of the world
    C. a few things
    D. a few areas of the world

18. The author is considering deleting the preceding sentence. Should the author make this deletion?
    F. Yes, it is irrelevant to the topic of the paragraph as a whole.
    G. Yes, it repeats information previously stated in the paragraph.
    H. No, it helps the reader understand how unique these waters are.
    J. No, it clarifies what differentiates the waters from other aquatic regions.

19. A. NO CHANGE
    B. on the U.S. in Texas
    C. to the U.S. from Texas
    D. within the U.S. and also to

20. F. NO CHANGE
    G. has only recently begun
    H. have only recently begun
    J. began

21. A. NO CHANGE
    B. constant
    C. committed
    D. continue

22. The author is considering deleting the underlined portion of the sentence. Should the writer make this deletion?
    F. Yes, the information distracts from the primary focus of the sentence.
    G. Yes, the information is repetitive.
    H. No, it clarifies a way that human activity plays a role in the demise of the turtle.
    J. No, it provides scholarly evidence of the damage that humans are doing to the turtle.

23. A. NO CHANGE
    B. affection
    C. impaction
    D. effect

24. Which of the following sentences would provide the best transition between the previous paragraph and the current paragraph?
   F. NO CHANGE
   G. Even though humans are the main cause of sea turtle decline, they are also part of the solution.
   H. Human beings have done much to harm the sea turtle, and should be held responsible.
   J. We humans must do all that we can to protect this beautiful creature.

25. A. NO CHANGE
   B. harvesting of turtles, is now illegal.
   C. harvesting of turtles is now, illegal.
   D. harvesting of turtles, is now, illegal.

26. F. NO CHANGE
   G. three criteria be met—first Florida in particular, must support
   H. three criteria be met. First, Florida must support
   J. three criteria be met: first Florida, must support

27. A. NO CHANGE
   B. successive
   C. next
   D. soon

28. F. NO CHANGE
   G. at the very minimum
   H. what is more
   J. more or less

29. A. NO CHANGE
   B. Atlantic Green Sea Turtles are also listed, in addition to being listed in the Endangered Species Act, in various other restrictive agreements.
   C. In addition to being listed in the Endangered Species Act and also listed in various other restrictive agreements, Atlantic Green Sea Turtles are found.
   D. Also listed in various other restrictive agreements, in addition to being listed in the Endangered Species Act, are Atlantic Green Sea Turtles.

30. Given that all of the choices are true, which of the following provides the clearest description of the timeframe, both in the short and long terms, within which human interference will occur?
   F. NO CHANGE
   G. a never-ending process, forever into the future.
   H. an ongoing process with no clear end in sight.
   J. a process that will be happening for many years.

Passage III

Children are corrupted by the temptations of modern society and need
<u>   </u>
                                        31
<u>accountability more than ever.</u> Children find it completely unfair when
                        31

they're reprimanded for taking cookies, staying up too late, or tracking mud

in the house. <u>However,</u> they believe punishment entirely justified when
                        32

their toy has been stolen, they get to tattle about something someone else

did, or just when they get downright bored. For <u>my siblings and I,</u> justice
                                                                    33

was served in the form of "Kitchen Court."

[1] Kitchen Court was a relatively simple concept. [2] The parents are

out; <u>how</u> will we entertain ourselves while the eldest sister babysits? [3] Why not
        34

do something humiliating to the youngest? [4] Somehow they would always try

<u>(and almost succeed in)</u> convincing her that my brother and I were fighting
                35

about something, and I was always the one <u>with error.</u> [5] My sister
                                                        36

would rise, assess the situation, and announce it was time for Kitchen Court.

[6] My brother would escalate the situation by confusing me using

a combination of talking stuffed animals, and subtle brain washing. 37

With the judge presiding from a wooden chair <u>placed atop the kitchen table,</u>
                                                                    38

my brother would prosecute me, the <u>defendant, whom</u> had no idea what
                                            39

was going on. Witnesses in the form of dolls and action figures were called in.

They'd give their testimonies in various voices invented by my siblings, and

all would indicate me as the perpetrator. <u>Just like the proper uneducated</u>
40
<u>trashy talk show participant</u>, I would yell and scream until eventually
40
<u>the end of Kitchen Court would come, along with my impending sentence,</u>
41
<u>due to the meat tenderizer gavel banging upon the cutting board.</u>
41

These sentences would fluctuate between chores <u>with</u> an assortment
42
of time outs. The most mundane being forced to sit in a chair (like most

kids received), <u>and the most fascinating activity being locked</u> in a dog cage.
43
In retrospect, I have no idea why I willingly accepted these punishments,

or why I never attempted to open the dog cage myself. Maybe it was only

with maturity that I recognized the wonder of opposable thumbs.

<u>Possibly I learned that it was within my power to open the cage!</u> 44

Perhaps it was out respect for the justice system that allowed Kitchen

Court to be the final decision making body. Our father was a lawyer after all.

31. Given that all of the choices are true, which one would most effectively introduce the main idea of this paragraph?
A. NO CHANGE
B. Children need to have firm discipline to set them on the path for success later in life.
C. It is remarkable how children think that they can get away with all sorts of mischief.
D. The way a child's mind interprets justice is a fascinating thing.

32. F. NO CHANGE
    G. Due to this
    H. Interestingly
    J. Surprisingly

33. A. NO CHANGE
    B. us
    C. my siblings and me
    D. we children

34. Which of the following alternatives to the underlined portion would NOT be acceptable?
    F. out. How
    G. out – how
    H. out. How on earth
    J. out, how

35. The writer is considering deleting the underlined portion from the sentence. Should the writer make this change?
    A. Yes, the information distracts the reader from the main idea of the paragraph.
    B. Yes, the information interrupts the flow of the sentence.
    C. No, the information clarifies the extent to which the narrator was convinced by her siblings.
    D. No, the information provides details about how her siblings convinced her of her guilt.

36. F. NO CHANGE
    G. with mistake
    H. on the wrong
    J. at fault

37. Which of the following represents the most logical arrangement of the sentences in the preceding paragraph?
    A. NO CHANGE
    B. 1, 3, 4, 2, 5, 6
    C. 1, 2, 3, 4, 6, 5
    D. 2, 1, 3, 4, 6, 5

38. F. NO CHANGE
    G. on a table
    H. on top of the table inside the kitchen
    J. within the kitchen

39. A. NO CHANGE
    B. defendant, who
    C. defendant whom
    D. defendant who

40. The author wishes to introduce this sentence with an introductory phrase that vividly describes the way she will conduct herself in the kitchen court. Given that all of the choices are true, which one best accomplishes this task?
    F. NO CHANGE
    G. Like a person who is going to act quite crazy
    H. Acting like a person who has lost her mind
    J. Behaving like someone who had totally lost control

41. A. NO CHANGE
    B. the meat tenderizer gavel would bang upon the cutting board, signaling the end of Kitchen Court and the coming of my impending sentence.
    C. the meat tenderizer gavel bang would provide the coming of my impending sentence and the end of Kitchen court would be signaled.
    D. the end of the Kitchen Court would come, due to the bang of the meat tenderizer gavel, and the impending sentence would soon follow.

42. F. NO CHANGE
    G. due to
    H. and
    J. from

43. A. NO CHANGE
    B. and the most interesting being locked
    C. and also being
    D. with the most terrible thing being locked up

44. The author is considering deleting the preceding sentence from the paragraph. Should the writer make this deletion?
    F. Yes, because the same information conveyed in this sentence is indirectly discussed previously in the paragraph.
    G. Yes, because this information is completely irrelevant to the main idea of the paragraph.
    H. No, because it conveys the passion that the author had in this situation.
    J. No, because it provides a detailed account of how the author dealt with the adverse situation of the Kitchen Court.

45. Suppose the writer had decided to write an essay that details the experiences of one person with the American judicial system. Would this essay fulfill the writer's goal?
   A. Yes, because it mentions the court throughout the passage.
   B. Yes, because it addresses a situation that is very similar to a real court.
   C. No, because it shows how someone's experiences with a fictitious court rather than the real courts of the country.
   D. No, because it is clear that the entire passage is imaginary, instead of based on the experiences of an actual person.

PASSAGE IV

   People with the best intentions often end up doing exactly the opposite

of what they intended. Alfred Nobel, born in 1833, invented dynamite, <u>along</u>
                                                                          46
355 other things. 47 His father disliked his interest in the humanities

and forced <u>Alfred Nobel</u> to study abroad for two years, 1873 and 1874 49.
              48
It was during this sabbatical that he <u>met, Ascanio Sobrero, the inventor</u> of
                                                              50
nitroglycerin, in Paris. <u>His introduction to the explosive liquid is what perked</u>
                                                   51
<u>his interest in creating a more predictable and controlled explosive</u>
                                        51
<u>using nitroglycerin.</u> In 1864 he was finally successful in creating
        51
nitroglycerin paste inserted into rods that became dynamite.

   <u>He</u> had originally wanted to help with building new businesses and
   52
developing land all over the world. <u>What is more,</u> he ended up creating one of
                                            53
the most deadly weapons of the time. It is said that Nobel decided to create

the <u>famous, Nobel Peace Prize named in his honor, after</u> a French newspaper
                                54
printed an incorrect obituary of Alfred after his brother Ludvig died in

Cannes. The paper said "The merchant of death is dead ... Dr. Alfred Nobel who became rich by finding ways to kill more people faster than ever before." $\boxed{55}$

The last will <u>which</u> Nobel wrote left a large portion of his wealth to the
        56
development of the Nobel Peace Prize. The will was so controversial that

it wasn't approved for several years after his death in 1896. Nobel left

31,225,000 Swedish kronor, <u>or the equivalent of 250 million U.S. dollars</u>, to
          57
supply the prize money. <u>The Nobel Prize honors men and women for work</u>
          58
<u>in peace and has added prizes in the fields of economics, physics, chemistry,</u>
          58
<u>medicine, and literature.</u> The first prize, awarded in 1901, was split evenly
     58
between Jean Henri Dunant, the Swiss founder of the International

Committee of the Red Cross, and Frédéric Passy, <u>the French Founder and</u>
          59
<u>President who was of the cardinal French Peace society.</u> Two of the recent
        59
prizes were given to Martii Ahtisaari for his significant labors over

thirty years and in many continents to help solve international problems,

and Barack Obama "for his extraordinary efforts to strengthen international

diplomacy and cooperation between peoples." $\boxed{60}$

46. **F.** NO CHANGE
    G. between
    H. within
    J. among

47. At this point in the paragraph, the author wishes to have a sentence that expresses the breadth and depth of Alfred Nobel's intellectual skills, as well as provides a smooth transition between the sentence before and after. Which of the following sentences would best accomplish this?
    A. His invention of dynamite would be later used in such useful tasks as road construction, but some harmful tasks such as trench warfare.
    B. In addition to excelling in chemistry and physics, he was also fluent in several languages and wrote poetry.
    C. He was a brilliant young man, by far one of the most talented in science of anyone in his peer group.
    D. While being truly gifted in the sciences, he had an interest in literature and the arts.

48. F. NO CHANGE
    G. them
    H. Nobel to make the choice to
    J. him

49. The author is considering deleting the years from the preceding sentence (i.e., the phrase "1873 and 1874"). What would the sentence NOT lose if the author were to make this deletion?
    A. An idea of the historical context of when Nobel lived and worked
    B. An understanding of when a turning point in Nobel's life occurred
    C. A perception of when Nobel ceased to be interested in the humanities
    D. Information that allows us to see how old Nobel was at the time of this change

50. F. NO CHANGE
    G. met Ascanio Sobrero, the inventor
    H. met Ascanio Sobrero the inventor
    J. met Ascanio Sobrero, the inventor,

51. The author wishes to have this sentence make a smooth transition between the previous sentence and following sentence to clearly demonstrate how his meeting with Sobrero sparked a desire to create dynamite. Which of the following changes, if any, would best accomplish his goal?
    A. NO CHANGE
    B. Ascanio Sobrero inspired Nobel to conduct more in-depth scientific research that would help the world become a far better place.
    C. After meeting Sobrero, Nobel decided to create a new invention.
    D. The meeting with Sobrero inspired Nobel to create dynamite.

52. **F.** NO CHANGE
    G. The inventor
    H. They
    J. Nobel

53. **A.** NO CHANGE
    B. However,
    C. Consequently,
    D. As a result,

54. **F.** NO CHANGE
    G. famous Nobel Peace Prize named in his honor after
    H. famous Nobel Peace Prize, named in his honor, after,
    J. famous Nobel Peace Prize, named in his honor, after

55. If the author were to delete the preceding sentence, what would the paragraph lose?
    A. An unbiased description of what Nobel did in his lifetime
    B. Information that helps us understand Nobel's change of heart
    C. An explanation of how Nobel turned his idea into a business empire
    D. An analysis of the way in which Nobel died

56. **F.** NO CHANGE
    G. when
    H. that
    J. within which

57. The author is considering deleting the underlined portion of the sentence. Should the writer make this deletion?
    A. Yes, because it provides information that has already been mentioned.
    B. Yes, because it distracts the reader from the focus of the paragraph.
    C. No, because without it, we would have no information about the amount of money left.
    D. No, because it helps the reader understand how much money was left.

58. **F.** NO CHANGE
    G. In the fields of physics, chemistry, medicine, economics, and literature, men and women are honored by the Nobel Prize, as they have always been honored for peace.
    H. Men and women who do work in the fields of economics, chemistry, medicine, and literature are honored for their work, just as the Nobel prize honors the peacemakers.
    J. Great honors for men and women have been given by the Nobel Prize over the years, which has gradually added chemistry, physics, medicine and literature to accompany peace as fields that it recognizes.

59. A. NO CHANGE
    B. the French Founder, and President of the cardinal French Peace society.
    C. the French Founder and President of the cardinal French Peace society.
    D. the cardinal French Peace society of the French Founder and President.

60. If the writer had been assigned to write a brief biography that showed the impact of a famous person in history, would this essay successfully fulfill the assignment?
    F. Yes, because it discusses both the life of Nobel and the influence that he had on later generations.
    G. Yes, because it focuses on the modern-day impact that the Nobel Prize has had.
    H. No, because it does not discuss the impact that Nobel has had on the world after his death.
    J. No, because it focuses on just the Nobel Peace Prize, instead of discussing Nobel's life as well.

PASSAGE V

[1]

The train swings slightly from side to side, like a rocking chair, easing

me into a delightful laziness. Aiding the train is the sun, shining through the

window, making me drowsier by making the fabric of my jeans hot. I've missed
                 61
the warmth of the sun since I've been gone. The temperature in this region
                                                                    62
of the country is typically about 20 degrees higher on average than the median
                                       62
temperature in the country as a whole. I snap myself awake as the train passes
                 62
a landmark I recognize, signaling that I am home.

[2]

I grew up in a small town, middle of nowhere Arizona. My parents

moved there just <u>when I was born, and fell in love with the hot sand, Native</u>
63
<u>American Culture, and arid climate</u>. My mother always detested the rain
63
for no reason I can find. My memory of the early years is limited to

an oppressive, skin-burning cloudless sky. I remember having a <u>dog—a golden.</u>
64
It used to <u>lay</u> on our wraparound porch, panting in the heat, in a futile
65
attempt to find relief from the consistent 90 degree weather. I remember wishing

I could cool myself down by sticking my tongue out just like the dog. [66]

[3]

I smile to myself as I reminisce. Nothing has changed. The low shrubs and

cactuses are the same ones that have been there since I was little, <u>but the</u>
67
exception that they might be even a little more dried out than they used

to be.

[4]

The train slows as it nears the station. The hiss of the brakes and the

steam from the engine make <u>their</u> way back to my seat in the coach section—
68
I just love my college student budget. I stick my head out the window

and take a deep breath. I swear Arizona air has a <u>specific taste; as soon</u> as it hits
69
your tongue, it curls back and dries out.

[5]

Struggling with my bags and climbing out of the boxcar, <u>you spot</u> the familiar
70

faces. Helping people off the train is an ancient <u>conductor; off</u> to the side,
71

a homeless man who has been standing on the bench preaching the end of

the world since I was 5. $\boxed{72}$ It's like this town is a microcosm of the world,

stuck in time and never changing. Every year more and more kids move away

to <u>fewer</u> trying areas that receive more than seven inches of rain per year.
73

As they leave they take the restaurants, jobs, schools, and almost every

other business <u>to other towns far away.</u> Maybe something is changing here.
74

But just like always getting off this train, there's the 1981 Toyota Corolla

waiting to take me home, like every year before. $\boxed{75}$

61. **A.** NO CHANGE
    B. which has made my jeans quite hot, which in turn has made me drowsier.
    C. heating the dark fabric of my jeans, and making me even lazier.
    D. that has heated the jeans' dark fabric thereby increasing my laziness.

62. **F.** NO CHANGE
    G. The temperature is about 20 degrees higher here than elsewhere
    H. It is much hotter here—about 20 degrees on average—than it is in other places in the country
    J. OMIT the underlined portion.

63. **A.** NO CHANGE
    B. when I was born and fell in love with the hot sand Native American Culture and arid climate
    C. when I was born, and fell in love, with the hot sand, Native American Culture and arid climate
    D. when I was born and fell in love, with the hot sand, Native American Culture and arid climate

64. Which of the following alternatives to the underlined portion would be most acceptable?
    F. dog a golden.
    G. dog; a golden.
    H. dog: a golden.
    J. dog (a golden).

65. A. NO CHANGE
    B. lie
    C. have lain
    D. had lain

66. The writer is considering deleting the preceding sentence from the paragraph. Should the writer make this deletion?
    F. Yes, because it is not consistent with the tone of the rest of the paragraph.
    G. Yes, because it is not relevant to the paragraph as a whole.
    H. No, because it provides a vivid description that ties together the previous two sentences.
    J. No, because it provides clear details about how hot the temperature was in Arizona.

67. A. NO CHANGE
    B. also
    C. with
    D. because

68. F. NO CHANGE
    G. its
    H. there
    J. its'

69. Which of the following alternatives to the underlined portion would NOT be acceptable?
    A. specific taste. As soon
    B. specific taste—as soon
    C. specific taste: As soon
    D. specific taste, as soon

70. F. NO CHANGE
    G. one spots
    H. we spot
    J. I spot

71. **A.** NO CHANGE
    B. conductor, off
    C. conductor off
    D. conductor. Off

72. At this point, the author wishes to include a sentence that conveys the bittersweet feelings that the author feels when looking at the current situation of her town. Which of these would best accomplish the author's goal?
    F. I sadly smile at my stagnant town.
    G. I am astonished at my town's downfall.
    H. My town is nothing more than a failed experiment.
    J. Things will surely improve for my town as the coming decades unfold.

73. **A.** NO CHANGE
    B. less
    C. more
    D. OMIT the underlined portion

74. **F.** NO CHANGE
    G. to the surrounding states of Nevada and California
    H. to areas that will not help me or my family prosper
    J. OMIT the underlined portion

75. The authors wishes to insert the following sentence in the passage:

    "There's no moisture in Arizona, especially not now."

    Where is the most logical place to put this sentence?
    A. At the end of paragraph 1
    B. At the end of paragraph 2
    C. At the end of paragraph 4
    D. At the end of paragraph 5

If there is still time remaining, you may review your answers.

MATH TEST

Time—60 minutes
60 Questions

> **Directions:** Determine the answer to each question, and then fill in the matching oval on your answer sheet. Do not spend too much time on any one problem. Solve as many as possible, then come back to ones that you have skipped. You are allowed to use a calculator on this section, but several of the problems are best completed without a calculator.
>
> Unless stated otherwise, assume that drawings are NOT necessarily to scale, geometric figures are in a two-dimensional plane, "lines" are straight lines, and "average" means the arithmetic mean.

1. For the equation: $3x - 4(x - 2) + 6x - 8 = 0$, find the value of x.
   A. -4
   B. 0
   C. 2
   D. 4
   E. 8

2. A coat has a list price of $325.00. During November, it did not sell, and the merchant marked it down 20 percent. Then in December, she marked it down an additional 10 percent. What would a Christmas shopper in December pay for the coat in dollars?
   F. $6.50
   G. $227.50
   H. $230.00
   J. $234.00
   K. $286.00

3. A pie chart is to be developed to display data about the plans of the senior class:

   15% plan to go directly to work
   40% will attend a state university
   35% will attend a private college or university
   10% will join the military

   How many degrees will the combined "going to college" take up on the pie chart?
   A. 35
   B. 75
   C. 126
   D. 270
   E. 306

4. Joseph has the following scores on tests in his class, which has only 100 point tests for assignments:

Test Number	Score	Relative Weight
One	86	15%
Two	70	15%
Midterm	90	30%
Final	??	40%

What must Joseph score on the final exam to attain at least an 82% B average for the class?

F. 70
G. 74
H. 79
J. 82
K. 124

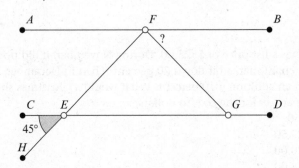

5. In the figure above, Points *A*, *F*, and *B* are collinear, and points *C*, *E*, *G*, and *D* are collinear. Lines *AB* and *CD* are parallel, and triangle *EFG* is isosceles with line segments *FG* and *EF* equivalent. If angle *CEH* is 45 degrees, what is the measure of angle *BFG*?

A. 30
B. 40
C. 45
D. 50
E. 55

6. Two numbers added together are 19. Their product is 70. What are the two numbers?

   F. 5, 14
   G. 7, 10
   H. 4, 15
   J. 3, 16
   K. 35, 2

7. $|-3|+|-2.5|=$?

   A. −5.5
   B. −4.5
   C. .5
   D. 5
   E. 5.5

8. Which of the following must be true for $\triangle ABC$ where $AB \cong BC$ and AC is 1.5 times the length of AB?

   F. $\angle BCA > \angle BAC$
   G. $\angle BCA > \angle CBA$
   H. $\angle ABC > \angle BCA$
   J. $\angle ABC < \angle BCA$
   K. $AB \cong AC$

9. Ten students take a biology test and receive the following scores: 45, 55, 50, 70, 65, 80, 40, 90, 70, 85. What is the mean of the students' test scores?

   A. 55
   B. 60
   C. 62
   D. 65
   E. 70

10. What is $\frac{1}{3}$ of 210?

   F. 0.3333
   G. 30
   H. 45
   J. 70
   K. 240

11. Given that the two trapezoids are similar to one another, having identical internal angle measurements, what is the area of the smaller trapezoid, assuming that the larger trapezoid has an area of 20 and a top base length of 6 units and the smaller trapezoid has a top base length of 3 units?

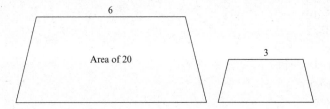

A. 5
B. 6
C. 8
D. 12
E. 15

12. Andrew is ordering books from a Sam's Bookstore. Each book is $8 at full price. If he purchases $100 or more of books, he receives a 20 percent discount on books above this threshold. What is the minimum number of books he needs to purchase in order to qualify for the discount?
F. 8
G. 12
H. 13
J. 16
K. 20

13. If x and y are directly proportional and $x = 3$ when $y = 8$, what is the value of x when $y = 13$?
A. 0.615
B. 4.875
C. 15
D. 34.667
E. 39

14. Which of these values is the smallest?

    F. 0.2222̄

    G. $\dfrac{2}{11}$

    H. $\dfrac{3}{16}$

    J. $\dfrac{8}{60}$

    K. $\dfrac{5}{26}$

15. If the ratio of the radii of two circles is 2:5, what is the ratio of their areas?

    A. 1:3
    B. 1:5
    C. 4:25
    D. 2:5
    E. 16:25

16. The longest side of a triangle is 10. Which of the following could NOT be the lengths of the other two sides?

    F. 4, 7
    G. 5, 5
    H. 3, 9
    J. 9, 8
    K. 7, 6

17. What is the product of the greatest even prime number and the least odd prime number?

    A. 6
    B. 9
    C. 11
    D. 14
    E. 18

18. A 14-inch diameter pizza has only cheese and pepperoni all the way to its edges so that there is no crust showing when one looks at it from above. The pepperoni consists of 100 circular slices of $\dfrac{1}{2}$ inch radius each. To the nearest whole inch, how many square inches of the surface of the pizza will NOT be covered by pepperoni?

    F. 9
    G. 16
    H. 16π
    J. 22π
    K. 24π

19. Assuming that all of the sides are straight lines and meet at right angles, what is the perimeter of the figure below?

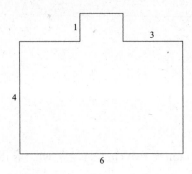

A. 14
B. 18
C. 20
D. 22
E. 26

20. The school principal has to have three different teachers speak at the graduation ceremony—one as the opener, one as the name-reader, and one as the closer. There are 85 teachers on staff. How many possible speaking lineups can the principal have?

F. 252
G. 255
H. 592,620
J. 592,704
K. 614,125

Questions 21–23 use the Calendar below.

January 2011

Sunday	Monday	Tuesday	Wednesday	Thursday	Friday	Saturday
26	27	28	29	30	31	1
2	3	4	5	6	7	8
9	10	11	12	13	14	15
16	17	18	19	20	21	22
23	24	25	26	27	28	29
30	31	1	2	3	4	5

21. January 2011 begins on a Saturday and ends on a Monday. What fraction of the days in January are on the weekend (Saturdays and Sundays)?

    A. $\dfrac{1}{3}$

    B. $\dfrac{10}{31}$

    C. $\dfrac{9}{30}$

    D. $\dfrac{13}{31}$

    E. $\dfrac{20}{31}$

22. Which of the following functions would provide the calendar date (i.e., the number of the day in the month of January) that each Wednesday of the month is, assuming that n represents the number of Wednesday that it is (i.e., 1 would be for the first Wednesday, 2 for the second)?

    F. $f(n) = 5n$

    G. $f(n) = 7n$

    H. $f(n) = 7(n - 1)$

    J. $f(n) = 5 + 7(n - 1)$

    K. $f(n) = \dfrac{5}{12}n$

23. February of 2011 has 28 days and March has 31 days. On what day of the week will next month, April, begin?

    A. Monday
    B. Tuesday
    C. Wednesday
    D. Thursday
    E. Friday

_____

24. For imaginary numbers $i = \sqrt{-1}$, what is the value of $\sqrt{4i^4}$?

    F. -1
    G. 0
    H. 2
    J. -4
    K. Undefined

25. Triangle *ABC* is a right triangle and the sides all have lengths that are consecutive odd integers. Given that *x* represents the smallest side, what would the lengths of the other two sides be?

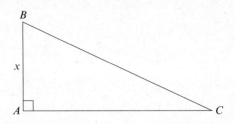

A. $X + 1, X + 2$
B. $X + 2, X + 4$
C. $X - 2, X - 4$
D. $X - 1, X - 2$
E. $(X + 2)^2, (X + 4)^2$

26. An equilateral triangle has sides of 12 inches. What is the approximate area of the triangle?
F. 62
G. 72
H. 84
J. 112
K. 144

27. Allison is on a walking tour through Paris, France. She has a device that can give her instantaneous information on her speed at any given time. Her first trip to a tourist site involved the following data:

- 15 minutes at 3 miles per hour
- 30 minutes at 4 miles per hour
- 15 minutes at 2 miles per hour

What was her average speed in miles/hour for this hour of walking?
A. 3
B. 3.25
C. 4.4
D. 6.15
E. 9

28. The result of $\sqrt{-3 \times -4} \times \sqrt{3} \times \sqrt{4}$ is:
    F. an irrational positive number.
    G. an irrational negative number.
    H. an imaginary number.
    J. a negative integer.
    K. a positive integer.

29. Dice have 6 sides a piece, with each side numbered 1, 2, 3, 4, 5, or 6. If a die is rolled two times in a row, what is the probability that the sum of the two rolls will be 2?
    A. $\dfrac{1}{36}$

    B. $\dfrac{1}{32}$

    C. $\dfrac{1}{24}$

    D. $\dfrac{1}{12}$

    E. $\dfrac{1}{6}$

30. $\sqrt{4x^4} \times \sqrt{16x^2} =$
    F. $64x^6$
    G. $4x^3$
    H. $16x^3$
    J. $8x^4$
    K. $8x^3$

31. The drawing below is represented by what equation or inequality?

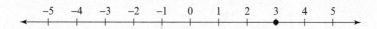

    A. $X < 3$
    B. $X > 3$
    C. $X = 3$
    D. $X \le 3$
    E. $X \ge 3$

32. The Theory of Relativity states that Energy (E) is equal to Mass (m) multiplied by the Velocity of Light (c) squared: $E = mc^2$. Which of the following would correctly express Mass (m) in terms of the other variables?

F. $m = E^2c^2$

G. $m = \dfrac{E}{c^2}$

H. $m = E \times c$

J. $m = \dfrac{c^2}{E}$

K. Cannot be determined with the given information.

33. The volume of a sphere is given by the equation $V = \dfrac{4}{3}\pi r^3$. If sphere A has 27 times the volume of sphere B, what is the ratio of the radius of sphere A to the radius of sphere B?

A. 3:1
B. 2:1
C. 1:9
D. 1:12
E. 27:1

34. The graph of $y = x^2 - 1$ is shown in the standard (x, y) coordinate plane below. For which of the following equations is the graph of the parabola shifted 2 units to the right and 2 units up?

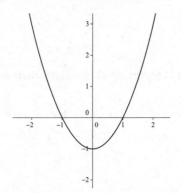

F. $y = (x - 2)^2 + 1$
G. $y = (x - 2)^2 - 1$
H. $y = x^2 - 2$
J. $y = (x - 4)^2 + 1$
K. $y = (x + 2)^2$

35. If there is a 70% chance that it will rain on a given day, what is the percent chance that it will NOT rain on that same day?
    A. 0%
    B. 30%
    C. 50%
    D. 70%
    E. 100%

36. If an equilateral triangle has a side of length 8, what will be the area of a square that has the same perimeter as this triangle?
    F. 9
    G. 16
    H. 25
    J. 36
    K. 49

37. All the items in this list have the same difference between them:
    1, 7, __ , __ , 25, with the 3rd and the 4th terms left blank.
    What would be the sum of the 3rd and 4th terms?
    A. 6
    B. 20
    C. 32
    D. 44
    E. 56

38. How many diagonals are in a regular octagon?
    F. 8
    G. 16
    H. 17
    J. 19
    K. 20

39. What is the shortest distance between the y axis and the point (2, 7)?
    A. 1
    B. 2
    C. 3
    D. 5
    E. 7

40. A particular whale's milk is 50% fat and a particular cow's milk is 3.5% fat. To the nearest whole cup, how many cups of the cow's milk would one need to drink in order to have at least the same amount of fat as there would be in one cup of the whale's milk?

    F. 4
    G. 7
    H. 12
    J. 15
    K. 17

41. $5x^3 - 15x^2 + 10x^4 =$

    A. $5x^2(x + 3 - 2x^2)$
    B. $5(x^3 - 3x^2 + 5x^4)$
    C. $5x^3(-2 + 2x)$
    D. $(5x^2 + 5)(x - 2)$
    E. $5x^2(x - 3 + 2x^2)$

42. In order to convert the area of a circle with radius R to the circumference of the same circle, the area should be multiplied by which of the following ratios?

    F. $\dfrac{4}{R^2}$
    G. 2
    H. $2\pi R$
    J. R^2
    K. $\dfrac{2}{R}$

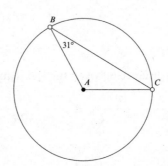

43. In the circle above, point A is the center of the circle, points B and C lie on the circle, and angle ABC measures 31°. What is the measure of angle CAB?

    A. 31
    B. 62
    C. 118
    D. 180
    E. 242

44. Jasmine takes 5 minutes to solve each math problem that she has for homework, and 2 minutes to read each page from her textbook. If she is assigned "X" math problems and "Y" total pages of her book, what equation expresses the total number of minutes it will take to complete the assignments?

    F. $3X + 2Y$
    G. $5X + 2Y$
    H. $10XY$
    J. $3XY$
    K. $3(X - Y)$

45. If Owen has blue jeans with a 32-inch waist, what will be the new jean waist size Owen has to wear (to the nearest whole inch) if his waist circumference increases by 15%?

    A. 34 inches
    B. 35 inches
    C. 36 inches
    D. 37 inches
    E. 38 inches

46. A ladder of length 20 feet leans against a building on level ground. The angle the ladder makes with the ground is 35°. Approximately how far up the building, in feet, does the ladder go?

    F. 8.4
    G. 11.5
    H. 13.5
    J. 15.1
    K. 20.2

47. If $x = 2t - 1$ and $y = 3t + 4$ then x equals which of the following in terms of y?

    A. $\frac{2}{3}y - \frac{11}{3}$
    B. $-\frac{3}{2}y - \frac{11}{3}$
    C. $t - 1$
    D. $\frac{2}{3}y + \frac{11}{3}$
    E. $2y - 1$

48. Morgan is on a social networking website. She has 60 female friends and 50 male friends and belongs to 5 social groups. If 30% of her female friends live in town and 40% of her male friends live in town, how many out-of-town friends does she have on the social networking site?
    F. 38
    G. 72
    H. 110
    J. 360
    K. 1800

49. Assuming that each sphere will touch adjacent spheres at a single point, what is the maximum number of spheres of radius 3 inches that can be placed in a cube of 6 feet on a side?
    A. 8
    B. 27
    C. 144
    D. 216
    E. 1,728

50. Which of the following is equivalent to this expression: $\sqrt[3]{-27x^9}$?
    F. $3x^3$
    G. $-3x^3$
    H. $-27x^3$
    J. $\frac{1}{9}x^9$
    K. $-3x^6$

51. If $\frac{A}{B}$ is the slope of line m, what is the slope of a line perpendicular to it?
    A. A
    B. B
    C. $\frac{A}{B}$
    D. $-\frac{B}{A}$
    E. $-\frac{A}{B}$

52. A right circular cylindrical paper tube has a height of 10 inches and a radius of 3 inches. Andrew unrolls the tube flat on a table. What is the area of the rectangle made by the unrolled paper tube in square inches?

    F. 18π
    G. 30π
    H. 60π
    J. 90π
    K. 900

53. Knowing that $\frac{\pi}{2} + \frac{\pi}{3} = \frac{5\pi}{6}$, what is the value of $\sin\left(\frac{5\pi}{6}\right)$ using the following information?

$$\sin(\alpha + \beta) = \sin\alpha\cos\beta + \cos\alpha\sin\beta$$

θ Value	Sin θ	Cos θ
$\frac{\pi}{3}$	$\frac{\sqrt{3}}{2}$	$\frac{1}{2}$
$\frac{\pi}{2}$	1	0
$\frac{\pi}{6}$	$\frac{1}{2}$	$\frac{\sqrt{3}}{2}$

   A. $\frac{\sqrt{3}}{2}$

   B. $\frac{5}{6}$

   C. $\frac{1}{2}$

   D. 0

   E. 1

54. Which of the following equations correctly uses the quadratic formula to solve for x in the following equation?

$$3x^2 - 4x + 2 = 0$$

F. $\dfrac{-3 \pm \sqrt{(-4)^2 - 4 \cdot 3 \cdot 2}}{2(-4)}$

G. $3^2 + (-4)^2 + 2^2$

H. $x(3x - 4) = -2$

J. $\sqrt{(-4)^2 - 4 \cdot 3 \cdot 2}$

K. $\dfrac{4 \pm \sqrt{(-4)^2 - 4 \cdot 3 \cdot 2}}{2 \cdot 3}$

55. What is the sine of angle A?

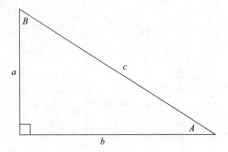

A. $\dfrac{a}{c}$

B. $\dfrac{A}{c}$

C. $\dfrac{b}{c}$

D. $\dfrac{a}{B}$

E. $\dfrac{A}{b}$

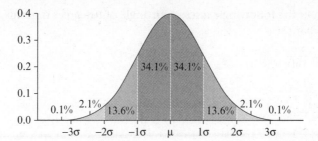

56. The plot of a normal distribution is provided above, with each band representing a value that is one standard deviation away from the mean. Suppose that researcher A does a study in which the standard deviation of the values is quite low and researcher B repeats the study, but the standard deviation of her values is relatively high. How would the bell curves of their data most likely compare?

    F. Researcher B's curve would be narrower than Researcher A's curve since the values would be closer to the mean, which they would roughly share.

    G. Researcher A's curve would be narrower than Researcher B's curve since the values would be closer to the mean, which they would roughly share.

    H. The curves would be of the same width and location.

    J. Researcher B's curve would be narrower *and* would have a greater mean than that of Researcher A.

    K. Researcher A's curve would be narrower *and* would have a greater mean than that of Researcher B.

57. A complex sphere is composed of three different materials. The inner portion is brass and has a radius of 10 centimeters; the middle portion extends an additional 6 centimeters radially from the inner portion; the outer portion extends an additional 12 centimeters beyond the middle portion. If the volume of a sphere is computed by using the following formula,

$$V = \frac{4}{3}\pi r^3$$

    then approximately what percent of the volume of the total sphere is made up of the middle shell portion?

    A. 6
    B. 9
    C. 12
    D. 14
    E. 17

58. Which of the following expresses an angle of θ degrees in terms of ϕ radians?

F. $\theta = \dfrac{\pi\phi}{180}$

G. $\theta = \dfrac{180\phi}{\pi}$

H. $\theta = 180\phi\pi$

J. $\theta = \dfrac{1}{180\phi}$

K. $\theta = 180\phi - \pi$

59. A checkerboard is a square that is divided into 8 squares by 8 squares, each of the same size. The squares are two colors: red and black, with half of the squares red and half of the squares black. The edges of the red squares do not touch those of any other red squares, although the red squares will touch the corners of other red squares. This is also the case for the black squares. If Pamela wants to randomly select a square, what are the odds that it will be a red square that does NOT lie on the border of the checkerboard?

A. 64

B. 16

C. $\dfrac{1}{2}$

D. $\dfrac{9}{32}$

E. $\dfrac{1}{4}$

60. What is the 8th term in the following sequence?

3, 5, 8, 13, 21 . . .

F. 34

G. 45

H. 55

J. 89

K. 144

If there is still time remaining, you may review your answers.

READING TEST

Time—35 minutes
40 Questions

Directions: There are several reading selections in this section, each of which is followed by questions. After you read a passage, determine the best answer to each question and fill in the matching oval on your answer sheet. Refer back to the passages as often as you need.

PASSAGE I

Prose Fiction—*And Magical Is Art*

The contraindications of nitroglycerine are a pulse below fifty or above one hundred beats per minute, a systolic blood pressure beneath ninety milli-meters of mercury, head trauma, and the prior administration of vasodilators.
Line That's what it says on the bottle. What it doesn't say is that nitroglycerine is
(5) what makes dynamite explode. It's a little funny—when I feel it coming; like my heart's on the brink of combustion, all I need to do is slip a little slice of dynamite under my tongue. Perhaps it works like a particle accelerator, smashing two equal and oppositely charged orbs together to obliterate them both. Perhaps my heart transcends Newtonian physics.
(10) And it's a little embarrassing, too. It's silly, but when I grew up girls weren't supposed to have chest pains. Or careers. Or rights, for that matter. Perhaps, as they say, it comes with the territory. But there are no little pink ribbons for women whose hearts are failing them. Though I suppose there's really no elegance in illness, anywhere. Still, I can't imagine myself being
(15) snuffed out by a bad heart—clutching my chest with rigid, digging fingers; collapsing like a domino behind two hundred years-worth of fat men who fell, gasping, to the floor and unbuttoned their badly tailored vests in lone-some offices and file rooms. Perhaps they built skyscrapers hoping to abridge the soul's ascent. Imagine a ghost who can't catch his breath.
(20) "Takotsubo cardiomyopathy"—medicine has a way of sucking all the po-etry out of death. I think most everyone would prefer to read in their obitu-ary that they had died of a broken heart. Now there's a fine way for a woman of fantastical predilections like myself to go; pining away for a lover lost at sea, or an only child estranged by famine and war. Suffering in solitude was
(25) once an honored virtue in a man, but it remains the unrewarded expecta-tion of a woman. Caitlin Macnamara—whose sorrow was marrying the poet Dylan Thomas—never *rage, raged against the dying of the light*, though she had more cause. People like to say that Shakespeare understood women—maybe in Rosalind and Beatrice, but I suspect they're just shades and shadows of
(30) the entire and true dark lady that tormented his heart; one austere, the other

fierce. Said Rosalind, "Women keep a special corner in their hearts for the sins they have never committed." Said Beatrice, "O God, that I were a man! I would eat his heart in the market-place." And what of Dickinson? "I heard a fly buzz when I died; the stillness round my form was like the stillness in
(35) the air between the heaves of storm." It's idyllic, and it's sinister; like me and my silent, strangling heart.

They say some women's heart attacks are silent; that they feel no pain, and their heart dies like a leaf in autumn, shriveling. I believe it. I can easily imagine myself holding hands with death, and never realizing it. Gypsies,
(40) quacks, and clairvoyants read the life line on our palms, and even skeptics, though they deny it, believe. That's how we see life—linear; climbing, pushing, staggering forward. But a line is nondirectional, so what we really see is an arrow; a line poisoned by the inflexible motion of time. Attached to the electrocardiograph, they trace my arrow on the Cartesian plane, and tell me
(45) I am approaching its flinty, tapered tip. It's divination: they scry the line like any ancient soothsayer, astragalomancing me with the knuckle bones of a forgotten king. Paul Simon sang that medicine is magical, and magical is art. Maybe I'd like my doctors more if they wore talismans instead of stethoscopes, and swapped their white coats for the trappings of a wandering
(50) shaman.

As it is, the only thing I can trust is my body, and even that is failing me. But I still feel; and in my mind I've raised huge, impervious cities of magnesium and white stone, suspension bridges that fasten together the self-same realms of sense and memory; the sort that no volume of dynamite will
(55) destroy. My life line moves in four dimensions, swirling to and fro like a cottonwood seed caught in a mercurial breeze. And my heart is like a troubled ocean; vast, mysterious, and dark.

1. The general style of this passage could best be described as:
   A. a dramatic dialogue.
   B. a feminist manifesto.
   C. an internal monologue.
   D. an anecdotal narrative.

2. The speaker seems to believe that people could benefit from approaching the idea of death with which of the following attitudes?
   F. Respect for its mysteriousness
   G. Scientific objectivity
   H. Fear of its inevitability
   J. Disregard for its reality

3. As used in line 23, the word "fantastical" most nearly means:
   A. feminine.
   B. bizarre.
   C. fanciful.
   D. exorbitant.

4. The quotations from Shakespeare in lines 31–33, "'Women . . . in the market-place,'" are used to illustrate the contrast between which of the following feelings in the hearts of women?
   F. Seriousness and passion
   G. Secretiveness and hunger
   H. Love and hate
   J. Sorrow and humility

5. The tone of the passage as a whole is best described as:
   A. militant.
   B. hopeless.
   C. pensive.
   D. fearful.

6. As used in line 14, the word "elegance" most nearly means:
   F. superiority.
   G. gracefulness.
   H. luxuriousness.
   J. excellence.

7. The likening of the speaker's life line to the motion of a cottonwood seed in the wind serves to:
   A. underscore the speaker's feelings of indignation and depression.
   B. suggest the speaker's feelings of uncertainty and transcendence.
   C. express the speaker's hope for a better future.
   D. identify the similarities between a seed and a person.

8. The underlying irony underscored in lines 1–7 is that:
   F. something scientifically serious can also be extremely humorous.
   G. what is written on a bottle is so different from what a medicine can do to one's body.
   H. scientific innovations can be used to help those with heart problems.
   J. something medically helpful can also be used for destructive purposes.

9. It can reasonably be inferred from the fourth paragraph, lines 37–50, that the author would be happiest if the doctors would give up the notion that they can be:
   A. knowledgeable about medicine.
   B. certain about their predictions.
   C. magical and artistic in their craft.
   D. able to feel the pain of their patients.

10. Which of the following does the passage NOT imply is a way that women as a whole have been thought of by society?
   F. They did not have rights.
   G. They were expected to suffer alone.
   H. They had quiet heart attacks.
   J. They never received pink ribbons.

PASSAGE II

Social Science—*Tristan the Warrior*

Throughout the Middle Ages, societies in Europe were governed largely by feudalism, a system that relies heavily on sworn agreements of the landowning elite. The development of the feudal system was facilitated by a growing
Line need within small communities for military and governmental protection
(5) against the invasions and territory-wars that were erupting with alarming frequency. For this reason, the emergent feudal social and political structures included a previously unseen ruling class of citizenry, dubbed the "warrior class," dedicated specifically to honing their skills in warfare.

In the feudal system, the bonds of loyalty, honor, and service among
(10) men—specifically between Lord and Vassal—were considered of utmost importance. Feudal Lords were men who possessed wealth, typically in the form of land. In order to maintain or expand his wealth, a Lord could offer a portion of his power to other men in exchange for their service and loyalty. Following a formal ceremony of Homage, these men were knighted, often
(15) given land, and became forever incorporated into the ruling social class. They became Vassals, and a Vassal's oath to serve, protect, and obey his Lord was meant to be the most sacred aspect of his life.

The Romance of Tristan provides us with a glimpse at the ideal feudal warrior as conceptualized by Lords in the Middle Ages, and demonstrates the
(20) model traits of loyalty, aptitude in combat, and selflessness most valued in the warrior class. Early in the narrative, Tristan responds to his Lord's call to fight Morholt, an Irish nobleman, so that the Cornish people will not have to pay a slave tribute to Ireland, and requests to be knighted for this specific task. Lord Mark consents, as his other Vassals are too cowardly, or too un-
(25) skilled to compete with Morholt. Later in this episode, Tristan reveals that, by

blood, he is the nephew of Lord Mark. Upon hearing this, Mark wavers and attempts to persuade Tristan against risking his life. However, Tristan insists on fighting, proclaiming that he has taken an oath of Homage to Lord Mark, and now must carry out his sacred duty.

(30) Later on, Tristan demonstrates further self-sacrifice on behalf of Lord Mark. Having revealed his relation to the Lord, other nobles at court become jealous of Tristan, claiming that if Mark does not find a wife with whom he can produce an heir, Tristan will inherit all of Lord Mark's wealth. Tristan responds to this claim by personally pledging to find his Lord a suitable wife,

(35) and sets out on a long journey to find such a woman. By and by Tristan slays a dragon, and upon doing so, is awarded with Yseut, the daughter of an Irish king. However, rather than taking the beautiful Yseut as his wife, Tristan claims her for Lord Mark and brings her home. Tristan's acts throughout these episodes—forsaking both a large inheritance and a bride—illustrate the

(40) degree of fealty expected of a warrior by his Lord.

Notably, while the *Romance of Tristan* encapsulates the ideal traits of a feudal warrior—strength, honor, loyalty to a Lord—it also reveals one of the darker aspects of feudalism. In the feudal system, women were frequently objectified and regarded as goods to be traded and used disposably. Often

(45) women were married off in order to secure and solemnize political arrangements. In general, one might say that the emphasis placed on the bonds of honor and loyalty between Vassal and Lord left little room for social bonds between men and women. Tristan embodies this unpleasant feudal quality as seamlessly as he fits the mold of the ideal warrior. The language used to

(50) describe his interactions with Yseut evinces the relationships between noblemen and noblewomen. Tristan first "wins" her from her father by performing a task; then he proceeds to "give" her to Lord Mark. At no point in the narrative is Yseut represented as a fully human character, but rather as a sort of inert currency to be exchanged among the men of the ruling classes.

(55) In a later episode, Tristan's treatment of the maid Brangain shows his lack of consideration for women in another way. Tristan engages Brangain for her body, convincing her to sleep with Mark on the night of his wedding to Yseut. Brangain is only valuable to Tristan for her virginity, which he sees ultimately as a tool to be used for his own advantage. These events in particular

(60) demonstrate how the feudal system conceptually disassembled women of the Middle Ages into their sexual components, representing them as somehow less than the sum of their parts.

11. Which of the following best describes the general structure of the passage?
    A. Analysis of a specific example to illustrate general social trends
    B. Discussion of a work of literature to show patterns in works of art
    C. Presentation of a biographical episode to provide examples of loyalty and courage
    D. An account of a Medieval historical event

12. What is the function of the second paragraph (lines 9–17) in the passage as whole?
   F. To provide definitions of obscure historical terminology
   G. To present examples illustrating the importance of loyalty and virtue in a Feudal society
   H. To give historical background of a general nature
   J. To analyze gender relations in Medieval Europe

13. It can reasonably be inferred that what may have significantly contributed to Tristan's different treatment of Brangain and Yseut?
   A. Tristan's evolving attitudes on gender relations
   B. A difference in their social classes
   C. Brangain's relative youth and Yseut's maturity
   D. Differences in their beauty and attractiveness

14. Based on the information in paragraph 3 (lines 18–29) and the passage as a whole, what does the author suggest is the accurately ordered hierarchy of medieval loyalties, from least important to most important?
   F. Homage, Family, Underprivileged
   G. Family, Underprivileged, Homage
   H. Homage, Underprivileged, Family
   J. Underprivileged, Family, Homage

15. The phrase "less than the sum of their parts" in line 62 serves to show that the general Medieval attitude toward women was:
   A. mathematically precise.
   B. consistently abusive.
   C. oppressive and indifferent.
   D. antiquated and progressive.

16. It can be reasonably concluded from paragraph 5 (lines 41–54) that women in Medieval society were generally treated most like:
   F. commodities.
   G. animals.
   H. slaves.
   J. enchantresses.

17. In line 35, the phrase "By and by" most nearly means:
   A. after many decades.
   B. after some time.
   C. as a result of.
   D. through and through.

18. The author of the passage would most likely be interested in further analysis of which of the following agendas of *The Romance of Tristan*?
   F. To tell entertaining stories about princesses and dragons that all members of society could enjoy
   G. To help justify inequality between men and women in society
   H. To demonstrate the proper forms of diplomacy among heads of state
   J. To illustrate what a normal knight would do when faced with an ethical dilemma

19. It is reasonable to conclude from the third paragraph (lines 18–29) that Lord Mark would not have objected to Tristan's desire to fight Morholt had Tristan not been Mark's:
   A. knight.
   B. nobleman.
   C. nephew.
   D. Lord.

20. According to the passage, the overall relationship between Lords and Vassals during the Middle Ages was one of:
   F. equitable partnership.
   G. unbalanced reciprocity.
   H. unwavering loyalty.
   J. hostile rebellion.

PASSAGE III

Humanities—*Passage A is a woman's tribute to her favorite poet, Gwendolyn Brooks. Passage B is a critic's response to one of Brooks' poems.*

PASSAGE A

The power of the poem, for me, is discovery. An effective poem doesn't tell us much of anything; it shows us one or more vivid images and allows us to uncover something on our own—something which contains shades of
Line both the author and the reader. In that way, the poem is different for every-
(5) one who reads it.

I found Gwendolyn Brooks in December of the millennial year, the day after she passed. I saw the headline on my MSN homepage: "First Black Author to Win Pulitzer Dies." There was a link to a few of her poems at the top of the page, and since I had an exam to study for, I clicked on it as a
(10) justification for further procrastination.

She struck me first as a bold combination of academic and activist, an objective protester of all that is unjust. Obsessed, she was, with perceptions of beauty, questioning ugliness and more often than not exposing the truly

ugly. Her work primarily focused on the Black urban poor, but she was not
(15) in the business of telling, even when her words were direct. Her poetics were
neither a lament nor a complaint nor a plea; she never became didactic.
Instead, it was her skill for creation that set her apart.

Born in Kansas in 1917, but spending most of her life in Chicago, Brooks
attended a myriad of white and black schools which worked to shape her
(20) thoughts on race very early. By thirteen she had published her first poem;
by sixteen she had published over seventy. And as she developed, so did her
poetry, becoming more and more politically inclined. By the time I had met
her, she was the matter-of-fact professor in glasses and a shapeless hat, an
image that complements the majority of her biographies.

(25)   Through Brooks, I had hard conversation after hard conversation. She
seemed intensely aware of racial and social injustice, but unwilling to freely
lend me her stance. Find it, she would urge. What else, she would probe.
There's more, she would rage. Somehow, I am a poet born through the inter-
rupted thoughts of a dead woman.

PASSAGE B

(30)   Gwendolyn Brooks' "The Lovers of the Poor" is a satirical poem that points
out the hypocrisy within a group of white, wealthy females who supposedly
love to give to the poor. In Brooks' representation, the rosy women work at
a soup kitchen not because they are particularly passionate about helping
the destitute and despairing, but because they have been trained to believe
(35) it is expected of them. Their "scented bodies" and "lovely skirts" are in stark
contrast to what the speaker calls "the puzzled wreckage/Of the middle passage." Intense imagery depicts the crude reality of poverty that surprises and
then overwhelms the not-so-altruistic guild.

Upon the arrival of the Ladies' Betterment League, an urban scene is
(40) depicted through "diluted gold bars across the boulevard," bars that the
privileged are free to walk in and out of, but which serve as a cage for others.
The "barbarously fair" love of the volunteers is symbolic of their immediate
contradiction: pale, innocent, and clean in appearance, they are far from
it in nature. Soon, it becomes clear that the women are utterly appalled by
(45) the smells and sights of poverty. Before the conclusion of the poem, the
women make a mad dash to escape their philanthropic duties—deciding that
it would be more fitting to send money rather than to create change themselves, and refusing even to breathe the same air as the indigent.

Brooks' poetic contrast is far from merely socio-economic. She uses lan-
(50) guage such as "pink paint," "milky chill," and "rose-fingers" to differentiate
the elite from their counterparts. For her, the class hierarchy is very much
related to racial hegemony. Race becomes a factor in what is beautiful, and
the author demands reconsideration.

The reader is liable to feel disgust at the disgust, repulse at the repulsion.
(55) Distasteful, and even shameful, is the privilege that is only willing to give on
terms of convenience and comfort. Yet, the speaker insists on the ugliness of

poverty, jumping from one vulgar image to another. Ultimately, the author makes sure to avoid the romanticizing of the poor that characterizes the affluent women's expectations in confronting the deprived. Interestingly, the
(60) women sought a "worthy poor," apparently worthy not by the extent of their need, but the extent of their beauty. Brooks mocks the naivety and arrogance of the well-to-do who pat themselves on the back for their compassion, but are all too often wrapped in a silk blanket of pretention.

Questions 21–24 are about Passage A.

21. It can be reasonably inferred that the narrator of the passage came across the poetry of Gwendolyn Brooks through
    A. focused research.
    B. happenstance.
    C. university coursework.
    D. review of periodicals.

22. According to the passage, the poet Gwendolyn Brooks was how old when she died?
    F. 61
    G. 68
    H. 76
    J. 83

23. The narrator suggests that if one were to read a poem from the early career of Gwendolyn Brooks, it would most likely have what political tone?
    A. Stridently conservative
    B. Rigidly liberal
    C. Relatively apolitical
    D. Passionately vocal

24. A teacher who tried to model her teaching style after Gwendolyn Brooks' own educational style, as portrayed by the narrator, would most likely
    F. draw contrasts between her views and those of others.
    G. use her own family life as a model.
    H. provide clear guidance on her expectations.
    J. try to show rather than tell.

Questions 25–27 are about Passage B.

25. The title that Gwendolyn Brooks chose for the poem analyzed in this passage is primarily intended to be
   A. ironic.
   B. skeptical.
   C. disconnected.
   D. appropriate.

26. The main purpose of the paragraph in lines 49–53 is to
   F. extend the scope of the narrator's analysis.
   G. introduce a contrasting theme into the essay.
   H. compare two seemingly unrelated situations.
   J. anticipate and address a likely reader objection.

27. The narrator of the passage would most likely be impressed by which type of charity?
   A. One that uses media contacts to motivate other donors through publicity
   B. One that gathers enormous sums of money from wealthy donors
   C. One with volunteers who are not afraid to get "dirty" as they help
   D. One with leaders knowledgeable about the latest poverty statistics

Questions 28–30 are about both passages.

28. The poem that is analyzed in Passage B is most nearly an example of which of the following as mentioned in Passage A?
   F. Lines 4–5, "In that way . . . reads it."
   G. Lines 12–14, "Obsessed . . . truly ugly."
   H. Lines 18–20, "Born in Kansas . . . very early."
   J. Lines 22–24, "By the time . . . biographies."

29. When compared to Brooks' poetry as portrayed in Passage A, Brooks' poetry as portrayed in Passage B is more
   A. balanced.
   B. forthright.
   C. mysterious.
   D. violent.

30. A theme of Brooks' writing that is discussed in depth in Passage B but only indirectly in Passage A is
   F. racial identity.
   G. autobiography.
   H. biography.
   J. economic class.

PASSAGE IV

Natural Science—*Impact Events*

Though one wouldn't know it by gazing at the sky with an unaided eye,
the Earth is under near constant bombardment by extraterrestrial fragments
of rock, metal, and ice. In fact, astronomers estimate that approximately 25
Line million meteoroids strike our atmosphere each day. The vast majority of
(5) these masses are small enough (less than a one tenth of a gram). that they
burn up long before reaching the Earth's surface; but even so, between 2,900
and 7,300 extraterrestrial bodies of 10 grams or larger fall to Earth each year.
After entering the atmosphere, space debris is classified by its general composition; masses comprised primarily of rock are called "chondrites," those
(10) comprised of metal are called "meteorites," and masses made of both are
called "pallasites." Comets, meanwhile, are composed of a loose conglomera-
tion of rock, dust, ice, and frozen gases. With the naked eye, chondrites are
distinguishable from terrestrial rocks by the presence of chondrules: dark,
internal specks about 1 millimeter in diameter that result from the cooling
(15) of free-floating droplets of molten minerals.
Though the degree of difference varies, all extraterrestrial masses are
chemically distinct from Earth's rocks and metals. These distinctions are a
consequence of our planet's differentiation and cooling phase, during which
the Earth separated into a crust, mantle, and core. About 4.5 billion years
(20) ago, gravitational and thermophoretic forces caused the majority of Earth's
dense, metallic elements such as iron and osmium to sink inward, followed
by siderophilic elements like iridium, gold, cobalt, and platinum. As a result,
extraterrestrial rocks and metals that enter the atmosphere today tend to
demonstrate a much higher ratio of siderophilic to lithophilic components
(25) than we find elsewhere on the surface of the Earth.
Although comet and meteorite impacts afford us some exciting opportunities for astrogeological study, there is also a more ominous—albeit rare—
aspect to these collisions. Asteroids are extraterrestrial masses too small to be
called planets, but much too large to be meteoroids. In general, they range
(30) from between 10 to 100 kilometers in diameter, and many follow a regular
orbit in our own solar system, especially between Mars and Jupiter. Some
asteroid orbits intersect with those of other asteroids and planets, and, occasionally, collide with them. Striking Earth, an asteroid with a diameter of
1 kilometer would result in a blast equivalent to a 20-megaton atomic bomb,
(35) and would leave a crater spanning nearly 100 square kilometers.
The notion of large-scale impact events on Earth may seem farfetched to
many, but since 1950 more than 30 "Apollo" asteroids have been observed
crossing the Earth's orbit, and both geological and historical evidence suggest that a significant impact occurred as recently as 100 years ago. In 1908, a
(40) massive air burst occurred near the Tunguska River in Siberia. The blast probably resulted from the explosion of a comet somewhere between 5 and 10 ki-

lometers above the Earth's surface, and released enough energy to flatten 250 square kilometers of dense forest. Most estimates place the event's power at about 1,000 times that of the atomic bomb detonated over Hiroshima, Japan.

(45)   Many scientists hypothesize that the tremendous impact of a Mars-sized asteroid with the newly-formed proto-Earth was responsible for the formation of the Moon, literally shearing off an entire portion of the Earth's surface. This mechanism would help to explain the nearly identical isotopic and elemental compositions of the Moon and Earth. Easily the most famous

(50) impact event hypothesis, however, is the Cretaceous-Tertiary extinction event that killed the dinosaurs, and rent open the path for the age of mammals. All over the world at the K-T rock boundary, scientists have found a thin layer of iridium in concentrations of up to 130 times the background levels, strongly suggesting an extraterrestrial origin. In addition to increased

(55) iridium levels, geologists have also discovered tremendous amounts of soot, ash, and shocked quartz at these sites. Quartz shocking is a planar deformation feature that can only occur under conditions of immense pressure, but limited temperature. On Earth, the only known examples of shocked quartz have resulted from meteorite impacts and the detonation of atomic bombs.

(60) In tandem with the coeval K-T extinction event, this evidence is a strong indicator that whereas large-scale impact events may be uncommon, they have already played a substantial role in the procession of life on Earth. What role they may play in the future we cannot yet say.

31. What best describes the author's primary purpose?
    A. To persuade
    B. To argue
    C. To inform
    D. To critique

32. According to the passage, what information would be most useful in determining whether a rock came from a meteoroid or Earth?
    F. Its relative location on the surface of the Earth
    G. The siderophilic to lithophilic ratio of the components
    H. If it is composed of rock, metal, or ice fragments
    J. A careful inspection of the texture of the substances

33. Based on the information in the first paragraph, approximately how many bodies of more than 10 grams hit the Earth per *day* on average?
    A. 25 million
    B. 10
    C. 2,900–7,300
    D. 8–20

34. The author uses the word "ominous" in line 27 primarily to suggest:
    F. the promise of extraterrestrial travel beyond the solar system.
    G. the disastrous potential effect of a collision event.
    H. the grave danger of the demise of mankind through nuclear conflict.
    J. something that is probably never going to happen.

35. Based on lines 36–39, the term "Apollo," if applied to an asteroid, would most likely indicate that it:
    A. has a large size.
    B. crosses the orbit of the Earth.
    C. causes a large blast.
    D. is a recent occurrence.

36. Based on the passage, scientists' relative understanding of the Moon's formation, the K-T extinction, and the Tunguska impact can be ranked from MOST to LEAST precise as:
    F. The Moon's formation, the K-T extinction, the Tunguska impact.
    G. The Tunguska impact, the Moon's formation, and the K-T extinction.
    H. The Tunguska impact, the K-T extinction, the Moon's formation.
    J. The K-T extinction, the Tunguska impact, the Moon's formation.

37. The term "shearing," as used in line 47, most closely means:
    A. breaking.
    B. pressurizing.
    C. shattering.
    D. creating.

38. Based on the last paragraph, it would be reasonable to expect the radiation levels of an average selection of the Earth's crust to be:
    F. 130 times that found on the surface of the Moon.
    G. 1/130th of those found on the surface of the Moon.
    H. 130 times that found in the K-T rock boundary.
    J. 1/130th of those in the K-T rock boundary.

39. The author primarily uses descriptions of atomic bombs throughout the passage to:
   A. minimize the significance of past asteroid collisions.
   B. provide historical evidence of extraterrestrial geological encounters.
   C. aid the reader in understanding the magnitude of an impact event.
   D. suggest a method for reducing the danger from asteroids.

40. Based on the last paragraph, what best describes the underlying tone of the last sentence of the passage?
   F. Caution with uncertainty
   G. Hope with confusion
   H. Dread with fear
   J. Doubt with playfulness

If there is still time remaining, you may review your answers.

SCIENCE TEST

Time—35 minutes
40 Questions

Directions: There are several passages in this section, each of which is followed by questions. After reviewing a passage, choose the best answer to each question and fill in the matching oval on your answer sheet. Refer back to the passages as often as you need. Calculators are NOT permitted on this test.

PASSAGE I

Chemists conducted an experiment to determine the reliability of a dietary tool— the "4-4-9" method. Dieticians recommend that dieters use the 4-4-9 method to estimate the Calories (i.e., kilocalories) per gram of nutrient, with 4 Calories per gram of protein and carbohydrates, and 9 Calories per gram of fat.

To conduct the experiments, chemists used a bomb calorimeter, which is drawn below. The substance being tested was placed inside the metallic "bomb" and then heated using a copper wire strung through the holes. The amount of Calories was determined by factoring in the mass of the substance in the bomb, and the amount of temperature change in the surrounding water.

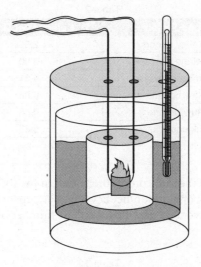

Figure 1

Experiment 1

The chemists first wanted to assess whether proteins, carbohydrates, and fats indeed had approximately 4, 4, and 9 Calories per gram, respectively. They did this by testing two proteins, two carbohydrates, and two fats that were about as close to pure in form as they could find in a grocery store. The substances used and resulting Calories per gram are recorded in Table 1.

Table 1

Substance Tested	Calories per Gram
Soy protein concentrate	3.31
Lean beef brisket	3.85
Wheat flour	3.63
Powdered sugar	3.89
Butter	8.76
Palm vegetable oil	8.62

Experiment 2

The chemists used the same procedure as in Experiment 1, but instead tested the Calories per gram of several foods that have mixtures of protein, fat, carbohydrates, and water.

Table 2

Food Tested	Calories per Gram
Turkey bacon	2.50
Cottage cheese	0.90
Parmesan cheese	4.31
Raw banana	0.89
Raw orange	0.46
Milk chocolate	5.35

Experiment 3

The chemists now used the same procedure to determine the Calories present in an equal volume of some popular nondiet beverages (1 cup, or 8 fl. oz). They wanted to determine which beverages provided the least number of Calories per volume, in order to satisfy dieters.

Table 3

Beverage Tested	Calories per Gram
Apple juice	117
Regular beer	153
Regular cola	136
Eggnog	343
Orange juice	105
Vegetable juice	46

1. Based on the information in Table 1, which of the following foods most likely consists primarily of fat?
   A. Soy protein concentrate
   B. Wheat flour
   C. Powdered sugar
   D. Palm vegetable oil

2. Based on the information in Table 2, which of the following foods consists of a pure form of protein, carbohydrates, or fat?
   F. Turkey bacon
   G. Cottage cheese
   H. Raw banana
   J. None of the above

3. A dieter is looking to find a drink that is filling (taking up a good bit of volume in the stomach) without having too many calories. Based on the information in Table 3, which of the following beverages would be the best fit for the dieter?
   A. Regular cola
   B. Regular beer
   C. Orange juice
   D. Apple juice

4. The parmesan cheese measured in Experiment 2 was placed in a very dry container for a period of 1 week. Which of the following values could represent the Calories per gram measurement of the cheese at the end of that week?
   F. 2.3
   G. 3.4
   H. 4.1
   J. 5.2

5. Based on the information in Experiment 1, if one is to use the 4-4-9 method to approximate Calories, it is most likely that the actual Caloric values of the foods tested are:
   A. Slightly higher than the 4-4-9 method would estimate.
   B. Slightly lower than the 4-4-9 method would estimate.
   C. Precisely predicted by the 4-4-9 method.
   D. Significantly different from what the 4-4-9 method would estimate.

6. A person is diagnosed with glucose intolerance. A dietician is trying to find a method for helping this person find a healthy diet. Would the 4-4-9 method be useful for helping this person?
   F. Yes, he should be primarily concerned about his fat intake.
   G. Yes, he should primarily be concerned about Calorie reduction.
   H. No, he won't be able to tell if he is eating carbohydrates or protein.
   J. No, he won't be able to tell if he is reducing his caloric intake at an adequate level.

PASSAGE II

Biologists often find it useful to classify organisms based on the source from which they derive their energy and nutrients. Of particular interest is the organism's source of carbon nutrients, and special substances utilized in the transfer of energy called "reducing equivalents." These classifications, called the "primary nutritional groups," are summarized in Figure 1.

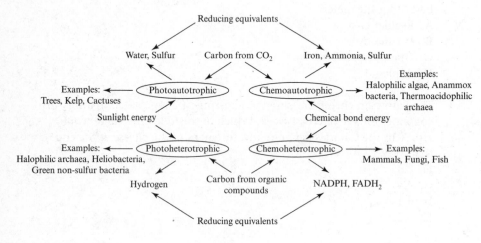

Figure 1

Mixotrophs are organisms that for various reasons cannot be classified in a single primary nutritional group. Most mixotrophs are unicellular; however, scientists have discovered that some large plants and even certain animals exhibit mixotrophic characteristics. Information on three mixotrophs is given in Table 1.

Table 1

Organism	Fixes carbon?	Uses organic carbon?	Captures energy from sunlight?	Energy from metabolizing chemicals?	Can survive without sunlight?	Inorganically synthesizes glucose?	Nitrogen deficient?
Euglena	Yes	Yes	Yes	Yes	Yes	Yes	No
Venus flytrap	Yes	No	Yes	No	No	Yes	Yes
Oriental wasp	No	Yes	Yes	Yes	No	No	No

7. Based on the information in Table 1, which of the following organisms could most likely survive for a prolonged period in a dark room?
   A. Euglena
   B. Venus flytrap
   C. Oriental wasp
   D. Cannot be determined from the information.

8. Using the information in Figure 1, what would most likely represent a sequence along a food chain?
   F. A chemoautotroph consumes a chemoheterotroph.
   G. A photoautotroph consumes a chemoautotroph.
   H. A chemoautotroph consumes a photoheterotroph.
   J. A chemoheterotroph consumes a photoautotroph.

9. Which of the following classifications of organisms is/are possibly able to use photosynthesis in the creation of energy?
   I. Mixotrophs
   II. Photoautotrophs
   III. Photoheterotrophs
   A. I only
   B. II only
   C. II and III only
   D. I, II, and III

10. Based on the information in Figure 1, how would we generalize the nature of the substances from which autotrophs and heterotrophs receive their carbon nutrients?
    F. autotrophs, simple; heterotrophs, simple
    G. autotrophs, simple; heterotrophs, complex
    H. autotrophs, complex; heterotrophs, simple
    J. autotrophs, complex; heterotrophs, complex

11. An astronomer is considering what the aftermath of Earth would be like if a catastrophic asteroid collision created a global dust cloud that lasted for several years. Based on the information in Figure 1, which organism would have the greatest chance of survival?
    A. Kelp
    B. Anammox bacteria
    C. Cactus
    D. Heliobacteria

PASSAGE III

To better understand the relationship among gravity, inertia, mass, and weight, an astronomy student conducted a series of mathematical experiments. The student knows from research that *weight* is the force exerted by two objects on each other due to gravity, *inertia* is an object's resistance to a change in acceleration, and that *Newton's second law of motion* relates mass and inertia in the equation shown in Figure 1. Additionally, Newton's law of universal gravitation is shown in Figure 2.

$$F = m(a)$$

F = net force applied to object
m = mass of object

a = acceleration of object

$$F = G\left(\frac{m_1 m_2}{r^2}\right)$$

F = gravitational force between masses
G = gravitational constant
$\quad$ (6.674×10^{-11} N · m^2 kg^{-2})
m_1 = first mass $\qquad m_2$ = second mass
$\quad r$ = distance between masses

Figure 1 $\qquad\qquad\qquad\qquad\qquad$ Figure 2

Experiment 1

Using the masses and diameters of the planets in our solar system, the student then calculated the weight of a 5.0 kg bowling ball on the north pole of each. The results are shown in Table 1.

Table 1

Planet	Diameter (km)	Mass (kg)	Weight of bowling ball (N)
Mercury	4,880	3.3022×10^{23}	18.9
Venus	12,103	4.868×10^{24}	45.3
Earth	12,713	5.9736×10^{24}	49.0
Mars	6,752	6.4185×10^{23}	18.8
Jupiter	133,708	1.8986×10^{27}	118.2
Saturn	108,728	5.6846×10^{26}	53.2
Uranus	49,946	8.6810×10^{25}	44.4
Neptune	48,682	1.0243×10^{26}	56.2

Experiment 2

The student imagined a situation in which the same 5.0-kg bowling ball descends into Earth's atmosphere from space. After illustrating the scenario in Figure 3, the student calculated the changes in gravitational force between the ball and the Earth at four different points. These values are summarized in Table 2.

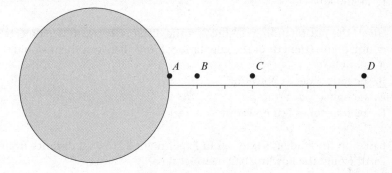

Figure 3

Table 2

Position	A	B	C	D
Distance from Earth's surface (km)	600	1,200	2,400	4,800
Gravitational force (N)	41.1	34.9	26.0	16.1

12. Based on the information in Table 1, which of the following correctly ranks the astronomical bodies in order of smallest to largest mass?
   F. Venus, Neptune, Uranus, Saturn
   G. Venus, Uranus, Neptune, Saturn
   H. Saturn, Uranus, Neptune, Venus
   J. Neptune, Saturn, Uranus, Venus

13. Based on the information in Table 2, as the ball's distance from Earth increases, the gravitational force between the two objects:
   A. increases only.
   B. decreases only.
   C. increases, then decreases.
   D. decreases, then increases.

14. Given the information in Experiment 2, at approximately what distance from the Earth's surface would the bowling ball experience a gravitational force of 18 N?
    F. 3,600 km
    G. 4,200 km
    H. 3,000 km
    J. 5,400 km

15. Given the information in Figure 2, if the distance between two objects is doubled, the strength of the gravitational force between them would:
    A. double.
    B. be four times as powerful.
    C. be half as powerful.
    D. be four times less powerful.

16. Based on the student's findings in Experiment 2, at what distance from the Earth would the bowling ball be weightless?
    F. 9,600 km
    G. 6,000 km
    H. The bowling ball will always have weight because weight is independent of distance.
    J. The bowling ball will always have weight because both the Earth and ball have mass.

17. Another scientist is skeptical of the results of Experiment 2. Which of the following would be a valid reason for her skepticism?
    A. The student used kilometers for measuring distance and Newtons for measuring gravitational force.
    B. The units of measurement are not consistent with scientific standards.
    C. The results in Table 2 are based on an imaginary situation rather than actual measurements.
    D. The lack of an atmosphere at the measured altitudes would skew the results since there would be no friction from air resistance.

PASSAGE IV

Allergic rhinitis, or "hay fever," results from a hypersensitivity of the immune system to certain types of weed or tree pollen, which results in an acute inflammatory response. The signaling cascade for an allergic rhinitis reaction is illustrated in Figure 1.

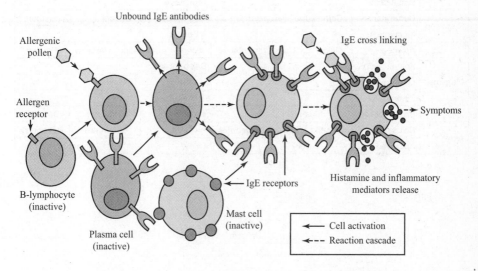

Figure 1

In a condition called "oral allergy syndrome" (OAS), people experience a mild allergic reaction in their mouth while eating many fresh fruits, nuts, and vegetables. However, unlike those with shellfish or peanut allergies, these people do not possess an allergy to the food itself but rather a pollen allergy that undergoes a "cross reaction," meaning that their pollen antibodies also bind to structurally similar food proteins, causing local inflammation. Table 1 summarizes the most common pollen-food cross-reactive patterns. Figure 2 shows an SDS-PAGE plate of the proteins detected in samples of birch pollen, apple, celery, aniseed, and peanut, separating the proteins according to their size. Each of the types of protein in Figure 2 has its lettered name to the right of it, labeled in lane 3.

Table 1

Pollen Type	Family	Cross-Reactive Foods						
Birch	Rosaceae	Apple	Peach	Plum	Pear	Cherry	Apricot	Almond
	Apiaceai	Carrot	Celery	Parsley	Caraway	Fennel	Coriander	Aniseed
	Fabaceae	Soybean			Peanut			
	Betulaceae	Hazelnut						
Ragweed	Cururbitaceae	Cantaloupe	Honeydew	Watermelon		Zucchini		Cucumber
	Muscaceae	Banana						
Mugwort	Apiaceae	Celery	Carrot	Aniseed	Fennel	Coriander	Caraway	Parsley
	Solanaceae	Bell pepper						
	Liliaceae	Garlic			Onion			
	Piperaceae	Black Pepper						
	Brassicaceae	Mustard		Cauliflower		Cabbage		Broccoli
Alder	Rosaceae	Almonds	Apples	Cherries	Pears		Strawberry	Raspberry
	Apiaceae	Celery		Parsley		Aniseed		

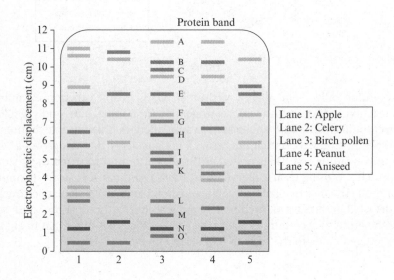

Protein band

Lane 1: Apple
Lane 2: Celery
Lane 3: Birch pollen
Lane 4: Peanut
Lane 5: Aniseed

Figure 2

18. If someone were allergic to Mugwort, Birch, and Alder pollens, what would be a food that the person would definitely want to avoid to prevent a possible cross-reaction?
    F. Cucumber
    G. Watermelon
    H. Honeydew
    J. Celery

19. What two pollen types shown in Table 1 likely share the most conserved proteins?
    A. Birch and Alder
    B. Ragweed and Mugwort
    C. Mugwort and Birch
    D. Alder and Ragweed

20. As indicated by its band in Figure 2, which protein is best conserved across the samples tested?
    F. Protein E
    G. Protein K
    H. Protein M
    J. Protein N

21. Based on the information in Figure 2, how many proteins are conserved across the two members of the Apiaceae family?
    A. 6
    B. 8
    C. 9
    D. 10

22. Allergists have designed immunotherapies that interrupt the reaction cascade at a number of intervals. Which of the following interventions would be LEAST likely to interrupt the cascade?
    F. Preventing secretion of IgE
    G. Activating mast cells prior to B-lymphocyte-allergen binding
    H. Inhibiting release of histamine
    J. Chemically inhibiting expression of IgE receptors

PASSAGE V

Two physics students are learning about special relativity. Their teacher explains that the equations of relativity for time and length involve two inertial reference frames: one in motion with respect to the event, and one at rest with respect to the event. Dilated time intervals and proper lengths are measured from the motional reference frame, whereas proper time intervals and contracted lengths are measured from the resting reference frame.

The teacher posits a scenario in which an astronaut is halfway between Earth and the star Proxima Centauri, traveling at 92% the speed of light. As measured by the astronaut, both students are asked to determine the distance remaining between the spacecraft and Proxima Centauri, and the amount of time it will take the astronaut to get there. Two relevant equations of special relativity are shown in Figure 1.

$$\Delta t' = \frac{\Delta t}{\sqrt{1 - v^2 / c^2}} \qquad\qquad L = L'_0 \cdot \sqrt{1 - \frac{v^2}{c^2}}$$

Where,

$\Delta t'$ = dilated time interval $\qquad\qquad L$ = contracted length

Δt = proper time interval $\qquad\qquad L'_0$ = proper length

v = relative velocity of the reference frames

c = speed of light in a vacuum (3.00×10^8 m/s)

Figure 1

Student 1

As measured by an observer on Earth, the distance remaining between the spacecraft and Proxima Centauri is 2.12 light years, or 2.0×10^{13} km. An observer on Earth is at rest with respect to the astronaut, who is in motion within the spacecraft.

Therefore, Earth is the resting reference frame, and the distance between the spacecraft and Proxima Centauri as measured by the astronaut is the proper length. Further, because the astronaut is traveling near the speed of light, time intervals measured aboard the spacecraft become dilated relative to those measured on Earth.

Student 2

Because they are traveling with the same velocity, the astronaut is at rest with respect to the spacecraft. Thus, the event, which is the time interval elapsing during the spacecraft's journey to Proxima Centauri, occurs in the same reference frame inhabited by the astronaut. The Earth and Proxima Centauri, meanwhile, are in motion with respect to the astronaut. Therefore, the time interval measured by the astronaut is the proper time interval. Further, just as the Doppler effect shortens the wavelength of a sound emitted in the direction of forward motion, the spacecraft's forward velocity causes the remaining distance between the astronaut and Proxima Centauri to contract.

23. Based on Figure 1, if the relative velocity of the reference frames in a given situation were zero, what would be the relationship between the contracted length and proper length in that situation?
    A. The contracted length would be greater than the proper length.
    B. The contracted length would be less than the proper length.
    C. The contracted length and proper length would be equal to one another.
    D. The contracted length and proper length would be undefined.

24. In the scenario outlined by the teacher, what would be the approximate speed of the spacecraft in meters per second?
    F. 3.0×10^8
    G. 2.76×10^8
    H. 2.0×10^{13}
    J. 2.12

25. Student 1 would think that time intervals measured aboard the spacecraft are:
    A. longer than those measured on the Earth.
    B. shorter than those measured on the Earth.
    C. equal to those measured on the Earth.
    D. directly proportional to those measured on the Earth.

26. A fundamental assumption of Student 2 with respect to the root cause of relativistic changes is that light waves behave much like:
    F. inertial reference frames.
    G. time.
    H. sound.
    J. motion.

27. Based on the information in the passage, how long will it take for the light from Proxima Centauri to reach Earth?
    A. 2.12 years
    B. 4.24 years
    C. 6.36 years
    D. 8.48 years

28. If the hypothetical measurements in the studies could be done with an extraordinary degree of accuracy, which of the following would most likely be a factor that the students would want to factor into their measurements that neither currently is?
    F. The position of the astronaut with respect to Proxima Centauri
    G. The movement of the Earth as it revolves around the Sun
    H. The impact of time dilation due to changes in inertial reference frames
    J. The relative velocity of the reference frames

29. Based on the passage as a whole, under the theory of relativity, as one gradually approaches the speed of light:
    A. time seems to speed up and distance seems to increase.
    B. time seems to speed up and distance seems to decrease.
    C. time seems to slow down and distance seems to increase.
    D. time seems to slow down and distance seems to decrease.

PASSAGE VI

A team of biologists studied the mercury content of fish in three of East Africa's rift valley lakes. It is known that in aquatic ecosystems, mercury content is often directly proportional to a specie's position on the local food-chain, with the greatest predator fish possessing two to three orders magnitude more mercury than the lower species. Comprised of about 30 bodies of water, the lakes of the rift valley are among the oldest on Earth, and vary significantly in their ecology and biodiversity, and in their *Secchi depth*, which is a measure of how deep one may see in a lake before there is no visibility. Further, the valley contains many alkaline lakes wherein species have specially adapted to survive under strongly basic conditions. Table 1 summarizes the chemical and physical properties of the three lakes studied.

Table 1

Lake	Secchi depth (m)	Volume (km³)	Number of Fish Species	Dissolved O_2 (mg/molecule)	Dissolved $CaCO_4$ (mg/molecule)	Surface chlorophyll (μg/molecule)	pH
Shala	0.15	36.7	14	7.4	10.0	136	10.0
Naivasha	1.1	4.6	5	7.1	3.3	72	7.1
Malawi	0.9	8,400	68	7.3	450	34	6.5

Though common in the tissue of fish, to humans mercury in levels exceeding 600 ng g^{-1} is a chronic neurotoxin. Muscle samples from various species of fish were purchased directly from local fisheries and subsequently tested for methylmercury (MeHg) via atomic fluorescence spectroscopy. Samples were degraded in a 1:4 solution of nitric-sulfuric acid at 225°C. An abridged summary of their results is illustrated in Table 2.

Table 2

Lake	Species	Food Source	Average Mass (g)	MeHg (ng g^{-1})
Shala	C. gariepinus	Fish	2,331	63.0
	P. aethiopicus	Mollusks	2,527	41.2
	N. shalaenis	Plants	207	11.9
	L. cylindricus	Macrophytes	36.2	76.0
Naivasha	T. zilli	Plants	173	14.5
	M. salmoides	Fish	1,142	56.7
	P. clarkia	Detrius	17.2	5.2
	H. paludinosus	Plankton	2.8	28.1
Malawi	D. noliticus	Detrius	1,067	19.7
	S. schall	Mollusks	128	75.5
	L. niloticus	Invertebrates	7,786	133
	H. forskahlii	Fish	837	307

30. Based on the information in Table 2, which of the following fish would be toxic for humans to eat?
    F. *N. shalaensis*
    G. *T. zilli*
    H. *S. schall*
    J. None of the above

31. Which of the lakes tested was the most alkaline?
    A. Shala
    B. Naivasha
    C. Malawi
    D. Cannot be determined from the information provided

32. A researcher hypothesized that the largest fish would feed only on other fish. Which species from Table 2 would provide the strongest evidence to disprove this hypothesis?
    F. *L. cylindricus*
    G. *L. niloticus*
    H. *H. paludinosus*
    J. *P. aethiopicus*

33. A fourth lake was studied and had a volume of approximately 1,000 km³. Based on the information in Table 1, what is the most likely range of the number of fish species in that lake?
    A. Less than 5
    B. Between 5 and 14
    C. Between 14 and 68
    D. Greater than 68

34. Based on the information in Table 2, which of the following fish is most likely to be at the highest point as a predator on a food chain?
    F. *C. gariepinus*
    G. *M. salmoides*
    H. *S. schall*
    J. *H. forskahlii*

35. Given the information in Table 1, what is the most logical possible explanation as to why the Secchi depth of the Shala lake was less than that of the other two lakes?
    A. The amount of surface chlorophyll associated with lots of plant life.
    B. The amount of water volume of the lake.
    C. The relatively high alkalinity of the lake's water.
    D. The relatively high number of fish species that would cloud the lake.

PASSAGE VII

Combustion is an exothermic reaction between an oxidant and a fuel compound. Combustion can be used simply to generate heat, as in the case of a campfire, or its energy can be harnessed to drive mechanical devices, as in the case of an automobile engine. In an ideal combustion, the energy released greatly exceeds the activation energy needed to initiate the reaction. Figure 1 illustrates the combustion of a "high explosive" and its reaction-energy diagram. Figure 2 shows the combustion and reaction-energy diagram of a "low explosive."

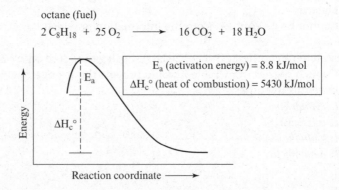

octane (fuel)

$$2\,C_8H_{18} + 25\,O_2 \longrightarrow 16\,CO_2 + 18\,H_2O$$

E_a (activation energy) = 8.8 kJ/mol
ΔH_c° (heat of combustion) = 5430 kJ/mol

Energy

Reaction coordinate

Figure 1

trinitrotoluene (fuel/oxidant)

$$4\,C_6H_2(NO_2)_3CH_3 + 25\,O_2 \longrightarrow 32\,CO_2 + 10\,H_2O + 6\,N_2$$

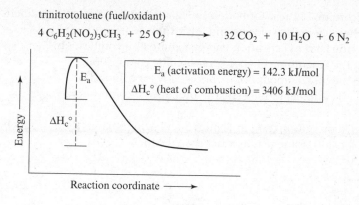

E_a (activation energy) = 142.3 kJ/mol

$\Delta H_c°$ (heat of combustion) = 3406 kJ/mol

Figure 2

The rate at which energy is released contributes significantly to a combustion reaction's efficacy, and the reaction rate is limited by the speed at which an oxidant can diffuse into the fuel. Figure 3 illustrates the reaction-rate diagram for the combustion of trinitrotoluene, and Figure 4 shows the diagram for octane. Both reactions are presumed to take place under standard temperature and pressure.

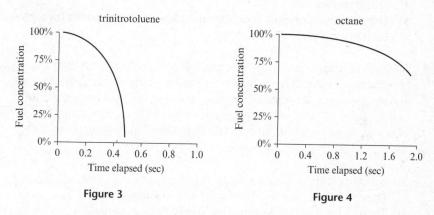

Figure 3

Figure 4

It is a common misconception that dynamite contains trinitrotoluene (TNT), but in fact dynamite's combustion is the result of the self-oxidation of nitroglycerine. Table 1 compares the combustion properties of nitroglycerine and trinitrotoluene.

Table 1

Compound	E_a (Kj/mol)	$\Delta H_c°$ (Kj/mol)	Detonation Velocity (km/s)
Trinitrotoluene	142.3	3406	6.94
Nitroglycerine	0.09	1529	7.58

36. According to the information in Figures 1 and 2, the main distinction between a high explosive and low explosive is:
    F. the level of activation energy required for combustion.
    G. the magnitude of energy released by combustion.
    H. the molar amount of fuel necessary for combustion.
    J. the number of molecular byproducts of combustion.

37. Based on information in Figures 3 and 4, approximately how much faster will trinitrotoluene fully react than octane?
    A. 0.7 s
    B. 1.3 s
    C. 1.9 s
    D. 3.5 s

38. If the military were to create a weapon that used one of the substances in the passage in a bomb designed to maximize explosive power while minimizing the size of the bomb as a whole, especially the fuel to spark an explosion, which of the following would be the best choice?
    F. Octane
    G. Nitroglycerine
    H. Trinitrotoluene
    J. They would all provide roughly equivalent explosive power for a given mass of explosive.

39. Given that detonation velocity is defined as the velocity at which a shockwave (a wave that changes the pressure of surrounding substances) travels through a detonated explosive, and that the heat of combustion is the energy released when a compound undergoes combustion, in the combustion of equal amounts of trinitrotoluene and nitroglycerine, on average which explosive's particles will travel farther?
    A. Trinitrotoluene
    B. Nitroglycerine
    C. They will travel approximately the same distance.
    D. There is not enough information in the passage to make a determination.

40. What is the most likely reason that octane is a more commonly used fuel source for mechanical devices than trinitrotoluene?
    F. Octane is more stable.
    G. Octane combusts at a slower rate than trinitrotoluene.
    H. Octane has a greater heat of combustion.
    J. Octane contains an efficient self-oxidizing agent.

If there is still time remaining, you may review your answers.

WRITING TEST

Time: 40 Minutes

Genetic Engineering

Scientists are increasingly able to manipulate the genetic codes of a wide range of living things. Famers can grow genetically modified crops designed to produce higher yields and require less water. Genetically modified bacteria might be created to accomplish tasks like consuming oil that has been spilled in the ocean. Genetic engineering can even be done on humans—parents who have the resources can select the gender of a child, and possibly even his or her eye color. Many fear, however, that genetic engineering will open up a "Brave New World" as technology potentially enables mankind to control a child's intelligence and attractiveness. With genetic engineering already having an ever-growing significant impact on technology and culture, the topic merits thorough analysis.

Read and carefully evaluate these points of view. Each puts forth a specific way of thinking about the impact of genetic engineering.

Viewpoint One	Viewpoint Two	Viewpoint Three
Humans have successfully used technology to make tremendous improvements in electronics, transportation, and other fields. It is unreasonably fearful to miss out on great scientific gains because of a fear of something new.	If one nation decides against allowing genetic engineering out of ethical concerns, other nations with surely go full speed ahead with whatever genetic enhancements technology can provide. Either embrace this change, or be left behind.	Genetic diversity is key to a species' survival and flourishing. If humans manipulate the gene pool to only have "favorable" genetic qualities, it will result in the most unfavorable consequence—a lack of genetic diversity to respond to new challenges.

ESSAY ASSIGNMENT

Compose a focused essay in which you consider multiple viewpoints on the potential consequences of genetic engineering. In your response, be certain to

- examine and assess the viewpoints provided
- express and develop your own point of view on the topic
- analyze the connections between your point of view and those provided

Your viewpoint may completely agree, somewhat agree, or not agree at all with any of those presented. No matter your perspective, provide clear, logical arguments supported by detailed examples to make your case.

Planning Your Response

Your prewriting notes on this page will not be considered in your score.

Use the following space to brainstorm ideas and map out your response. You may want to think about the following as you analyze the given prompt:

Strengths and weaknesses of the three viewpoints

- What good points do they make, and what potential objections do they ignore?
- Why might they be convincing to readers, and why might their perspectives fall short?

Your previous experience, background knowledge, and personal values

- What is your viewpoint on this topic, and what are the pros and cons of this viewpoint?
- How will you craft an argument in support of your point of view?

ANSWER KEY

English

1. C	16. H	31. D	46. J	61. C
2. J	17. D	32. F	47. B	62. J
3. B	18. G	33. C	48. J	63. A
4. F	19. A	34. J	49. C	64. H
5. D	20. H	35. C	50. G	65. B
6. H	21. B	36. J	51. A	66. H
7. B	22. H	37. C	52. J	67. C
8. F	23. D	38. F	53. B	68. F
9. C	24. G	39. B	54. J	69. D
10. J	25. A	40. F	55. B	70. J
11. A	26. H	41. B	56. H	71. B
12. H	27. B	42. H	57. D	72. F
13. B	28. F	43. B	58. F	73. B
14. G	29. A	44. F	59. C	74. J
15. C	30. H	45. C	60. F	75. C

Mathematics

1. B	13. B	25. B	37. C	49. E
2. J	14. J	26. F	38. K	50. G
3. D	15. C	27. B	39. B	51. D
4. H	16. G	28. K	40. J	52. H
5. C	17. A	29. A	41. E	53. C
6. F	18. K	30. K	42. K	54. K
7. E	19. D	31. C	43. C	55. A
8. H	20. H	32. G	44. G	56. G
9. D	21. B	33. A	45. D	57. D
10. J	22. J	34. F	46. G	58. G
11. A	23. E	35. B	47. A	59. D
12. H	24. H	36. J	48. G	60. J

Reading

1. C	9. B	17. B	25. A	33. D
2. F	10. J	18. G	26. F	34. G
3. C	11. A	19. C	27. C	35. A
4. F	12. H	20. G	28. G	36. H
5. C	13. B	21. B	29. B	37. A
6. G	14. J	22. J	30. J	38. J
7. B	15. C	23. C	31. C	39. C
8. J	16. F	24. J	32. G	40. F

Science

1. D	9. D	17. C	25. A	33. C
2. J	10. G	18. J	26. H	34. J
3. C	11. B	19. A	27. B	35. A
4. J	12. G	20. G	28. G	36. F
5. B	13. B	21. C	29. D	37. C
6. H	14. G	22. G	30. J	38. G
7. A	15. D	23. C	31. A	39. D
8. J	16. J	24. G	32. G	40. H

ACT SCORING GUIDE

(These norms are based on sampling classes of students, not on a nationwide sample.)

Calculate your overall composite score by adding the individual scores from each of the four sections and dividing by 4. You can round up.

Score	English	Math	Reading	Science	Score
36	75	60	40	40	36
35	74	58–59	38–39	38–39	35
34	72–73	56–57	36–37	36–37	34
33	71	54–55	35	35	33
32	70	52–53	34	34	32
31	69	50–51	33	33	31
30	68	49	32	32	30
29	66–67	48	31	31	29
28	65	46–47	29–30	30	28
27	63–64	44–45	27–28	29	27
26	61–62	42–43	26	28	26
25	59–60	40–41	25	26–27	25
24	57–58	38–39	23–24	24–25	24
23	55–56	36–37	22	23	23
22	53–54	34–35	21	21–22	22
21	50–52	32–33	20	20	21
20	47–49	30–31	18–19	18–19	20
19	44–46	28–29	17	16–17	19
18	42–43	25–27	16	15	18
17	40–41	22–24	15	14	17
16	37–39	19–21	14	12–13	16
15	35–36	16–18	13	11	15
14	33–34	12–15	12	10	14
13	30–32	9–11	10–11	9	13
12	28–29	7–8	8–9	8	12
11	25–27	6	7	7	11
10	23–24	5	6	6	10
9	20–22	4	5	5	9
8	17–19	3	–	4–5	8
7	14–16	–	4	3	7
6	12–13	2	–	–	6
5	9–11	–	3	2	5
4	6–8	1	2	–	4
3	4–5	–	1	1	3
2	2–3	–	–	–	2
1	0–1	0	0	0	1

ACT WRITING RUBRIC

Ideas and Analysis: Considers multiple perspectives. Develops a clear and sophisticated thesis. Provides a useful context for analyzing the issue. Analyzes the implications, complexities, and underlying assumptions of different viewpoints.						
6: Excellent	5: Skillful	4: Adequate	3: Fair	2: Weak	1: Poor	____ /6

Development and Support: Provides an insightful and well-supported argument, placing the issue in a broad context. Uses reasoning and illustration to express the significance of the issue. Demonstrates an understanding of the complexity of the topic.						
6: Excellent	5: Skillful	4: Adequate	3: Fair	2: Weak	1: Poor	____ /6

Organization: Shows a skillful overall organizational approach. Has a clear, sustained position, accompanied by a logical sequence of ideas that builds the writer's argument. Provides clear and logical transitions between sentences and paragraphs.						
6: Excellent	5: Skillful	4: Adequate	3: Fair	2: Weak	1: Poor	____ /6

Language Use: The essay's language is well-suited to the argument. Vocabulary choice is precise and appropriate. Sentence structure is clear and varied. Tone, voice, and style are effective. Grammar, usage, and mechanics issues are minimized and do not interfere with the reader's understanding.						
6: Excellent	5: Skillful	4: Adequate	3: Fair	2: Weak	1: Poor	____ /6

Essay Raw Score:	____ /24

Multiply your Essay Raw Score by 1.5 to get your approximate ACT Writing Scaled Score: Essay Raw Score: _____ × 1.5 = _____ out of 36 possible points.	
ACT Writing Scaled Score:	____ /36

ANSWER EXPLANATIONS

English

1. **(C)** If we were to delete this sentence, we would not have a logical contrast with the narrator's concern over linguistic expression that follows in the next sentence.

2. **(J)** is consistent with the first-person (i.e., "I"), wording we see elsewhere in the paragraph and essay as a whole.

3. **(B)** puts commas around a phrase, "if someone wished to insult me," that is a helpful piece of information, but is not essential to this being a functional sentence.

4. **(F)** provides helpful details without being unnecessarily wordy like (H). (G) would remove the statement of "idiocy" from the original phrase, and (J) would omit any descriptive details.

5. **(D)** No verb is needed here since it would interrupt the introductory phrase, "With its earliest recorded usage in the 1300s."

6. **(H)** is the only option that gives a transition that expresses a needed logical contrast between the preceding sentence and the current sentence.

7. **(B)** appropriately uses an adjective to describe "definition" instead of an adverb, as (A) and (D) do. (B) also correctly compares two things (i.e., the "original definition" and the "dulled version"), while (C) would be used to compare three or more things.

8. **(F)** is concise and is a contraction for "It is." (G) is used to show possession, and (H) and (J) are too wordy since it is clear that we are discussing "tattle-tale," the last noun mentioned.

9. **(C)** "Between" is used when discussing a range of time.

10. **(J)** The question states that readers would have the background knowledge that "the bard" refers to "Shakespeare," so it would be unnecessary to make this change, especially since "Shakespeare" is immediately mentioned in the following sentence.

11. **(A)** uses the dash to provide a heavy pause before the clarification of "apex." (B), (C), and (D) all put an unnecessary comma after the word "golden."

12. **(H)** We generally use "fewer" when discussing things that *can* be counted, which the number of words would be. "Less" is generally used when discussing noncountable things, such as "love" or "happiness."

13. **(B)** "Was" is needed here since the subject is the singular "innovation" (not "times") and the events take place in the past.

14. **(G)** The essay as a whole deals with the history of insults and also spends a good deal of time discussing Shakespeare's contribution to this history. (G) would best focus on this subject matter and also maintain its scholarly tone.

15. **(C)** puts the paragraphs in the correct historical chronological order.

16. **(H)** connects two seemingly contradictory things, namely the fact that the story of the Sea Turtle is tragic, and that, despite this, it is not without hope.

17. **(D)** is neither too wordy nor too vague. (A) and (B) are too wordy, and (C) is too vague.

18. **(G)** This information about the uniqueness of these areas has already been stated in the second sentence of this paragraph.

19. **(A)** It is idiomatically correct to say "coast of" rather than any of the other options.

20. **(H)** Because we are talking about times since 1981, we would use the past perfect tense of "have only recently begun" to indicate that this began in the past but is continuing up to the present day. "Have" is needed rather than "has" since the subject of the sentence is the plural "they."

21. **(B)** properly uses an adjective to provide needed description of the word "peril." (A) is an adverb, and (C) does not make sense, since how can "peril" be committed? Choice (D) is incorrect because if it said "continued" it could work, but "continue" is a verb that would not be proper in this context.

22. **(H)** This portion helps provide details to expand on the previous sentence's assertion that human activity is having a negative effect on the turtles. It is not at the level of "scholarly evidence," as in (J), but is more of a casually asserted fact that does not provide precise information on the damage humans are causing turtles. The information provided is neither distracting nor repetitive, making (F) and (G) incorrect.

23. **(D)** "Effect" is generally used as a noun, whereas "affect," as in (A), is generally used as a verb. "Affection," as in (B), means "a general fondness," which does not fit. "Impaction," as in (C), means more of a physical collision.

24. **(G)** The primary idea of the previous paragraph is that human activities have had a negative impact on sea turtles. The current paragraph focuses on changes to environmental laws to help sea turtles survive. (G) is the only answer that provides a logical connection between these two general themes. (F) and (H) focus more on the previous paragraph, and (J) focuses more on the current paragraph.

25. **(A)** We do not want to separate the subject, "harvesting of turtles," from the verb, "is," with a comma. Also, no break is needed in the phrase "is now illegal."

26. **(H)** provides a clean break before the paragraph begins a three sentence list of the criteria. (F) puts unneeded commas around "Florida." (G) and (J) could work if we had a comprehensive list within the sentence, but the listing of criteria involves three sentences, so a larger pause is needed. In addition, (G) would need a comma between "Florida" and "in," and (J) would need to remove the comma after "Florida" and put one after "first."

27. **(B)** correctly indicates that this would take place for 6 of the years that followed. (A) could work if we said "of the following," and (C) could work if we

said "for the next 6 years." Choice (D) does not work because "soon" cannot properly modify the word "years."

28. **(F)** is contextually correct phrasing—we would say "sustain at least." (G) is too wordy, (H) is used like the word "furthermore," and (J) would change the criterion to being approximately 50% instead of at least 50%.

29. **(A)** puts the wording in the most logical sequence without any interruption, as in (B), or lack of subject clarification until later in the sentence, as in (C) and (D).

30. **(H)** is the only choice that focuses on the short term, by saying "an ongoing process," as well as the long term, by saying "with no clear end in sight." The other choices all focus solely on the long-term timeframe.

31. **(D)** The paragraph goes on to discuss how children hate being punished for their own misbehavior but are quick to demand punishment of those who have hurt them. (D) is the only answer that addresses this thought process.

32. **(F)** is the only answer that provides the correct logical transition between the opposite ideas expressed in the previous sentence and the current sentence, namely that kids find it unfair when *they* are punished but they *love* to see other kids punished.

33. **(C)** provides needed clarification, which (B) lacks, and treats the phrase as an object of the sentence. (A) and (D) would be used if this were the subject of the sentence. Although the wording is inverted, the subject is "justice."

34. **(J)** The question asks for what would NOT be acceptable, and (J) would be a comma splice, having a complete sentence both before and after the comma with no transitional word. (F), (G), and (H) all provide the necessary break.

35. **(C)** Without this phrase, we would not understand that the narrator was very nearly convinced by her siblings. We don't have any details as to *how* her siblings convinced her, so (D) would not work.

36. **(J)** is the correct idiomatic expression, "one at fault." If (F) said "in error," if (G) said "mistaken," and if (H) said "in the wrong," those could work.

37. **(C)** The sentences are in a logical, chronological order, except for the last two, which need to be switched so that the brother's escalating comments would happen before the sister's decision to hold kitchen court.

38. **(F)** provides clarifying details that (G) and (J) lack. (H) is too wordy.

39. **(B)** The phrase "the defendant" needs to be set off with commas because it is a clarification of the word "me." Because of this, a comma is needed after "defendant." Also, we would want to say "who" because it functions as a subject within this small part of the sentence. We would say "he had no idea," not "him had no idea," remembering that he/who go together and him/whom go together.

40. **(F)** gives the most vivid description of how she will conduct herself in the kitchen court. (G), (H), and (J) are all too vague.

41. **(B)** puts the words in the most logical, chronological sequence. (A) and (D) both have interruptions in their sentence flow, and (C) mixes the sequence of the impending sentence and the end of Kitchen Court.

42. **(H)** It is idiomatically correct to say "between chores and an assortment." "Between" demands the use of an "and" when mentioning the two items compared.

43. **(B)** gives a parallel structure to the sentence: *most mundane being. . . most interesting being.* (A) and (D) are too wordy, and (C) would lack a parallel structure of comparing a mundane thing and a fascinating thing.

44. **(F)** Although it is not directly stated, the implication from the previous sentence, "Maybe it was only with maturity that I recognized the wonder of opposable thumbs," is that it was indeed within the writer's power to open the cage. Having opposable thumbs enables one to grasp objects.

45. **(C)** "Kitchen Court" is an imaginary court of children, not a part of the actual American court and judiciary system. So, this essay would not fulfill this potential prompt.

46. **(J)** Since we are placing dynamite in the context of everything else that Nobel invented, it would be appropriate to use the word "among" since the author is referring to hundreds of items. "Between," as in (G) would be used in comparing two things. (H) would be used with one item, and (F) would be used if we said "along with."

47. **(B)** provides specific elaboration on Nobel's depth of scientific skill and the breadth of his intellectual interests, discussing his passion for literature and poetry. (A) does not transition to the next sentence, (C) doesn't specify his intellectual skills, and (D) is too vague.

48. **(J)** is fine, since there is no doubt that the pronoun would refer to Alfred Nobel. It would be needlessly repetitive to say his name again, as in (F), particularly giving his full name. His full name was already provided in the previous sentence. (G) uses the incorrect pronoun, and (H) is too wordy.

49. **(C)** Be certain you read the question carefully and don't miss that it asks you to determine what the sentence would NOT lose. It would not lose any information about when he ceased to be interested in the humanities because these years were when Nobel was forced to study abroad. Had he chosen to study abroad of his own accord, then this could indicate a lack of interest in the humanities.

50. **(G)** places a comma after the name of the person Nobel met and before a detailed description clarifying who this person was.

51. **(A)** Being introduced to the explosive liquid would provide a logical explanation as to why he wanted to conduct further research into making the more stable and controllable dynamite. (B) and (C) are too vague, and (D) would not provide a clear demonstration of how Nobel's meeting with Sobrero inspired his research.

52. **(J)** Since this is a new paragraph, we need to clarify the subject again by stating the person's name.

53. **(B)** expresses the logical contrast between the previous sentence, which mentions Nobel's hope in helping people, and the current sentence, which discusses how he ended up creating a deadly weapon.

54. **(J)** We need to keep "famous" directly connected to what it modifies, "Nobel Peace Prize," and so we would not want a comma between "famous" and "Nobel." Also, we need to isolate the clarifying phrase, "named in his honor," and then pick up the sentence directly afterward without a breath or pause.

55. **(B)** Earlier in the paragraph it mentions that Nobel created the Nobel Peace Prize after reading an incorrect obituary about himself. Giving direct evidence of what the obituary said helps us more clearly understand why he would have been motivated to create such a prize—namely, in order to redeem his public image.

56. **(H)** "That" is used to begin an essential characteristic of something, and if we simply said "last will," we would not know that it is the last will that Nobel wrote.

57. **(D)** Providing the equivalent of the amount of money in U.S. dollar terms would likely help the reader better understand how much money was left. It is not (C) because we *would* have information about how much money was left, albeit in a less used currency, the Swedish kroner.

58. **(F)** puts the sentence in a logical sequence. While (G), (H), and (J) contain the same information as (F), they present it in a convoluted, confusing way.

59. **(C)** preserves the original meaning while not being too wordy, as is (A). (B) inserts an unnecessary comma, and (D) inverts the word order.

60. **(F)** The first half of the essay discusses Nobel's personal life, and the second half focuses on the long-term impact of his legacy, the Nobel Prize. As such, it would successfully both provide a biography and show the impact of a famous historical figure.

61. **(C)** gives the sentence a parallel construction of "shining," "heating," and "making."

62. **(J)** (F), (G), and (H) all would insert irrelevant information that would conflict with the more informal, narrative tone of the paragraph.

63. **(A)** has a comma that provides a break between the first half of the sentence, ending with "born," and also puts commas in the list of things that the narrator loved about Arizona. (B) is too jumbled since it has no commas. (C) goes too far in the other direction, being too choppy. (D) incorrectly places a comma between "love" and "with."

64. **(H)** uses a colon to set off a clarification of the type of dog, just as the dash does in the original sentence. (F) gives no pause, (G) would require a complete sentence after the semicolon, and (J) makes the phrase not have the

significance that it does in the current sentence because it surrounds it with parentheses.

65. **(B)** uses the correct wording, "lie," since the dog is physically reclining. "Lay," as in (A), means "place or set." The sentence is already in the past tense, with the word "used," so changes in the tense that we see in (C) and (D) are incorrect.

66. **(H)** The previous two sentences mention how the narrator has a dog and how it is quite hot outside. The sentence in question would indeed provide interesting details that would be consistent with the tone of the paragraph.

67. **(C)** gives the correct idiomatic expression, "with the exception."

68. **(F)** refers to the "hiss" and the "steam," which would be plural and require the plural possessive word, "their."

69. **(D)** The question asks for what would NOT be acceptable as an alternative. Since we have an independent clause (complete sentence) both before and after the possible punctuation, a comma would not be strong enough, resulting in a comma splice.

70. **(J)** is consistent with the first-person use of "I" throughout the rest of the essay.

71. **(B)** provides a needed break before the dependent clause that follows. The clause "Off to the side, a homeless man who has been standing on the bench preaching the end of the world since I was 5" cannot stand on its own because the word "who" prevents it from being a complete sentence. This makes (A) and (D) not work, since they must have a complete sentence follow their particular punctuations. (C) would not provide a needed break, having no comma whatsoever.

72. **(F)** expresses both bitter and sweet feelings by saying "sadly smile." (G) and (H) are too negative, and (J) is too optimistic.

73. **(B)** works because we cannot easily quantify how "trying" an area would be. We generally use "less" with nonquantifiable things and "fewer" with quantifiable, countable things. (C) would give an inconsistent meaning, and (D) would take away a helpful description.

74. **(J)** It is not necessary to put a phrase here, since it is implied that if the businesses "leave," as stated earlier in the sentence, they would be going to other places.

75. **(C)** would be the most logical placement, since the sentence right before it would discuss the dryness of the Arizona air.

Mathematics

1. **(B)** $3x - 4 (x - 2) + 6x - 8 = 0$
$$3x - 4x + 8 + 6x - 8 = 0$$
$$5x = 0$$
$$x = 0$$

2. **(J)** After the end of November, the price would go down by 20%. This would equal $325 \times 0.2 = 65$.

   We can subtract 65 from 325 to get the price at the end of November: $325 - 65 = 260$.

   Now, find 10 percent of the end-of-November price: $260 \times 0.1 = 26$.

   Then subtract this from the end-of-November price to get the December price:

   $$260 - 26 = 234$$

3. **(D)** The "going to college" group will be 40% + 35% = 75%. There are 360° in a circle, so figure out what 75% of 360 is: $360 \times 0.75 = 270$.

4. **(H)** All of the relative weights add up to 100%. So, you can figure out how many points he will need to get from the final in order to have an overall total of 82%.

   $$86 \times 0.15 + 70 \times 0.15 + 90 \times 0.3 = 50.4$$

   The total remaining number of points needed is $82 - 50.4 = 31.6$.

   Then, realize that 31.6 is the points given from the final exam. Determine what score is necessary on the final exam by using this equation, where x represents the score on the final exam:

   $$0.4x = 31.6$$
   $$x = 79$$

   Alternatively, you could just plug in the values from the choices into the table and calculate the grade until it averages out to 82%.

5. **(C)** Label all the angles you can. The triangle is isosceles, and the angles are thus 45° as labeled. The angle in question is equal to 45° because it is an alternate interior angle that will be the same as angle *FGE*:

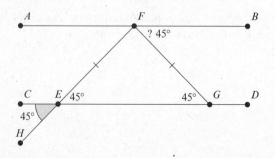

6. **(F)** Using x and y as the two numbers, the equations would be:

$$x + y = 19$$
$$x \cdot y = 70$$

While you could solve this through substitution, it will likely be faster to just plug in the numbers. The only pair that fits these conditions is $x = 5$ and $y = 14$.

7. **(E)** $|-3| = 3$ and $|-2.5| = 2.5$ so $3 + 2.5 = 5.5$

8. **(H)** Here is the triangle with the conditions as described:

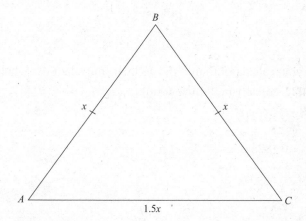

Angles *BAC* and *BCA* are the same, since the triangle is isosceles. Since angle *ABC* is across from the longest side, it will be the longest angle.

9. **(D)** The mean of a set of numbers is equal to the sum divided by how many numbers are in the set: $\dfrac{\text{Sum}}{\text{Number}} = \text{Mean}$.

In this case, the mean can be calculated as follows:

$$\frac{45 + 55 + 50 + 70 + 65 + 80 + 40 + 90 + 70 + 85}{10} = \frac{650}{10} = 65$$

10. **(J)** $\dfrac{1}{3} \times 210 = 70$

11. **(A)** The area of a trapezoid is $\dfrac{B_1 + B_2}{2} \times \text{Height} = \text{Area}$. The height on the new trapezoid will be half what it was in the original, and the lengths of the bases all together will be half what it was in the original. So, the new area will be $\dfrac{1}{4}$ what it was in the original trapezoid: $20 \times \dfrac{1}{4} = 5$.

12. **(H)** $\dfrac{100}{8} = 12.5$. Since you cannot purchase half of a book, you need to round up to 13.

13. **(B)** When x and y are directly proportional, their relationship can be expressed with the equation: $y = kx$ where k is the constant of proportionality. We can use the first set of xy values to determine what k is:

$$y = kx$$
$$8 = k \times 3$$
$$\frac{8}{3} = k$$

So, the equation including the proportionality constant k is $y = \frac{8}{3}x$.

Now, plug 13 in for y into this equation and solve for x:

$$13 = \frac{8}{3}x$$

$$x = 13 \times \frac{3}{8} = 4.875$$

14. **(J)** Use your calculator to find the decimal equivalent of each answer:

F. $0.222\overline{2}$ (already in decimal form)

G. $\frac{2}{11} = 0.181818$

H. $\frac{3}{16} = 0.1875$

J. $\frac{8}{60} = 0.1333$

K. $\frac{5}{26} = 0.2$

15. **(C)** The area of a circle is πr^2. Take the area of one circle and divide it by the area of the other:

$$\frac{\pi 2^2}{\pi 5^2} = \frac{4}{25}$$

16. **(G)** The lengths of the two shorter sides in a triangle must add up to more than the length of the longest side of the triangle. 5, 5 would NOT work because $5 + 5 = 10$, which is the length of the triangle's longest side.

17. **(A)** The greatest even prime number is 2 (it is the only even prime number) and the least odd prime number is 3 (1 is not a prime number). The product of the two numbers is $2 \times 3 = 6$.

18. **(K)** Subtract the area of all the pepperonis from the area of the pizza as a whole. The area of the pizza as a whole is $\pi 7^2 = 49\pi$ since the pizza has a radius of 7. The area of each pepperoni is $\pi\left(\frac{1}{2}\right)^2 = \frac{1}{4}\pi$. There are 100 pepperonis, so the area of all the pepperonis put together is

$$100 \times \frac{1}{4}\pi = 25\pi$$

$$49\pi - 25\pi = 24\pi$$

19. **(D)** Fortunately, we don't need to figure out what each individual side is in the figure because the sides all meet at right angles. So, you can figure what the sides add up to as in the figure below:

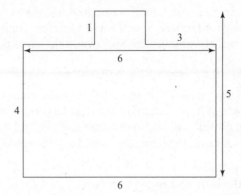

The vertical sides all add up to 5 + 5 = 10 and the horizontal sides all add up to 6 + 6 = 12. So the perimeter of the entire figure is 10 + 12 = 22.

20. **(H)** Since the number of choices goes down by one each time, solve this as follows:

$$85 \times 84 \times 83 = 592,620$$

21. **(B)** Use the calendar and count up the number of days that are on the weekend: a Saturday or Sunday. There are a total of 10. Divide 10 by the total number of days in January to get the fraction: $\frac{10}{31}$.

22. **(J)** Rather than trying to create a function from scratch, you will likely find it easiest to plug sample values into the choices to see which function correctly. Pick a value for the date of a Wednesday and plug it into the different options. Let's try 3 because it is less likely that an unusual number like 3, as opposed to 1, will result in equivalent answers. The third Wednesday is on the 19th.

F. $f(n) = 5 \times 3 = 15$

G. $f(n) = 7 \times 3 = 21$

H. $f(n) = 7(3 - 1) = 14$

J. $f(n) = 5 + 7(3 - 1) = 19$

K. $f(n) = \frac{5}{12} \times 3 = \frac{15}{12}$

(J) is the only option that equals 19 when we plug in 3 for x.

23. **(E)** You could count this all the way up, but you can save time if you take the total number of days that will have gone by in February and March, 28 + 31 = 59. Then divide 59 by 7 to see what the remainder is. $7\overline{)59}$ with a remainder of 3. So, we can go 8 full weeks forward and 3 days from the last day of January, which was a Monday. Then, the next day will be the day on which April begins. This would therefore be a Friday.

24. **(H)** $i^4 = \left(\sqrt{-1}\right)^4 = 1$. So, the $\sqrt{4i^4} = \sqrt{4 \times 1} = 2$.

25. **(B)** Since X is the smallest side and the other sides are consecutive odd integers with respect to X, the length of the next larger side will be 2 more than X, and the largest side will be 4 more than X. (3, 5, and 7 are all consecutive odd integers, for example). The other side lengths would therefore be $X + 2$ and $X + 4$.

26. **(F)** Label all the sides and angles as follows:

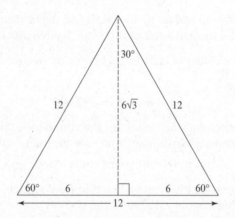

The height of the triangle is $6\sqrt{3}$ since it is one leg of a 30-60-90 triangle. The area of the triangle is $\frac{1}{2}BH$ so the area is $\frac{1}{2} \times 12 \times 6\sqrt{3} \approx 62$.

27. **(B)** The chunks of walking time all add up to 1 full hour, so if we figure out how many miles Allison has walked, that will give us the miles/hour. Instead of minutes, convert each bit of time to its part of an hour (e.g., 15 minutes equals 0.25 hours).

$$0.25 \times 3 + 0.5 \times 4 + 0.25 \times 2 = 3.25 \text{ miles total,}$$
$$\text{so } 3.25 \text{ miles per hour.}$$

28. **(K)** $\sqrt{-3 \times -4} = \sqrt{12}$ and $\sqrt{3} \times \sqrt{4} = \sqrt{12}$.

$\sqrt{12} \times \sqrt{12} = 12$, which is a positive integer. (Irrational numbers cannot be expressed as a ratio, e.g., $\sqrt{2}$.)

29. **(A)** Each die roll has 6 total possible values: 1, 2, 3, 4, 5, or 6. With the two rolls, there are $6 \times 6 = 36$ total combinations. Out of these total combinations, there is only one possible combination that will give a total of 2—when both die rolls result in a 1. So, the probability is 1 divided by 36, or $\dfrac{1}{36}$.

30. **(K)** $\sqrt{4x^4} \times \sqrt{16x^2} = \sqrt{64x^6} = 8x^3$

31. **(C)** The only highlighted point is 3, so the expression is simply $x = 3$.

32. **(G)** Take the initial equation, $E = mc^2$, and divide both sides by c^2 to get m by itself:

$$\frac{E}{c^2} = \frac{mc^2}{c^2}$$

The c^2s will cancel on the right side, leaving you with $m = \dfrac{E}{c^2}$.

33. **(A)** The only thing that will change from one sphere's volume to the other's is the radius. If the volume of one sphere is 27 times the other, that means that $r^3 = 27$ times the r^3 of the other. Take the cube root of 27 to get 3, making 3:1 represent the ratio of the radius of the larger sphere to the radius of the smaller sphere.

34. **(F)** In order to move the parabola to the right two units, the x value must have 2 subtracted from it. In order to move the parabola up 2 units, add 2 units to the right-hand side of the equation. This makes

$$y = (x - 2)^2 + 1 \text{ correct.}$$

35. **(B)** $100\% - 70\% = 30\%$

36. **(J)** The triangle will have a perimeter of 24. If the square has the same perimeter, it will have individual sides of $\dfrac{24}{4} = 6$. The area of the square will be $6 \times 6 = 36$.

37. **(C)** Here is the sequence, making sure there is the same difference between each term: 1, 7, <u>13</u>, <u>19</u>, 25. The sum of the 3rd and 4th terms will be $13 + 19 = 32$.

38. **(K)** Use the formula $\dfrac{(n-3)n}{2}$, where n represents the number of diagonals in a polygon. Put in 8 for n: $\dfrac{(8-3)8}{2} = 20$.

39. **(B)** The shortest distance between the y axis and the point $(2, 7)$ is 2, as you can see from the graph below:

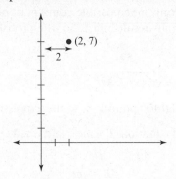

40. **(J)** $\dfrac{50}{3.5} = 14.28$ and round up to 15 full cups to have at least as much fat as there would be in 1 cup of whale milk.

41. **(E)** Factor out the common term of $5x^2$. This results in $5x^2(x - 3 + 2x^2)$.

42. **(K)** $\pi R^2 \times \dfrac{2}{R} = 2\pi R$

43. **(C)** Sides AB and AC are identical, since they are both radii of the circle. This makes the triangle isosceles, with angles ABC and BCA both equal to 31 degrees. We can solve for the measure of angle BCA as follows: $180 - 31 - 31 = 118$ since there are 180 degrees in a triangle.

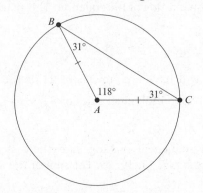

44. **(G)** Each of the X math problems takes 5 minutes, and each of the Y pages takes 2 minutes. So, to compute the total number of minutes, use this expression: $5X + 2Y$.

45. **(D)** To have a 15% increase, multiply the original amount by 1.15 to get the new amount: $32 \times 1.15 = 36.8$ which rounds up to 37 inches.

46. **(G)** Here is a drawing of the ladder configuration, with the height up the building represented as x:

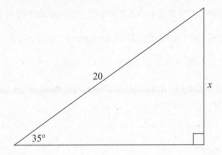

To solve for x, use $\sin 35 = \dfrac{x}{20}$

$\sin 35 \times 20 \approx 11.5$

47. **(A)** $y = 3t + 4$

$$\frac{y-4}{3} = t$$

Plug this in for t in the x equation:

$$x = 2t - 1$$

$$x = 2\left(\frac{y-4}{3}\right) - 1$$

$$x = \frac{2y}{3} - \frac{8}{3} - 1$$

$$x = \frac{2y}{3} - \frac{11}{3}$$

48. **(G)** The number of social groups is irrelevant. Calculate the number of out-of-town friends on the social networking sites—70% of the females live out-of-town since 30% live in town, and 60% of the male friends live out-of-town since 40% of the males live in town. So, calculate the total as follows:

$$0.7 \times 60 + 0.6 \times 50 = 72$$

49. **(E)** Each sphere will take up a cube of its own with a volume of 6 inches on each side. Why? The radius of the sphere is 3 and it needs to be doubled to provide the diameter. The volume of these minicubes will be $6 \times 6 \times 6 = 216$ cubic inches. The volume of the large cube can be found by taking each of the 6 foot sides and converting them to inches, and then multiplying the length, width, and height of the cube together: $72 \times 72 \times 72 = 373{,}248$. Then, calculate the number of spheres that can fit into this large cube by dividing the volume of the large cube by the volume of the small cubes:

$$\frac{373{,}248}{216} = 1{,}728$$

50. **(G)** The cube root of –27 is –3, and the cube root of $x^9 = x^3$. So, the expression is equal to $-3x^3$.

51. **(D)** To find the slope of a line that is perpendicular to a given line, take the slope of the given line and find its negative reciprocal. With $\frac{A}{B}$, this will be $-\frac{B}{A}$.

52. **(H)** The unrolled cylinder will have the same height as the cylinder and will have the circumference as its base:

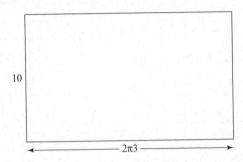

The area of the rectangle formed by this unrolled roll of paper is $10 \times 2\pi3 = 60\pi$.

53. **(C)** $\sin(\alpha + \beta) = \sin \alpha \cos \beta + \cos \alpha \sin \beta$

$$\sin\left(\frac{5\pi}{6}\right) = \sin\left(\frac{\pi}{2} + \frac{\pi}{3}\right) = \sin\left(\frac{\pi}{2}\right)\cos\left(\frac{\pi}{3}\right) + \cos\left(\frac{\pi}{2}\right)\sin\left(\frac{\pi}{3}\right)$$

Then plug in values for these expressions from the given table:

$$= 1 \times \frac{1}{2} + 0 = \frac{1}{2}$$

54. **(K)** $x = \dfrac{-b \pm \sqrt{b^2 - 4ac}}{2a}$ and $a = 3$, $b = -4$, and $c = 2$. So, $\dfrac{4 \pm \sqrt{(-4)^2 - 4 \cdot 3 \cdot 2}}{2 \cdot 3}$

would be used to solve for the values of x.

55. **(A)** $\sin A = \dfrac{\text{opposite}}{\text{hypotenuse}} = \dfrac{a}{c}$

56. **(G)** From the graph or from your background knowledge, you can see that the greater the standard deviation, the farther the curve will be stretched since the values of σ will be larger and larger. Therefore, Researcher A's curve would be narrower since the standard deviation is lower. Also, since they are studying the same information, it is most likely that the mean of both the curves of Researcher A and Researcher B would be quite close to one another.

57. **(D)** Visualize the cutaway of the sphere with this diagram:

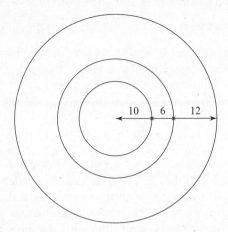

To get the volume of the sphere in the middle portion, we need to subtract the inner volume of the sphere (radius 10) from the middle volume of the sphere (radius 16). To calculate this percentage of the whole, take this amount and divide it by the entire sphere that has a radius of 28.

$$\frac{\left(\frac{4}{3}\pi 16^3 - \frac{4}{3}\pi 10^3\right)}{\frac{4}{3}\pi 28^3} = \frac{16^3 - 10^3}{28^3} \approx 0.14, \text{ which would convert to 14\%.}$$

58. **(G)** There are 180 degrees in Radians so do a conversion as follows:

$$\phi \text{ Radians} \times \frac{180°}{\pi \text{ Radians}} = \text{Degree measure of } \theta \text{ in terms of } \phi \text{ Radians}$$

59. **(D)** There will be 64 squares total on the 8 × 8 checker board, and half of them will be red, making for 32 total red squares. To determine how many red squares are NOT along the borders, let's figure out how many ARE along the borders. This graph below represents a checkerboard, with the black squares marked with a "B" and the red squares marked with an "R":

R	B	R	B	R	B	R	B
B	R	B	R	B	R	B	R
R	B	R	B	R	B	R	B
B	R	B	R	B	R	B	R
R	B	R	B	R	B	R	B
B	R	B	R	B	R	B	R
R	B	R	B	R	B	R	B
B	R	B	R	B	R	B	R

There are a total of 14 red squares along the borders of the board. So, there are 32 – 14 = 18 red squares NOT along the border. Now, determine the odds it will be a red square that DOES NOT lie on the border by doing $\frac{18}{64} = \frac{9}{32}$.

60. **(J)** The pattern is formed by each term after the first two terms equaling the sum of the previous two terms. For example, 8 = 3 + 5, 13 = 5 + 8, and 21 = 8 + 13. To get the 8th term, continue the sequence:

$$3, 5, 8, 13, 21, 34, 55, \underline{\mathbf{89}}.$$

Reading

1. **(C)** Throughout the passage, the narrator is having a conversation with herself about the nature of her illness while making a variety of poetic and literary references. This is best described as an "internal monologue." It is not (A) because there are not two characters interacting, as would be needed for a "dialogue." It is not (B) because although some elements of feminism are present in the second paragraph, the essay as a whole does not address this theme. Finally, it is not (D) because it is not a narrative, which would take on more the form of a story rather than the in-depth analysis of a personal situation present in the essay.

2. **(F)** The final paragraph focuses on a respect for the mysteriousness of death, given that the narrator recognizes that her knowledge about her illness is limited—"the only thing I can trust is my body" (line 51). In the final paragraph she also mentions how she has created mental imagery that enables her to visualize herself as transcending the limits of physical reality, creating nonphysical, indestructible connections between "sense and memory." With her saying this, it is possible to infer that she respects the mystery of death because she is trying to cope with its inevitability. Process of elimination can be of great help on this particular question. It is not (G) because she makes no claim of having scientific expertise, much less scientific objectivity. It is not (H) because she is apparently *not* fearful of death because throughout the passage, she analyzes illness and death with intellectual rigor and humor. Finally, it is not (J) because she certainly understands that death is real, according to lines 38–39, where she states "I can easily imagine myself holding hands with death."

3. **(C)** Based on the context surrounding lines 22–23, we see that the narrator would prefer to look at death in a more poetic way. She would rather have her death portrayed in a romantic, "fanciful" fashion than to have it portrayed in a clinical, scientific way. It is not (A) because the example of being "an only child estranged by famine and war" is not related to femininity. It is not (B) because that would imply more of a negative connotation than the narrator would intend to have in describing her own preferences. Finally, it is not (D) because "exorbitant" implies great financial expense, to which her thoughts do not relate.

4. **(F)** is the only logical option based on the content of the quotes—the first from Rosalind talking about being serious and restrained and the second from Beatrice about being passionate and intense. Also, in lines 30–31, the narrator previews this comparison by saying "one austere, the other fierce."

5. **(C)** The narrator gives an introspective, highly analytical internal discussion of the nature of illness and death. This can best be described as "pensive," or thoughtful. (A), "militant," would be far less contemplative and far more action-oriented and passionate. (B), "hopeless," and (D), "fearful," are not possible given the narrator's discussion in the last paragraph of creative approaches she is taking to extend her mind and soul beyond the limits of the physical world.

6. **(G)** In lines 14–18, the narrator vividly portrays having a heart attack as lacking any dignity, making "gracefulness" something this experience would definitely lack. (F), "superiority," does not capture the sense of her feelings as closely as "gracefulness" does. (H) could be true in other contexts, but is totally off the mark in describing one's emotional reaction to an illness. (J), "excellence," is far too vague.

7. **(B)** Consider the context surrounding this phrase: "My life line moves in four dimensions, swirling to and fro like a cottonwood seed caught in a mercurial breeze." The idea of moving in four dimensions as opposed to three implies a sense of transcendence. The idea of moving around in a mercurial breeze implies a feeling of uncertainty. The tone of this sentence is more neutral, making the more negative (A) and the more positive (C) incorrect. This is a metaphorical comparison, making the literal comparison in (D) wrong.

8. **(J)** The ironic idea in the first paragraph is that the same substance that is helping the narrator live—nitroglycerine—is the same substance used to destroy things in the form of dynamite. There is nothing the narrator believes to be humorous about her illness, making (F) incorrect. What is written on the bottle *is* an accurate indication of what the medicine can do to the narrator's body, so (G) is wrong. (H) is true, but it is not ironic.

9. **(B)** Throughout the paragraph, the narrator dismisses the certainty that her doctors have in their analysis of her electrocardiograph by comparing their work to fortune tellers. In the last sentence, she expresses that she would feel happier if her doctors portrayed themselves more as shamans than as scientists. She knows that they are indeed knowledgeable about medicine, (A), but it is the degree of certainty they have about their findings that bothers her. She would like them to be more magical and artistic in their craft, (C), so this would not be something they would "give up." (D) refers to a small snippet from the passage that has no relevance to this question.

10. **(J)** Be sure you notice the NOT in this question. In lines 12–13, the implication is that there would be pink ribbons for women suffering from *other* illnesses than heart problems. We see evidence of (F) in line 11, evidence of (G) in lines 33–35, and evidence of (H) in lines 37–38.

392 • Pass Key to the ACT

11. **(A)** After a general historical background, the author uses the in-depth example of *The Romance of Tristan* to give evidence of general social trends in feudal society. It is not (B) because the focus is on feudalism, not on works of art in general. It is not (C) because the biographical episode of Tristan is a relatively small part of the passage. It is not (D) because *The Romance of Tristan* was a fictional narrative, not a historical account.

12. **(H)** The second paragraph functions to provide a general historical background about the nature of relationships in feudal society. (F) does not work because there is not an explicit definition of terms, and even if there were, that would not illustrate how the paragraph functions in the passage as a whole. (G) is incorrect because the example illustrating loyalty and virtue comes later in the essay with the discussion of *The Romance of Tristan*. (J) is also done later in the passage, not in the second paragraph.

13. **(B)** Yseut is the "daughter of an Irish king" (lines 36–37), and is treated with great respect. Brangain is treated as an object rather than a respected person as portrayed in the last paragraph. It is reasonable to infer that the two women were treated differently because of their difference in social class, with Yseut being an elite person and Brangain being a maid. It is not (A) because Tristan does not present evidence that his *views* on gender have changed—just his treatment of the two women is quite different. It is not (C) because there is no clear indication of the exact ages of the women, other than that they were both likely young since Yseut was of marrying age and Brangain was a virgin. It is not (D) because, given Tristan's actions, it is likely he found both women to be attractive.

14. **(J)** Treatment of the underprivileged is clearly the least important, especially considering how the maid Brangain was treated in the last paragraph. Treatment of family is the next in importance, but the example of Tristan and Lord Mark illustrates that even though the bonds of family relations were strong—Tristan was Mark's nephew—the obligations of feudal homage were stronger, given Tristan's sacrifices. Additionally, lines 16–17 explicitly state that "a Vassal's oath to serve, protect, and obey his Lord was meant to be the most sacred aspect of his life."

15. **(C)** Based on the context of the paragraph, we can see that women were treated as objects. Lines 59–61 state: "These events in particular demonstrate how the feudal system conceptually disassembled women of the Middle Ages into their sexual components." There is an attitude of using women for the advantage of men, which indicates oppression, and a lack of consideration of their feelings, which indicates indifference. (A) does not take into account that this is a sociological analysis, not math. (B) is persuasive, but is a bit too extreme to fit what is presented here. While there is definitely evidence of abuse, having an example of one person is not sufficient to demonstrate consistent abuse of all women. In fact, earlier in the essay the princess Yseut was

treated with respect. (D) is contradictory—their treatment was antiquated, but it was not simultaneously progressive.

16. **(F)** Lines 43–44 best illustrate this: "In the feudal system, women were frequently objectified and regarded as goods to be traded and used disposably." This is synonymous with a commodity. Although animals (G) and slaves (H) could be described in this way, "commodity" provides the most precise definition of what is presented. There is no discussion of witchcraft or enchantment in this paragraph, making (J) incorrect.

17. **(B)** Based on the context of this paragraph, it is apparent that after setting out on a long journey, Tristan is able to slay a dragon. The best fit for this would be "after some time," since it is clear that the dragon slaying did not occur until the journey was well underway. (A) is too precise a time period. (C) would repeat the transition later in the sentence, "upon doing so," which already expresses cause and effect. Also, it would fail to connect to the previous sentence because it is not as a direct result of going on his journey that Tristan slays the dragon. (D) would be too imprecise to describe what is happening because it could refer to time or a physical location.

18. **(G)** Even though the other themes would certainly be possible based on the story of *The Romance of Tristan*, it is clear that an exploration of the theme of gender inequality in the text would most appeal to the author. Why? Because the author spends the last two paragraphs of the essay focusing on this theme. If the author had demonstrated an interest in one of the other themes, we could infer that he would find that to be worthy of further investigation.

19. **(C)** is the only logical answer based on direct evidence from the passage in lines 25–27: "Later in this episode, Tristan reveals that, by blood, he is the nephew of Lord Mark. Upon hearing this, Mark wavers and attempts to persuade Tristan against risking his life." Based on the surrounding context, Mark clearly had no issue with Tristan going on such a risky journey when he thought Tristan was just another knight who had paid homage to Mark.

20. **(G)** Based on the second paragraph, vassals received a bit of power from their Lord, while the Lord received unquestioned obedience. Unbalanced reciprocity is the best fit because the relationship between the two is not balanced, with the Lord far more powerful than the vassal, and because there is reciprocity, with the Lord helping the vassal and the vassal helping the Lord. This is hardly an equitable partnership (F). There is also not unwavering loyalty (H), because the *unwavering* loyalty only works in one direction: from the vassal to the Lord. There is not hostile rebellion (J) because the vassals follow the Lord obediently—they do not rise up against him.

21. **(B)** The paragraph in lines 6–10 indicates that the narrator came across the poet while surfing the internet and procrastinating for an exam. "Happenstance" is therefore an excellent description of the method whereby the narrator discovered the poet, since it was through an unplanned, random

occurrence. The other choices all imply a more determined effort to seek out information than the narrator actually demonstrates in the passage.

22. **(J)** Line 18 states that she was born in 1917, and line 6 states that she died in the "millennial year," which can reasonably be inferred as the year 2000. 2000 – 1917 = 83. If you are ever asked to do anything quantitative on the reading section, know that only the most basic mathematical skills will be required. You certainly won't need a calculator.

23. **(C)** Lines 21–22 state, "And as she developed, so did her poetry, becoming more and more politically inclined." So, as she became older, her poetry became more political; it is reasonable then to conclude that when she was young, her poetry was likely NOT political. "Apolitical" means politically disinterested, so this would be an appropriate fit. The other choices all indicate much stronger political views than she would likely have demonstrated in her early work.

24. **(J)** Lines 14–15 state that Brooks "was not in the business of telling, even when her words were direct," and lines 25–27 state that Brooks "seemed intensely aware of racial and social injustice, but unwilling to freely lend me her stance." These excerpts show that Brooks was not interested in trying to directly tell her students what they should do, but more in presenting thoughts that her students could use for independent discovery. All of the other options involve more direct advising than Brooks was likely to give.

25. **(A)** "The Lovers of the Poor" is a quite ironic title for a poem that highlights the hypocrisy of some wealthy women who actually have great contempt for the poor. Choice (B) does not work because Brooks was trying to portray the wealthy women in a negative light—there is no indication that she was wavering or skeptical in her estimation of them. It is not choice (C) because the title is connected to the subject of the poem, since the women are doing charitable work. It is not choice (D) because the wealthy women did not in fact "love" the poor but are instead dismissive of those poor who do not fit their romanticized ideas.

26. **(F)** This paragraph moves the analysis from simply focusing on socioeconomic elements of the poem to focusing on the racial aspects of it. It therefore "extends" the range of the narrator's analysis to racial language. It is not choice (G) because this analysis complements rather than contrasts with the analysis up to this point. It is not choice (H) because the author states that the themes of socioeconomic division and racial difference are interwoven. It is not choice (J) because, even though this could be a minor reason for including this paragraph, it is not the main purpose of its inclusion.

27. **(C)** Lines 55–56 state that "Distasteful, and even shameful, is the privilege that is only willing to give on terms of convenience and comfort." In other words, the narrator disapproves of those who want to be disassociated from those they are supposedly helping; instead, the narrator would likely approve of those willing to throw themselves whole-heartedly into volunteerism,

even if what they see conflicts with their preconceived romanticized ideas. The other choices suggest a desire on the part of givers to remain distant from those they help.

28. **(G)** These lines state, "Obsessed, she was, with perceptions of beauty, questioning ugliness and more often than not exposing the truly ugly." The poem analyzed in Passage B, "The Lovers of the Poor," highlights what Brooks sees as the ugliness of those who claim to be interested in helping those less fortunate but are actually pretentious and self-absorbed. It is not choice (F) because the author of Passage B is emphatic that readers will come to a shared "disgust" at the behavior portrayed. It is not choice (H) because these lines emphasize biography, not poetry. It is not choice (J) because these lines emphasize the appearance of Brooks, not her writing.

29. **(B)** Lines 15–16 state that "her poetics were neither a lament nor a complaint or a plea." This implies that her poetry was more open to interpretation. Contrast this with the poem analyzed in Passage B, in which Brooks paints a picture that is designed to generate universal feelings of disapproval toward the pretense of the wealthy women. It is not choice (A) because the poem analyzed in Passage B is much more one-sided. It is not choice (C) because the poem is clearer in what it is trying to express. It is not choice (D) because emotions and social/racial structure are analyzed—violence is neither presented nor analyzed.

30. **(J)** Economic class is a major theme of Passage B, with Brooks presenting a portrait of the pretention of the wealthy. Line 26 of Passage A mentions "social injustice," which is indirectly associated with economic class. It is not choice (F) because racial identity is clearly mentioned in both passages. It is neither choice (G) nor choice (H) because autobiographical and biographical themes are discussed more in Passage A than in Passage B.

31. **(C)** The essay as a whole *informs* us about the science and geologic history of impact events. With its objective focus on presentation of facts and differing hypotheses, it cannot be said to *primarily* focus on persuasion (A), argumentation (B), or critique (D).

32. **(G)** Lines 22–25 clearly state that rocks that originate from outer space tend to have a much higher ratio of siderophilic to lithophilic components. Location (F) would not be enough, since no mention is made of the relative position on the *surface* of the Earth making a difference. If a rock were found in a particular layer of the Earth, such as the K-T boundary, that might give more evidence of its extraterrestrial origin. (H) is incorrect because simply finding that a rock is made of rock, metal, or ice fragments would not give precise information about its exact chemical composition, making it virtually impossible to determine its origin. (J) is incorrect because there is no mention of using the texture of the substances to evaluate their origin.

33. **(D)** Lines 6–7 state that "between 2,900 and 7,300 extraterrestrial bodies of 10 grams or larger fall to Earth each year." So, if you divide 2,900 and 7,300

by 365 days in a year, it comes closest to 8–20 extraterrestrial bodies per day. Since you don't have a calculator, how can you figure out this problem? Simply notice that the passage gives a *range* of possible impacts, which would eliminate (A) and (B) since they only give particular numbers. (C) is wrong because it gives how many there are in a year instead of just a day. This would be an easy question to misread, so be sure you are being extremely careful to avoid any key words.

34. **(G)** The paragraph elaborates on the term "ominous" by pointing out that the impact of a massive asteroid would have the same effect as a nuclear bomb detonation. This would clearly be a "disastrous potential effect." It has nothing to do with extraterrestrial travel (F). It uses the nuclear bomb as a way to compare two different events—it does not make any commentary about manmade nuclear conflict (H). And it is certainly not (J) because lines 31–33 state that "Some asteroid orbits intersect with those of other asteroids and planets, and, occasionally, collide with them."

35. **(A)** Based on the context of the sentence in lines 36–39, impact events are referred to as "large scale"—the author goes on to discuss these same events as "Apollo" asteroids. So, having a large size is a necessary condition of being an Apollo asteroid. It is not (B) because there is no indication in the passage that an Apollo asteroid *necessarily* must go through the orbit of Earth. It is not (C) because the author discusses these asteroids as going through Earth's orbit—not necessarily impacting the Earth or other astronomical bodies, causing a large blast. It is not (D) because, whereas the author states that only a handful of these asteroids have been observed in the past few years, we can infer that asteroids of this size existed well before the present day, especially given the discussion of the evidence in support of the K-T rock boundary.

36. **(H)** Lines 40–44 give many clear details about the exact size and scope of the Tunguska River impact, so this is known with the most precision. Lines 49–63 give relatively fewer details about the K-T extinction, but still enough to make it more well understood than the Moon's formation, an explanation of which in lines 45–49 is described as merely a hypothesis.

37. **(A)** The sentence in lines 45–48 describes the hypothetical process for the formation of the Moon as involving a huge asteroid impacting the early Earth and essentially *breaking* off a large chunk of it to form the Moon. "Pressurizing" (B) would not indicate that a separation occurred. "Shattering" (C) would convey that the impact resulted in lots of small parts rather than a large Moon. "Creating" (D) is persuasive, but it is too vague to work to precisely describe how "shearing" is used in the context of this sentence.

38. **(J)** Lines 52–54 state that "All over the world at the K-T rock boundary, scientists have found a thin layer of iridium in concentrations of up to 130 times the background levels." We can infer from this that in a typical portion of the Earth's surface that the radiation would be 1/130th of the radiation found in the K-T boundary.

39. **(C)** With the impact of an asteroid having potentially catastrophic consequences, the author uses atomic bomb comparisons in order to illustrate how
significant an impact an asteroid collision could have. Comparing an asteroid
impact to an atomic bomb blast hardly minimizes it (A). It does not provide
historical evidence (B) because an atomic bomb blast would provide no proof
of an asteroid collision. Although an atomic bomb could potentially be used
to destroy a dangerous asteroid, the passage has no discussion of this (D).

40. **(F)** The last sentence of the passage states "What role they (asteroid impacts)
may play in the future we cannot yet say." Leading up to that, the paragraph
discusses how an asteroid collision may have contributed to the extinction of
the dinosaurs. This is a serious subject, for it is possible that another asteroid
impact like this could happen in the future so it is something about which
we should be cautious, but also something that involves quite a bit of uncertainty because it is not definite that this will occur. So, (G) and (J) would
not work because such a possibility does not inspire "hope" or "playfulness."
However, the tone is more measured, not going to the extreme of "dread"
and "fear," making (H) incorrect. We would be more fearful and full of dread
if we knew an asteroid impact were about to happen with a great degree of
certainty.

Science

1. **(D)** Look for the food that has a Calories per gram value closest to 9. Palm
vegetable oil with a Calories per gram value of 8.62 is the only one close to
9.

2. **(J)** None of these foods comes close to even an approximation of 4 Calories
per gram for protein and carbohydrates and 9 Calories per gram for fat.

3. **(C)** Since all of the values in this table have the same volumes—cups—look
for the beverage that has the fewest Calories per cup. Orange juice, at 105, is
lower than that of all the other beverages.

4. **(J)** As a result of being in a very dry container, it is most likely that the
cheese would dry out. If it dries out, its Calories per gram would increase
because less of its volume would come from water, which has no Calories. (J)
is the only option that would involve an increase in Calories per gram over
the original amount.

5. **(B)** All of the foods tested in Experiment 1 come *under* the 4-4-9 whole number estimates, so it would be logical to generalize that this same trend would
hold for other types of food.

6. **(H)** The 4-4-9 method would do a nice job differentiating between the caloric values of fatty foods and other foods, but it would not help someone
differentiate between carbohydrates and protein since both of these food
types have Calories per gram values of approximately 4.

7. **(A)** According to Table 1, Euglena is the only one of the three organisms that can survive without sunlight, so it would be the organism most likely to survive for a prolonged period in a dark room.

8. **(J)** Using basic background knowledge from biology, it would be reasonable to conclude that a chemoheterotroph—a mammal, fungi, or fish—would consume a photoautotroph—trees, kelp, cactus. The other sequences would not be expected.

9. **(D)** According to Figure 1, Photoautotrophs and Photoheterotrophs both receive energy from sunlight. According to Table 1, all three types of mixotrophs given are able to capture energy from sunlight. Because of this, it would be reasonable to conclude that all three options are possible organisms that use photosynthesis.

10. **(G)** Based on Figure 1, Autotrophs gather their carbon from the more simple CO_2, and Heterotrophs gather their carbon from what would be the more complicated "organic compounds."

11. **(B)** To survive a global dust cloud, an organism would have to be able to survive without sunlight. According to Figure 1, anammox bacteria are chemoautorophs that would gather energy from chemical bonds. The other organisms get energy from sunlight. So, the anammox bacteria would have the best chance of survival in such a catastrophe.

12. **(G)** This puts the planets in order from smallest to largest based on their mass values from Table 1. Be careful with the scientific notation.

13. **(B)** Based on Table 2, as the ball's distance *increases* from 600 km to 4,800 km, the gravitational force *only decreases* from 41.1 N to 16.1 N.

14. **(G)** 18 N would fall between Position C and Position D, making it have a distance that would be between the distances of C (2,400) and D (4,800). (G), 4,200, falls between 2,400 and 4,800 and is closer to the 4,800, just as 18 N would be closer to the value of Position D's gravitational force, 16.1 N.

15. **(D)** Look at Figure 2, which has the Universal Gravitation equation. If you double the r on the bottom of the equation, the F on the left-hand side will be $\frac{1}{4}$ as large since you would square the r.

16. **(J)** Taking into account the Universal Gravitation equation in Figure 2, as long as two objects have mass, they will exert *some* gravitational force on one another no matter how far apart they are. (F) and (G) are too small for the gravitational force to be insignificant, much less approach zero. (H) is not true because weight *would depend* on the distance between the objects.

17. **(C)** The first sentence of Experiment 2 states that "The student imagined a situation. . ." It would be reasonable to be skeptical of an experiment that was not actually conducted but was merely theoretical. (A) is not true because it is perfectly fine to use these units for measurement. (B) is not correct because the units of measurement are commonly used in scientific practice. (D) is not correct because although there would be a lack of friction from air resistance,

this would actually make the experiment *better* at determining the validity of Newton's theory, since gravity, and not air resistance, would be the only force acting on the bodies.

18. **(J)** Celery is listed as a cross-reactive food for all three of the pollen types, so it would be the one you would want to avoid. The other three options are not present in all three of the pollen types.

19. **(A)** Birch and Alder share the same families—Rosaceae and Apiaceae—so it stands to reason that they would most likely share the most conserved proteins. The other choices do not have the same level of similarity among their families and cross-reactive foods that Rosaceae and Apiaceae do.

20. **(G)** Protein K is the only option that is present in all five lanes. In other words, Protein K is found at about 4.7 cm along the electrophoretic displacement and is represented in the Apple, Celery, Birch pollen, Peanut, and Aniseed.

21. **(C)** According to Table 1, Celery and Aniseed are both members of the Apiaceae family. Looking at Figure 2, there are a total of 9 proteins for which Celery (lane 2) shares the same electrophoretic displacement level with Aniseed (lane 5).

22. **(G)** Based on Figure 1, there are other IgE receptors that can be a part of this reaction given the two arrows pointing out of the "IgE receptors" label. So, activating mast cells prior to B-lymphocyte-allergen binding would be the LEAST likely of these options to interrupt the cascade since there is an alternative way that this part of the reaction can come about. For all of the other options, there is only *one* way they can come about so they would all serve to interrupt the reaction cascade.

23. **(C)** Based on Figure 1, if the velocity were zero, the v^2 would equal zero. If this is the case, the L'_0 would simply equal the L on the right-hand side.

24. **(G)** The second paragraph states that the spacecraft is traveling at 92% the speed of light. Figure 1 states that the speed of light is 3.0×10^8 m/s, so if we estimate what 92% of this would be, it would be closest to 2.76×10^8 m/s. The other options are far enough off the mark that even without a calculator, you should be fine in making this estimation.

25. **(A)** The last sentence of Student 1's paragraph states that "time intervals measured aboard the spacecraft become dilated relative to those measured on Earth." A "dilated" interval would be an increased one, so (A) is the only logical choice.

26. **(H)** Student 2 refers to the "Doppler effect" and explicitly compares the spacecraft's motion to that of "the wavelength of a sound."

27. **(B)** Student 1 states that the distance remaining between the spacecraft and Proxima Centauri is 2.12 light years, meaning it will take 2.12 years for the light from Proxima Centauri to reach the spacecraft. The second paragraph of the passage states that the imagined scenario involves an astronaut "halfway

between Earth and the star Proxima Centauri." So, we would *double* the 2.12 years of time to 4.24 to give us the number of years it takes for light from Proxima Centauri to reach the Earth.

28. **(G)** As it is currently designed, the thought experiments assume that the Earth maintains its position. In actuality, the Earth will be in motion around the Sun, so if we were to conduct this experiment with an extraordinary degree of accuracy, the movement of the Earth would need to be factored into the calculations. The amounts of time and distance being considered are so vast that the Earth's movement would be relatively insignificant. (F), (H), and (J) are all currently being considered to some extent.

29. **(D)** As one approaches the speed of light, the v (velocity) in Figure 1 will become closer and closer to c (the speed of light). If we then consider what will happen to the values of the time interval and the length as v gets closer and closer to c based on the equations in Figure 1, the value of time will seem to slow down and the distance will seem to increase.

30. **(J)** According to the second paragraph of the passage, the level at which mercury is toxic to humans is in excess of 600 ng g^{-1}. None of these fish has a mercury level in excess of this level.

31. **(A)** Based on background knowledge from physical science, you should know that something that is *more* alkaline is *less* acidic. On the pH scale, lower numbers indicate higher acidity and higher numbers indicate higher alkalinity. So, Shala would be the most alkaline since its pH is the highest of the three lakes listed in Table 1.

32. **(G)** *L. niloticus* is the largest fish in the table and feeds on invertebrates, which are not fish. Fish are vertebrates since they have backbones. So, this would provide the *strongest* evidence to disprove this hypothesis.

33. **(C)** A lake with a volume of 1,000 km³ would be between Shala and Malawi in volume. There is a positive correlation between the number of fish species and the volume of the lakes, based on the data in Table 1. So, it would be reasonable to conclude that this lake would have a number of fish species somewhere between 14 and 68, which are the number of fish species present in Shala and Malawi, respectively.

34. **(J)** According to the second sentence of the paragraph, the greatest predator fish along a food chain will often have two to three orders of magnitude more mercury than the lower species. So, the *H. forskahlii* is the most likely to be a predator given its high mercury content.

35. **(A)** The first paragraph defines "Secchi depth" as the measure of how deep one may see in a lake before there is no visibility. We need to consider what about the Shala lake differentiates it from the other lakes in a way that would lower its visibility. Shala's high level of surface chlorophyll would be associated with more abundant plant life than would be found in lakes with lower surface chlorophyll. More surface plant life would likely cloud the lake's sur-

face, making its Secchi depth lower. The other choices would be largely irrelevant to contributing to a lack of water visibility.

36. **(F)** The passage states that Figure 1 illustrates a high explosive, and Figure 2 illustrates a low explosive. The clearest difference between the two is that a high explosive has a far lower activation energy than that of low explosive. This makes sense, since a high explosive would have a higher likelihood of exploding than a low explosive. (G) is associated with the heat of combustion, but the difference in heat of combustion between the high and low explosives is not nearly as significant a relative difference as the activation energy represents. (H) and (J) have little to no clear association with whether something is a high or low explosive.

37. **(C)** Following the trends of Figures 3 and 4, trinitrotoluene would reach 0% fuel concentration at approximately 0.5 seconds, and octane would reach a fuel concentration of 0% at approximately 2.4 seconds. 2.4 − 0.5 = 1.9 seconds. The other options are far enough apart that a solid estimate for your answer will be sufficient.

38. **(G)** To maximize the explosive power while minimizing the size of the bomb, nitroglycerine would be the best choice given its extremely low activation energy. It would take very little fuel to ignite this explosive.

39. **(D)** There is insufficient information to make this determination because although we know that there are differences among the shockwave speeds between the compounds, given their different detonation velocities, we do not know how quickly their *explosive particles* actually travel. Why? Because although the shockwaves change the pressure of the gases around the explosion, we don't know how quickly the particles from the actual explosives would travel.

40. **(H)** In order for a substance to be a preferred fuel source, it would need to create a great deal of heat to provide mechanical energy. Octane's high heat of combustion would make it the preferred fuel source. The other options would have no bearing on making octane a preferred fuel source.

Sample Top-Scoring Writing Response

A world without difference is no world at all. If history has shown anything, it is the inhumanity involved in attempts to differentiate or create a dominant race. From colonialism to eugenics, the lesson prevails: difference is something to be embraced.

While it might be appealing to consider genetic engineering for agricultural purposes to say, feed a starving world, it is more problematic to think about its implications for the human genome.

402 • Pass Key to the ACT

Currently, parents deliberate on the possibilities for choosing gender and eye color, and even protecting their children from genetic disorders or health issues. But what happens when this "artificial selection" is, in fact, possible? Do parents then get to choose a preferential complexion, height, weight, and intelligence level? And how does society figure into this when we (as we always have in the past) characterize one skin tone, one sexual orientation, one gender classification, etc. as superior to others? If it's starting to sound a bit too Hitler-like, that's because it is. If it's starting to sound like a Sci-Fi movie gone wrong, that's because a super-human army wouldn't be so fantastical.

Genetic engineering is a technological advancement of great import. Nobody can deny its role in the future. Consider the cow that makes twice as much milk, or the sheep with twice as much wool. Consider crops that can withstand drought or flood. The possibilities for the treatment of cancers and other life-threatening diseases or disabilities are probably the greatest appeal of genetic engineering. Certainly, many would argue that its evolution is inevitable and something to be encouraged, like in the first and second viewpoints. However, this technology is not that of the computer or smart phone. To see genetic modification only as an exciting innovation of endless opportunities that archaic technophobias are merely afraid of is to narrow and simplify it greatly. We are talking about altering the most fundamental biological components of ourselves, essentially refashioning the human race.

Viewpoint Three is the only perspective to reflect on the severity of naming certain traits more favorable than others and using science to manipulate genetic diversity. Innovation, diversity, individual difference and artistic aesthetic are only some of the cultural staples that will collapse when we have created little more than a population of clones. These risks are easiest to perceive when one considers the multitude of books and their subsequent films that deal with this very issue. In the recent Hunger Games ries, Suzanne Collins imagines what the future could look like when a small, wealthy portion of the population has access to genetic engineering, but the working class is left out, used as mere laborers and treated less than humane. Ray Bradbury's celebrated <u>Fahrenheit 451</u> envisions a future of coerced conformity and book burning that ultimately suppresses all individualism.

Despite its advantages, genetic engineering is a technology that must be approached cautiously and reservedly, especially when it involves manipulating human chromosomes.